CAMBRIDGE TEXTS IN THE
HISTORY OF POLITICAL THOUGHT

———

WILLIAM OF OCKHAM
*A Letter to the Friars Minor
and Other Writings*

CAMBRIDGE TEXTS IN THE HISTORY OF POLITICAL THOUGHT

Series editors

RAYMOND GEUSS

Lecturer in Philosophy, University of Cambridge

QUENTIN SKINNER

Regius Professor of Modern History in the University of Cambridge

Cambridge Texts in the History of Political Thought is now firmly established as the major student textbook series in political theory. It aims to make available to students all the most important texts in the history of western political thought, from ancient Greece to the early twentieth century. All the familiar classic texts will be included, but the series seeks at the same time to enlarge the conventional canon by incorporating an extensive range of less well-known works, many of them never before available in a modern English edition. Wherever possible, texts are published in complete and unabridged form, and translations are specially commissioned for the series. Each volume contains a critical introduction together with chronologies, biographical sketches, a guide to further reading and any necessary glossaries and textual apparatus. When completed the series will aim to offer an outline of the entire evolution of western political thought.

For a list of titles published in the series, please see end of book

WILLIAM OF OCKHAM

A Letter to the Friars Minor and Other Writings

EDITED BY

ARTHUR STEPHEN McGRADE

University of Connecticut

AND

JOHN KILCULLEN

Macquarie University

TRANSLATED BY

JOHN KILCULLEN

CAMBRIDGE
UNIVERSITY PRESS

CAMBRIDGE UNIVERSITY PRESS
Cambridge, New York, Melbourne, Madrid, Cape Town,
Singapore, São Paulo, Delhi, Tokyo, Mexico City

Cambridge University Press
The Edinburgh Building, Cambridge CB2 8RU, UK

Published in the United States of America by Cambridge University Press, New York

www.cambridge.org
Information on this title: www.cambridge.org/9780521358040

© Cambridge University Press 1995

This publication is in copyright. Subject to statutory exception
and to the provisions of relevant collective licensing agreements,
no reproduction of any part may take place without the written
permission of Cambridge University Press.

First published 1995
Reprinted 2001

A catalogue record for this publication is available from the British Library

Library of Congress Cataloguing in Publication Data
William, of Ockham, *c.* 1285-*c.* 1347.
[Selections. English. 1995]
A letter to the Friars Minor, and other writings / William of
Ockham ; edited by Arthur Stephen MGrade and John Kilcullen;
translated by John Kilcullen.
p.   cm. -(Cambridge texts in the history of political
thought)
Includes bibliographical references and index.
ISBN 0 521 35243 6. - ISBN 0 521 35804 3 (pbk.)
1. Church and state. 2. Poverty - Religious aspects - Catholic
Church. 3. Catholic Church - Doctrines. 4. Popes - Primacy. 5. Holy
Roman Empire - Kings and rulers. 6. Political science - Philosophy.
I. McGrade, Arthur Stephen. II. Kilcullen, John, 1938- .
III. William, of Ockham, *c.* 1285-*c.* 1347. Epistola ad Fratres
Minores. IV. Title. V. Series.
BV629.W62213   1995
322´.1´09023 - dc20   94-43248 CIP

ISBN 978-0-521-35243-7 Hardback
ISBN 978-0-521-35804-0 Paperback

Cambridge University Press has no responsibility for the persistence or
accuracy of URLs for external or third-party internet websites referred to in
this publication, and does not guarantee that any content on such websites is,
or will remain, accurate or appropriate. Information regarding prices, travel
timetables, and other factual information given in this work is correct at
the time of first printing but Cambridge University Press does not guarantee
the accuracy of such information thereafter.

Contents

Preface

The *Epistola ad Fratres Minores* and extracts from *Opus nonaginta dierum* and *Octo quaestiones de potestate papae* are translated, with the publisher's permission, from the Latin texts established by H.S. Offler and others in *Guillelmi de Ockham opera politica* vols. I (rev. edn.) and II (Manchester: Manchester University Press, 1974, 1963). The translation of III *Dialogus*, II.3, chapter 6, is made, with the permission of the editor of the journal, from H.S. Offler, "The Three Modes of Natural Law in Ockham: A Revision of the Text," in *Franciscan Studies*, 37 (1977), 207–18. The remaining extracts from the *Dialogus* are translated from the text published by Melchior Goldast in volume II of *Monarchia S. Romani Imperii* (Frankfurt: Conrad Biermann, 1614; photographic reprint Graz: 1960). The numerous departures from the Goldast text of the *Dialogus* are listed in the Appendix. See the Appendix also for the practice followed in rendering specifically political terms.

Notes for the present volume have been kept to little more than the minimum necessary for tracking Ockham's explicitly cited sources and the turns of his own argument.[1] The chief exception is that references have been provided to the passages in Marsilius of Padua's *Defender of Peace* which Ockham was clearly arguing against in his discussions of conciliar authority and the authority of Peter over the other apostles. The reader will find fuller information on historical and theological context and fuller comparisons of Ockham's views

---

[1] For *A Letter to the Friars Minor, The Work of Ninety Days*, and *Eight Questions on the Power of the Pope*, the references to sources derive from Professor Offler's edition.

with those of other political thinkers in our edition of his *Short Discourse on Tyrannical Government* in this series.[2]

However we assess Ockham – whether we condemn him for shattering medieval Christian spiritual-political unity or praise him for constructively disengaging religious and secular institutions from one another – there can be no doubt that the disproportion between an author's importance and his availability to readers of English is greater in his case than in that of any other western political thinker. The present volume, along with the *Short Discourse*, does much to remedy this lack of access. This is especially true for the *Dialogus*, the text of which as printed in the early editions of Treschel and Goldast requires much correction. We are grateful to Jeremy Mynott and Quentin Skinner for making possible so substantial a presentation of Ockham and are grateful again to Professor Skinner for essential diplomatic aid in bringing the possibility to life.

John Kilcullen, who is responsible for the translation, notes, appendix, and indexes and for the collation of Goldast's text with manuscripts of the *Dialogus*, also wishes to thank: Professor George D. Knysh for the proposed textual emendations credited to him in the Appendix; John Scott, who checked the translation and Appendix and checked the reading of the manuscripts, suggesting innumerable corrections and improvements; the staff of the Macquarie University Library, Marilyn Wagstaff in particular; the staff of the libraries which supplied microfilm of manuscripts; Sue Folwell, Hilary Hatfield, and Maureen Mosely, who word-processed various parts of the translation; and the Australian Research Council, which supported the work financially. A. S. McGrade, who is responsible for general editing and for the introduction, wishes to thank his wife for many helpful suggestions and for unfailing moral support.

A. S. McGRADE
JOHN KILCULLEN

---

[2] In our edition of the *Short Discourse*, references to the present volume are made under the working title *Selections from the Major Political Works*.

A note on references

Most citations are by author's name or short title of the work cited; the full title will be found in the Bibliography beginning on page 371.

Books of the Bible are cited according to the Vulgate, the version Ockham used. Biblical names are as in the Douay version, which was translated from the Vulgate. Ockham gives chapter references only; verse numbers have been added. Bible references in square brackets have been added by editors or translator.

In Aristotle's works the medieval book and chapter divisions are not always the same as in modern editions. We have given the Bekker numbers in footnotes.

References in the text which include the symbols "q." or "dist." are to material included in the first of the various medieval compilations together sanctioned by Pope Gregory XIII in 1580 as the body of canon law (*Corpus iuris canonici*): the *Decretum* of the twelfth-century Bolognese jurist Gratian. Ockham uses the form "X.," expanded here to *Extra* (the books "outside" the *Decretum*), in citing both the second and third parts of the *Corpus iuris canonici*: the five books of *Decretales* promulgated by Gregory IX between 1230 and 1244, and the additional book of decretals (*Liber sextus*) added by Boniface VIII in 1298. The letter "v." indicates a reference to the gloss. Canon law references are separately indexed on page 385, with volume and column of the standard modern edition of A. Friedberg. Footnote references for both text and gloss are to the edition of Lyons, 1671 (Cambridge University Library).

References to Roman civil law, the *Corpus iuris civilis* promulgated in the early sixth century by the emperor Justinian, are keyed to the edition of Mommsen and Krueger with the English translation of Alan Watson (Philadelphia, 1985) for the *Digest*; to the edition of Mommsen, Krueger, and Schoell (Berlin, 1954) for the *Institutes, Code*, and *Novels* (cited by Ockham as *Auth.* = *Authenticum*), and to the edition of Lyons, 1627, for the gloss.

The three major parts of Ockham's *Dialogue* are cited in the form "I–III *Dial.*," with a following Roman numeral (I or II) for the two tracts of Part III and arabic numerals for book and chapter. Thus, "III *Dial.* 1.2.7" refers to chapter 7 of Book 2 of Tract I of Part III. References to works published in the Manchester edition of Ockham's *Opera politica* (ed. H.S. Offler and others) are given in accordance with the conventions of that edition. References to the *Short Discourse* are by page in our edition.

The book and chapter titles at the beginnings of sections in this volume have been provided by the editors.

Abbreviations

Auth.	*Authenticum* (= *Novellae*), part of *Corpus iuris civilis*
EFM	Ockham, *Epistola ad Fratres Minores*
Extra	The five books of *Decretales* of Gregory IX and, in Ockham's references, the sixth book added by Boniface VIII (li. 6, *Liber sextus*)
OND	Ockham, *Opus nonaginta dierum*
Gloss	See *Corpus iuris canonici* and *Corpus iuris civilis* in the Bibliography
OQ	Ockham, *Octo quaestiones*
Short Discourse	Ockham, *A Short Discourse on Tyrannical Government*

Introduction

William of Ockham is largely responsible for the widely held modern conviction that religious institutions and secular governments should normally operate independently of one another. In Ockham's view, the separation is not absolute. Secular government does not "regularly" have authority in religious matters, but "occasionally" it does. Conversely, church leaders should not ordinarily have political authority. In extreme cases, however, when secular processes have failed, they must intervene. This complex conception of normally but not invariably independent spiritual and temporal powers is central in the selections included in the present volume.

Partly because of its complexity, Ockham's political thought is controversial. To be sure, Ockham's institutional dualism can be seen as a conservative rationalization of traditional power relations – namely, of the *de facto* independence of priestly and lay authority from one another which was responsible for much of the dynamism of medieval life. Despite frequent expressions of mutual respect, however, medieval ecclesiastical and secular rulers were often far from agreeing in the basic understanding of their relationship. The natural impulse of kings and emperors to assume control of all significant activities within their domains came up especially hard against papal claims to more than ceremonial recognition of Christ's superiority (and Christ's vicar's superiority) to every earthly power. By the time Ockham addressed the issues, the papalist or hierocratic side had achieved unsurpassed theoretical development in such authors as James of Viterbo, Giles of Rome, and Augustinus Triumphus. Among the more moderate thinkers, John of Paris came closest to asserting the balanced dualism Ockham would develop further. The most radical anti-hierocratic treatise in circulation was Marsilius of Padua's *Defender of Peace*, which assigned all coercive jurisdiction to the (theoretically popularly controlled) lay ruler. The appearance of conservatism of Ockham's position is thus somewhat misleading. In appealing to biblical theology and newly current Aristotelian political ideas in order to distinguish religious and secular authority, Ockham challenged simpler views on both sides.

A further source of controversy is the fact that a number of Ockham's political works are directed against a reigning pope. Ockham's career in politics began with this confrontation.

The poverty controversy and the
Letter to the Friars Minor

As the leading Franciscan thinker at Oxford in the generation after Duns Scotus, Ockham produced important texts in logic, natural philosophy, metaphysics, and theology. These have no overt political content. Ockham was required, however, to defend the orthodoxy of some of his early theses on grace and divine power before an examining commission at the papal court in Avignon. These views were never formally condemned, but while he was at Avignon in the mid-1320s Ockham became convinced that Pope John XXII was himself a heretic on points of doctrine central to Franciscan belief and practice.

In the religious order founded by Francis of Assisi in the early years of the thirteenth century, renunciation of both individual and communal ownership came to be a central commitment. In the course of the century, the ideal of gospel poverty achieved increasing doctrinal recognition in papal pronouncements on the poverty of Christ and his apostles which closely reflected Franciscan teaching. The common belief of the friars in Ockham's time was that Nicholas III's bull *Exiit qui seminat* (1279) indisputably defined the complete poverty of Christ and the apostles as part of the Christian faith.

The Franciscan understanding of Christ's poverty was not, however, a part of John XXII's faith. In a series of bulls promulgated during the 1320s, John rejected a previous arrangement whereby the papacy had held ownership of goods used by the friars, and he declared it heretical to deny that Christ and the apostles had

had rights of ownership in the things they used. Through much of this period the Franciscan Minister General Michael of Cesena was in residence at the papal court, trying, in increasing desperation, to bring the pope to a position clearly consistent with earlier Franciscan and papal teaching. It was at this time that Ockham read John's constitutions. As he explains in the first selection translated here, he found many of John's pronouncements "heretical, erroneous, silly, ridiculous, fantastic, insane, and defamatory" (p. 3). Accordingly, in the spring of 1328, Ockham, Michael of Cesena, and a few other friars, fled Avignon and sought refuge with Ludwig of Bavaria, whom John had excommunicated in 1324 for functioning as Roman emperor without papal approval of his disputed election ten years before.

Ockham was excommunicated for leaving Avignon without papal permission, and he was regarded as a heretic by John XXII and succeeding popes for rejecting John's teachings on poverty. He thus became the first major western theologian to enter into protracted dispute with the papacy on matters of Christian doctrine – at first the doctrine of poverty and then the less well-defined doctrines of supreme spiritual and temporal power.

Our first selection is the account of his actions which Ockham addressed to the Franciscans assembled at a general meeting of the Order in 1334. Some of the seventy propositions in John XXII's bulls which Ockham lists as erroneous in the *Letter to the Friars Minor* are discussed in the next selection. The import of others can be grasped only in the light of detailed further argumentation which cannot be reviewed here. In its framework, however, the *Letter* is grippingly accessible: the opening, closing, and a brief central narrative passage express in the clearest possible terms both the depth of Ockham's conviction that John XXII had deviated from the Christian faith and the strength of his own determination to oppose John's errors to the utmost of his means and ability.

The Work of Ninety Days

When he wrote his *Letter to the Friars Minor*, Ockham had already completed, in the time indicated by its title, the next work represented in this volume, *The Work of Ninety Days*. Here he deals at length with errors listed in the *Letter* and attacks several hundred subordinate assertions by John XXII which he regarded as heretical or erroneous. *The Work of Ninety Days* is the first of three "impersonal" works which together make up the bulk of Ockham's political writing. The discussion is carried on through alternating passages from John XXII's *Quia vir reprobus* with arguments by unnamed "attackers" of John's doctrine, who uphold the position of "the appellant," Michael of Cesena, to whose appeal against John's earlier bulls *Quia vir* was a detailed response. John is referred to simply as "the attacked." Despite this involuted format, Ockham succeeds in laying out a coherent statement of the Franciscan position on gospel poverty as this had existed prior to John XXII's blitzkrieg against it. In so doing, he also advances a number of important propositions about property, power, and natural rights.

Some of the issues in dispute are vividly stated at the beginning of chapter 2. In the remainder of this chapter Ockham surveys the various senses of the key terms in which these issues had been stated: "using," "use of fact," "use of right," "right of using," "simple users," "things consumed by use," "lordship," "property," and words such as "mine," "yours," and "his." Points debated in later chapters typically turn on the meanings of one or more of these terms.

In chapters 26–8, for example, the senses of lordship and the nature of property are crucial. Michael of Cesena had held that in their renunciation of temporal possessions the apostles had returned, as far as property was concerned, to the state of innocence described early in the book of Genesis. In that state, he contended, there had been use of material things without any property or lordship. John XXII argued, to the contrary, that God's order to Adam and Eve to subject and dominate the earth was clear proof of human lordship in the state of innocence and that, before Eve's creation, Adam was sole proprietor of the world.

Ockham's reply on behalf of the Michaelist attackers is that Adam and Eve did indeed have a lordship of effective control over material things, but not the exclusive lordship of owners (chapter 26). Even if Adam alone was in charge of the world initially, this would not show that his lordship was proprietary (chapter 27). Lordship is not ownership because of belonging *in fact* to one person. It is ownership only when appropriated to one person in such a way that it cannot belong to anyone else without the owner's gift, other act of transfer, or death. Ockham illustrates this distinction by reference to the possession of property in a traditional monastic house. If someone founded a monastery and endowed it with many goods, the first monk there would not have exclusive lordship over those goods. He would not be their owner, since if a second man became a monk in the same monastery, he too would have some kind of lordship over the monastery's goods without any special act of transfer from the first monk.

The application of this example to the state of innocence is clear. Whatever lordship Adam may have had when he was alone in the world, it was not exclusive to him. It was for Eve and their posterity, since no act of his was necessary to make Eve a participant in that lordship. Eve was not an economic creature of her husband, nor are later generations economic creatures of those before them, gleaning whatever is left from the previous generation's enjoyment of its own private property.

In chapter 65 it is the concept of a right (*ius*) that is crucial. John XXII presented the Michaelists with a dilemma. Did Franciscans have a right to their food, clothing, and shelter, or did they not? If they did, then their claim to have renounced all ownership was void. But if they did not have a right to the things they used, then their use of them was unjust (*iniustum*) and wrong.

Ockham's response is one of the most important texts on natural rights to be found in his work. He distinguishes between a right of the forum or law-court (*ius fori*) and a right of heaven (*ius poli*), essentially a natural right. The latter is that by which persons living without positive legal institutions can licitly use material things for their preservation or comfort. The effect of property rights embodied in positive legal institutions (rights of the forum) is to abridge the original common right of heaven, so that ordinarily (the case of extreme need is an exception) no one can licitly use anything belonging to another without the owner's permission. The effect of the "licences to use" granted by others to the Franciscans is not to confer a positive legal right on the friars but to cancel the abridgment of their original common natural right. The proof of this distinction is that, if a donor withdrew his licence, the friars would have no recourse in a court of law, as they would if a legal right had been granted them.

Thus the response to the dilemma posed by John XXII is that the friars' mode of possessing and using material goods – one of several modes of possession other than ownership which Ockham considers in this chapter – is not unjust, for it is in accord with the right or law of heaven. But neither do the friars have positive legal rights. Their poverty is intact.

According to John XXII's attackers, as we have seen, there was no property in Paradise. How, then, did property come into the world? Ockham defends five conclusions on this matter in chapter 88 of *The Work of Ninety Days*. (1) There was no exclusive lordship or property in the state of innocence. (2) After the fall, the first exclusive lordship of temporal things was introduced by human law, or by human ordinance or will. The first exclusive lordships Ockham finds indicated in the Bible were those of Cain, a farmer, and Abel, a shepherd, but since there is no suggestion that the property division implied by this division of labor was made by divine command, the inference is that it was a product of human ordinance or will. (3) Distinct lordships over many things were introduced at various times by human laws other than the laws of kings. Ockham argues that we need not think of all property divisions as having been made by rulers: perhaps Cain and Abel divided property on their own authority, just as Abraham and Lot seem to have divided territory between themselves on their own authority. (4) In course of time *some* lordships of temporal things *were* introduced by direct divine ordinance. To the many texts cited by John, Ockham adds the divine grants of Mount Seir to the children of Esau and of Ar to the sons of Lot (Deuteronomy 2:4 and 9). Ockham is far from questioning God's authority to grant ownership of whatever He pleases to whomever He pleases, but he denies that all property titles have such a direct theological foundation. In particular, (5) after the promulgation of the gospel, all new property divisions have been made by human law, not by divine law or by any special grant of God.

Ockham's secularization of property rights in chapter 88 of *The Work of Ninety Days* is complemented in chapter 93 by what might be called, from a secular standpoint, an impoverishment and marginalization of Christ and the apostles. In *Quia vir* John XXII had argued that Christ was universal king and lord of all temporal things, and this not merely insofar as he was divine, but even insofar as he was a mortal man. Ockham's attempt to prove the manifest heresy of this position forms the longest single chapter of *The Work of Ninety Days*.

He begins by distinguishing relevant senses of the words "king" and "lord." Of the many possible senses of *rex* (relating to *regendo*, "ruling"), three are especially pertinent. The term may apply (1) to one person ruling others temporally, and here there are many modes, including the supreme mode associated with monarchical rule of a whole community; (2) to someone who rules others in spiritual matters; or (3) to someone who rules himself and his movements and acts by right reason. The term "lord" is also equivocal. Someone may be called a lord in recognition of some power he has (in relation to the senses of lordship enumerated in chapter 2 or the kinds of ruling noted in the present chapter) or as a prerogative of holiness, virtue, wisdom, riches, or the like.

Ockham's next step is to explain what the Michaelists regard as the truth concerning Christ's kingship and lordship. The pattern of argument is the same in the two cases. (1) First Ockham affirms Christ's authority as God. As God Christ was king of all, just as the Father is king of all. Similarly, Christ as God was lord of all, just as God the Father is lord of all. (2) This is followed by a denial or restriction of Christ's worldly power or wealth as a human being. As mortal man Christ was not a king in the supreme mode of temporal rule (although he was a temporal king in a more limited sense, because he ruled the apostles temporally). Similarly, Christ as mortal man was not lord of all temporal things by a lordship exclusive to himself (although he was lord of all by the common lordship God gave to the whole human race, if it is not permissible for anyone to renounce such lordship). (3) Finally Ockham explains the appropriateness of applying terms such as "king" and "lord" to Christ even as a human being – if the terms are taken in the correct senses. Thus, Christ was supremely a king from ruling *spiritually*, because for this he came into the world, to govern the faithful who believe in him with respect to spiritual matters. Again, as a mortal man Christ did not have legal ownership of anything, but he could nevertheless be called lord because of the union of human nature in him with the divine nature and because of his holiness and other graces.

In short, the Michaelists' position on the kingship and lordship of Christ rested on two distinctions: (1) between Christ as God and Christ as man and (2) between secular political or economic senses of kingship and lordship on one hand and spiritual, moral, or theological senses on the other. On the basis of these two distinctions, Ockham argues in the third and longest section of chapter 93 that John XXII's assertions of Christ's kingship and lordship "smack of manifest heresy." One need not accept this judgment to find much of value in Ockham's discussion of texts such as John 18:36 (Christ's statement to Pilate: "My kingdom is not of this world") and in his consideration of the implications for Christian life and leadership to be drawn from the Franciscan view of a poor and politically powerless Christ.

Tract I of Part III of the *Dialogue* (III *Dialogus* I)

Ockham's conviction that John XXII had fallen into grave error was also the motive for his next major work, the massive Part I of a *Dialogue* between Master and Student (I *Dialogus*), a discussion of heresy, "especially papal heresy." Part II of the *Dialogue*, apparently never written, was to have considered the content of John's teachings. Part III, from which the next two selections in the present volume are taken, was originally planned as a series of tracts on the deeds of six individuals (including Ludwig of Bavaria and himself) involved in the current altercations about the faith. Two preliminary treatises are all that survive, one on the power of the pope and clergy (III *Dialogus* I) and one on the power and rights of the Roman Empire (III *Dialogus* II).

The second book of III *Dialogus* I, translated here in its entirety, is a pioneering attempt to discuss the government of the Church in the joint contexts of biblical theology and Aristotelian political theory. To achieve a clearer understanding of the proposition that Christ appointed Peter head of all believers (a proposition which Ockham accepted), the Student determines to discuss first whether it is beneficial for the community of the faithful to *have* a single head. The pursuit of this question is intertwined with treatment of two related questions: what qualifications must a head of all believers have, and may the community of the faithful change its form of government?

On balance, the thirty chapters of III *Dialogus* 1.2 provide substantial "political" as well as scriptural support for the medieval western church's acceptance of papal authority as universal. This support is reinforced in the remaining two books of III *Dialogus* I by a critique of the doctrine of conciliar supremacy (Book 3) and by a defense of the traditional belief that Christ himself conferred chief authority in the Church on Peter and, through him, his successors (Book 4). Ockham's endorsement of papal monarchy is, however, carefully nuanced. Although Book 2 supports the view that a monarchical regime is *ordinarily* or *regularly* best for the Church, circumstances are envisaged in which one or another alternative form of government would be more beneficial. In such circumstances, Ockham argues, the community of the faithful may temporarily set papal government aside.

Ockham discusses constitutional change in Church government as a question about the power of "the community of the faithful" to effect such change. He conspicuously does not propose formal institutional procedures whereby the community of believers might deliberate and decide upon such a momentous step. Some of the cases considered in which structural change in Church government would be indicated assume that significant multitudes of Christians who were for good or bad reasons unwilling to accept papal monarchy would accept some other regime. The suggestion seems to be that in such cases it would be, objectively speaking, beneficial to suspend papal rule for a time. Ockham might expect reasonable individuals ("kings" in the third sense of the term recognized in chapter 93 of *The Work of Ninety Days*?) to assess the situation correctly and act accordingly. There is, however, no basis for supposing that he thought any formal procedure could guarantee that any particular set of individuals would be thus reasonable.

Whatever the explanation for his failure to recommend formal procedures by which the community of the faithful might determine whether to change its form of government, Ockham clearly did not hold that a general council of the Church was infallible in doctrine or, presumably, in action. This is evident from Book 3 of III *Dialogus* I, where he discusses the thesis, presented by Marsilius of Padua and taken up by later writers, that a general council of the Church has authority as great as or greater than the pope's.

Ockham respects the efforts of general councils through the ages to define Catholic truth, but he is unwilling to interpret Christ's promise to be always with "the Church" as a promise to be with any particular Christian or set of Christians, lay or clerical, scholar or prelate. Christ's promise would, he says, be fulfilled even if there were only one orthodox Christian at any given time. Like Adam before the creation of Eve, or like the first monk in chapter 27 of *The Work of Ninety Days*, a single individual might for a time bear sole responsibility for what is normally, and by right, a great community.

Ockham contests another part of Marsilius's position in the next and final book of III *Dialogus* I. He argues here that Peter was appointed by Christ to feed all his sheep, including the other apostles (III *Dialogus* 1.4.8) and St. Paul (chapter 9), and that this ministry entrusted to Peter involved power and authority, not merely words, examples, and physical support (chapter 10). Later in the book (chapter 22) the Master argues that what has been believed since the time of the apostles by prelates and doctors of the Church in continuous succession and by the people subject to them should be held firmly by all Catholics. But all these have believed that Peter was superior to the other apostles.

For Ockham, a pope's authority over all Christians is distinctly and specifically spiritual. It must respect the rights of others, both rulers and individuals. Papal authority includes a measure of coercive power but does not involve a right to command anything not contrary to divine or natural law. It does not require great wealth or show itself in magnificence. Interpreted in this way, papal authority has a unique claim to the respect of all Christians. But this interpretation sets a standard from which flagrant deviation need not be tolerated, and it proposes a style of leadership which, even when legitimate, does not impose itself at the cost of great conflict among believers.

Tract II of Part III of the *Dialogue* (III *Dialogus* II)

The conception of lay political authority which emerges from the second tract of III *Dialogus*, on the rights of the Roman Empire, is distinctly and specifically secular. At the beginning of the tract, the Student proposes an ambitious program. After a first book devoted to fundamental questions about the value and basis of a world empire and the qualities needed in an emperor, there is to be a second book on the emperor's rights in temporal matters, a third on possible imperial rights in spiritual matters, a fourth on the question of whether an emperor has a strict religious obligation to defend the Empire's rights, and a fifth on various sorts of enemies of the Empire. After an understandable moment of hesitation, the Master agrees to embark. The tract (and with it the work) breaks off at chapter 23 of Book 3, after a discussion of the emperor's jurisdiction over clerics. The last argument, reminiscent of chapter 93 of *The Work of Ninety Days*, is that the pope's coercive jurisdiction is inferior to the emperor's, because Christ as a mortal man was inferior in coercive jurisdiction to the emperor and other secular judges of his time.

The questions about secular government which Ockham discusses in the 17 chapters translated from Book 1 of the second tract of III *Dialogus* II are similar to the questions about spiritual government discussed in III *Dialogus* I. What is the best form of government? What qualities are needed in a leader? Is constitutional change permissible? The most strongly defended answers are sometimes similar in the two discussions, sometimes different. In both, the question of right or legitimacy is significantly qualified by considerations of benefit to the population governed, either the community of the faithful or the totality of mortals. The thesis that a monarchical regime is ordinarily, but not invariably, the most beneficial dictates in each case that at least temporary variation in form of government is permissible, although the difference between the divine origin of the papal office and the human origin of secular government places a higher value on ecclesiastical than on secular monarchy. There are major differences in the functions to be served by the two governments and in the qualifications needed in the persons who are to head them. The settlement of disagreements and the correction of subordinate officials is a common task for both monarchs, but positive, nurturing functions are more important for the papacy, while the first argument for secular monarchy is that it is the regime under which wrongdoers may best be restrained and the good allowed to live quietly among the bad. A pope should be holy and wise; although it is not necessary that he be greatly superior in these respects to everyone about him, a less worthy person sins if he does not give way for the office to a more worthy. An emperor, on the other hand, should above all have good sense and be, or become, conversant about secular affairs and natural law. It is appropriate that he be literate in Scripture, but expertness here (or indeed in the technicalities of civil law) is not strictly necessary. Since the pope is not responsible for punishing secular crimes, he does not need great riches. An emperor is and does.

The interplay of benefit and right begins in chapter 1, with the Student's assertion that the Roman Empire's rights would not *be* rights if it were not beneficial for all mortals to be under one secular ruler in temporal matters. But *is* this beneficial? Ockham presents five opinions on this question in the first five chapters of the book, beginning with a simple affirmative and concluding with the opinion that what is beneficial varies with the quality and necessity of the times. He notes at the beginning of chapter 6, however, that the first and last opinions need not be regarded as contrary, and the following eight chapters defend a position which combines them: it is *ordinarily* best for the world to have a single leader in secular matters, but there are cases in which another regime would be more beneficial – and hence deserve more support.

Ockham's declaration that the first and fifth opinions are not necessarily opposed – since, he argues, monarchy is ordinarily or regularly but not always the best form of world government – dictates a double approach in the second, critical phase of the discussion. The next few chapters qualify the arguments in favor of monarchy, showing that they do not invariably hold good, by specifying cases in which some other regime is more beneficial. The response to arguments for the regular superiority of other forms of government is that anything another regime can do, monarchy can (ordinarily) do better.

The first argument for monarchy in chapter 1 was that wrong-doers are best restrained under a single ruler and the good can live more quietly among the bad. Two general cases in which this argument fails are presented in chapter 6, and they set a pattern for Ockham's qualifying responses to other pro-monarchical arguments. One case in which a single ruler is not most effective in restraining the bad occurs when the bad are actually stirred up by the attempt to institute a monarchy. The Master cites (if the passage is authentic) the civil wars among the Romans in the time of Julius Caesar. The object of Caesar's ambition – the predominance of one man, himself – is not criticized, but under the circumstances it was not right to pursue this aim. In considering other arguments, Ockham returns to this theme more than once. The likelihood of substantial resistance to monarchy may make it wrong to attempt to institute such a regime if it does not exist, or wrong to attempt to enforce monarchical prerogatives previously acknowledged as legitimate. The other principal instance in which bad people are less well restrained by monarchy than by an alternative regime occurs when the world ruler himself "rages with tyrannical cruelty." Nero is given as an example.

After offering similar qualifications to the ten further arguments for monarchy from chapter 1, the Master responds in chapters 11–13 to the arguments offered earlier for other positions. Of special interest are his replies to arguments for an aristocratic world government, a regime of many wise men ruling together. These replies supplement a similar comparative discussion of regimes in III *Dialogus* 1.2.19. A single ruler can take advantage of the greater wisdom of a multitude by seeking advice, and no one should be made ruler unless there is a strong probability that he will indeed do this when it is necessary and beneficial. To the argument that a group of rulers would be less corruptible than a single ruler, the reply here is different from the somewhat tortuous response in the earlier chapter. Here the Master argues that errors and faults arising from bad will and negligence are more likely with several rulers than with one, since humans, especially those with power, are prone to conflict with one another, but no one is in conflict with himself.

The Master has now established that a world monarchy in temporal affairs is ordinarily beneficial for the totality of mortals – ordinarily but not always. The Student's initial assertion about the rights of the Roman Empire has been skilfully modulated. Those rights would not be rights, he had said, if such a government were not beneficial. To the extent that world monarchy is beneficial, then, a Ludwig of Bavaria would have a good basis for pressing his legitimate claims as emperor and asserting imperial authority. But the unwillingness of an increasing number of other secular rulers to acknowledge the Empire's overlordship would qualify as a case in which it would not be right to press those claims too far. The secular political program dictated by Ockham's discussion would seem to be a prudent one of working toward the best outcome – a just and effective world government exercised over a substantially willing human community and concerned primarily with the restraint of wrongdoers rather than with a spiritual mission of its own – but with due regard for the human costs involved in asserting even the best attested legal titles.

The second major question considered in III *Dialogus* II.1 has to do with the "excellences or graces, virtues and characteristics" in which the head of a world government should be outstanding. The Student begins by asking, in chapter 14, whether a world monarch in temporal matters is obliged to be a Catholic. No doubt he is, the Master replies, for every adult mortal having the use of reason is so obliged. Or did the Student mean to ask whether someone can be a true emperor who is not a Catholic? On this question there are different opinions, which will be dealt with later. Ockham's situation as a controversialist did not encourage defense of a possible future non-Christian world monarch, but his insistence on the biblically attested legitimacy of the pagan Roman Empire in the time of Christ indicates clearly enough the direction his treatment of the question would have to take.

Chapter 15 is an important discussion of a good world governor's intellectual qualifications, with a section on advice which should be added to the discussion of this topic in III *Dialogus* 1.2.19 and chapter 4 of the present book. The Student begins by asking whether an emperor should be expert in two traditional branches of learning, theology and civil law. With regard to the first of these, one opinion presented by the Master is that an emperor should indeed be expert in sacred literature, both on the model of Old Testament kings and because he is obliged to defend the Christian faith and should therefore understand it. The Master does not respond to these arguments, but it seems clear from the sequel that Ockham prefers a second opinion: it is fitting that the ruler be able to read Scripture and understand its literal meaning (the basis of other meanings that can be found in it), but this is not essential, since without such skill he can usefully and justly manage temporal affairs. Ockham is also willing to settle for an emperor with less than professional competence in civil law, for there have been just and even saintly emperors and kings lacking such knowledge (who would have acquired it if it had been necessary). Also, an emperor or king, in contrast with inferior judges, is not tied by the laws. An emperor who lacks profound knowledge in theology or civil law should therefore not devote himself so much to remedying these shortcomings that he neglects the responsibilities of government that have been entrusted to him.

The personal qualities most necessary in an emperor are natural sense, discretion, energy, and judgment of reasoning. A new emperor or king should apply himself to gaining expertise in secular affairs and knowledge of natural law, especially "natural law about which the learned can err or doubt." The Student is puzzled by this last clause. As he understands natural law, there is no excuse for being ignorant of it, but if there are natural laws about which experts can err or be uncertain, there could be excuses for ignorance concerning those laws. This objection leads to a significant elaboration of Ockham's conception of natural law. There are, the Master explains, three kinds of natural laws. (1) There are, first, self-evident principles and propositions following so closely from such principles that they cannot fail to occur to us when we are obliged to do or omit something in accordance with them – unless we simply refuse to think of what we are about. One cannot fail to see, for example, that it is wrong to kill a harmless innocent human being. (2) There are other natural laws which are drawn plainly and without great consideration from first principles. Ignorance is no excuse for violating either of these two types of rational norms. (3) There are, however, other natural laws which can indeed be inferred from the first type, but only with great attention and study and through many intermediate propositions. These laws are inferred by few people, even among the experts, and "about these the experts sometimes have conflicting opinions, some thinking them just, others unjust." As this reference to justice indicates, Ockham follows scholastic tradition in conceiving of natural laws as rational dictates concerning right and wrong. The knowledge he wishes his ruler to cultivate is not an amoral proficiency in calculating ways to achieve his own ends. Although the difficulty of determining the rights and wrongs involved here may provide an excuse for ignorance of them, natural laws of this third type are objective. In enjoining rulers to acquire knowledge of such natural laws, Ockham

aims at a politics guided by natural justice in detail, not only at
the level of general principle.

To acquire skill in natural laws and secular affairs, the emperor
should have many wise advisers. The mention of advisers leads
the Student to cite Ecclesiasticus: "Let only one in a thousand be
your adviser." The Master, in turn, offers advice about advice.
There are, he says, various subjects on which, or reasons for which,
advice may be sought. Sometimes the matter at hand is secret and
dangerous to reveal. At other times it may be public, so it can be
revealed without danger. The point of seeking advice may be to
secure the advisers' agreement and thus make the decision more
authoritative and effective. Or the decision may be one which is
to be carried out by the advisers. In this case and in cases where
confidentiality is needed, the cautionary maxim from Ecclesiasticus
applies. In the other cases already mentioned – and also when
knowledge of law or fact is sought or when the discretion, prudence,
faithfulness, affection, or intentions of the advisers are being
tested – advisers should be many. Indeed, advice should sometimes
be sought from the unskilled or malevolent.

Chapter 16 has less to do with an emperor's personal qualities
than with the policies he should follow in the administration of
justice. Indeed there may sometimes be a tension between desirable
policy and the desirable personal quality of mercy, since Ockham
seems to make the common good and the safety of subjects
(especially the good ones) the criterion for policy. Accordingly,
sometimes an emperor should forbear or defer pursuing justice,
sometimes he should temper justice with mildness, but sometimes
he has a strict obligation to be rigorous. Similarly, with respect to
inflicting penalties for crimes, if the emperor knows that a criminal
is perfectly reformed, mercy is permissible. Otherwise, mercy toward
the criminal is cruelty to subjects.

The last chapter on the qualities required in an emperor is also
externally oriented, although the discussion of truth, the first trait
considered, suggests that it is a virtue of character which should
be carried over into the ruler's public personality. As to the fulfillment of promises, the Master asserts, presumably because the
emperor's primary responsibility is for the common welfare, that
he should not fulfill promises badly made or even those licitly

made if they have begun to be harmful. Finally, there arises the question of wealth and power. A pope, as we have seen, does not need to be rich, according to Ockham. The case is different for an emperor. The Master reports that some think – and since he offers no other opinion, Ockham apparently agrees – the imperial office cannot be well administered without riches. Such authority is nothing without coercion, but coercion cannot be exercised without power (*potentia* here, not *potestas*, Ockham's more usual term). Power is most strengthened by riches, for it is with riches that a ruler acquires and retains friends, or at least obedience. Friends and obedience will not be secured by riches, however, unless the wealth is poured out liberally (presumably not prodigally). Thus, in the Franciscan Ockham's political theory the virtue of liberality, a habit leading to intrinsically good acts by prosperous individuals in Aristotle's *Ethics*, becomes an instrumental virtue of secular statecraft. There is also a contrast with Ockham's own account of spiritual government. Different motives are effective in the two spheres. The pope should be a wise and holy example but need not be rich. Ockham's last touch on the qualifications of an emperor is to say that he will need resoluteness (the courage that is a virtue of soul) to use his resources to carry out the policies required by the common good. Bodily fortitude is not so necessary.

Ockham's contribution to the Mirror of Princes genre in III *Dialogus* II.1.14–17 is neither voluminous nor elegant, but it fits the conception of secular government laid out earlier in the book. The restraint of wrongdoers and the other functions of secular government can ordinarily be carried out most effectively and justly by a single ruler. The qualities needed in such a ruler differ from those required in a spiritual leader because his responsibilities differ. Knowledge, including a quite refined knowledge of right and wrong, is required, but this knowledge, as well as an understanding of existing secular realities, is distinct from the knowledge needed in a spiritual leader. The distinction between spiritual and temporal in Ockham's thought is sharp enough to allow for the possibility of a non-Christian world emperor, but it by no means consigns secular politics to a realm of amorality and mere force. Indeed, as we shall now see, Ockham claims positive divine warrant for a secular politics which pursues a rationally defined peace and justice.

The last excerpt from the *Dialogue* included in this volume is Ockham's defense of an emperor's eligibility to be sole elector of the pope. In these three chapters from the incomplete third book of III *Dialogus* II, Ockham does not base the emperor's capacity for this role on any sort of responsibility for religion inherent in the imperial office. Although he argues strongly for the legitimacy, in principle, of a practice engaged in by more than one medieval emperor as grounded in his office, Ockham makes the emperor's right to choose the pope contingent, ultimately, on the cooperation of other Catholic Christians. There is a further wrinkle of contingency in the Master's concession that the papacy itself was the proximate source of some past emperors' possession of this right. The chief point of these chapters, however – a point in the making of which Ockham deploys a novel and suggestive threefold conception of natural law – is that in this matter of papal election the right of those whom the pope is to govern is more fundamental than the right of the pope himself. The Romans have not been given the right to decide how a pope will be elected by the papacy. Rather, the papacy must be regarded as having this right (when it does have it) by consent of the Romans.

The Student objects that the Romans do not have such a right, because they do not have it by either divine law or human law. The response to this objection is a division of natural law which, besides doing much to reconcile a number of apparently contradictory remarks on the subject by Isidore of Seville (remarks enshrined in the canon law), sheds further light on the role of reason in Ockhamist politics.

The Master proposes in chapter 6 that the Romans have the right to elect the highest pontiff "by divine law, extending divine law to include all natural law." There are three modes of natural law, he explains: (1) that which is in conformity with natural reason that in no case fails; (2) that which is to be observed by those who use natural equity alone without any custom or human legislation; and (3) that which is gathered by evident reasoning from the law of nations or another law or from some act, divine or human, unless the contrary is enacted with the consent of those concerned.

As examples of the first, unfailingly obligatory natural law, the Master gives two of the Ten Commandments: do not commit adultery, do not lie. There is no suggestion that the Romans, the emperor, the pope, or anyone else has electoral rights on so absolute a basis as this. The second mode of natural law is that which governed the state of innocence. Under natural law in this sense, for example, there is no private property and no servitude. But even though this second mode of natural law has some application in the fallen condition of human nature (for example, material things are common to all in the sense that all are obliged to treat them as common *unless* for reasonable cause they decide on the contrary), it is more an ideal standard than a categorical norm. The third mode of natural law, which the Master calls natural law "on supposition," is a matter of rational response to existing contingencies. The obligation to return a deposit to its owner, for example, arises from the fact that the deposit has been made. Again, the right to repel violence by force is an example of natural law in this sense. Finally, the particular right under discussion is an example of natural law in this third mode. For *supposing* someone is to be set over certain persons as prelate, ruler, or rector, it is inferred by evident reason that unless the contrary is decided on by some higher authority those who are to be ruled have the right to choose their ruler.

Natural law in all of these three modes can be called divine law both because it is from God, the creator of nature, and because it is contained in Scripture either explicitly or implicitly, for in Scripture there are certain general propositions from which, alone or with other (presumably factual) propositions, every natural law can be inferred. The particular natural-divine right in question here can also be thought of as a matter of human right, for the principle that a community is entitled to choose its rulers is included in the law of nations. One could therefore say that the Romans have the right to elect the pope by both divine law and human law.

According to Ockham, the right of a community to choose its leaders is not inalienable. In chapter 7 the Master concedes that at some time in the past the Romans probably transferred this right and power to the pope. Yet, as he will argue in the following chapter, if the pope should become a heretic, the right to elect a true pope would devolve upon the Romans again, "reverting to its own nature."

Ockham was first and foremost a theologian, one who undoubtedly considered God's will the supreme norm of action for any creature. The passages on natural law included in the present volume indicate, however, that he did not regard divine will as hostile to human reason. Quite the contrary. For secular political purposes there is a perfect harmony between reason and the biblical revelation of God's will. God the creator of nature also affirms, in revelation, the principles of natural reason.

Eight Questions on the Power of the Pope

Ockham's conspicuous lack of interest in promoting popular participation in either ecclesiastical or secular government leaves us at this point with two normally independent monarchical institutional structures. This is not a neat result. From the standpoint of modern political theories built on one or another conception of sovereignty, Ockham seems to have ignored the one thing necessary in a system of political thought: identification of a single supreme locus of control. Whether or not this is a defect in Ockham, it is certainly no accident. The *deliberately* dualistic character of his thought comes out clearly – indeed, it is the whole point – in the last selection in the present volume, Question III of *Eight Questions on the Power of the Pope*.

In this question Ockham asks whether all legitimate secular rule depends on papal authorization. He gives most attention throughout the question's thirteen chapters to a monistic premise held in common by papalists and Marsilians, the premise that "a community . . . in which all or many are prone to discord, dissensions, and disputes is not best ordered unless it is subject to one supreme rector, judge, and head, upon whom the jurisdiction of all others depends" (p. 305). This premise is first stated in an argument for universal papal secular jurisdiction in chapter 1, but it is also used in chapter 3 to defend the most extreme anti-papalist position presented in the intervening chapter. That obviously Marsilian position concedes that no community is best ordered unless it is subject to one supreme judge but insists that that judge should be appointed by the totality of mortals, or by the greater or sounder part of them, and should not be the pope. The great interest of Question III lies in Ockham's clear recognition that his own advocacy of a regular dualism of spiritual and secular governments requires him to deal, not only with papalism, but also with a secularism or laicism that would bring religion completely under civil control.

Ockham offers a single positive argument against the monistic premise. A community is *not* best ordered if it is subject in all things to one supreme judge, "because in such a community that supreme judge could destroy justice by his wrongdoing and even endanger the whole community." The rest of Question III, except for a brief concluding chapter giving replies on behalf of papalism to the arguments for secular independence, is devoted to explaining how this anti-unitarian position can coherently be maintained. To do this Ockham embarks on an explanation of some of the things required by, incompatible with, or consistent with (though not essential to) the best regime.

The first requirement for the best regime (chapter 4) is that it be established for the common good of its subjects and not for the ruler's own good. A second requisite is that it be monarchical (chapter 5). Although Ockham indicates that many arguments could be given for this, he contents himself with one: a single ruler is best for preserving friendship, peace, and concord, and for removing discord, among those who are subjects.

In chapter 6 Ockham turns to things which conflict with the best regime. The one point made is that it conflicts with the best regime to have only slaves as subjects. Accordingly (chapter 7), it conflicts with the best regime for the ruler to have the fullness of power sometimes attributed to the pope: power to command and impose on his subjects anything not in conflict with immutable natural law or with divine law.

What is compatible with the best regime although not of its essence? As a basis for answering this question, Ockham argues that the "most principal" function of a (secular) ruler is to correct and punish wrongdoers (chapter 8). Accordingly, it is compatible with the best regime for the jurisdiction of some person or persons within the community to be independent of the supreme ruler, provided that no member of the community who does wrong is thereby able to escape just and due punishment (chapter 9). It is not inconsistent with the best regime for someone in the community to be regularly exempt from the supreme ruler's coercive power, provided he is subject to it occasionally, so that he cannot do wrong insolently (chapter 10). Thus, the Empire does not "depend" on the papacy, and the papacy does not "depend" on the secular ruler: the authority of one is not derived from the other. The normal exemption of the pope (and perhaps others subject to the pope) from secular authority does not conflict with the optimal ordering of the community.

After briefly presenting his characteristic thesis that regimes may properly vary and that in some circumstances the best regime may need to be given up (chapter 11), Ockham replies in some detail to monistic arguments presented earlier. He argues that the unity required in an optimally ordered community is sufficiently attained if no one is absolutely and in all cases exempt from the supreme secular ruler's jurisdiction. Even in cases where the supreme spiritual power needs correction, it is reasonable that others besides the supreme secular ruler should have primary responsibility for the task. Conversely, when the supreme secular ruler needs correction, primary responsibility lies with the laity. In extreme circumstances, however, action across normal jurisdictional lines may be called for.

Marsilius of Padua had posed the dilemma of a person subject to independent supreme rulers who is summoned by each to appear before him at the same time. Ockham's response does not make the dilemma go away. If reasons are given for each summons, these can be assessed, but no general rule can be given for the assessment. If no reasons are given, there is a presumption (for the sake of peace?) in favor of the secular summons. All in all, Ockham's response may require free individual subjects to think for themselves.

A classic modern criticism of earlier political thought is that it is preoccupied with what ought to be, instead of facing what is. Some modern theorists then attempt to contain things as they supposedly are within a single system of control. If checks and balances or countervailing powers are needed, these must be accommodated within a single institutional framework. If something simply will not fit within the framework, it must be regarded as fundamentally private or inner, lacking any legitimate claim to interfere with what is public and real. Beyond the realm of such theory, however, a recognition persists that things neither are nor ought to be quite so neat. Ockham deserves a considerable measure of credit for transforming this recognition from a dynamic fact of medieval life into an intellectually respectable view of our wayfaring human condition.

Principal dates in Ockham's life

1285?   Born, perhaps in Ockham, Surrey.

By 1324   Studied and taught theology at Oxford and else-
               where in England; lectured on the *Sentences* of
               Peter Lombard and wrote extensively on theology,
               logic, and Aristotelian physics.

By 1328   Examined by a papally appointed commission at
               Avignon concerning theses in his theological works
               suspected of being heretical – never formally con-
               demned in this connection.

26 May 1328   Flees Avignon with Michael of Cesena and a
               few other friars opposed to John XXII's teachings
               on the poverty of Christ and the apostles, eventu-
               ally finding refuge with Ludwig of Bavaria, first
               in Pisa and then, for the rest of his life, in
               Munich. Ludwig had been elected Roman
               emperor in 1314 in a disputed election. In 1324
               John XXII excommunicated him for refusing to
               submit his election for papal examination and
               approval. In 1327 Ludwig asserted his imperial
               rights by invading Italy. He returned to Germany
               in 1330.

6 June 1328   Ockham is excommunicated by John XXII for leav-
               ing Avignon without permission and refusing to
               return when summoned. He is implicitly con-
               demned as a heretic by the clause at the end of
               John's bull *Quia quorundam* (1324) condemning

those who rejected his earlier bull on evangelical poverty, *Cum inter nonnullos.*

1332–4   Ockham writes the *Opus nonaginta dierum (OND, The Work of Ninety Days)*, a massive, formally neutral presentation of the issues between John XXII and his attackers in the poverty controversy, but a presentation in which the Michaelist side always has the last word.

Spring, 1334   Writes the *Epistola ad Fratres Minores in capitulo apud Assisium congregatos (EFM, A Letter to the Friars Minor Gathered in Chapter at Assisi),* an explanation to his fellow Franciscans of his break with John XXII, with lists of John's errors on evangelical poverty and other matters.

By late 1334   Writes Part I of *A Dialogue* (I *Dialogus),* a work still more massive than the *OND* and also formally impersonal; a discussion of heresy, "especially papal heresy."

1334–47   Produces other political works attacking the orthodoxy of John XXII and his successors, defending the legitimacy of Ludwig of Bavaria's authority as Roman emperor, and examining more generally the basis and functions of ecclesiastical and secular governmental institutions. These works include *Contra Benedictum (Against Benedict* [XII]), which attacks John XXII's successor for tolerating or confirming John's errors and the errors of others and for decreeing that no one should venture to approve either side of a controversy under examination by the pope prior to papal decision. Book VI is Ockham's first approach to the problems of papacy and empire.

III *Dialogus.* Another impersonal work, apparently never completed. What survives of Part III of the *Dialogue* is Ockham's most systematic contribution to political theory.

Octo quaestiones de potestate papae (Eight Questions on the Power of the Pope). An impersonal discussion, in which Ockham's views can be readily identified, of various questions concerning the pope's authority over the Empire.

Breviloquium de principatu-tyrannico super divina et humana, specialiter autem super Imperium et subiectos imperio, a quibusdam vocatis summis pontificibus usurpato (A Short Discourse on the Tyrannical Government Over Things Divine and Human, but Especially Over the Empire and Those Subject to the Empire, Usurped by Some Who Are Called Highest Pontiffs).

De imperatorum et pontificum potestate (On the Power of Emperors and Pontiffs). A direct, final discussion of papal power.

April 1347   Ockham dies in Munich, unreconciled; is buried in the Franciscan convent.

October 1347   Ludwig of Bavaria dies in a hunting accident.

1356   The emperor Charles IV promulgates the Golden Bull, defining procedures for imperial elections independent of papal supervision.

Suggestions for further reading

Translations of Ockham's earlier works, besides those listed in the bibliography to this volume, include William of Ockham, *Quodlibetal Questions*, 2 vols., translated by Alfred J. Freddoso and Francis E. Kelley (New Haven and London, 1991). Several passages from Ockham's political works are translated in Ewart Lewis, *Medieval Political Ideas*, 2 vols. (London, 1954). The initial stages of Ockham's involvement in political controversy are traced in detail by Jürgen Miethke in *Ockhams Weg zur Sozialphilosophie* (Berlin, 1969). Also see the article by George Knysh cited below. The tradition that Ockham sought reconciliation with the papacy at the end of his life is shown to rest on a confusion of Ockham with another "brother William of England" by Gedeon Gál, "William of Ockham Died *Impenitent* in April 1347," *Franciscan Studies*, 42, Annual 20, 1982:90–5. For an assessment of the direct influence of Ockham's ideas, see H.S. Offler, "The 'Influence' of Ockham's Political Thinking: The First Century" (in *Die Gegenwart Ockhams*, W. Vossenkuhl and R. Schönberger, eds., Weinheim, 1990, pp. 338–65).

For a general presentation of Ockham's political ideas, see Arthur Stephen McGrade, *The Political Thought of William of Ockham: Personal and Institutional Principles* (Cambridge, 1974). Marilyn McCord Adams, *William Ockham*, 2 vols. (Notre Dame, 1987), provides an acute presentation of the other major portion of Ockham's thought. Also see Gordon Leff, *William of Ockham: The Metamorphosis of Scholastic Discourse* (Manchester, 1975) and, for ethics, Lucan Freppert, *The Basis of Morality according to William*

Ockham (Chicago, 1988) and Taina M. Holopainen, *William Ockham's Theory of the Foundations of Ethics* (Helsinki, 1991). For negative assessments of Ockham's philosophical and political ideas, see E. Gilson, *The Unity of Philosophical Experience* (New York, 1937) and Georges de Lagarde, *La naissance de l'esprit laïque au déclin du moyen âge*, new edn. (Paris, 1956–70). The classic positive assessment of nominalist theology is H.A. Oberman's *The Harvest of Medieval Theology: Gabriel Biel and Late Medieval Nominalism* (Cambridge, MA, 1963). For relevant larger contexts see Norman Kretzmann, Anthony Kenny, and Jan Pinborg, eds., *The Cambridge History of Later Medieval Philosophy* (Cambridge, 1982); Quentin Skinner, *The Foundations of Modern Political Thought*, 2 vols. (Cambridge, 1978); J.H. Burns, ed., *The Cambridge History of Medieval Political Thought* (Cambridge, 1988); Anthony Black, *Political Thought in Europe* (Cambridge, 1992); James M. Blythe, *Ideal Government and the Mixed Constitution in the Middle Ages* (Princeton, 1992); and Jaroslav Pelikan, *The Christian Tradition*, vol. IV, *Reformation of Church and Dogma (1300–1700)* (Chicago and London, 1984).

Ockham's contribution to thinking about rights is discussed in A.S. McGrade, "Ockham and the Birth of Individual Rights," in Brian Tierney and Peter Linehan, eds., *Authority and Power: Studies on Medieval Law and Government Presented to Walter Ullmann on His Seventieth Birthday* (Cambridge, 1980), pp. 149–65; and in two articles by Brian Tierney, "Villey, Ockham and the Origin of Individual Rights," in J. Witte and F.S. Alexander, eds., *The Weightier Things of the Law: A Tribute to Harold J. Berman"* (Atlanta, 1988), pp. 1–31, and "Origins of Natural Rights Language: Texts and Contexts, 1150–1250," *History of Political Thought*, 10.4, Winter 1989:615–46.

The third volume of *Franciscan Studies* devoted to papers presented at the international Ockham colloquium held at St. Bonaventure University in 1985 *(Franciscan Studies, 46, Annual 24, 1986)* consists largely of papers concerned with Ockham's ethics and political thought. See especially Marilyn McCord Adams, "The Structure of Ockham's Moral Theory" (pp. 1–35); George Knysh, "Biographical Rectifications Concerning Ockham's Avignon Period" (pp. 61–91); Alberto Melloni, "Ockham's Critique of Innocent IV" (pp. 161–203); Wolfgang Stürner, "Die Begründung der *Iurisdictio temporalis* bei Wilhelm von Ockham" (pp. 243–51); and the papers on Ockham and papal infallibility by John J. Ryan (pp. 285–94) and Brian Tierney (pp. 295–300). On this last topic also see John Kilcullen, "Ockham on Infallibility," *Journal of Religious History*, 16, 1991:387–409.

A Letter to the Friars Minor

A Letter to the Friars Minor

To the religious men, all the Friars Minor[1] gathered at Assisi in the year of our Lord 1334 on the feast of Pentecost, brother William of Ockham [writes] to defend faithfully the orthodox faith. Divine Scripture suggests, the examples of the saints show, right reason dictates, human laws command, and fraternal charity persuades, that an account should be given of everything. Accordingly, so that I may follow in every way the footsteps of the glorious Apostle blessed Paul,[2] I desire to give, as well as I can, an account to you all, Catholic Christians and heretics, of what I have done, am doing, and will do. Know, then, and may all Christians know, that I stayed in Avignon almost four whole years before I recognized that the one who presided there had fallen into heretical perversity; because, not wishing to believe too readily that a person placed in so great an office would define that heresies should be held, I did not care either to read or to possess his heretical constitutions. Presently, however, when some occasion arose, at the command of a superior I read and diligently studied three of his constitutions – or rather, heretical destitutions – namely *Ad conditorem, Cum inter,* and *Quia quorundam.* In these I found a great many things that were heretical, erroneous, silly, ridiculous, fantastic, insane, and defamatory, contrary and likewise plainly adverse to orthodox faith,

---

[1] "Friars Minor" is the traditional translation of *fratres minores,"* "lesser brothers," the official name of the Franciscan Order.

[2] Cf. Paul's speech in Acts 22:1 ff, beginning, "Men, brethren and fathers, hear ye the *account* which I now give unto you."

3

good morals, natural reason, certain experience, and fraternal charity. I have decided that some of them should be inserted here.[3]

The first error in the constitution *Ad conditorem* that should be drawn to attention here is that the brothers' renunciation of property, by which, when they make their profession, they renounce property by a vow of poverty, "can contribute nothing to perfection if the same solicitude" concerning temporal things "persists as was in them before." From this it follows evidently that if after making their profession the brothers are just as solicitous about temporal things as they were in their novitiate, their vow of poverty can contribute nothing to perfection. And thus he seems here to fall manifestly into the error of those who say that a good deed done with a vow is not more meritorious than it would be if done without a vow; because, without that, the argument by which he strives to prove that the brothers' renunciation of property has not helped them toward perfection would lack all plausibility, as is plainly proved in other arguments.

And after the above assertion he adds, saying and asserting, that after the clarifying declaration of Nicholas III[4] the brothers "were not less solicitous, in court and out of court, in acquiring and keeping those goods," namely, those mentioned in the declaration, "than other mendicant religious are, who have some things in common." In this statement he seems to censure the brothers for transgressing the declaration of the Rule and their vow.

The second assertion contained there[5] is that "by not having the lordship" reserved to the Roman Church the brothers are not "poorer than if they had the things themselves together with the lordship they say they do not have." From this it seems to follow that the Order has renounced in vain and uselessly the lordship of all temporal things reserved to the Roman Church. And yet that assertion conflicts alike with the divine Scripture and with natural reason, as is shown evidently in many works.

The third assertion is that "the lordship reserved to the Roman Church" is "simple" – that is, hidden, bare, and obscure, as he

---

[3] To understand the meaning of these propositions, and to understand why Ockham regards them as heretical, it will in some cases be necessary to read the relevant parts of *OND*. For references see the footnotes to H.S. Offler's edition of *EFM*.

[4] The constitution *Exiit qui seminat* was issued "to clarify [*declarare*] some things that could have seemed doubtful in that Rule"; Friedberg, vol. ii, col. 1111.

[5] In *Ad conditorem*.

explains below, and consequently useless – because "no temporal gain has so far resulted from it to that church, and it is not hoped that any might result in future." This error is most plainly refuted in the decretal *Exiit*. There it is plainly asserted that the "retention[6] of such lordship, together with a grant of use made to poor persons, is accounted so much the more useful as it exchanges temporal things for eternal." But the retention of a lordship hidden, bare, and obscure must be regarded as more harmful than useful. From this assertion it likewise seems to follow that everything must be thought useless from which no temporal gain results and it is not hoped that any might result in future. That this is heretical every believer knows.

The fourth assertion is that in things consumable by being used, use of fact cannot be separated from ownership or lordship. From this it follows evidently that whenever the brothers use things consumable by use, they have ownership or lordship of those things, at least in common. This assertion plainly conflicts with divine Scripture, natural reason, and certain experience. For we see that thieves and robbers and others use such things without lordship and ownership, though, as we know, some use them licitly and some illicitly.

However, to prove, provide a basis for, and defend that assertion he brings in many things that seem to me fantastic, which need no refutation. He defines, pronounces, and affirms, first, that "simple use of fact, which is not a servitude, and for which there is no right of using, cannot be established or had" in things consumable by use. Also, "that no one can use a thing from which, while its substance is preserved, no advantage can come to him, such as things consumable by use certainly are." Also, that "in things consumable by use an act of using cannot be established or had without some right." Also, that "although in things consumable by use neither a right of using nor using itself can be established or had, nevertheless someone can 'use them up.' "[7] Also, that "using presupposes that, with the use, the substance of the thing is preserved." Also, that " 'using up' requires that, with the act, the substance of the thing be consumed." Also, that the act of

---

[6] That is, by the Roman Church.

[7] *Abuti* can mean either "use up" or "misuse." See *OND*, 33.64–9, pp. 510–11. See also Justinian, *Digest*, 7.5.5.1.

using "does not exist in reality either before it is performed, or while it is being performed, or after it is completed"; and that "when the act is in progress it still does not exist in reality." In support of the above assertion he brings forward these and many other things that seem ridiculous, but are, nevertheless,[8] contrary to the sacred Scriptures; and unless they are taken in their obvious meaning they are quite irrelevant to the intended conclusions.

In the same constitution he also definitively determines, asserts, and affirms many other assertions destructive of our Rule and of ecclesiastical poverty. I pass over them for the sake of brevity and because they are carefully discussed in other works.

And in the constitution *Cum inter nonnullos*, intending (as he testifies himself) to impose an end to the dispute which was taking place in the schools, where some were asserting that Christ and the apostles had no right of ownership and lordship (particular or even common) while others were affirming the contrary, he determines that the negative side is heretical. Yet Pope Nicholas III held that negative side, on the basis of the divine Scriptures.

Also, in the same constitution he pronounces definitively that unless Christ and the apostles had had the right to use, sell, and give the things they had and to acquire other things by means of them, their uses and actions would have been unjust. This seems manifestly heretical. From this it also follows that, since the Friars Minor do not have those rights in the things they are said to have, their uses and actions would be unjust, and thus the status of the Friars Minor would be plainly heretical.

In the constitution *Quia quorundam* I have also found a great many assertions that seem to me erroneous. Here I will draw attention to a few of them.

The first is that "gospel truth and apostolic statements testify in a great many places" that after their return from preaching the apostles carried money. Through this error he seems to impose on divine Scripture something plainly false. For although we read that Judas carried a purse, we never read that after their return from preaching the apostles carried money.

The second assertion is that Christ's statement when he said to the apostles that they should not carry money "was not a command-

---

[8] The implication of "nevertheless" seems to be that though these statements are ridiculous they must be taken seriously in this respect, that they are heretical.

ment, but a [granting of] power to accept necessaries from those to whom they preached the Gospel, which it was permissible for the apostles to observe, or, also, not to observe."

The third assertion is that he[9] had "a purse in respect of ownership."

The fourth assertion is that "to have some things in common in respect of ownership does not detract from the highest poverty."

The fifth is that Christ did not himself practice renunciation of the right to the ownership of any thing whatever and did not impose it on the apostles, and the apostles did not accept it under vow.

The sixth is that it does not belong to faith or morals "that Christ and the apostles had only simple use of fact in the things they had."

The seventh is that Nicholas III revoked some of the things that Gregory IX, Innocent IV, and Alexander IV had declared and determined concerning the poverty of the Friars Minor.

In proof of this he asserts and brings forward certain things that seem to me fantastic, which nevertheless smack of manifest heresy.[10]

The first of these is that the Order of Friars Minor "is an imaginary and represented person";[11] and consequently, by the same reasoning, the Church and every congregation, multitude, and people would be an imaginary and represented person.

The second is that those [things][12] "that are of fact cannot truly befit the Order"; and by the same reasoning, [things] that are of fact cannot befit the Church or any group or multitude. And thus the Church cannot make definitions concerning questions of faith or exercise jurisdiction, and it could not decide litigation or make any statutes whatever.

---

[9] That is, Christ.

[10] On the meaning of the three propositions following see Miethke, *Ockhams Weg*, pp. 502–4, and the gloss to *Quia quorundam*, in *Corpus iuris canonici*, vol. III, cols. 161–2.

[11] *Representata* here probably means "in the mind." This is what Ockham takes it to mean; see *OND*, 62.213, p. 568. (Compare: *esse in opinione . . . in intellectione . . . exemplatum . . . cognitum . . . repraesentatum, quae omnia aequivalent*; Duns Scotus, *Ordinatio*, I, dist. 35, q. un., *Opera omnia* vol. VI, p. 284.)

[12] In Latin *illa*. "Things" is supplied because in such a context English requires some noun. "Things" here has a broad, vague meaning, covering actions and rights as well as possessions.

The third is that although [things] that are of fact cannot befit the Order, nevertheless "those that are of law can befit the Order."[13] From this it follows that, according to him, [things] that are of law can befit a represented and imaginary person, and some *right* of using can belong to someone to whom, however, an *act* of using is, by the nature of the thing, altogether incongruous.

Taking note, therefore, that the three constitutions spoken of above were sprinkled with the heresies and errors listed and a great many others (so that I do not remember ever seeing so small a writing of any heretic or pagan that contained so many errors and heresies or was so devoid of theological or philosophical truths), and considering that the author had also pronounced definitively that everything taught as dogma in them should be held, I did not at all doubt that he was a heretic. Accordingly, knowing that all heretics "have nothing of power or right," that they are bound by a sentence of excommunication, and that they should be avoided by all Catholics and also, as far as each person's state permits, effectively attacked (because "an error not resisted is approved"), and knowing that according to the canon laws a question of faith, when it is certain that the assertion conflicts with a truth of faith, concerns not only a general council or prelates or even the clergy "but also the laity and absolutely every Christian," dist. 96, c. *Ubinam* (where the gloss takes the argument, "What touches all should be dealt with by all," from which it follows evidently that a question of faith concerns even Catholic and believing women, on the example of many holy women who with the utmost constancy underwent death and martyrdom for the defense and confession of the orthodox faith), I gladly left Avignon to devote myself, in my small measure, to attacking that heretic and his heresies. Making my way to the city of Pisa, I joined in the appeal against this heretical pseudo-pope prudently entered by brother Michael, the

---

[13] In the language of the civil law, "of law" either means "in the sense the term has in the law," or suggests that something is the case (or is treated as if it were the case) because of some legal rule or judgment. "Fact" seems to mean either an act of a human person, or what is the case apart from any legal rule or judgment. According to John XXII a represented person cannot have "use of fact" because a mental entity cannot perform any act of a human person, but the law (which sometimes treats a group as if it were a person) may attribute to it "use of law" (i.e., "use" in the sense the term has in the law, a certain legal right). Ockham denies that a group is a mental entity; a group is its members (ordered in a certain way – see Miethke, pp. 512–13), and it acts when its members act (in some appropriate way).

Minister General (though according to some it is not simply necessary to appeal in a case of faith, since no sentence passed against the Catholic faith can become definitive [*res judicata*]).

Afterwards, however, when this manifestly heretical pseudo-pope answered the appeal entered by brother Michael, the Minister General, and drew up and published the constitution *Quia vir reprobus*, he strengthened us in many ways and firmly united us in our purpose; for joining new heresies to old, he made explicit a great many things we believed he would never assert and clearly excluded many answers and evasions he could have made to some of our attacks.

And in the constitution *Quia vir reprobus* he taught as dogma the assertions written below, which seem to me erroneous.

The first of these is that in things consumable by use a right of using cannot be had.

The second is that in things consumable by use an act of using cannot be had.

The third is that things consumable by use cannot be used, only "used up."

The fourth is that all things common to believers in the primitive Church that are mentioned in chapters 2[:44] and 4[:32] of Acts were common to them in respect of the same sort of lordship as they had before their conversion.

The fifth is that houses, fields, and other immovables were common to the converted believers mentioned in chapters 2 and 4 of Acts and to the apostles, in respect of lordship and ownership.

The sixth is that after the sending of the Holy Spirit the apostles had estates in Judaea, in respect of lordship and ownership.

The seventh is that it was permissible for the apostles after the sending of the Holy Spirit to possess estates both in Judaea and among the gentiles.

The eighth is that after the division of the common things mentioned in chapters 2[:45] and 4[:35] of Acts, each of the apostles and other believers was the particular owner and lord of the money and other things assigned to him.

The ninth is that the vow of living without property does not extend to the things that human life necessarily requires.

The tenth is that when Peter said, "See, we have left everything" [Matthew 19:27], he did not mean that they had left everything in respect of lordship and ownership.

The eleventh is that the apostles did not vow the renunciation of ownership, not even of particular ownership, of all temporal things.

The twelfth is that the apostles afterwards sold the estates of which they had[14] had lordship and ownership in Judaea after the sending of the Holy Spirit.

The thirteenth is that gospel poverty, even in its most perfect degree, by no means excludes lordship and ownership of things.

The fourteenth is that the blessing "Increase and multiply" related in Genesis 1 was given to Adam outside Paradise before Eve was formed.

The fifteenth is that before Eve was formed Adam had the lordship of temporal things that is now called ownership.

The sixteenth is that a slave actually lending his lord's money has neither the use nor the "using up" of the money.

The seventeenth is that the words of Pope Nicholas III when he defines in the decretal *Exiit* that the Friars Minor have use of fact of all the things they use without lordship and ownership should be understood of things not consumed by use, and if the constitution *Exiit* defined that in things consumable by use the Friars Minor have simple use of fact, it defined the impossible.

The eighteenth is that use of fact in things consumable by use is not had by an enactment of God.

The nineteenth is that in things consumable by use the act of consuming cannot be separated from lordship.

The twentieth is that Nicholas III did not grant the brothers simple use of fact of things consumable by use, and if he did grant it his constitution contained an impossibility.

The twenty-first is that a successive act does not exist in reality and cannot exist.

The twenty-second is that every human law by which temporal lordships are possessed is contained among the laws of kings, as kings are distinguished from other public powers.

The twenty-third is that in respect of temporal things the civil law brought in formulas of action, and not lordship.

---

[14] Deleting *non* (which is in the manuscript; but see *OND*, 18.18–19, p. 454). Or keep *non* and translate: " ... (of which they had *not* had lordship and ownership) ..," taking the parenthesis as Ockham's contradiction of what John had said (McGrade).

The twenty-fifth [*sic*] is that Christ, as a mortal wayfaring man, was from the instant of his conception the temporal lord of all temporal things.

The twenty-sixth is that Christ, as God, had kingship and universal lordship of things eternally by the very fact that the Father begot him.

The twenty-seventh is that Christ had lordship of clothing, food, shoes, and even of a purse, not from the instant of his conception but afterwards successively in other ways, such as by gift of the faithful or by purchase.

The twenty-eighth is that Christ, as a wayfaring man, could not have renounced temporal kingship and universal lordship of things.

The twenty-ninth is that Christ was not a poor man by not having lordship of things, but by not taking the fruits of things.

The thirtieth is that bare lordship perpetually separate from any taking of gain from a thing does not make the person having it rich.

The thirty-first is that every lordship stripped of the taking of temporal gain must be regarded as useless.

The thirty-second is that before the apostles were sent to preach they did not relinquish the lordship or ownership of any temporal thing.

The thirty-third is that Christ gave to the apostles no other law of living than he gave to the other disciples (including under the name of disciples all Christian men and women).

The thirty-fourth is that the commandment given to the apostles of not possessing gold etc., was temporary, only for the time of that [preaching] journey.

The thirty-fifth is that after their return from preaching the apostles had bread, fish, money, cloaks, and swords, in respect of ownership or lordship.

The thirty-sixth is that it was permissible for the apostles to contend and litigate in court for temporal things as for their property.

The thirty-seventh is that the words of Matthew 5[:40], "He who wishes to contend with you in court," etc., and of Luke 6[:29], were not said to the perfect, but only to the imperfect. (This is erroneous, because they were given to both, though they can be understood in different ways as said to the perfect and to the imperfect.)

The thirty-eighth is that the twelve apostles were not apostles at the time when the commandments spoken of in Matthew 5 and Luke 6, "He who wishes to contend with you in court," etc., were given to them.

The thirty-ninth is that in 1 Corinthians 6[:1–9] the Apostle forbade or dissuaded the Corinthians only from fraudulent and unjust actions or litigation in the courts of unbelievers and did not reprehend or even recommend against other litigations, but instead wished them to litigate.

The fortieth is that the key of knowledge is in no way a key of the Church or of the kingdom of heaven, because it is neither the same as, nor distinct from, the key of power.

The forty-first is that the Roman pontiff can in respect of things pertaining to faith and morals revoke the definitions and determinations of the pontiffs his predecessors and define contrary assertions.

After the constitution *Quia vir reprobus*, he preached and taught many assertions contrary to truths he is obliged to believe explicitly.

The first of these is that in the divinity there are not three distinct persons.

The second is that God can do by his absolute power nothing except what he does by his ordinate power; and that [the statement] that God may do something other or otherwise than he does includes a contradiction; and that all things happen of necessity, so that [the statement] that something not pre-ordained by God may happen includes a contradiction.

The third is that the souls of the saints in heaven do not see God and will not see him before the day[15] of general judgment.

The fourth is that the souls of the reprobate are not and will not be in hell before the day of general judgment.

The fifth is that the demons are not punished and will not be punished before the day of general judgment.

The sixth is that Christ will not be king after the day of judgment.

Because of the errors and heresies written above and countless others, I withdraw from the obedience[16] of the pseudo-pope and

---

[15] Substituting *diem* for *idem*.

[16] That is, from the set of persons who obey. See *The Oxford English Dictionary*, "obedience," 2.b.

of all who support him to the prejudice of the orthodox faith. For it has been shown to me evidently by men of outstanding learning that because of the above errors and heresies this heretical pseudo-pope must be regarded as having been deprived of the papacy and excommunicated by the law itself, without any new sentence, because he manifestly falls under the canons "of sentence passed," both of general councils and of highest pontiffs. To prove these things several volumes have been published, and concerning the heresies and errors listed and those annexed to them I myself, from my slender abilities, have written by my hand fifty sexterns of the common form of paper, and I still have forty and more to write.[17] For against the errors of this pseudo-pope "I have set my face like the hardest rock,"[18] so that neither lies nor slurs nor persecution of whatever sort (that does not physically touch my person), nor the multitude, however great, of those who believe or favor or even defend him will ever at any time be able to prevent me from attacking and refuting his errors as long as I have hand, paper, pen, and ink. For before I would regard all the above errors as compatible with the faith, I would think that the whole Christian faith, and all Christ's promises about the Catholic faith lasting to the end of the age, and the whole Church of God, could be preserved in a few, indeed in one; and I would judge that all other Christians erred against the Catholic faith, on the example of the prophet Elias, who, though he believed that he was God's only worshiper left,[19] nevertheless did not at all desert the true faith: though I do not doubt that in fact many "thousands of men" and women "have by no means bent the knee" of their faith "before Baal."[20]

Anyone, therefore, who wishes to recall me or anyone else of those withdrawing from the obedience of the pseudo-pope and his supporters should attempt to provide a basis for his constitutions

---

[17] A sextern consists of six sheets folded together to form twelve folios, i.e., twenty-four pages; how much a folio contained depended on the handwriting. Presumably *The Work of Ninety Days* is one of the works Ockham had been writing; in the only complete manuscript extant this work occupies 163 folios, in the modern printed edition 551 pages. The first part of the *Dialogue*, written at about the same time, occupies roughly 200 folios. These two works, therefore, account for about two-thirds of the fifty sexterns.

[18] Isaias 50:7.

[19] See 3 Kings, 19:10.

[20] 3 Kings, 19:18.

and sermons and show that they agree with the divine Scriptures; or else he should show by sacred texts or by manifest arguments that a pope cannot fall into heretical perversity, or that someone knowing that a pope is a notorious heretic should obey him. Let him not allege the multitude of his adherents or rely on insults. For those who try to arm themselves with a multitude, lies, insults, threats, accusations, and calumnies show themselves to be naked of truth and reason. Let no one think, therefore, that because of the multitude of this pseudo-pope's supporters or because of arguments that are common to heretics and to the orthodox, I would wish to abandon acknowledged truth. For I prefer the divine Scriptures to a man who is a simpleton in sacred literature, and I prefer the teaching of the holy fathers reigning with Christ to the deliverances of those living in this mortal life. And I consider that the general chapter of Perugia, in which the brothers acted, though with fear, yet from conscience, should be preferred to all later gatherings of the brothers, in which they were moved by fear, ambition, or hatred, and that all the brothers, each and every one of them, at the time when they held the truths of faith and of the Order, are worth more than themselves if they have abandoned those truths.

But if someone shows me plainly that the constitutions and sermons of the pseudo-pope do not deviate from Catholic truth, or, alternatively, that one should obey an heretical pope knowing that he is a heretic, I will not be slow to return to the brothers who support him. No one, however, who can prove neither of these things either by argument or by authorities should be hostile either to me or to anyone who does not obey the said heretic.

I have given you an account, therefore, of the reason for my absence from the multitude of the brothers. I am not afraid to give an account also, before a just judge, of any other statements and actions of mine whatever, although I am not ignorant of the wickedness of men. For I think I have learned[21] more in these last four years about the characters of our contemporaries than if I had had continual dealings with them for forty years without this quarrel. I understand better the generalizations of the sacred Scriptures describing the characters of men, when I see them being

---

[21] Substituting *me advertisse* for *evertisse* (the sole manuscript reads *evertisse*).

verified by experience every day. For in this time of testing, the thoughts of the hearts of many are being revealed. But do not "blow the nose" too much,[22] for, since he who now reigns is mortal, you do not know what the days to come will bring forth. May the Omnipotent deign to turn evil portents to good! Amen.

---

[22] An allusion to Proverbs 30:33, "He that violently bloweth his nose bringeth out blood." This verse seems to have been taken to mean that evils sometimes have to be tolerated; see *Extra, De renunciatione,* c. *Nisi cum pridem,* col. 235.

The Work of Ninety Days

The Work of Ninety Days

The Work of Ninety Days

Chapter 2

[John XXII] In the first place, then, this heretic tries to attack
the constitution *Ad conditorem canonum* in this, that the said
constitution, "intending to prove that the Friars Minor, pro-
fessing to live without property in things that are consumed
by being used, are not to be regarded as simple users," asserts
the following: "To say that use of right or of fact separate
from ownership or lordship can be established[1] in such things
as are consumed by use conflicts with law and goes against
reason ... In things consumable by use neither a right of using
nor a use of fact separate from ownership or lordship of the
thing can be established or had." These are the words of the
constitution, which, so this heretic says, "clearly go against
sacred Scripture, the sacred canons and definitions of the holy
doctors, and also the determinations of the holy Roman Church.
That they conflict with sacred Scripture is proved clearly from
chapters 2 and 4 of Acts. For in chapter 2 it is said: 'All the
believers were together and had all things common. They sold
their possessions and property and distributed them to individuals as each had need' [Acts 2:44–5]. In chapter 4 it is written:
'The multitude of believers were of one heart and soul, and
none of them said that anything he possessed was his ... Nor

---

[1] *Constitui*, which might also be translated "created," "brought into existence," or
"set up." For example, the right called usufruct (a right to use something that
belongs to someone else) could be created (*constitui*) by legacy, if the testator left
ownership of land to one person but the right to farm it to another; see Justinian,
Digest, 7.1.1.3.

was there among them anyone in want. For those who possessed fields and houses sold them and brought the price of the things they sold and put it at the feet of the apostles. They distributed to individuals as each had need . . . They broke bread in their homes, and took food with rejoicing' [Acts 4:32–46]. The word 'his' the saints explain thus: 'His, that is, proper [belonging exclusively to him],' as is clear in 12, q. 1, c. *Scimus*, c. *Nolo*, and c. *Non dicatis*, and para. *Sic ergo*, and in Augustine's *Rule* (near the beginning). And the ordinary gloss on the words 'they had all things common' says: 'It is a sign of brotherly love to possess all things and have nothing proper [exclusive to oneself].' These words," so this heretic says, "clearly suggest that the believers did not have ownership of any temporal thing, whether consumable by use or not consumable by use. For they sold their things not consumable by use – namely possessions, fields, houses, and property (gloss: 'that is, flocks') – and did not keep them, either individually or in their community; and those things which the law (*Inst.*, *de usufructu*, para. *constituitur*) says are consumable by use – namely monies taken as the price of things sold and bread (particularly mentioned here) – they had in common, and they 'distributed to individuals as each had need'; and 'none of them said that anything was his,' that is, proper, but 'among them all things were common.' Thus each of them had use of things consumable by use without ownership and lordship" – that is, separate from ownership and lordship. From this he concludes that "the said assertion and teaching contained in the said constitution goes against divine Scripture and destroys and confounds every religious order that has a vow renouncing the ownership of temporal things, for it implies that when any religious used things consumable by use he would have to be regarded as an owner." These are the words of this heretic, which undoubtedly include many falsehoods. We will answer them in what follows.

[Ockham] These are the words of the constitution [*Quia vir repro-bus*]. This part begins the body of the constitution, which is divided into three main parts. The first part answers objections against the constitution *Ad conditorem*, the second answers objections against the constitution *Cum inter*, the third answers objections against the constitution *Quia quorundam*. The second part begins at "Again, this heretic tries to attack the constitution *Cum inter nonnullos*" [chapter 82], the third begins toward the end, at "Again, this heretic tries to attack the constitution *Quia quorundam*" [chapter

120]. The first part is divided into five parts corresponding to the five matters in *Ad conditorem* that brother Michael tries to disprove as erroneous. The second begins at "Again, this heretic says that the aforesaid constitution" [chapter 33], the third at "Again, the said heretic says that the said constitution" [chapter 59], the fourth at "Again, this heretic tries to attack the said constitution" [chapter 67], the fifth at "Again, the said heretic tries to attack the said constitution" [chapter 74].

The first part is further divided into seven parts, answering the seven objections against the first assertion taken from the constitution *Ad conditorem*. The second part begins at "Again, to prove that the assertion" [chapter 10], the third at "Further, this enemy of truth" [chapter 19], the fourth at "Again, he tries" [chapter 21], the fifth at "Further, that heretic says" [chapter 25], the sixth at "Further, to show" [chapter 29], the seventh at "Again, he says that this assertion" [chapter 31]. The first part is further divided into two parts. For first the attack is reported and then it is answered in the part immediately following, at "For we say" [chapter 3].

In the first part, then, it is shown that in things consumable by use neither use of fact nor use of right can be separated from ownership or lordship. This is asserted in the constitution *Ad conditorem*, and in his appeal brother Michael attacks it by means of the statement of chapters 2 and 4 of Acts, "Among them all things were common" [Acts 4:32; cf. 2:44]. For he says that since according to the truth of Scripture "Among them all things were common," they did not have ownership of any thing consumable by use; yet certainly they had use of fact of things consumable by use; in things consumable by use, therefore, use of fact can be separated from ownership and lordship. This is the force of the attack reported above, which the attackers try to defend.

They say that since the attacked labors to bring in errors and destroy truth under the ambiguities of terms, they will, to clarify what is to be said, explain certain terms often used in this constitution, namely: "use," "use of fact," "use of right," "right of using," "simple users," "things consumable by use," "things not consumable by use," "lordship," "ownership," and the words "mine," "thine," "his," and the like.

Concerning the first, namely what is meant by **use**, they say that writers take the word "use" in various ways. It can be taken in four ways. In one way "use" is taken as distinguished from enjoyment, insofar as use and enjoyment are acts of will by which something is taken in the faculty of will. It is seldom or never taken in this way in legal science. In another way use is taken for the act of using some external thing, and it is taken in this way in every discipline which uses the word "use." "Use" is taken this way in Judges 19[:19], where it is said, "Having bread and wine for use by your maidservant and myself." In a third way "use" is taken for being accustomed to do something. It is taken in this way in 1 Kings 17[:39], when David, when he put on the armor, said, "I cannot go like this, for I do not have the use." It is also taken this way in dist. 11, c. *Consuetudinis*, and *Extra, De consuetudine*, c. *Cum consuetudinis*. In a fourth way "use" is taken for a certain particular right by which one can use things belonging to another, preserving their substance. They say that "use" is taken this way in the legal sciences and in writings which imitate the manner of speaking of the legal sciences. They do not recall, they say, that "use" is ever taken this way in theology or philosophy. They say, therefore, that the noun "use" can be taken in these ways, without denying that it may be found taken in some other way.

Concerning **use of fact**, they say that use of fact is the act of using some external thing – for example, an act of living in, eating, drinking, riding, wearing clothes, and the like. They illustrate this from divine Scripture, from legal science, and also from sayings of the attacked himself. For Judges 19 (quoted above) says, "Having bread and wine for use by your maidservant and myself": this use was, certainly, to eat the bread and drink the wine; "use" therefore is sometimes taken for the act of eating or drinking. Again, *Inst., de usu et habitatione*, para. 1, says: "Whoever has the bare use of a farm is understood to have no more than this, that he may use, for everyday use, the vegetables, fruit, flowers, hay, straw, and wood." In these words, when it is said "he may use, for everyday use," "use" does not mean a right, since it would be unsuitable to say "he may use, for everyday right." It is therefore taken here for the act of using to[2] which someone has this right, called "bare use," by which he can use the vegetables, fruit, and suchlike. But the act by which someone uses vegetables and fruit is the act of eating. The act of eating is therefore called "use" also in the civil

---

[2] Substituting *pro* for *quo*.

law, and by the same argument the acts of drinking and wearing and the like can be called use.

Again, that the act of eating may be called "use of fact" is shown also by statements of the attacked himself. For in this constitution *Quia vir reprobus* he says: "Use of fact is proper to the user in such a way that it cannot be said to be another's or to be communicable to another; for it is clear that Peter's act of eating was in such a way proper to him that it could not be said to be common to others." These words clearly establish that this act of eating is called a use of fact; and by the same reason acts of drinking, wearing, and the like can be called uses of fact. Thus, therefore, every act anyone performs in relation to an external thing, such as eating, drinking, wearing, writing, reading in a book, riding, and the like, is called a use of fact, "fact" being added to distinguish such use from use of right. But [the attackers] do not deny that "use of fact" can be taken in some other way.

Concerning **use of right**, they say that use of right is a certain determinate positive right, established by human ordinance, by which one has the licit power and authority to use things belonging to another, preserving their substance.[3] Accordingly, it is defined in the law thus: "Use is the right of using the things of another, preserving their substance." Use in that sense can be divided into bare use and usufruct. **Bare use** is when one has the right of using something that is another's, preserving its substance, but cannot sell, rent, or give this right for nothing to another. Thus one who rents a house has the right to live in the house with his family, but he cannot sell, give, or rent it to another. Similarly, one who has bare use of a farm has the right to stay on the farm, if he wishes, and also the right to gather certain crops growing on the farm, as determined by the civil law; but he cannot sell, give, or rent this right to anyone else. **Usufruct** is a fuller right in another's things, preserving their substance; for whoever has usufruct not only can use the thing but also sell, give, and rent all his right to another. So when use is called bare, the "bare" is added to distinguish it from usufruct. And thus "use of right" is sometimes taken generally, and in this sense it is common to bare

---

[3] On the right of use and usufruct see Justinian, *Institutes*, II.4 and 5, and *Digest*, Book VII.

use and usufruct, and sometimes it is taken more specifically for bare use as distinct from usufruct (just as the word "custom" is sometimes taken generally for human law both written and not written and sometimes specifically for human law that is not written, as can clearly be gathered from *Decreta*, dist. 1). In whichever way "use of right" is taken, therefore, it is always a right and not an act of using. Thus whoever rents a house to live in has use of right in the house even while he is outside the house and not actually living in it. "Of right" is added to distinguish it from use "of fact," which is a certain act performed in relation to an external thing, as this term is taken in the law – as it is often also found taken in theology.

Fourth, they explain **right of using**, saying that a right of using is a licit power of using an external thing of which one ought not be deprived against one's will, without one's own fault and without reasonable cause, and if one has been deprived, one can call the depriver into court. "Licit power" is included to distinguish it from the illicit power by which a thief often uses another's things; and many others also often use their own things by an illicit power. "Of which without one's own fault," etc., is included to distinguish it from a grace, by which a licit power to use something is often granted to someone, of which, however, he can licitly be deprived at the granter's discretion, without any fault of his or any reason, solely because the granter revokes the power granted. Thus poor people invited by a rich man have the licit power to use food and drink put before them, but the inviter can if he pleases take them away, and, if he does so, those invited cannot for this call the person who invited them into court; they have no action against him. In the law such a power is often called a "grace." Thus the ordinary gloss on 10, q. 3, *Cavendum*, notes that "if a bishop has funds he can spend, he ought not burden others, for these things seem to be sought *of grace rather than of right*." The gloss to *Extra, De postulatione praelatorum*, c. *Bonae memoriae*, also notes that if someone is called to some election "of grace" he does not acquire for himself any right or advantage. Thus a distinction must be made between a right and a grace. A right of using, therefore, belongs to those who have bare use and to those who have usu-fruct – and not to them only, but it often belongs to whoever has lordship and ownership of the thing. Thus in the definition of "use" a right of using is put as the genus, when it is said that

"use is *a right of using* another's things, preserving their substance."
It is quite clear from this that not every right of using is a "use,"
for if it were, the first part of the definition of use, which is put
in place of the genus, would be convertible with what is defined
and the remaining parts would be superfluous. Therefore, although
every use of right is a right of using, not every right of using is
the use of right that is distinguished from ownership and lordship;
but every right of using things *belonging to another, preserving their
substance*, is a use.

If it be said that a right of using is a servitude, but no one has
a servitude in a thing of his own, therefore whoever has lordship
of a thing does not have a right of using the thing of which he
has lordship; again, sometimes a person has lordship and ownership
of some thing yet cannot licitly use it (for example, if he rents
something of his own to someone else he cannot use it, except
illicitly), therefore lordship of a thing or ownership is not a right
of using:

To the first of these the attackers say that although it is found
in the law that every *use* is a servitude and that every servitude is
a right of using, nevertheless it is perhaps not found that every
right of using is a servitude; and if this were found, they would say
that there "right of using" was taken more narrowly and not as a
general term for every kind of right of using (which would not be
unsuitable, because as St Augustine shows by many examples in
De Trinitate, Book xv, the same word is taken sometimes generally,
sometimes specifically or narrowly). They say, therefore, that
although no one has a servitude in a thing of his own, a person
nevertheless has a right of using a thing of his own. For not all
who use their own things use them unjustly, nor do they use them
always by others' grace; they therefore use them of right, since
whoever uses anything uses it either unjustly and illicitly, or by
another's grace, or by a right he has in it. Thus, therefore, the
lord of a thing in which another has no right uses it by a right
he has in it, since he does not use it unjustly and illicitly or by
another's grace. Therefore he has a right of using in that thing,
though he does not have a servitude in the thing, because not
every right of using is a servitude (though the converse is true).

To the second they say that although lordship of a thing is not
a right of using it whenever one wishes, yet often a person who
has lordship has, along with lordship, a right of using it when he

pleases; sometimes, however, he keeps the lordship and grants the right of using to another, either for nothing or for a price. And so, granting that lordship of a thing or ownership is not a right of using, one need not grant that someone who has lordship does not have a right of using, though sometimes he who has lordship of the thing does not have a right of using at that time (though he may have a right of using at another time, for example, when the other ceases to have a right of using the thing).

Fifth, they explain what they understand by **simple users**. They say that "user" is made from "use" and therefore, just as "use" is taken in two ways – namely for use of right and for use of fact, though it may be taken also in other ways – so also "user" can be taken in two ways: in one way as corresponding in meaning to "use" taken for use of right, as one is called a user who has use of right (just as one is called owner who has ownership of the thing); and then a *simple* user is someone who has bare use, or at least has no right beyond use of right. In this way, the attackers say, the Friars Minor are not simple users, because they are not users in this way, since they do not have the use of right spoken of in the legal sciences (and never in theology). In another way "user" can be taken as corresponding in meaning to "use" taken for use of fact; thus one is called a user who has use of fact of the thing, and a *simple* user is one who has, or can have, use of fact of the thing by not having any right by which (either in his own name or in the name of his group[4]) he could litigate in court for the thing or for use of fact of the thing. They say that in this way the Friars Minor are simple users.

Sixth, they explain which things are **consumable by use** and which not consumable by use. They say that things consumable by use are those which are consumed by the use itself – that is, by the act of using: either consumed altogether (as far as the user is concerned), or generally are made to deteriorate and are at length consumed. These include food and drink, medicines, ointments, money, clothes, and the like. For although in its substance money is not consumed or even made to deteriorate when something is bought with it, yet as far as the buyer is concerned it is consumed – that is, it totally ceases to be his, as if it were consumed

---

[4] *Collegium*, meaning any set of people acting as a body.

in its substance. Clothes, also, although they are by no means consumed by the first use of fact, generally begin to deteriorate and are at length consumed. Other things that can be used are called things **not consumable by use**; for example, a house, which is not made to deteriorate by being lived in, except perhaps accidentally, and other like things, are said to be not consumable by use.

Since someone might say that the attacked takes "things consumable by use" more narrowly and therefore according to him money and clothes should not be counted as things consumable by use (which would exclude many objections appearing against him concerning clothes and money), the attackers therefore show that the attacked himself thinks clothes and money should be counted among things consumable by use. Concerning clothes, indeed, he says so plainly, for in the constitution *Quia vir reprobus* he says it in these words: "It is certain that everyday clothing is counted among things consumable by use." Concerning money he suggests the same in the answer to the sixth objection, as will be clear there. Clothes and money, therefore, even according to the attacked himself, are to be counted among things consumable by use.

Seventh, the attackers show what should be understood by **lordship**. They say that such words as *dominium* [lordship], *dominus* [lord], *dominator* [lord], *dominari* [to be lord over, to dominate], and the like are taken in different disciplines equivocally and in different ways. For they are taken in one way in moral philosophy, in another way in natural philosophy, in another way sometimes in common speech, and in another way in legal science; and therefore, since according to Augustine theology in a way includes all the sciences, these words are taken equivocally in various places in divine Scripture.

Thus "lordship" is often taken in moral philosophy for the power by which someone can freely do opposite acts; and in this way they say that man is lord and has lordship over his acts, whereas brutes do not have lordship over their acts. "To dominate" is also taken in this way, according to one exposition, in Genesis 4[:7], when the Lord says to Cain, "Your appetite will be under you, and you will dominate it." Such words are taken in another way for the virtuous habit by which someone rules his passions according to right reason. "To dominate" is taken in this way in Proverbs

16[:32]: "Better is the patient man than the strong man, and he who rules [*dominari*] his soul than the destroyer of cities." Such words are taken in another way for violent and usurped rule over others who cannot or dare not resist it. Such lordship Peter prohibits to the elders in his first epistle, chapter 5. He says: "Feed the Lord's flock which is in your charge, caring for them not by constraint but willingly according to God, not for the sake of shameful gain but voluntarily, not as dominating your charge, but being a wholehearted example to the flock" [1 Peter 5:2–3]. So also in common speech it is sometimes said that a wife dominates her husband, a servant his master, a companion his companion. Such words are taken in another way for the power of ruling some thing in a due way, and thus a boy is sometimes said to dominate his lord's horse.

In natural philosophy some of these words are taken in another way for the power of changing another thing. In this sense it is said that in every mixture there is some predominant element. However, they [the attackers] say that they do not remember reading that the word "lord" is found with such a meaning.

In the legal sciences these words are taken in another way: for a specific power of laying claim to some temporal thing and defending, holding, and controlling it. They say "a specific power" because, although some power of laying claim to a temporal thing (etc.) is called lordship in the law, not every such power of laying claim to a thing (etc.) is called lordship. For whoever rents a house has, in a certain way, power to lay claim to the house if he is driven out illicitly and also to defend it if someone tries to take it from him, and he also has power to live in the house and otherwise control the house, yet he is not for that reason understood to have lordship. Therefore not every power of laying claim to a temporal thing (etc.) is called lordship. Yet it is certain that lordship is a power of laying claim to a temporal thing (etc.). It is therefore necessary to search for a definition or proper description of the lordship often spoken of in the law.

Now the attackers say they have not read a definition or proper description of lordship in any authoritative writing, and therefore, wishing to give a definition of lordship, they draw distinctions concerning lordship as the term is taken in the law. They say that of lordships over temporal things, one is divine, with which they are not concerned at present. Another is human lordship, and that is twofold. For one lordship belonged to men in the state of innocence by natural or divine law; concerning this lordship it is said to our first parents in Genesis 1[:28], "Have lordship over the fish of the sea and the birds of the air and over all living things that move upon the earth." Another lordship belongs to mankind by positive law or by human establishment, and this lordship is often spoken of in civil and canon law. And lordship in that sense can be taken in two ways, namely generally or broadly, and specifically or narrowly.

Taking lordship generally or **broadly**, the attackers define or describe it as follows: "Lordship is a principal human power of laying claim to and defending some temporal thing in a human court." "Human power" separates this lordship from the divine lordship; "principal" separates lordship from bare use and usufruct and from every other right held from a principal lord, and also from the power of an agent, who has power to lay claim to something in another's name. Thus, although one who has bare use and usufruct has power to lay claim to the thing and also to defend it, yet he had that power from another who granted him the use or usufruct, keeping the first right to himself without acquiring a new right. Thus, also, although a creditor has power to lay claim to a thing pledged, indeed sometimes even has power to sell it and transfer the lordship, nevertheless he does not have lordship of the thing, because he had it from another who, keeping the first right to himself, has not acquired another right. The phrase "in a human court" separates this lordship from that which belongs to a man by natural law or by primary divine law; it also separates this lordship from every grace and permission to use a thing, though graces and permissions are also excluded, strictly speaking, by "laying claim to."

Taking "lordship" in this general sense, the attackers say that prelates and ecclesiastics have lordship in church property. They try to make this clear from the sacred canons. For blessed Gregory, as quoted 12, q. 2, c. *Ecclesiasticis*, says: "Because, therefore, we have learnt that Theodore, a most eloquent man and one of our councillors, is without the assistance of slaves, therefore we command that the boy Acosimus, a Sicilian, be given and handed over into his right and lordship. Since he already possesses him, handed over by our own will, it was necessary for this to be supported by authority, for evidence in the future and for the confirmation of the grant, so that, with the Lord's protection, he can possess him as lord, securely, always, and without any suspicion of his being taken back." From these words it appears that Theodorus had the right and lordship of a slave, whom he possessed as lord; and by the same reason the clergy have lordship of other church property. Gregory also seems to suggest this, as we read in 16, q. 4, in the penultimate chapter, when, writing to Peter the Subdeacon, he says: "We want you to go to the city of Palermo and investigate the question on that basis, that is, with lordship of the thing remaining with the possessor, as it has been possessed until now." These words imply that a church[5] possessed lordship of the thing in dispute.

Further, the attackers say that whoever has ownership of a thing has lordship of it; but prelates and ecclesiastics have ownership of church property, on the testimony of blessed Gregory, who (as quoted 12, q. 2, last chapter) commanded that a certain house, garden, and lodging be handed over to a certain religious woman to be possessed by right of ownership; that religious woman could therefore control temporal things by right of ownership. Bishops also are understood to have their own churches, as is clear from 3, q. 1, c. 1, and q. 2, c. *Audivimus*; and we read in many places that bishops and monks have their own property; prelates and ecclesiastics therefore have lordship of church property. We read this also explicitly in a decretal of Nicholas III, *Exiit qui seminat*, that he takes all the things the Friars Minor use into the lordship and ownership of the Roman Church.

It is proved also by argument. For it is certain from the sacred canons that prelates and ecclesiastics have a right in temporal things. But running through the various rights by which temporal things are possessed, in many things they have no right except lordship. For although in some things they may have usufruct and in others use (as can be inferred from the words of Augustine, quoted 17, q. 4, last chapter), nevertheless they by no means have such a right in many other things which are known to have been alienated from every right of laymen. It seems, therefore, that in those things they have some sort of lordship.

---

[5] Or a monastery. The parties to the dispute were a church and a monastery.

The attackers therefore say that in many of the Church's things prelates of the Church and ecclesiastics have lordship. Thus the Church, in them, has lordship in some way over things of the Church which have been given to the Church by the faithful freely and without condition. For although in such things the Church does not have as full a power of management as laymen have in theirs, ecclesiastics nevertheless have as full a power of laying claim in court in the name of the Church; and the Church should not be deprived of those things without a reason, just as laymen should not be deprived of theirs – though some ecclesiastical persons can be deprived for a reason more easily of things assigned to them. And so, since they have power to lay claim to and defend church property in court and such power does not belong more principally to anyone else than it does to them, it follows that in some way they have lordship.

In another way human lordship is taken more **narrowly**, the attackers say. They define lordship taken in the narrowest sense thus: "Lordship is a principal human power of laying claim to a temporal thing in court, and of treating it in any way not forbidden by natural law." That last clause excludes the right the clergy are understood to have in temporal things; for, although they have the principal power of laying claim (etc.), nevertheless they cannot treat church property as they please, and laymen can manage their temporal things in many ways absolutely forbidden to the clergy.

That, therefore, is the definition of lordship in the narrowest sense, according to them, and the more some right in temporal things falls short of that definition the more it falls short of the fullness of lordship. Thus it is certain that the more (or the less) people are limited to certain ways of managing and treating their things, the more (or the less) lordship they have in them. For this reason often a man has fuller lordship of some of his things and less full in others. For example, in many places some have fuller lordship in movable things, which they can freely and blamelessly give, sell, and bequeath, and less lordship of their immovable things, because they cannot give, sell, or bequeath those things, since they cannot disinherit their heirs of immovable things. And perhaps it has been established reasonably by human ordinance that no one should have in any of his things such full lordship that no ways of treating them can be forbidden to him for a reason.

Commonly, however, lordship (especially in movables) as it is taken more often and perhaps always in civil law and more commonly in canon law, includes power to sell, give, and bequeath. Tharasius, bishop of Constantinople, testifies concerning the power to sell; as we read in 1, q. 1, c. *Eos*, he says: "For every lord sells what he has, if he wishes, whether it be a slave or some other of his possessions." *The Canons of the Apostles* clearly enough suggest the power of bequest; as we read, 12, q. 1, c. *Sint manifestae*, they say, "Let the things proper to the bishop (if he has things of his own) be clear, and clear the things which are the Lord's, so that the bishop when he dies may have power to leave things proper to him as he wishes to whom he wishes." The civil and canon laws clearly speak also of the power of giving.

But ecclesiastics do not have such lordship in any of the temporal things the faithful have offered to God. For the clergy are all limited to certain ways of managing church property, inasmuch as they sin mortally if they manage or treat them otherwise, unless perhaps they can be excused by ignorance or in some other way; also, if they have given, bequeathed, or alienated church property in any other way than has been granted to them, those things can be recalled by a judge. The canon laws often speak of this sort of lordship when they say that the clergy are by no means the lords of church property but agents or stewards; this could be fully proved by reference to many sacred canons, as will appear elsewhere.

Eighth, the attackers show what they understand by **ownership**. For they say that the words *proprium* ["proper," "one's own"], and *proprietas* ["ownership," "property"] are taken in one way in logic and in another in the legal sciences. How they are taken in logic need not be discussed here. In the legal sciences, that is in civil and canon law, "ownership" is usually taken for lordship of a thing, so that lordship and ownership are the same, though perhaps it is also taken differently sometimes. And just as lordship is taken in two ways, so therefore is ownership, corresponding to the last two ways of taking lordship.

Ninth, they say that the words **"mine," "yours," "his," "to have,"** and other words of corresponding meaning are in various places taken equivocally. For sometimes they imply lordship and ownership, as the attacked also affirms, and it therefore seems unnecessary to prove it by examples. Sometimes such words imply a licit power of using some thing, or use of the thing, or the assignment of some thing to someone's use; thus in common speech it is said that someone invited to a lodging "has" the lodging, and often he says "This is *my* lodging," although he does not have lordship and ownership of it. Many examples of this way of taking such words will be given below [chapter 9.876–907] when the lordship and kingship of Christ is discussed, and so for the present I pass on. And these words can be taken, and are taken, in other ways which will be spoken of below.

These distinctions the attackers put forward because, they say, through them it will be clear what both the attacked and his attacker, brother Michael, mean, and how the attacked tries to bring in errors under the ambiguity of words, and how the answers of the attacked are easily disproved and the attacker's reasons appear evidently as unanswerable. They say also that some of these words can be taken in other ways; but these are enough for them at present.

With these things seen, the attackers say that from the foregoing it evidently follows that the above words that they attack contain two plain errors. The first is that a use of fact separate from lordship or ownership of the thing cannot be had in things consumable by use; the second is that a right of using separate from ownership or lordship of the thing cannot be had in such things. But since the attacked asserts and confirms these two propositions, which the attackers regard as erroneous, in his answer to the objection reported above, they defer their attacks on them to the following part, in which his answer is set out.

But the attackers concede a third point contained in those words, namely that in certain things consumable by use it is not possible to have use of right separate from ownership or lordship – they concede it taking "use of right" in its proper sense. For they say that this negative proposition has a true reason why it is true, which is this: in such things consumable by use it is not possible to have a use of right, because a use of right is a right of using another's things, preserving their substance; and therefore, in many things consumable by use, a use of right in the proper sense cannot

33

be established or had; and, consequently, in such things a use of right separate from lordship or ownership cannot be had, because in them no use of right in the proper sense can be had.

Following from this they say that they do not mean to deny in every sense the proposition, "The Friars Minor are not to be regarded as simple users in things consumed by use," and they do not mean to concede its opposite in every sense. For as has been said, if the word "user" corresponds in meaning with the word "use" as it is taken for use of right, then they grant that in this sense the Friars Minor are not simple users, either in things consumed by use or in things not consumed by use, because in neither the former nor the latter are they users, because they have no use of right in anything. But if the word "user" corresponds in meaning with the word "use" as it is taken for use of fact, then they concede that in this sense the Friars Minor are simple users, that is, they use things without having any right by which they could litigate in court.

[On the letter] After this we must look at the letter. *Use of right or of fact*: From this it is clearly established that even the attacked distinguishes between use of right and use of fact. Let him explain, therefore, what is use of fact and what is not use of right; he will not be able to, except by saying that acts of using, such as acts of eating, drinking, living in, riding, and the like, are uses of fact. *Neither a right of using*: Here he should show what is the right of using that is put into the definition of use of right. *Said was his*: Here the word "his" is taken as implying lordship or ownership of the thing, though it can be taken in another sense. *The saints explain thus: "His, that is, proper"*: It is true that they explain it thus in that place, but in some other places they explain the word "his" in other ways. *Without ownership and lordship*: This is true of the lordship which includes the power to give, sell, and bequeath.

Chapter 26

[John XXII] To this it must be said that his statement that in the state of innocence our first parents did not have lordship of anything but only simple use of fact (at least after the blessing, "Increase," etc.) expressly contradicts sacred Scripture. For we read in Genesis 1[:28] that the Lord said to our first parents, "Increase and multiply, and fill the earth and subject it." (In place of "subject it" another reading has "and dominate it"; Augustine follows this reading in his *Literal Commentary on Genesis,* and in his *City of God,* Book XIV, chapter xxi.) The passage continues, "And dominate the fish of the sea and the birds of the air, and all living things that move upon the earth." From this it appears evident that after the blessing our first parents had lordship [*dominium*] in the state of innocence over the earth, the fish of the sea, the birds of the air, and all living things that move upon the earth.

[Ockham] In this part the attacked tries to answer the foregoing objection. First he answers the point assumed about the state of innocence, that our first parents had the use of things consumable by use without having lordship and ownership of them. Second, he answers the chapter of Clement, at "There is no objection" [chapter 28]. The first part is divided into two: first he shows that in the state of innocence our first parents had lordship of temporal things; second he asks what sort of lordship, common or exclusive [*proprium*], and shows that the first man had exclusive lordship of such things. The second part is at "And if it be asked" [chapter 27].

First, therefore, answering the objection, he says that our first parents, at least after the blessing "Increase," etc., had lordship of things. He proves this by the words of Genesis quoted above. But the attackers say that the attacked here argues frivolously and does not go to the appellant's meaning. For the appellant meant to speak of lordship exclusive to some person or particular group. To indicate this plainly, he always or frequently adds a reference to ownership when he speaks of lordship – e.g. "lordship or ownership" (or something equivalent) – to make it understood that he speaks of the lordship which in the legal sciences is called ownership. Now the lordship called "ownership" in the legal sciences and in writings that observe the manner of speaking of the legal sciences is something exclusive to some single person or particular group in virtue of which he or they can litigate in court, as plaintiff or defendant, against another person or group claiming or detaining the thing in which the lordship is had. They try to prove that the lordship called ownership or exclusive lordship is of this sort.

To make this clear they say that it must be known that just as everything called "*proprium*" [his, her, their own; exclusive] belongs to some and not to another or others, so it is also of *proprietas* [ownership, property], which is so called because it belongs to some and not to another or others. The lordship, therefore, which is called "ownership" is so called either [1] because it belongs to some man or men and not to another man or men, or [2] because it belongs to a man or men and to no other or others outside the human race. If the first is granted the point is established, that the lordship the appellant speaks of is exclusive to some single person or to some particular group. The second cannot be said, because man does not have lordship of any thing without there being someone outside the human race who also has lordship of the same thing. This is indeed certain of God, because "The Lord's is the earth and its fullness." It seems also to be true of the angels, extending "lordship" to the kind of lordship our first parents had in the state of innocence, because the whole of the rest of creation is no less subject to the angels now than it was then to our first parents. The lordship called "ownership" therefore did not exist in any way in the state of innocence and never would have existed if our first parents had not sinned, because nothing would have been appropriated in such a way to any single person or particular group.

And so, since the lordship pertaining to our first parents is to be called "lordship" equivocally with respect to the lordship of which the appellant spoke and the laws speak, it is clear that the attacked argues against him frivolously, without at all touching his meaning. It must be conceded, therefore, that our first parents did have lordship of temporal things, just as it can be said that the angels have lordship over the demons and over temporal things because the demons and temporal things are subject to the angels, who dominate them; but the appellant's appeal does not mention such lordship.

[On the letter] *In the state of innocence our first parents did not have lordship of anything:* Although this has a true sense – because according to them it is true if we take "lordship" for the lordship that gives rise to human contracts and to court actions, because our first parents did not have any lordship of this kind (for in the state of innocence there were no such contracts, such as purchase, sale, gift, lease, loan, and the like, or court actions, and therefore they did not have any lordship of this kind) – nevertheless in those words the appellant does not say this. He says, "The first man, and his posterity, if they had not fallen, would have had the use of things consumable by use without ownership and lordship of them." In these words he indicates clearly that he speaks of the lordship which in law is called "ownership"; and our first parents had no such lordship in the state of innocence. Thus, although it must be conceded that in the state of innocence our first parents had lordship, in some sense, over temporal things, nevertheless it should not be conceded that they then had ownership of temporal things: this is because just as the term "*dominium*" [lordship] has some meanings which the term "*proprietas*" [ownership, property] does not have, so conversely the term "*proprietas*" has some meanings which the term "*dominium*" does not have, though in the legal sciences "*proprietas*" is perhaps never taken in those meanings.

But only simple use of fact: The appellant here makes absolutely no mention of this, although it is true inasmuch as simple use of fact excludes every right by which one can litigate in court: for there was no such right in the state of innocence. *Expressly contradicts sacred Scripture*: They say that there is no contradiction. For a contradiction is an opposition of one and the same reality and name (not only name), according to the opinion of the wise man.[6] But the appellant takes "lordship" in one way and in that passage of Genesis 1 divine Scripture takes it in another (though in many other places divine Scripture uses the term "lordship" in the way the appellant does here, and thus it was permissible for him to use the word "lordship" in that way, since the sacred Scripture and the legal sciences use it thus). *Dominate*: That is, use them effectively. *Had lordship in the state of innocence*: This is true of the lordship which is effective strength of ruling and using them for comfort and in other permissible ways; but mortals do not now have this kind of lordship over many temporal things. But it is not true of the lordship which is called ownership of temporal things, because such lordship did not then exist.

[6] Aristotle, *Sophistical Refutations*, ch. 5, 167 a23.

Chapter 27

[John XXII] And if it be asked whether that lordship was exclusive or common, it seems it must be said that, if at the time of the blessing spoken of above only Adam had been formed and not Eve (as the order of sacred Scripture indicates evidently, since that blessing was given to Adam when he was outside Paradise, but Eve was formed when Adam was put into the garden, as is clear in Genesis, chapters 1 and 2) – it seems that before Eve was formed the lordship of temporal things was exclusive to Adam, not common. Indeed it could not have been common, since at that time he was alone, and in respect of one who has never had any fellows nothing can be called common. This seems to be said explicitly in Ecclesiasticus 17[:1], where it is said: "God created man from the earth and made him according to his own likeness ... He gave him power over things upon the earth and put fear of him upon all flesh, and he dominated the beasts and birds." From this it is clear that he dominated by himself. And from this it follows that for that time he had lordship by himself, because according to Dionysius, *De divinis nominibus*, chapter 12, "From 'lordship' [*dominium*] is derived 'lord' [*dominus*], 'dominating,' and 'dominator.' " Accordingly, since it is said of Adam by himself that he dominated the beasts and birds, it follows that he was lord by himself. And that Eve had not then been formed is clear, because immediately after these words, "And he dominated the beasts and birds," it continues, "He created from him a helper like himself." Damascene also seems to be of this opinion in Book II, last chapter, where, speaking of our first parent, he says: "The creator made this human being as a male, appointed and gave to him his own divine grace, and through this put him in communion with himself. Accordingly he made him dominator,[7] prophetic namer of the animals, as of his own gifts" – another reading has: "as of his own slaves." It continues: "He made from him his own helper," etc.

[Ockham] Now that it has been shown, according to the attacked, that in the state of innocence our first parents had lordship and ownership of temporal things, here he asks what kind of lordship they had, that is whether exclusive or common. And he determines

---

[7] Substituting *dominatorem* for *dominator*.

that Adam at first had exclusive lordship over all temporal things. He proves this by the argument: Lordship belonging to one by himself, who has never had fellows, is exclusive lordship. But Adam had lordship before Eve was formed; he proves this by texts from Ecclesiasticus 17, and John Damascene. Therefore Adam had exclusive lordship of temporal things.

But the attackers say that the foregoing words contain two errors chiefly: the first is that the blessing, "Increase," etc., was given to Adam outside Paradise before the creation of Eve; the second is that Adam had exclusive lordship of temporal things before Eve was formed.

That the first must be regarded as erroneous they try to show by means of a passage from Genesis 1. For there it is written thus: "God created man in his own likeness; in God's likeness he made him, male and female he created them. And God blessed them, saying, 'Increase and multiply, and fill the earth, and subject it. Have lordship over the fish of the sea and the birds of the air and over all living things that move upon the earth.' " It is quite clear from these words that God made them male and female, and to these he gave the blessing; and thus all the clauses of the blessing are expressed in the plural, not in the singular. The blessing was therefore given after Eve was formed. And that this was fitting is proved by an argument: A commandment about the multiplication of offspring is included in that blessing; but offspring could not be multiplied by a man without a woman; therefore it was fitting that the commandment be imposed after the woman was formed, and so the blessing was not given before Eve was formed.

The second error, they say, is that before Eve was formed Adam had exclusive lordship of temporal things. To support this they say that it must be known that lordship is not called "*proprium*" [exclusive] because it belongs in fact to one by himself: for then, if all the monks of an abbey were to die or be killed except one, he by himself would have exclusive lordship of all the goods of the abbey and would then have to be regarded as its owner, which must be reckoned altogether false. Lordship is therefore not called exclusive because it belongs in fact to one by himself. Rather, it is called exclusive when it is appropriated to one person in such a way that it cannot belong to anyone else without his gift, sale, bequest, or

some other human contract by which lordship of a thing is transferred to someone else, or at least by some act of his or by his
death. For this reason, if someone founded a monastery and gave
it many goods, the first to be made monk in that monastery would
not have exclusive lordship of those goods and should not then be
regarded as its owner: because without his donation, sale or any
other human contract by which lordship of a thing is transferred
to someone else, and without any act of his or his death, if another
becomes monk in the same monastery, the second has some kind
of lordship of the same things, just like the first.

From this they conclude that, if Adam had some kind of lordship
of temporal things (not the kind men now have) before Eve was
formed, he did not on this account have exclusive lordship of those
things. Because lordship of things is not exclusive to someone if
it can come to another without any gift, sale or other human grant
by which lordship of a thing is transferred to another, and without
his act or death. But lordship of temporal things could come to
Eve without any grant of Adam's, or his act or death: indeed in
the state of innocence it would never have come to her by his
grant, because in the state of innocence one person would never
have transferred lordship of anything from himself to another, but
anyone, whenever he found something suitable to his use, or, also,
to his comfort, would have taken it without any grant by another.
Adam therefore did not have exclusive lordship before Eve was
made.

This argument is confirmed: Adam ought not to have been
deprived of any exclusive lordship without his fault; but when Eve
was formed she had lordship of all things just as Adam did;
therefore, when Eve was formed, Adam did not then have exclusive
lordship, and consequently he did not have exclusive lordship before
Eve was formed, because if he had had it, when Eve was formed
he would have been deprived of this exclusive lordship without any
fault of his. Thus, therefore, they say that even if lordship of things
had been given to Adam before Eve was formed, nevertheless he
did not then have exclusive lordship, because that lordship was not
given to him for himself alone, but for himself and the woman to
be formed from him and all their posterity, and it did not pertain
to him to confer any lordship upon Eve when she was formed.

The support which the attacked brings for his assertions will be answered in the comments upon the letter.

[On the letter] *It seems it must be said*: Although here he does not at all seem to speak assertively, afterwards he manifestly asserts it. *At the time of the blessing spoken of above*: that is, "Increase and multiply," etc., because he had not previously mentioned any other blessing. *Only Adam had been formed*: They say that this is erroneous, as has been shown above.

As the order of sacred Scripture indicates evidently: Here they note two things. First, that here he manifestly asserts what he seemed before to put forward not as an assertion but conditionally: for to say that the order of Scripture indicates something evidently is to hold to it firmly, if the speaker does not doubt the truth of Scripture. Second, they note that what he says is plainly false, since the order of Scripture does not indicate this, and the words of Scripture plainly show the opposite, as clearly appears by the words of the blessing mentioned above.

If it be said that the order of Scripture indicates that the blessing was given before Eve was formed because [1] in Scripture it is put before the description of the way Eve was formed (because the blessing is put in Genesis 1, while the formation of Eve is described in chapter 2); also, because [2] the blessing was given before the commandment about eating all the trees of Paradise and before the commandment about not eating the tree of the knowledge of good and evil; but that commandment was given to Adam alone before Eve was formed, and therefore the blessing was given before Eve was formed: To the first of these they say that, just as the blessing is put in the text before the description of the way Eve was formed, so also, before the description of the way Eve was formed, it is said, "Male and female he created them," yet it is certain that the Lord created no woman before Eve, because she was the first woman created by God. And therefore, just as before the description of the way Eve was formed it is said by anticipation that God created the female, so it is said by anticipation that God blessed the male – and the female. To the second it seems to some that it must be said that the blessing was not given before the commandment about eating, etc., though lordship was given previously, because it seems to them that that lordship was merely a natural or concreated power of effectively using and governing the things of which they had lordship, and thus Adam had this sort of lordship from the beginning. Accordingly, it seems to them that when the Lord said, "Dominate the fish of the sea," etc., this was more a commandment concerning the exercise of lordship than a conferring of lordship, just as when he said, "Multiply," he did not confer the power to multiply offspring, but gave a commandment concerning the exercise of a power previously conferred. And thus, whatever may be true of the time of conferring lordship, it is certain that the blessing was given after Eve was formed.

Since that blessing was given to Adam when he was outside Paradise: They say that this lacks all truth. For the blessing was not given before the commandment about eating, and yet that commandment was given when Adam was in Paradise. It is no objection that the blessing is spoken of before that commandment, because, as has been shown above and will be shown more fully below, the order of the text does not always follow the order of events.

It seems that before Eve was formed the lordship of temporal things was exclusive to Adam, not common: This does not follow from the foregoing, even if he had lordship before. *Indeed it could not have been common*, etc.: Here they say that something is called common because it is to be communicated. Thus the gloss, dist. 1, says, "Say common things, that is, to be communicated in time of need." In another sense, what in fact belongs to many is called common. That lordship was common in the first way even if we suppose that Adam had lordship before Eve was formed, because it was to be communicated to Eve (not by Adam but by God) and Adam could not appropriate it to himself; and therefore it was common, that is, to be communicated. And outside the time of need, "common" in this sense is distinguished from "exclusive," according as lordship is divided into common and exclusive. Whether in fact and actuality it belongs to many or not is inessential; but if, outside the time of need, some lordship is to be communicated (not by a human contract of the one who has lordship), it is called common, according as common is distinguished from exclusive.

In respect of one who has never had any fellows nothing can be called common: This is false of what is called common because it is to be communicated. Thus, just as something can be called common which belongs to one who in fact has no fellows, as is clear if only one monk were to survive from a monastery, who would not on this account be the owner, so something can be called common in respect of one who in fact has never had fellows – and this because it is to be communicated to others, and when others have come he cannot appropriate it to himself.

He gave him power, namely to use at will and to rule or manage. *And he dominated the beasts*, etc., that is, had power to manage at will the beasts and birds of the air. *From this it is clear that he dominated by himself*: They say here that he was then the only actual dominator in fact; but from this it does not follow that he then had exclusive lordship. For exclusive lordship implies that the thing in which there is exclusive lordship is not to be communicated to another outside the time of need except by the grant of whoever has the exclusive lordship. And therefore in the state of innocence there would have been no exclusive lordship. But it seems to some that Adam was not a dominator then because what is said there in Ecclesiasticus is said by anticipation.

And from this it follows that for that time he had lordship by himself: They say that even if it were conceded that at that time he alone had lordship in actuality, it does not follow that he had exclusive lordship, just as it does not follow from this that he was the owner; just as it does not follow, "One monk alone has in fact (when the others are dead) lordship of the things of a particular monastery, therefore he is the owner." *Since it is said of Adam by himself that he dominated the beasts and birds, it follows that he was lord by himself*: He argues badly, they say, because something is often said in one place of one person alone yet is not on that account denied of others. Of Jesus alone it is said in Matthew 21[:17], "Leaving them, he went forth out of the city to Bethany," but it does not follow here that he went out of the city by himself alone without his disciples. And there are countless examples of this, in which something is said of one alone yet is not on that account denied of others.

And that Eve had not then been formed is clear, because immediately after these words, "And he dominated the beasts and birds," it continues, "He created from him a helper like himself": Here they say that he argues badly, because he argues on the basis of the rule, "This is written later, therefore it was done later," to which there are infinite

43

counter-instances. For the written order does not always follow the order of events, as they show evidently by the text of Ecclesiasticus [17:1–5] quoted above. It is written there: "God created man from the earth and made him according to his own likeness. And again he turned to him and clothed him in strength like himself. He gave him the number of the days and the time, and gave him power over things upon the earth and put fear of him upon all flesh, and he dominated the beasts and birds. He created from him a helper like himself; likewise tongue, eyes, ears and heart he gave them." It is certain that in these words the Wise Man by no means keeps to the order of events in every respect. For first he tells us that God gave man the number of the days and time, before he mentions woman; yet it is certain that Eve was formed before Adam had the number of the days, because she was formed on the same day as Adam was created. Thus the order of Scripture does not always follow the order of events. This is evidently shown also from 1 Machabees 3[:1–3], where we read: "Then there rose up Judas, called Machabeus, his son, in his place; and all his brothers helped him, and all who had joined themselves to his father, and Israel fought the battle joyfully. And he increased the glory of his people and put on a breastplate like a giant and girt himself with warlike armor in battles and protected the camp with his sword." Here it is certain that the order of events is not followed in every respect, for Israel did not fight joyfully first and afterwards Judas arm himself. It is certain therefore that in the Scriptures the order of events is not always kept. And therefore from the fact that after the words, "And he dominated the beasts and birds of the sky," it adds, "He created from him a helper like himself," it cannot be proved that before Eve was formed Adam had lordship of things – though some concede this, saying, however, that that lordship was not to be regarded as exclusive, because he did not receive it only for himself but also in some way for others.

Damascene also seems to be of this opinion: They say that Damascene was not of this opinion. *Accordingly he made him dominator, prophetic namer of the animals, as of his own gifts*: They say that this was said by anticipation. But some concede that he had lordship then, but it was not exclusive lordship but common, that is to be communicated and in no way appropriated. *He made from him his own helper.*

Some say that this was done before, although here it comes later in Damascene's narration.

Chapter 28

[John XXII] There is no objection from c. *Dilectissimis*, which was quoted on the other side. For that does not prove that our first parents did not have lordship of temporal things, but that they did not have it dividedly. Indeed, from the text of the philosopher that blessed Clement quotes in that chapter it is inferred evidently that they had lordship in common. For he says that "just as air and sunlight cannot be divided, so the other things given to be possessed in common should not be divided either." From these words it appears clearly that the philosopher said that those temporal things were given to all to be possessed in common. And if they were given by him who could give them, since he was God, and to him who was capable of having them, namely man, it follows that a lordship of them was made. The philosopher introduces the comparison of air and sunlight with temporal things not in respect of lordship – as if, just as they did not have lordship of air and sunlight, so they should not have lordship of temporal things – but only in respect of their not being divided. For he says this: "And just as air and sunlight cannot be divided, so the other things given to be possessed in common should not be divided either, but should be possessed as common things." But of air blessed Augustine says this in Book II of *On Free Will*: "You can breathe in some of the air that I breathe out, but you cannot breathe in the part that has gone to nourish me, because I cannot return it. (For doctors say we take nourishment through the nostrils.) When I breathe only I can feel this nourishment, and I cannot return it by breathing out for you to breathe it in and feel it with your nostrils."

[Ockham] In this part the attacked replies to the chapter of Clement, by which the appellant wished to prove that the first man and his posterity, if they had remained steadfast in the state of innocence, would have had the use of things consumable by use without ownership and lordship of them. He says first that from that chapter it can be inferred that our first parents had lordship in common, because the text of the philosopher which blessed Clement quotes shows that temporal things were given to men to be possessed, and consequently belong to their lordship. Second, at "The philosopher," he answers a certain objection. Someone may say that this philosopher compares air and sunlight to temporal things, and therefore, just as air and sunlight do not belong to the lordship of mortals, so also they should not have lordship of temporal things. To this he answers that the philosopher does not introduce the comparison in respect of lordship, but in respect of not being divided. Third, at "But of air," he quotes a text of Augustine that seems to prove that each person has exclusive lordship of air in respect of some part.

But the attackers say that here, as elsewhere, he argues frivolously. For the appellant does not deny in every sense that our first parents had lordship of temporal things in the state of innocence. He denies that they had the lordship called "ownership," by virtue of which one can say, "This is in such a way mine that it is not yours, and that is in such a way yours that it is not mine." And thus he speaks in agreement with the thought of blessed Clement, who says: "For use of all the things in this world should have been common to all men. But through iniquity one said that this was his, and another that that was his." By these words we are given to understand evidently that before iniquity no one should have said that this is his, and another that that is his. But the words "mine" and "his" relate (though not always) to the lordship which is called "ownership"; before iniquity, therefore, no one had the lordship called ownership. And that is the appellant's meaning; for he did not mean to prove more than this, that use of fact of things consumable by use can be separated from all lordship called ownership. But the lordship that our first parents had in the state of innocence is of altogether another nature than that lordship; and their lordship does not seem to have been exclusive to our first parents, but it seems to have been common to them and the angels. For if, according to the Savior's judgment, the devil is called "ruler of this world" because of the power he exercises in it by usurpation, it seems that much more could the angels be called rulers and lords of these temporal things because of the power they are known to have over them. And it does not seem that they have less power over them than our first parents had in the state of innocence, which their posterity would have had if they had remained steadfast in that state (though the angels do not need things in the way mankind would have needed them; but lordship does not require need of anything, because God, who needs nothing, is most perfectly the lord of all things). It is therefore certain that the appellant speaks of the lordship which is called ownership, and of that it is true, according to the attackers, that use of fact in things consumable by use can be separated from all such lordship. Something will be said about the other matters in the comments on the letter.

[On the letter] *For that does not prove that our first parents did not have lordship of temporal things*: That is not true, they say, of the lordship called ownership, of which the appellant spoke. But of another lordship, such as the angels have and had in common with men, it can be conceded: but then it is not to the point. *But that they did not have it dividedly*: They concede this, because it is negative. *Indeed, from the text of the philosopher that blessed Clement quotes in that chapter it is inferred evidently that they had lordship in common*: It does not prove anything of the lordship called ownership. In the meaning of the philosopher, who did not know about the state of innocence, it does not prove anything about the lordship that our first parents had in the state of innocence, but it applies to the lordship that is power to divide and appropriate temporal things, which our first parents had after sin and before the division of things (though the philosopher did not know of this). But the appellant did not speak of this kind of lordship. *Just as air and sunlight cannot be divided, so the other things given to be possessed in common should not be divided either*: These words show clearly, they say, that the philosopher does not speak of any lordship other than the lordship that is a power to divide and appropriate. But that kind of lordship did not exist in the state of innocence, and would not have existed if they had remained steadfast in it, because the whole human race would not have had power in that state to divide and appropriate temporal things. And thus he does not speak of the lordship that existed in the state of innocence.

Given to all to be possessed in common: This is true; and therefore after sin they had power to use all things as common without any appropriation. *If they were given by him who could give them, since he was God, and to him who was capable of having them, namely man, it follows that a lordship of them was made*: They say that although the conclusion is true in one sense, nevertheless he argues badly. For taking "giving" in one sense, it sometimes does not follow, "This is given by him who can give, and to him who is capable of it, therefore he is made lord." For often someone gives lodging to another – that is, gives him accommodation to stay in for a while – yet the other is not made lord, though he is capable of lordship. They say, therefore, that, using equivocal words, here and often elsewhere, he commits in his arguments the fallacy of equivocation. And no other answer is to be made, for the right answer to sophisms that are faulty through equivocation is to explain the ambiguity of the words.

Just as they did not have lordship of air and sunlight, so they should not have lordship of temporal things: Our first parents did not have lordship of air and sunlight, yet they had lordship of other things, though not the lordship called ownership. *Introduces the comparison only in respect of their not being divided*: Some concede this, because just as they could not divide the air and appropriate it while it remained in its place, nor the sunlight, so, if all men had been good, they should not have divided temporal things and appropriated them; after sin, however, they were able to divide temporal things and appropriate them. And so they had a lordship over temporal things such as they did not have over air and sunlight. "*Some of the air that I breathe out,*" etc.: Augustine means that the air remaining in its place outside the human body cannot be appropriated; however, air taken in as nourishment is in some way appropriated, like other nourishment.

Chapter 65

[John XXII] Besides, this heretic will say that he to whom a licence to use some thing is granted uses the thing justly or unjustly, or he uses the thing neither justly nor unjustly. If he says unjustly, that is certainly in harmony with the constitution spoken of above, which says that whoever uses without right uses unjustly. If he says that he uses it justly, it follows consequently that he uses it also by right; because what is done justly is done also by right; [see] *Extra, De verborum significatione*, c. *Ius dictum*; 14, q. 4, c. *Quid dicam*. But if he says that he to whom the licence to use is granted uses neither justly nor unjustly, this is false. For it is impossible for an individual human act to be indifferent – that is, neither good nor bad, just nor unjust. For since that act is called human which proceeds from deliberate will, and consequently is done for some purpose (which is of course the will's object), if the purpose of the act is good the act must be good also, but if the purpose is bad the act must be bad; for as Augustine says in his book *De moribus ecclesiae*, according as the purpose is praiseworthy or culpable, so our works are praiseworthy or culpable.

[Ockham] In this part he brings forward a second argument to prove that a person who has licence to use something has a right of using that thing. And first he states it; and second, in the immediately succeeding part, he answers an objection which could be brought against it. The argument is this. Whoever uses something by another's licence, without a right, uses it either justly, or unjustly, or neither justly nor unjustly. If unjustly, that is in harmony with the constitution *Ad conditorem*. If justly, then by right: *Extra, De verborum significatione*, c. *Ius dictum est*, and 14, q. 4, c. *Quid dicam*. If neither justly nor unjustly – this cannot be said, for every human act is either just or unjust.

But the attackers say that he tries to refute Catholic lovers of truth, arguing frivolously under the ambiguity of terms. Accordingly, for the unraveling of this argument they first draw a distinction concerning a right; second, they show what right the appellant and the attacked spoke of before; third, they show how temporal things are said to belong to different people in different ways, and how different people are said to possess temporal things in different ways; fourth, they briefly repeat a certain distinction concerning the terms "just," "justice," and "justly"; and fifth, they formally answer the above argument.

Concerning the first, they say that the word "right" is sometimes taken for a right of the forum and sometimes for a right of heaven.[8]

---

[8] *Ius fori*, the right of the law courts, *ius poli*, the right of the pole or heavens. (For use of these expressions in the *Decretum* see Reuter and Silagi; see also gloss to *Digest*, 1.1.3, v. *Nam iure*.) The distinction is, in effect, between positive law (including divine positive law) and natural law. In the Latin text *ius* sometimes clearly means a right as distinct from a law (as in the next paragraph) and sometimes (for example in passages quoted from older writers) it clearly means

This distinction is gathered from the words of Augustine, *De vita clericorum*, which are included in 17, q. 4, last chapter. He says: "The bishop had the power not to return them, but by right of the forum, not by right of heaven." The same distinction is found in the same *causa* and *quaestio*, para. *Sed notandum*. To make the distinction clear it should be known that "the just" that is established by human or explicit divine pact or ordinance is called **"the right of the forum"**; accordingly, the right of the forum can also be called the right of custom, taking "custom" in a broad sense. Of this right it is said in the *Decretum*, dist. 6, "The right of custom had its beginning after natural law, when men gathering into one began to live together." By these words we are given to understand that this right is established by human pact or ordinance. After this pact or ordinance [has been] confirmed by custom or law, it should not be violated at the will of anyone at all, as Augustine testifies in Book II of his *Confessions*, quoted dist. 8, c. *Quae contra*. He says: "Affronts to the customs of mankind are to be avoided according to the diversity of customs, so that a pact made among themselves confirmed by the custom or law of a people or city should not be violated by the licentiousness of any citizen or stranger." By these words we are given to understand that a right established by human pact should not be violated at the will of anyone at all (though in some cases something can licitly be done against such a right on the authority of a superior, as Augustine makes clear in the same place).

That a right established by human action also should not be violated at will is shown. For according to Isidore, as we read in the *Decretum*, dist. 1, "Every right stands firm by laws and customs." But laws and customs should not be violated at will; therefore it is not licit to violate at will a right established by human action, without the authority of a superior. That it is not licit to violate customs at will is clear from the chapter of Augustine quoted above, *Quae contra*. The same is clear also of laws, also from Augustine, *De vera religione*; as we read in dist. 4, c. *In istis*, he

a law. Sometimes it might mean either a right or a law, and in those cases we have translated it as "right."

On the distinction between the two senses of *ius* involved here see the articles on Ockham's contribution to thinking about rights by Tierney and McGrade listed in Suggestions for further reading (p. xxxix).

says: "In the case of these temporal laws, although men judge them when they establish them, nevertheless, once they have been established and confirmed it will not be licit for the judge to judge them, but [he must] judge by them." By these words we are given to understand that laws established by human action should not be violated at the will even of judges; and thus also rights established by human action should not be violated at will. It follows further that a licence, which by the law of the forum can be revoked by the granter at will, should not be regarded as being among the rights of the forum. (This is especially known to be true when the granter of the licence is not the superior of the person to whom the licence is granted; this is said on account of a ruler granting someone a privilege which he can revoke at will and which, nevertheless, not with respect to the ruler but with respect to subjects, has the force of law.)

But the natural equity that is, without any human ordinance or any merely positive divine ordinance, in harmony with right reason – in harmony either with purely natural right reason or with right reason taken from things revealed to us by God[9] – is called **"the right of heaven"**. Accordingly, this right is sometimes called "natural right," for every natural right pertains to the right of heaven. Sometimes it is called divine right, for many things are in harmony with right reason taken from things revealed to us by God which are not in harmony with purely natural reason. For example, it is in harmony with right reason taken from the articles of belief that those who preach the gospel should be sustained from the goods of those to whom they preach (at least if they do not otherwise have means of sustenance), yet this cannot be proved by a purely natural argument, just as it cannot be sufficiently proved by such an argument that the things they preach are true, useful, and necessary to those to whom they preach.

Second, they say that the appellant and the attacked, when they disagree whether use of things without a right of using can be licit, are speaking of a right of the forum. That the appellant speaks thus is certain, and he himself concedes it. That the attacked speaks thus is certain from the fact that in this part he speaks of

---

[9] Compare the second alternative here with the third kind of natural law in III *Dial.*, II 3.6, translated below (pp. 287–8).

the right of using in the way in which the attackers he is answering in his constitution *Quia quorundam* speak of the right of using, and in the way in which Nicholas III speaks of it in his decretal *Exiit*, when he says that "in temporal things we must consider ownership, possession, usufruct, the right of using, and simple use of fact," and when he says, "This use, I say, having the name not of right, but only of fact, offers to the users only what is of fact in using, nothing of right." That he [the attacked] speaks in the way that these [the attackers and Nicholas III] do is manifestly clear from chapters 2, 6, 31, 32, 37, 42, 55, 58, and 60; but these speak of a right of using that exists by the right of the forum. That the attackers speak of such a right is plain and certain, for they speak there of the right by which one can litigate in court, and such a right is a right of the forum; therefore, etc. That Nicholas also speaks of such a right in the above words is clear, for denying to the brothers[10] a right of using he does not deny them a right of heaven but explicitly concedes it; he therefore does not speak of the right of heaven but of the right of the forum. It is certain, therefore, that the words of the attacked should be understood of the right of the forum. For otherwise he would not refute except sophistically the attackers he is answering in the constitution *Quia quorundam* or the appellant or the Friars Minor who say that they have nothing of right in the things they use; for all these refer to a right of using that is understood to pertain to the right of the forum.

Third, they show how temporal things are said to belong to different people in different ways. [1] They say that temporal things are said to belong to some people from worthiness of merit. In this way everything belongs to the just – that is, the just are worthy to possess everything; and in this way no temporal thing belongs to the wicked, for a wicked man is not worthy even of the bread he eats. And therefore, because God made everything for the sake of the just, it is said that in a way everything belongs to the just by divine law, as Augustine says in *Ad Vincentium*, quoted 23, q. 7, c. 1: "Although no earthly thing whatever can rightly be possessed by anyone except either by divine law, by which everything belongs to the just," etc. – that is, only the just are worthy of all temporal

---

[10] That is, to the Friars Minor.

things. [2] In another way earthly things are said to belong to some people by the necessity or the moral integrity of a debt, namely because they are due to them by right reason. In this way the superfluities of the rich belong to the poor and needy, namely because the rich are obliged to donate their superfluities to them. In this way the words of Ambrose [rather, Basil] should be understood, quoted dist. 47, c. *Sicut hii*, when he says: "The bread you keep belongs to the hungry; the clothes you shut away belong to the naked; the money you hide in the earth is the ransom and release of the unfortunate." In this way also the property of the Church is said to belong to the poor. Things said to belong to someone in this way can be said to be theirs by divine law, for by divine law those who possess them are obliged to give them up to the poor. [3] In a third way temporal things are said to belong to some people by right of heaven, and sometimes at the same time by right of the forum and in good conscience. In this way things someone uses in a situation of extreme necessity are his, whether they are his by right of the forum or not. [4] Fourth, things are said to belong to someone by sincerity of conscience. In this way temporal things are said to belong to those who are known to have them, not from avarice or bad intention, but moved by reason; but they do not belong in this way to those who keep them from avarice or bad intention. Thus Ambrose says in the same place, "But the avaricious man says, 'Why is it unjust, if I do not invade what belongs to another, if I look after my own with diligence?' O shameless saying! What do you call your own? Which things? From which hidden places have you brought them into this world? . . . Let no one call his own what is common, what is more than is sufficient for his expenses, what has been obtained by violence . . . Who is so unjust, so avaricious, as someone who makes the food of many not his use, but his abundance and pleasure?" [5] Fifth, some temporal things are said to belong to someone by right of the forum only. And this way [of belonging] is divided into many. For things belong to someone by right of the forum either in respect of ownership and lordship or in respect of bare use or in respect of usufruct, and perhaps in other ways. In this way some things can belong to some persons although they do not belong to them in any of the four previous ways, and thus the avaricious have many things by right of the forum of which they are unworthy, which are owed not to them but to others, which they keep for themselves not from a right conscience but only from avarice.

From these points it is clear that different people are known to possess temporal things in different ways: for some possess temporal things by right of the forum, such as those who possess temporal things by human laws or divine positive laws; some possess temporal things by right of heaven, such as those who in a time of extreme necessity possess temporal things, which they also use; some possess them in good conscience; some possess temporal things by no right and not in good conscience, such as tyrants, usurers, and others who possess temporal things unjustly.

Fourth, they repeat[11] a distinction about "justice," "just," and "justly." Some justice is particular, in distinction from the other virtues, some is legal justice, and some is the justice by which an action is conformed with right reason. And correspondingly an act is said to be just or unjust in three ways, and something is said to be done justly or unjustly in three ways.

Fifth, by means of the foregoing the attackers formally answer the argument of the attacked, as follows. They say that when it is taken [as a premise] that "someone to whom a licence (namely a licence that is not a right) has been granted to use something uses it either justly, or unjustly, or neither justly nor unjustly," they say that if "justly" is taken in the first way, as something is said to be done justly because it is done by the particular justice that is a virtue distinct from the other virtues, in that sense he uses it neither justly nor unjustly; for taking "justice" and "just" that way, there are many acts, even meritorious or demeritorious acts, which are neither just nor unjust (though they are good or bad, praiseworthy or blameworthy), for even an act of chastity is in that way neither just nor unjust. But if "justly" is taken in the third way, in that way they say that he uses the thing for which he has the licence to use justly, because he uses it in conformity with right reason. And for that reason they concede that he uses by right – not indeed by right of the forum, but by the right of heaven; for everything done rightly without a right of the forum is done by

---

[11] From 60.120–60. There Ockham quotes Thomas Aquinas, *Summa theologiae*, 2-2, q. 58, a. 2. See also Aristotle, *Nicomachean Ethics*, v.2, 1130 a13–15.

right of heaven. Thus to do by right in this way is simply to do well morally, to use by right is to use well morally, and to possess by right is to possess well morally.

But perhaps someone will say that it is not by right of heaven that such a person uses the thing granted to him, just as he does not possess it by right of heaven, because no one uses any thing by right of heaven except one who uses such a thing in a time of extreme necessity. Nicholas III seems to suggest this when he says in the decretal *Exiit*: "And indeed, if these all fail (as is not to be presumed in any way), the way of providing for the sustenance of nature in a situation of extreme necessity that is granted by the law of heaven to all caught in extreme necessity is not closed to the brothers, just as it is not to others." These words seem to suggest that no one is permitted to use things by right of heaven unless he is living in a situation of extreme necessity. To this they say that although Nicholas says that it is permitted by the law of heaven to everyone living in a situation of extreme necessity to use things necessary to sustain life, nevertheless he does not deny that some may in other cases use things by right of heaven.

To make this clear, they say, it must be known that to use temporal things pertains to a right of nature that no one can licitly renounce. However, it does not pertain to natural right in such a way that it cannot in many cases be limited and in some way restricted and impeded so that it does not licitly issue in an act. In this way, according to Isidore, as we read in dist. 1, c. *Ius naturale*, "The common possession of all things and the one liberty of all" pertain to natural right, and yet that right is in a way restricted, because, also, temporal things are appropriated and many people are subjected to servitude. However, this natural right cannot be emptied totally, because temporal things can never be appropriated in such a way that it is not true that they ought to be common in time of necessity. Thus the power to use temporal things can in a way be restricted by human law and by a free man's own will and can sometimes be impeded so as not to issue in any act of using (for thus one can by vow resolve that one will abstain from flesh, thus also men are prohibited from using the things of others), but the power to use temporal things cannot be eradicated totally. And therefore, anyone can use by right of heaven any temporal thing whatever that he is not prohibited from using either by natural law or by human law or by divine law or by his own act. And therefore, in time of extreme necessity, anyone can use by the law of heaven any temporal thing whatever without which he cannot preserve his own life; for in this case he is not obliged not to use a temporal thing by any law whatever or by his own act.

But when someone is prevented from using some determinate temporal thing only by the fact that it is another's (for except in case of extreme necessity one ought not to use another's thing in which one has no right, apart from natural right, against its owner's will), the mere permission of the owner, expressed through a licence, is enough for him to use that thing by right of heaven. The permission, and consequently the licence, merely removes the impediment preventing one who has a natural right of using from going on to an act of using, and does not give him any new right. Therefore, one who has such a permission or licence can by right of heaven use the thing which is another's. That no new right is conferred on someone given a licence is proved by the following argument. Every right is either divine or human, and, if human, is a right either natural and of heaven or positive and of the forum. But it is certain that such a permission or licence does not confer any divine right or a right of heaven or natural right. If, therefore, a right is conferred on one having the licence, such a right pertains to the right of the forum, and therefore he would use the thing by a right of the forum. This is certainly false. For by every right of the forum one can litigate in court; but such a person does not have any right by which he can litigate in court; therefore he does not use the thing by right of the forum. He uses it therefore only by right of heaven. But it is when he is licensed or permitted that he first uses the thing licitly by right of heaven and not before then; for what prohibits the natural right from issuing into an act of using has now been removed, and it was by no means removed before. And from this it is clear that, if they have in things no positive right common to themselves and all other believers, the Friars Minor use whatever things they licitly use by right of heaven and not by right of the forum, however much they may be outside a situation of extreme necessity: for they cannot renounce the natural right of using, yet they can by vow resolve that they do not wish to have any thing of their own or any right of their own in temporal things, and therefore they cannot use any thing by a right of the forum. If they ought to use another's thing, what prohibits their doing so must be removed; it is removed by the permission or licence of the person to whom it pertains to give permission or licence; and when it is removed, the right of heaven can issue into an act. If they use anything that is granted to whoever takes it[12] or is regarded as abandoned, they use it by right of heaven, because with respect to such a thing there is no impediment prohibiting their natural right of using from issuing into an act of using.

[On the letter] *Whoever uses without right uses unjustly*: Here the attacked supposes that someone can use something without a right. This should be understood of the right of the forum, for no one can use any thing without any natural right, since natural right is common to all, dist. 1, c. *Ius naturale*; and so it is certain that the attacked speaks of the right of the forum. *If he says that he uses it justly, it follows consequently that he uses it also by right*: It is true that it follows that he uses it by right of heaven or by right of the forum. *Because what is done justly is done also by right*: It is true that it is done by right of heaven or by right of the forum; but it need not always be done by right of the forum.

"Extra," "De verborum significatione," c. "Ius dictum"; 14, q. 4, c. "Quid dicam": The attackers say that since the words in these chapters on which he bases his position seem obscure, they wish to quote them and explain how they ought to be understood. They are as follows: "For this is possessed by right which justly, this justly which well." These words suggest two propositions, namely that everything which is possessed well is possessed justly and that everything which is justly possessed is possessed by right. From these a third follows, namely that everything that is possessed well is possessed by right; from this it seems to follow that everyone who uses some thing well uses it by right, and thus a good act[13] of using cannot be separated from a right of using.

But they say that the chapters listed above speak disjunctively (or equivalently) of the right of heaven and the right of the forum. Now the right of heaven is nothing but a power conforming to right reason without a pact; the right of the forum is a power

---

[12] That is, something able to be appropriated but not yet appropriated.
[13] Substituting *actus* for *usus*.

resulting from some pact, sometimes conforming with right reason and sometimes not. And no one possesses a thing well unless he possesses it according to right reason. And so whoever possesses well possesses either by right of heaven or by right of the forum, and whoever possesses by right of heaven possesses well but not everyone who possesses by right of the forum possesses well. From this it follows that the above words cannot be understood only of the right of the forum; for many things are possessed by right of the forum which are not possessed well, and many things are possessed well which are not possessed by the right of the forum. That many things are possessed by right of the forum which are not possessed well is quite clear [1] in the case of the avaricious, who possess many things by right of the forum which they do not possess well, and also [2] in the case of the many things they possess by right which nevertheless they use badly and in consequence do not possess well, as Augustine testifies in the chapter referred to, *Quid dicam*, when he says, "But he possesses badly who uses badly," and Isidore, in the chapter referred to, *Ius dictum est*, says, "He possesses badly who uses his own badly, or encroaches upon others' things." From these words we gather evidently that some possess their own thing badly, and consequently many things are possessed by right of the forum which are nevertheless possessed badly. That, also, many things are possessed well which are by no means possessed by right of the forum is clear. For whoever legitimately prescribes possesses well another's property before the prescription is complete, yet before the prescription is complete does not possess by any right of the forum; therefore many things are well possessed which are not possessed by any right of the forum. The chapters listed above therefore do not speak only of the right of the forum but also of the right of heaven, and so it cannot be inferred from them that whoever uses another's thing by the other's licence uses it by right of the forum; it is enough that he uses it by right of heaven. But in proving that licit use can be separated from a *right* of using, the appellant does not speak of the right of heaven but of the right of the forum, as he often explains clearly. The foregoing argument against the appellant therefore proves nothing.

Neither justly nor unjustly: If "justly" and "unjustly" are taken in the first way there is no unsuitability. Accordingly, someone who gives another something out of generosity, not because of some debt, does not give justly or unjustly in that sense, for he is not obliged to give to him and therefore does not perform an act of particular justice but of generosity; and he is not obliged not to give and therefore does not give unjustly. However, taking "justly" and "unjustly" in the third way, it must not be conceded in that sense that he does not use justly or unjustly. *Neither good nor bad*: This they concede without distinction. *Just nor unjust*: This they concede in one sense and deny in another, as appears from the foregoing. *If the purpose of the act is good the act must be good also*: They say that since he is not at all instructed in difficult matters of theology, in which nevertheless he rashly intervenes, therefore they pass over this statement of his and his statement about the object of the will.

Chapter 88

[John XXII] Sacred Scripture evidently says the contrary, namely that it was rather by divine law, and not human, that lordship was introduced. For divine law is what we have in the divine Scriptures, as we read in dist. 8, c. *Quo iure*, in the beginning, where it is said that "divine law" is what "we have in the divine Scriptures, human law" what we have "in the laws of kings." But in the divine Scriptures we read that before the laws of kings existed, indeed even before kings existed, some things were someone's; therefore, by divine law someone was able to say that something was his. The major [premise] is clear from the chapter *Quo iure* quoted above. The minor is proved also by[14] the state of innocence. For it seems that in the state of innocence, before Eve was formed, Adam alone had lordship of temporal things. For he could not for that time have had common lordship, since he was by himself, since sharing [*communio*] obviously requires several. And that he was lord before Eve was formed seems to be proved expressly by Ecclesiasticus 17[:1–4]. For there it is said, "God created man from the earth ... He put fear of him upon all flesh, and he dominated the beasts and birds." It says therefore that he dominated [*dominari*], from which it follows that he had lordship [*dominium*]: for according to Dionysius *De divinis nominibus*,

---

[14] That is, by what was the case (in John's opinion) in the state of innocence, before there were kings.

chapter 12, from "lordship" [*dominium*] is derived "lord" [*dominus*], "ruler" [*dominator*], and ruling [*dominans*]; from this it follows from the fact that he dominated that he had lordship. And that Eve had not then been formed is clear; for immediately after the words "and he dominated the beasts and birds" it continues, "He created from him," namely, from Adam, "a helper like himself," namely Eve. Wisdom 9[:1–2] supports the same conclusion, where it says, "O God of our fathers and lord of mercy, you made all things by your word, and by your wisdom you appointed man to rule over your creation, which was made by you," etc. And Damascene expressly says this, in Book II, last chapter, as has been said above [chapter 27]. Also, that after the fall of our first parents, before the flood, and before there were kings, someone was able to say, "This is mine," is proved by Genesis 3[:19], where the Lord said to Adam, "In the sweat of your brow you will eat *your* bread"; therefore it is clear that Adam was able then to call the bread his, and yet kings did not then exist, nor indeed other men except our first parents alone. Concerning Abel also, the second child of our first parents, it is said in Genesis 4[:4] that "Abel . . . offered from the first-born of *his* flock"; from this it is clear that Abel was able to say, "This flock is mine." Also, it is clear that after the flood, without the law of kings, someone was able to call something his. For we read in Genesis 9[:20–1] that Noah planted a vine and drank the wine it produced. I think that no sensible person will deny that he was lord of the vine, and also of the wine; and yet we do not read that any king existed then. Again, in Genesis 12[:7] the Lord said to Abraam when he was in the land of Canaan, "I will give this land to your seed," which he also did. And it is certain that those who were of his seed were able to say, "that land is ours," and not by the laws of kings; for they had it by a grant of God, not of kings. Again, in Genesis 26[:1–3] when Isaac went down to Gerara, the Lord said to him, "I will give the whole of these regions to you and to your seed"; his seed had lordship of these regions not by the law of kings, but by God's grant. Moreover, in Numbers 31[:53] it is said that "what" each one "had taken as booty was his," which it was not by the laws of kings, since the Israelite people did not then have any king, but its leader was Moses alone. Also, in Numbers 33[:51–4], the Lord said to Moses, "Command the children of Israel, and say to them: 'When you have passed over the Jordan and enter the land of Canaan, scatter all its inhabitants. I have given it to you for a possession, which you will divide among you by lot,' " and this they also did, as we read in Joshua 13[:7ff]. Therefore, each of them, after the division of that land, was able to say of the portion that came to him that it was his – and this not by the law of kings but by divine law, since at that time, as has been said, that people was not ruled by kings. Again, in Numbers 35[:2–3], the Lord said to Moses, "Command the children of Israel that they give the Levites out of their possessions cities to live in and suburbs round them, that they may live in the towns, and the suburbs be for their flocks and beasts of burden"; this they also did, as we read in Joshua 14[:4]. From these things it is clear that when the Lord commanded the children of Israel to give to the Levites out of their possessions, the children of Israel could, before they gave the possessions, call them theirs, and the Levites [could call them theirs] from when they were given to them – and not by the laws of kings, since they did not have kings, but by divine ordinance. From all of these things it is clear that we find in the sacred Scriptures that someone, both in the state of innocence and after the fall of our first parents, both before the flood and after the flood, was able to say, without the law of kings, that something was his. And in 23, q. 7, c. 1, it is proved that there are some lordships by divine law.

[Ockham] In this part the attacked, disproving the appellant's assertion concerning the question previously spoken of, puts forward his own opinion. It is divided into two parts: first he puts forward his own assertion; second he answers the texts adduced in favor of the contrary assertion, at "From the foregoing, therefore" [chapter 91]. The first part is divided into three: first he shows that lordship of temporal things was introduced not by human law, but by divine law; second he shows that lordship of temporal things could not have been given to men by human law, but only by divine law; third he shows what human law introduced concerning the lordship of temporal things. The second begins at "Further, that . . . by no law," [chapter 89], the third at "It is true, however" [chapter 90].

In the first part, therefore, he proves the first conclusion by the following argument. Divine law is what we have in the divine

Scriptures, human law what we have in the laws of kings. But in the divine Scriptures we read that, before there were kings, temporal things belonged to the lordship of some persons; therefore lordship of things was introduced by divine law, not by human law. He shows the major [premise] by means of a text of Augustine, which is included in dist. 8, c. *Quo iure.* Concerning the proof of the minor premise he shows first by means of three texts that exclusive lordship of things was introduced in the state of innocence, and not by kings; certainly, therefore, by God. Second, at "Also, that after the fall," he proves by means of two texts that lordship of temporal things was introduced after the fall and before the flood, without the laws of kings. Third, at "Also . . . after the flood," he proves by means of one text that lordship of things was introduced after the flood, without the laws of kings. Fourth, at "Again, in Genesis 12," he proves by means of two texts that lordship of some things was introduced directly by God. Fifth, at "Moreover, in Numbers 31," he proves by one text that lordship of some things was introduced without the laws of kings. Sixth, at "Also in Numbers 33," he proves by means of three texts that lordship of some things was introduced directly by God.

But the attackers, regarding many things said here as erroneous, proceed as follows: [1] First they attempt to prove five conclusions which they believe are Catholic; [2] second they try to show that many errors are contained in this passage; [3] third, running through the letter, they endeavor to answer every text.

[1] Concerning the first they say, [i] first, that in the state of innocence there was no exclusive lordship. This conclusion was treated above, in chapters 26, 27, and 28; therefore it is passed over at present. [ii] The second conclusion, which they prove, is that the first exclusive lordship of temporal things was introduced after the fall by human law, or by human ordinance or will. They prove this as follows. The first division of lordships that we read of in Scripture was between Abel and Cain. For in Genesis 4[:2–5] we read as follows: "Abel was a shepherd of sheep, and Cain a farmer. And it came to pass after many days that Cain offered gifts to God from the fruits of the earth. Abel also offered some of the first-born of his flock and some of their fat; and the Lord looked favorably upon Abel and his offerings, but he did not look favorably upon Cain and his offerings." From these words we

gather that these two men had distinct lordships of things that had been divided. But we do not read that the division was made by divine commandment; therefore the first division of lordships was introduced by human will.

But perhaps someone will object against this, in two ways. First, because before Cain or Abel was born, the Lord said to Adam, "In the sweat of your brow you will eat *your* bread," as we read in Genesis 3[:19]; therefore, Adam had his own bread before he had children. Also, in the same chapter we read, "The Lord God made Adam and his wife coats of skin, and clothed them"; by these words we are given to understand that by God's gift each of them had his or her own coat; therefore, not only was there a distinction of lordships before the birth of Cain and Abel, but also the distinction of lordships was introduced directly by God.

But they [the attackers] answer to both of these objections that, although there was between our first parents a division of things in respect of use, nevertheless all things were common in respect of lordship of some kind. This seems probable enough because of the bond of marriage and the concord and love between them. For while love and concord existed between them, it does not seem that they should have been moved by any reason to divide temporal things between them in respect of lordship or ownership. They say also that, if they had divided temporal things between them in respect of lordship (and thus the first division of lordships would not have been between Cain and Abel), nevertheless the first division of lordships would still have been introduced by human will. For before Adam ate bread and before the Lord gave them coats of skin, we read that "when they recognized they were naked, they sewed together fig leaves and made themselves girdles" [Genesis 3:7]. And it does not appear that they appropriated to themselves the coats more than the girdles. Therefore, if the coats and other things were divided among them in respect of lordship, it follows that the girdles were divided among them in respect of lordship; and not by special divine commandment, but by human will. Therefore the first distinction of lordships was introduced by human will.

[iii] The third conclusion is that distinct lordships of many things were introduced, and at various times, by human law without the laws of kings (as kings are distinguished from dukes, counts, barons

and other secular rulers). This is quite clear of the division made among the children of the children of Noah, in Genesis 10[:5]. Of them it is said, "The islands of the nations in their regions were divided by them." Many other things are added there concerning the division of lands; this division was made by human will and ordinance.

[iv] The fourth conclusion is that diverse and distinct lordships of some temporal things were introduced by direct divine ordinance. This is clearly proved by many texts quoted by him [the attacked]. It is also clearly shown from Deuteronomy 2[:4–5], where the Lord said to Moses: "You will pass by the borders of your brothers the children of Esau, who live in Seir, and they will fear you. Take great care, therefore, not to move against them; for I will not give you of their land as much as a foot's breadth, because I have given Mount Seir as a possession to Esau." And afterwards [Deuteronomy 2:9]: "Do not fight against the Moabites and do not go to battle against them, for I will not give you any part of their land, because I have given Ar as a possession to the sons of Lot." From these [passages] it is clear that lordships of the regions of Seir and Ar had been given by special divine ordinance to the sons of Esau and Moab. And if it were said that this happened only by hidden inspiration or approval, and not by special commandment, this cannot be said of certain other cases. For as we read in Exodus 12[:36], when the children of Israel went out from Egypt they despoiled the Egyptians by commandment of the Lord, and thus they acquired lordship of the spoils by special divine ordinance and commandment. And thus lordship of some things was introduced by divine law. This could be plentifully proved by means of others texts of divine Scripture, but let the above suffice.

[v] The fifth conclusion is that, after the promulgation of the gospel and the abolition of the legal [observances, i.e. of the Old Law], new exclusive lordships of all temporal things existed by human law and not by divine law or by any special grant of God. This is proved: For from that time neither Jews nor Christians nor pagans newly possessed anything by divine law; therefore, from that time there was no new lordship by divine law, since all were then either Jews, Christians, or pagans.

[a] That the Jews did not after that time[15] newly possess anything by divine law is clear. For by divine law other things were not

---

[15] Substituting *ex tunc* for *tunc*.

newly possessed by the Jews besides those they acquired by the commandment of divine Scripture; but those commandments had already ceased; therefore, they did not newly possess anything by divine law.

[b] That Christians also did not newly possess anything by divine law is clear. For they did not acquire particular lordship[16] of any thing by special grant of God, for in the whole New Testament we do not read that God gave any temporal thing to Christians in respect of particular lordship, unless you say that Christ fed the crowds: but it does not follow from this that, after the promulgation of the gospel and the abolition of the legal [observances], he gave anything particularly to Christians. Also from the fact that he fed the crowds it does not follow that he gave them lordship of the loaves and fishes, because he did not give them these loaves and fishes except for eating.

But perhaps you will say that the clergy acquire lordships of things by divine law, since by the New Testament they are owed stipends, as Christ said in Luke 10[:7], "The laborer is worthy of his pay," and in 1 Corinthians 9[:7] the Apostle says, "Who ever serves at his own expense?" and in the same place [1 Corinthians 9:13–14], "Those who serve the altar share with the altar. So also the Lord has ordained that those who preach the Gospel should live from the Gospel." By these words we are given to understand that by divine ordinance temporal stipends are due to those who preach the Gospel; therefore, temporal things are possessed by divine law.

To this they [the attackers] say that that ordinance of God is a general ordinance that determines no particular temporal thing, and therefore things are not said because of such a general ordinance to be possessed by divine law as we are speaking of it now. For just as, although by a general ordinance of God the rich should give alms to the poor and nevertheless alms given to the poor are not said to be possessed by divine law, but by human law, since in that general ordinance of God no temporal thing is specified: so, although by a general ordinance of God the faithful are obliged to give necessaries to those who preach the Gospel and to the other clergy who devote themselves to divine service, nevertheless

---

[16] "Particular lordship" translates *dominium in speciali*, in contrast with "common lordship," which translates *dominium commune*.

the things given to them are not for this reason said to be possessed by divine law, but by human law, since it results from human will that those temporal things and not others have been given; and thus such things are possessed by the clergy by human law.

Again, although the faithful are obliged by God's ordinance to provide necessaries to preachers of the Gospel and to other clergy, they are not, however, obliged to confer on them lordship of temporal things; for them to fulfill the said commandment it is enough if they give them necessaries without lordship. That they transferred to them some sort of lordship of temporal things depended in the beginning on the will of those who conferred them, and afterwards, in respect of some temporal things, it was established by the human law of highest pontiffs and general councils. Thus whatever the clergy possess they possess by human law, because God did not give one penny to the clergy, either in particular or in common, though he ordered that the faithful should provide them with necessaries. However, it must be known that, as the gloss says, dist. 8, c. *Quo iure*, sometimes " 'divine law' is taken for canon law." And in that sense it must be conceded that something is now possessed by the clergy by divine law; but we are not now speaking of divine law in that sense.

[c] That the pagans also did not from that time possess the lordship of any things whatsoever by divine law, but by human, need not be proved, since it does not appear that God gave anything to them in particular, except as "he makes his sun arise upon the good and the bad" [Matthew 5:45]. It is clear, therefore, that after the promulgation of the Gospel and the abolition of the legal [observances], all new temporal lordships have existed by human law, and not by divine law, except as all lordships exist by divine law because everything that is just is contained in the general divine commandments.

[2] Second, from the foregoing the attackers say that three errors are contained in the foregoing passage. The first is that every human law by which lordships of temporal things are possessed is contained in the laws of kings, according as kings are distinguished from other public powers and rulers. That he says this is explicitly clear, since from the premise that before the flood and after the flood there were in the Israelite people no such kings he tries to prove that they possessed the things they then had not by human

law but by divine. But that this is erroneous is quite clear. For only those lordships existed by divine law and not by human law that were possessed by a particular gift of God manifested by a particular revelation, as is clear of the spoils the Hebrews took from the Egyptians and of many other things spoken of in divine Scripture. But it is manifest that the Hebrews and others justly possessed the lordships of many things which, nevertheless, they by no means possessed by gift of God manifested by a particular revelation. This is clear of Abel and Cain, in Genesis 4, and of Abraam, who by right of purchase possessed a tomb in which he buried his wife. Jacob also acquired many things through his labor and industry, as is clear in Genesis 25, 30, and 31. The same could be plentifully proved by divine Scripture of Isaac, Joseph and other fathers of the Old Testament, and of many pagans. Therefore, they possessed such things by human law, and yet those laws were not contained in the laws of kings. Therefore the human laws by which temporal things were possessed were not all contained in the laws of kings.

The second error is that all lordships spoken of in divine Scripture existed by divine law and not by human law. That he means this is quite clear, since he proves that some things are possessed by divine law by the argument that we have divine law in the sacred Scriptures, and in the sacred Scriptures we find that some things were possessed. From this it follows, according to him, that all the lordships spoken of in the sacred Scriptures existed by divine law, and not by human law. But it is clear that this is erroneous: for the lordship of the Romans, and of many other pagans, is spoken of in sacred Scripture, and yet their lordships existed by human law, not divine law. How we should understand the text of Augustine that he quotes in his favor will be clear in the comments on the letter.

The third error is that before Eve was formed Adam had the lordship of temporal things that is ownership or exclusive lordship. This error has been spoken of above, in chapters 26, 27, and 28.

The fourth error is that, before he had children, Adam had exclusive lordship of the bread he ate. They think that this is probably erroneous, though they do not know how to demonstrate this completely. However, they hold this as probable because there seems no reason that could have moved Adam to appropriate to himself the bread he ate in respect of lordship, since such appropriating of bread in respect of lordship is seldom or never done between man and wife, between whom there is often less love and concord than there was between Adam and Eve. And thus it does not seem that Adam appropriated to himself the bread he ate, in respect of lordship, excluding Eve from that lordship.

[On the letter][3] Third, running through the letter they answer all the texts brought forward. *Rather by divine law*: This can be conceded in one sense; for every lordship was introduced by divine law in the way of speaking in which the Apostle says, in Romans 13[:1], "There is no power except from God." In that sense there is no lordship except in some way from divine law, since all lordship is from God. But he [the attacked] is not speaking in that way, since he distinguishes between the lordships that exist by divine law and those that exist by human law. And therefore, as has been said, that lordship is here said to exist by divine law which is possessed by a gift of God manifested by a special divine revelation, and in that sense not all lordships are by divine law.

Not human, that lordship was introduced: This negative statement is false in every sense, as has been proved above, because exclusive lordship was first introduced by human law. Thus let those who hold the doctrine of Thomas take note of what he says. For in [*Summa theologiae*] 2-2, q. 66, a. 2, he says, "The division of possessions is not in accordance with natural law, but according to human enactment, which belongs to positive law, as was said above. Thus ownership of possessions is not against natural law but is added to natural law by an invention of human reason." Therefore, according to him, exclusivity [*proprietas*] of lordships was introduced by an invention of human reason.

For divine law is what we have in the divine Scriptures: Nevertheless, not every law mentioned in the divine Scriptures is a divine law, except in the way all laws are divine because everything just is from God indirectly or directly. *As we read in dist. 8, c. "Quo iure"*: To these things it is answered that although natural law is contained in the Law and in the Gospel, nevertheless not everything contained in the Law and in the Gospel is found to be bound up with natural law. *"Human law what we have in the laws of kings"*: This was true for Augustine's time, in reference to which he was speaking against the heretics of his time, because at that time all nations had been subjected to kings (by the word "king" in no way excluding emperors); and therefore at that time all temporal lordships were possessed by the law of emperors or kings. But for many other times it was not true, except by extending the word "kings" to all who hold any power over others. (However, this was perhaps not true in the first division of things, because perhaps Cain and Abel divided some things between them on their own authority, without the authority of their father, just as Abraham and Lot, as we read in Genesis 13[:5–12], seem to have divided the regions between themselves on their own authority.) For it is quite clear that human law was not always in the laws of kings, taking the word "king" thus strictly: for, as we read in *Decretum*, dist. 1 [c. 8], "Every people and city has power to establish its own law for itself"; therefore, without kings, people and cities and other communities have power to establish human laws for themselves. It is certain that many peoples and cities have done so; and thus the Romans at one time did not have kings and yet used human laws and also at that time made human laws and at that time possessed some things by their laws.

But in the divine Scriptures we read that before the laws of kings existed, indeed even before kings existed, some things were someone's: This is true; for before the times of kings some things were possessed by divine law, and some by human law, though not by the law of kings. *Therefore, by divine law someone was able to say that something was his*: This must be conceded, though it does not follow from the premise taken by itself. But from this affirmative proposition the negative, "Nothing was then possessed by human law," does not follow. *The major [premise] is clear, etc.*: From the major and the minor, since both are affirmative, the negative "that before kings lordship was not introduced by human law," does not follow; also, by virtue of the form of the argument this affirmative, "Before kings someone was able to say that something was his by divine law," does not follow: for the premises are not arranged in mood and figure, or in any due form of argument, as is quite clear to those practiced in the elements of dialectic. However, since the conclusion he expresses in words is true, if properly interpreted, it is not necessary to explain the defect of the argument.

Adam alone had lordship: Although he alone had lordship before Eve was formed, nevertheless the lordship was not for that reason exclusive: just as, if all the monks of some monastery died except one, he alone would then have lordship of the goods of the monastery, and yet that lordship would not be exclusive, but common, i.e. to be communicated, and he would not then be the owner, as was said above in chapter 27. *Since sharing obviously requires several*: Unless by chance there is some impediment.

And that Eve had not then been formed: This has been answered above, in chapter 27. *"You appointed man to rule over your creation,"* etc.: Here "man" is taken for both male and female, and thus it cannot be inferred from that text that before Eve was formed Adam had temporal lordship; and although he then had lordship, he nevertheless did not then have the lordship that is ownership. *And Damascene expressly says this*: This is answered in chapter 27. *That after the fall of our first parents, before the flood, and before there were kings, someone was able to say, "This is mine"*: This must be conceded; but it does not follow from it that that lordship was not introduced by human law, though it follows that it was not introduced by the law of kings. The appellant does not say that lordship was first introduced by the law of kings, but that it was introduced by human law; and there have been many human laws that were not laws of kings. *"You will eat 'your' bread"*: That bread was Adam's as to use and as to a lordship in some way common, though not as to a lordship exclusive to himself. *"Offered from the first-born of 'his' flock"*: The flock was his by human law, though not by the law of kings. *That after the flood, without the law of kings, someone was able to call something his*: This must be conceded, for then also someone was able to say by human law that something was his. *Noah planted a vine*: That vine was Noah's, though perhaps not exclusively his, without the law of kings, and perhaps without human law. It is consistent with this, however, that the first division of lordship was made by human will. *"I will give this land to your seed"*: From this it follows evidently that the lordship of some temporal things was introduced by divine law, without human law; but that was not the first exclusive lordship. *"I will give the whole of these regions to you and to your seed"*: The same answer is given to this text as to the previous one. *" 'What' each one 'had taken as booty was his' "*: From this it does indeed follow that those lordships did not exist by the laws of kings. *"I have given it to you for a possession, which you will divide among you by lot"*: As before, it must be conceded that those lordships did not exist by the laws of kings. *"That they give the*

Levites out of their possessions": It is conceded that those possessions were not possessed by the laws of kings. Nevertheless, it is consistent with this that the first division of lordships was introduced by human law.

From all of these things it is clear that we find in the sacred Scriptures that someone, both in the state of innocence and after the fall of our first parents, both before the flood and after the flood, was able to say, without the law of kings, that something was his: This conclusion has a true sense. For in the state of innocence, without the law of kings, Adam was able to say that something was his as to power of using and as to lordship; and after the sin of our first parents, without the law of kings, someone was able to say that something was his as to use and as to a lordship in some way common (namely, to both Adam and Eve), and another, without the law of kings, was able to say that something was his as to an exclusive lordship introduced by human law. After the flood, without the law of kings, some persons were able to say that some things were theirs by divine law; and some were able to say that some things were theirs by human law, and yet without the law of kings. And thus it is clear that this conclusion does not detract in any way from the appellant's assertion. For he did not mean that every division of lordships was introduced by the law of kings, as kings are distinguished from other powers; he meant that the first division of lordships was introduced by human law, or by the law of kings (with the term taken thus), but afterwards some lordships were introduced by divine law. And in the time of blessed Augustine all lordships existed by the law of kings, including emperors under the term "kings," for then all regions had been subjected to kings. And thus, if he knew how to distinguish lordships and times, he could harmonize the written sources.

And in 23, q. 7, c. 1, it is proved that there are some lordships by divine law: This chapter is wrongly adduced here. For the words of the chapter from which the above assertion could be taken are these: "Although no earthly thing whatever can rightly be possessed by anyone except either by divine law, by which all things belong to the just, or by human law, which is in the power of the kings of the earth." But in these words we do not find that some lordships are by divine law; for then, according to these words, all things would belong to the just in respect of lordship, which, however is false. For if all things belonged to the just in respect of lordship, others would not have just lordship in them, which is false. Augustine therefore did not mean that by divine law all things belong to the just in respect of lordship, but he meant that by divine law all things belong to the just in respect of worthiness to have: that is, the just are worthy of all things, the wicked are not worthy of anything, though they have true and just lordship of many things, a just lordship of which, however, they are unworthy.

Chapter 93

[John XXII] Second, it is asked whether Christ had lordship of any temporal thing, and what kind of lordship. That he did have lordship of temporal things sacred Scripture, both in the Old Testament and in the New, testifies in many places. For instance, many prophets prophesied that he would be the king of the Israelite people, and consequently would have lordship of a kingdom. Isaias, for instance, prophesied of him in Isaias 33[:22] thus: "See, the Lord is our judge, the Lord is our lawgiver, the Lord is our king; he will come and will save us." Also, God spoke thus through the mouth of the prophet Jeremias, in Jeremias 23[:5, 6], "I will raise to David a just shoot, and a king will reign, and he will be wise . . . And this is the name they will call him, The Lord our Just One." For he is "the stone cut out of the mountain without hands," to whom "the God of heaven" gave "a kingdom that will forever not be scattered," as we read in Daniel 2[:44–5]. Also, in Zacharias 9[:9] he is spoken of thus: "Rejoice greatly, daughter of Sion, shout for joy, daughter of Jerusalem; behold, your king will come to you, just and a savior; he is poor, and riding upon an ass, and upon a colt, the foal of an ass." Concerning this David prophesied in many places. Thus in one place he spoke in his person thus: Behold, "I am made king by him over Sion," etc. [Psalm 2:6], and in many other places he prophesied that he would be a king. Thus in the whole of the psalm *Eructavit* [Psalm 44] he speaks of that king and his spouse, namely the Church, and many other psalms speak clearly enough of such a king. Concerning this also Solomon, in Canticles 3[:11], spoke thus: "Go forth, daughters of Sion, and see King Solomon," etc. Of this man, even before he was conceived, the archangel Gabriel said, as we read in Luke

1[:32], "The Lord God will give him the throne of David his
father, and he will reign," etc. Also, when he was born the
angel said to the shepherds, in Luke 2[:11], "This day is born
to you a savior, who is Christ the Lord," that is, king and
lord. When he was born the three wise men of the Gospel,
Matthew 2[:2], also bore witness to this, saying, "Where is he
who has been born king of the Jews?" Also, Nathaniel, the
true "Israelite in whom there was no guile," said to him, in
John 1[:49], "You are the son of God, you are the king of
Israel." Pilate, also, in a notice above the cross, wrote, "Jesus
of Nazareth, king of the Jews." He made this notice indeed
not without divine inspiration: when the Jews urged that he
should not write "King of the Jews" but "He said 'I am king
of the Jews,'" he would not listen to them, but answered,
"What I have written, I have written." This our Savior also
confessed, in John 18[:36–7]. For when Pilate asked him
whether he was the king of the Jews, he answered him, "My
kingdom is not of this world." Making an inference from this,
Pilate said, "You are a king, then?" and Jesus answered, "My
kingdom is not from hence." He did not say, "It is not here,"
but "It is not from hence," as if to say, "I do not have my
kingdom from the world" – as indeed he did not have it, but
rather from God, as the angel had foretold to his mother,
when he said in Luke 1, "The Lord God will give him the
throne of David," etc. And blessed Peter explicitly testifies to
this in Acts 2[:36], when he says, "Let the whole house of
Israel know most certainly, that God has made him both Lord
and Christ, this Jesus whom you crucified." In these words
Peter clearly enough implies two things about Jesus our Lord,
namely [a] that he did not have his kingdom from the world,
but from God, since he says that the Lord made Jesus "Christ,"
that is, "king": for by "Christ" we understand "king," because
"Christ" is translated "the anointed," and since it was the
custom to anoint kings, by "Christ" we understand "king."
Thus Rabanus in the same place says, "Clearly, Peter shows
from this psalm that Christ's kingdom is not earthly but heavenly." Also, [b] Peter implies by the words above that Christ
was made lord and king as man subsisting in a divine subject:
for it is certain that he was not crucified as God, but as man;
and therefore, since he was made king and lord as crucified,
and was crucified as man, it follows that God granted him both
kingship and lordship also as man. The angel also supposes this

73

in speaking to the shepherds when he was born: "This day is born to you a savior, who is Christ the Lord," that is, king and lord. We should notice here that what the angel Gabriel had said in the future tense when Christ was not yet born, when he said to Mary, "The Lord *will* give him the throne of his father David," etc., the angel said to the shepherds when he was born in words of present tense, "Today is born to you a savior, who *is* Christ the Lord." Augustine explicitly testifies to this in his book *The Harmony of the Gospels*, in the preface, "The Lord Jesus Christ is a true king and a true priest," and shortly afterwards he says, "As man, indeed, Christ was made both king and priest, to whom 'God gave the throne of David his father, and his reign will have no end.'" Also, it seems that the Savior was lord of all temporal things. For it is said of him in Isaias 16[:1], "Send forth, O Lord, the Lamb, the dominator of the earth," etc. Also, in Micheas 5[:2] it is said of him, "And you, Bethlehem Ephrata, are by no means the least among the princes of Juda. For from you will go forth he who will be the dominator in Israel, and his going forth is from the beginning, from the days of eternity." And Malachias 3[:1] speaks of him thus: "Immediately the Dominator, whom you seek, and the Angel of the Testament, whom you desire, will come to his holy temple." Also, in John 13[:13] Truth himself says, "You call me Master, and Lord, and you say the truth, for so I am." Also, in Matthew 21[:2–3] he said to the disciples, "Go into the village in front of you, and immediately you will find an ass tied up, and its foal with her; untie them and bring them to me; and if anyone says anything to you, say that the Lord has need of them, and immediately he will let them go." This also blessed John testifies, in Apocalypse 19[:16]: "He has written on his garment, 'King of kings and lord of lords.'" Moreover the apostles confess this in their creed: "And in Jesus Christ, his only son, our Lord." This also the holy fathers expressly confess in the creed sung at mass, at "And in one lord Jesus Christ the only-begotten son of the Lord." But the foregoing, namely kingship and universal lordship, Jesus had as God from eternity, by virtue of the fact that God the Father begot him, and as man from a time, namely from the moment of his conception, by God's gift, as is clear from the above.

[Ockham] After discussing in the preceding part the law by which lordship of things was introduced, here he approaches the main question, asking whether Christ and his apostles had lordship of any temporal thing. It is divided into two parts: first he treats of this matter concerning Christ, and second concerning the apostles, at "But now we must see concerning the apostles" [chapter 97]. The first is divided into two: first he shows that Christ as man had kingship and universal lordship of temporal things; second he shows how, despite this, Christ was a poor man. The second begins at "But this heretic says" [chapter 96]. The first is divided into three: first he shows that from the moment of his conception Christ had kingship and universal lordship of all temporal things by God's gift. Second, he shows that, not from the moment of his conception, but afterwards, he acquired lordship of certain other things by other means. Third, he shows that Christ never renounced kingship and universal lordship. The second begins at "And likewise he had lordship" [chapter 94], the third at "And if he wants to say" [chapter 95]. The first could be divided into three parts: first he shows by fifteen texts that Christ as man was a king in temporal matters; second, he shows by eight texts that Christ as man was lord of all temporal things, at "Also, it seems that the Savior was lord of all"; third he determines when Christ had kingship and lordship of all things, at "But the foregoing".

And first he asks a question; second he decides it, showing that Christ had lordship of all temporal things because he was a king, which he shows by fifteen texts. But the attackers say that two manifest heresies are contained here: the first of them is that Christ as wayfaring man was a king in temporal matters; the second is that Christ as wayfaring man was lord of all temporal things from the instant of his conception. To convict [him of] these heresies more plainly they proceed thus: [1] first they try to make clear the equivocations of the words "king" and "lord"; [2] second they explain what they regard as the truth concerning the above matters; [3] third they try to prove that the two assertions stated above smack of manifest heresy.

[1] Concerning the first, they say that since the word "king" [*rex*] derives from "ruling" [*regendo*], someone can be called "king" in various ways, according to the various modes of rule [*regimen*]. Thus – not to mention divine rule over the angels, and also rule such as is found among irrational things – among men is found, besides others, three kinds of rule.

One is that by which one person rules others temporally, i.e., in respect of temporal things and actions known to relate to temporal things; and in this way, taking the word "king" in the broadest sense, emperors, kings, dukes, counts and barons, and heads of households could be called kings; and thus sometimes it is commonly said that every head of household is a king in his own home. However, according to a common way of speaking, those alone are called kings from this way of ruling who are known to hold the supreme mode of such ruling (in which, however, there can be degrees), and thus kings are distinguished from dukes, counts, barons, and other secular powers.

Another is spiritual rule, by which someone rules others concerning spiritual things. And in this way the pope and any prelate can be called a king. For if (as will be explained afterwards) anyone who rules his movements and sensual passions by reason can be called a king, much more can one who rules others concerning spiritual matters hold the name of king.

The other is the rule by which someone rules himself and his movements and his acts by right reason, and from that rule anyone at all who lives reasonably can be called a king. And thus for this reason blessed Remy asserts that all Christ's elect are kings. Explaining the words of Apocalypse 1[:6], "He has made us a kingdom and priests to God and to his Father," he says: "By this statement all are shown to be priests who have above been called kings. For because the head, the Son of God, is king and priest, appropriately the members of the head are also called kings and priests. It is said to them by Peter, 'You are an elect people, a kingly priesthood.' For they are kings, they are also priests and sacrifice and altar; for they rein in as kings the revolts of carnal pleasures rising up against them, and they offer up to God a sacrifice of praise and mortification and mortify their body from the desires of the present world, so as to become living sacrifices. Therefore the only-begotten Son of the Father, king and priest, makes us his elect kings and priests, whom he has appointed as kings of the earth and shown to be priests by that work." It is clearly shown by these words that someone can be called king from ruling his own desires and sensual movements. And thus in the written sources the word "king" is taken in various ways.

Second, they say that the word "lord" is taken in the written sources equivocally. For in one way someone is called a lord on account of some power recognized in him, and this way is divided into many, which were spoken about above in chapter 2. In another way someone is called "lord" because of a prerogative of holiness, virtue, or wisdom, or riches or some other superiority. For just as rich and powerful men and great lords often call priests and religious and many others "lords" because of a prerogative of holiness, religion, order, wisdom or some other superiority that they observe in them or regard as preeminent in them, so also many rich men call some persons "lord" to whom they nevertheless do not believe themselves to be subject. And this way of speaking is found not only in common speech but also in the divine Scriptures. For as we read in 3 Kings 18[:13], Abdias said to Elias the prophet, "Has it been told you, my lord, what I did?" Here Abdias called Elias his lord because of the prerogative of prophecy and holiness which he knew in him. Thus the Sunamite woman who had made a guestroom for Elias called him "lord" because of his prerogative of holiness, as we read in 4 Kings 4[:16], "Do not, I beseech, my lord, man of God, do not lie to your handmaid," and afterwards [4 Kings 4:28], "Did I ask my lord for a son?" And so this woman called Elias "lord," to whom, however, she was not temporally subject.

[2] Second (principally),[17] the attackers explain what they regard as the truth about the poverty of Christ, saying that Christ as God was king of all, just as the Father is king of all, and by the same rule as that by which the Father rules all things. Second, they say that as mortal man Christ was not a king [as the name is taken] from ruling temporally and according as someone is called king because of a supreme mode of ruling others temporally (though he was a king temporally because in some way he ruled the apostles temporally, who lived with him practically all the time). Third, they say that Christ was king from ruling spiritually, because "for this he came into the world," namely to direct [*gubernare*] the faithful who believe in him in respect of spiritual matters. Fourth, they say

---

[17] That is, second in the main series of sections, which are numbered in the translation.

that Christ as God was lord of all, just as God the Father is lord of all. Fifth, they say that Christ as mortal man was not lord of all temporal things by a lordship exclusive to himself, though he was lord of all by the common lordship that according to many was given by God to the whole human race (if it is not permissible for anyone to renounce such lordship). Sixth, they say that, although Christ as mortal man did not have of any thing that lordship which in the written sources is called ownership, nevertheless he could be called antonomastically[18] "lord" because of the prerogative of the union of human nature in him with the divine, and of holiness and other graces. From these points they say that it is clear that the attacked, deceived by the equivocation of words, falls into the heresies stated above.

[3] Third (principally), therefore, they try to prove that the two assertions stated above smack of manifest heresy. To make this evident they first explain what the attacked meant, saying that he meant not only that Christ as mortal man was a king because of his spiritual rule, and not because of [just] any way of ruling temporally, but [precisely] because of power to rule in the supreme mode of ruling temporally: so that not only as God, but as mortal man, it belonged to him, by the office committed to him, to judge concerning temporal matters, to divide inheritances, to establish secular laws, to subject murderers, robbers, and other wrongdoers to due punishment, to provide temporal help to the pilgrim, orphan, and widow when oppressed by the powerful, and to perform other things that belong to the duty of secular kings. And also he did not mean only that Christ was lord of all in the way in which anyone at all is in some way lord of all if the whole human race has common lordship of all, but he also meant that all things were Christ's as mortal man in the same way, or more truly, as cities and castles are some king's: in such a way that he had particular lordship, and not only lordship in common.

Now that we have seen this, they [i] first prove that Christ as mortal man was not a king in temporal matters [as the name is taken] from the supreme mode of ruling temporally; [ii] second,

---

[18] "When a term stands precisely for the individual it fits most of all, as in 'the Apostle [meaning Paul] says this,' 'the Philosopher [meaning Aristotle] denies this,' and the like"; Ockham, *Summa logicae*, p. 237. Thus Jesus is called "the Lord" because, although there are many other lords, the term fits him most of all.

they show that he was not lord, in that way, of all temporal things. The first point they show [a] first by authoritative texts, and [b] second by arguments.

[i.a] The first authority by which they show that Christ was not king in that way is that of Christ himself, when he said in John 18[:36], "My kingdom is not of this world"; by these words it is established that the kingdom of Christ as man was not a temporal kingdom.

But the attacked answers this. He says that Christ did not mean to deny that his kingdom was temporal and worldly but meant to say that he did not have his kingdom from the world but from God, because the world did not give him the kingdom and did not choose him as king, but God did. Thus, as is clear above, the attacked brings this text in support of his own assertion, proving by it that Christ was a king, though he did not have a kingdom from the world but from God. Thus, and for this reason (he says), Christ said, "My kingdom is not from hence," and did not say "It is not here," giving us to understand from this that he did not have the kingdom from the world, but from God.

But they say that here "he interprets divine Scripture in another way than the sense of the Holy Spirit demands," [Jerome], dragging the divine Scripture – most clearly resisting – to his own sense. For it is quite clear from the relevant words of the Gospel that Christ meant to assert by the above words that he did not have a temporal kingdom or one such as worldly people try to acquire. For, as is certain from the Gospel text, the chief accusation the Jews put forward before Pilate against Christ, by which they wished especially to provoke Pilate against Christ – indeed, by which they finally in a way compelled Pilate to pass sentence against Christ – was concerning Christ's kingship: they said that Christ asserted that he was the king of the Jews. Thus in Luke 23[:2] it is written concerning the Jews: "And they began to accuse him, saying: 'We have found this man subverting our nation, and forbidding tribute to be given to Caesar, and saying that he is Christ the king.'" And in John 19[:12] we read thus: "Pilate sought to let him go. But the Jews cried out, saying: 'If you let this man go, you will not be Caesar's friend; for everyone who makes himself a king speaks against Caesar.'" And later [John 19:15]: "Pilate says to them: 'Will I crucify your king?' The chief priests answered: 'We have no king but Caesar.' Then therefore he handed him over to them to be crucified." From these words we gather evidently that the main accusation of the Jews against Christ was that he made himself king – speaking of a temporal king, such a king as Caesar was not willing to tolerate unless he would acknowledge his kingship as being from him. For this reason they said, "Everyone who makes himself a king speaks against Caesar." And by this accusation they finally in a way compelled Pilate against his will to pass sentence of death against Christ, as is clear from the words quoted above. But Christ did not deny that he was a king, indeed he asserted it; and nevertheless he adequately excluded the accusation of the Jews before Pilate, who did not want to tolerate a king of the Jews besides Caesar, in that way of using the word "king" in which the Jews accusing Christ spoke of a king. Therefore, it is manifestly clear that Christ declared before Pilate that he was a king in another way than the Jews were speaking of a king, and that he was not a king in the way in which the Jews were speaking of a king. Since therefore they were referring to a temporal king reigning temporally, or wishing to reign temporally, it follows that when Christ said, "My kingdom is not of this world," he showed that he was not a king temporally, and not one having an earthly kingdom.

Here it is necessary to prove three points. The first is that the Jews accusing Christ were referring to a king reigning temporally, or wishing to reign temporally. The second is that Pilate did not want there to be any king of the Jews besides Caesar, in the Jews' sense of "king". The third is that Christ satisfied Pilate by adequately excluding the accusation of the Jews. From these it is plainly inferred that Christ was speaking of king and kingdom in another way than the Jews were, and consequently did not assert that he was a king in temporal matters, but in another way.

The first point is clear enough, for otherwise they would never have provoked Pilate against Christ by that accusation. For the Romans and their agents seem at that time to have cared little about things pertaining to the law of the Jews, and they did not judge anyone worthy of death on account of a transgression of the law. Thus, as we read in Acts 23[:29], when the tribune Lysias sent blessed Paul to the governor Felix he wrote, "Whom," namely Paul, "I found to be accused concerning questions of their law, but having nothing charged deserving death or bonds." And, as we read in chapter 25, Portius Festus speaking of Paul said: "Concerning whom, when the accusers stood up, they made no accusation of matters concerning which I suspected evil. But they had against him certain questions concerning their own superstition, and concerning a certain Jesus, deceased, whom Paul affirmed was alive" [Acts 25:18]; and later: "But I have found that he has done nothing deserving death" [Acts 25:25]; and in chapter 26 we read: "And the king arose, and the governor, and Bernice, and their assessors. And when they had drawn apart they spoke to one another, saying, 'This man has not done anything deserving death or bonds' " [Acts 26:30]. From these words we gather evidently that at that time the Romans regarded no one as deserving of death or bonds on account of diverse and conflicting assertions of Jewish law, even if some should say that some man was God, as Paul confessed that Christ himself was God. Therefore, however much the Jews accused Christ to Pilate of saying that he was God, or a king in another way than temporally and not to the prejudice of Caesar's temporal kingdom, they would never have provoked Pilate against Christ, but Pilate would have regarded their accusation as frivolous; for he would not have regarded him as being against Caesar or against the temporal public peace. Therefore the Jews were speaking of a temporal king.

The second point also, namely that Pilate did not want there to be any temporal king of the Jews besides Caesar, is manifest. For he knew that Caesar claimed for himself the lordship of all kingdoms and thus did not want anyone to be king of the Jews unless he would acknowledge the kingdom as being from him.

The third, namely that Christ satisfied Pilate by excluding the said accusation of the Jews adequately and plainly, is shown clearly by the Gospel text. For after the said accusation of the Jews and Christ's answer, in which he had conceded that he was a king and had expressed the way in which he was king, Pilate said, as we read in John 18[:38], "I find no case against him," and in John 19 Pilate said, "Behold I bring him forth, that you may know that I find no case against him"; and afterwards: "You take him and crucify him; I do not find any case against him." From these words it is clear and plain that Pilate regarded the accusation of the Jews as adequately excluded by Christ's answer. For since the Jews had accused Christ before Pilate of saying that he was the king of the Jews (and without doubt they meant this of a king ruling, or wishing to rule, temporally, for otherwise it would have been in no way prejudicial to Caesar – which, however, they most manifestly claimed, saying, "Everyone who makes himself a king speaks against Caesar"); and since by his answer Christ had most manifestly conveyed that he did not mean to claim for himself a temporal kingdom that would be "of this world," but the other, spiritual, one spoken of before, and thus had very clearly shown Pilate the multiplicity [of senses] and the equivocation of the word "king," and consequently that he had called himself king in a far different way than the Jews had meant in their accusation; and since Pilate had seen that the Jews were not able to prove that Christ had called himself king to Caesar's prejudice: Pilate himself regarded their accusation as frivolous. For as he testifies in Matthew 27[:18], "He knew that they had handed him over out of envy," and for this reason, as we read in the same place [Matthew 27:24], "Taking water, he washed his hands in front of the people, saying, 'I am innocent of the blood of this just man' "; and in Mark 15[:9] we read that Pilate said, " 'Do you want me to release to you the king of the Jews?' for he knew that they had handed him over out of envy." From these words we gather plainly that Pilate clearly understood that the Jews accusing Christ of saying that he was king of the Jews, and Christ conceding that he was king of the Jews, were taking the word "king" equivocally. For if Christ had said he was king in the way the Jews accusing him took the word, Pilate would have regarded him as quite deserving of death, as having confessed in court a crime most deserving of death, namely usurping a temporal kingdom without Caesar's will.

But someone will ask, How did Pilate perceive that Christ meant that he was king in another way than the Jews meant in accusing him? It must be said that he perceived this from Christ's words when he said, "My kingdom is not of this world. For if my kingdom were of this world my servants would certainly fight so that I would not be handed over to the Jews. But as it is my kingdom is not from hence" [John 18:36]. By these words he indicated that he did not have a kingdom of the kind of which the Jews made accusation, for if he had had such a kingdom his servants would have fought for him so that he would not be handed over to the

Jews. But still by these words Pilate does not seem to have understood plainly whether Christ was confessing that he was king here or elsewhere, nor what sort of kingdom he had. And therefore, as if in wonder, he drew the inference, "You *are* a king, then?" as if to say, "Then you concede that you are a king, although not such a king as the Jews speak of. Where therefore is your kingdom, and what sort of kingdom do you have?" And Christ answered these questions that Pilate in some way seemed to have in mind, explaining where his kingdom was and what sort it was. He said: "You say that I am a king. For this I was born, and for this I came into the world, to bear testimony to the truth, and everyone who is of the truth hears my voice" [John 18:37]. Here Christ first confesses that he is a king, saying, "I am a king." Second, he shows where his kingdom is, namely here, when he says, "For this I was born, and for this I came into the world," as if to say, "I was born to reign in this world." Third, he shows of what kind his kingdom was and in what way he had come to reign, saying, "To bear testimony to the truth," as if to say, "I came to reign, but I did not come to reign temporally, but spiritually, by bearing testimony to the truth." Fourth, he shows who belongs to his kingdom, namely those who believe in him; and therefore he says, "Everyone who is of the truth hears my voice," as if to say, "All those who believe the truth belong to my kingdom." And thus by these words Pilate was fully informed that, although Christ regarded himself as a king here, he nevertheless did not regard himself as a temporal king; and therefore Pilate did not regard Christ as being in any way opposed to Caesar, who sought temporal kingdoms. He therefore regarded him as innocent, and as meaning that he was a king in another way than the Jews meant.

And this truth explained thus by means of the words of the Gospel, namely that Christ was a king in another way than the Jews accusing him meant, is confirmed by authoritative texts of the saints. Thus Augustine says upon John: The Christian faithful are "his kingdom which is now gathered, indeed is purchased, by Christ's blood"; therefore in Pilate's time only Christians belonged to Christ's kingdom. But if Christ had been king in the way the Jews spoke of a king in accusing Christ, not only Christians but all the Jews living in the kingdom of Judaea would have belonged to Christ's kingdom: which is false, according to Augustine. Therefore according to Augustine Christ was a king in another way than the Jews meant.

Chrysostom also testifies to the same effect, commenting upon the text, "My kingdom is not from hence." He says, "He does not deprive the world of its providence and rule, but shows that his kingdom is not human or corruptible." By these words it is plainly established that Christ did not have a kingdom of the same kind as a worldly and human kingdom, and thus he was not king in the way the Jews meant.

And Augustine clearly teaches this, commenting upon John 19: "Hear, Jews and gentiles; hear, circumcised, hear, uncircumcised; hear, all kingdoms of the earth. I do not hinder your lordship in this world, because 'My kingdom is not of this world.' Do not fear that most vain fear that Herod the Elder felt and killed so many infants, too cruel through fear more than anger. 'My kingdom,' he says, 'is not of this world.' What more do you want? Come to the kingdom that is not of this world. Come through faith, and do not rage through fear. He says indeed in prophecy of God the Father: 'And I am appointed by him king over Zion, his holy mountain, preaching his commandment'; but Zion and that mountain are not of this world. For what is his kingdom except the believers, to whom he says, 'You are not of this world, just as I am not of this world': although he wished them to be in the world, and for this reason he said of them to the Father, 'I do not ask you to take them from the world, but to preserve them from evil.' And thus he did not say here, 'My kingdom is not in this world,' but 'It is not of this world.' When he proves this – saying: 'If my kingdom were of this world, my servants would indeed fight so that I would not be handed over to the Jews. But now, my kingdom is not from hence' – he does not say, 'It is not here,' but 'It is not from hence.' For his kingdom is here until the end of the world, having tares mixed in with it until the harvest. For the harvest is the end of the world, and then the reapers will come, that is, the angels, and 'they will gather out of his kingdom all scandals.' This would indeed not happen if his kingdom were not here. But, nevertheless, it is not from hence, because it is on pilgrimage in the world." From these words we clearly gather three things. The first is that the manner of Christ's rule in no way impeded earthly domination and domination by earthly men: from this it follows that Christ did not come to reign in a temporal or secular way, but only spiritually; for if he had involved himself in secular rule he would have impeded the domination of secular [rulers] and would have provoked them to the utmost. The second is that one does not arrive at Christ's kingdom through secular subjection, but through faith, because by believing; and consequently Christ's kingdom is not secular, governed in a secular way, but spiritual, governed spiritually. The third is that believers are Christ's kingdom, for the Church is the kingdom of Christ; thus, just as Christ is the king and bridegroom, so the Church is the kingdom and his bride. And for this reason the Church of Christ present in this world is in the Gospel often called the kingdom of heaven, as Gregory testifies; in his homily *Of the Common of Virgins* he says, "We must know that in sacred language the Church of the present time is often called the kingdom of heaven. The Lord in another place says about it, 'The Son of Man will send his angels, and they will gather all scandals out of his kingdom.'" The kingdom, therefore, of which Christ said, "My kingdom is not of this world," is his Church, including believers, good and bad; and thus that kingdom is often called the kingdom of heaven.

From the foregoing it is quite clear that Christ's kingdom was not Judaea, inasmuch as Judaea included all Jews living there, as the Jews meant who accused Christ of saying that he was king of the Jews. Rather the kingdom of Christ was Christ's Church, including only believers in Christ; and thus Christ's kingdom was not a secular kingdom but a spiritual kingdom – that is, it was the Church of Christians, to be governed by him spiritually.

The second main text that proves that Christ was not a king in secular matters is taken from Luke 1[:32–3], where the angel, describing his kingdom and way of reigning, says, "The Lord God will give him the throne of his father David, and he will reign in the house of Jacob eternally, and of his kingdom there will be no end." By these words we are given to understand that Christ would be king in the way in which he would reign in the house of Jacob and in no other way. But Christ as man, as long as he was yet to live in this mortal life, was not going to reign in a secular way, but only spiritually; therefore he was not going to be king in respect of secular matters, but in respect of spiritual matters only.

Here it seems it should be proved that Christ as mortal man did not reign in a secular way, but only spiritually. But this does not need to be proved. For Christ never intervened in secular rule, especially in the supreme secular rule from which someone is called a king, as we are now speaking of a king in temporal matters. For he neither held parliaments and courts nor judged concerning temporal matters nor did justice to malefactors nor did battle with enemies nor paid out military stipends, and he did not in any way perform other things pertaining to secular rule. Christ's kingdom, therefore, was not secular, but spiritual. This the gloss on the words given above clearly testifies. It says, " 'The Lord God will give him the throne of his father David' – that is, the Israelite people, to whom David and his sons provided the government of the temporal kingdom. The spiritual kingship of this has been given to Christ, when it was determined by God that he should become flesh of the seed of David, to call that nation his kingdom perpetually. And 'He will reign' not only in that people of the Jews but 'in the house of Jacob eternally' – that is, in the whole Church, which through the faith and confession of Christ belongs to the line of the patriarchs, whether in those that are born from the line of the patriarchs, or in these that have been cut out of the wild olive and grafted into the good olive." It is quite clear from these words that Christ's kingdom was not a temporal but a spiritual one, to which only believers belonged, whether from among the Jews or from among the gentiles.

Also, Bede testifies that the kingdom of Christ was not earthly, secular, or worldly, in a passage included in the gloss on the text of Mark 11[:10], "Blessed be the kingdom that comes of our father David." He says: "According to John, when the crowds wanted to seize Christ and make him king, he fled, and did not want a kingdom while he had time yet to live. But now, on the point of suffering, he does not shrink from saying that he is a king. He does not restrain hymns worthy of the Son of God and a king, does not restrain those who sing of the restoration of David's kingdom in him and of the gifts of the ancient blessing; because, of course, he was the king of an empire not temporal and earthly, but eternal and in heaven, to which he would come through contempt of death, the glory of resurrection, and the triumph of ascension. Thus he said to the disciples after his resurrection, 'All power is given to me in heaven and on earth.' " From these words it is clear that the kingdom of Christ was not earthly and temporal.

Pope Leo agrees with this, in a sermon about the Epiphany: "But Herod, hearing that the prince of the Jews had been born, suspected a successor, and was much afraid . . . O blind wickedness of stupid envy, that you should think that the divine plan would be disturbed by your fury. The lord of the world does not seek a temporal kingdom, but offers one that is eternal." From these words we gather that Christ as man did not have a temporal kingdom.

Also, Saint Fulgentius in a sermon about the Epiphany says, "The gift of gold shows that our Lord Jesus Christ was a true king: not at all the kind of king who takes his image on coins, but one who seeks his image in men themselves." These words plainly establish that Christ was not a king of the kind who seek their images on coins, and thus he was not to be regarded as a king in temporal matters. Rabanus testifies to this same [assertion], as he [John] quotes him, as will appear in the comments upon the letter.

[i.b] It remains now to show the same assertion by means of arguments fortified by sacred authorities. The first argument is as follows. Anyone who is not a judge of secular litigation or a divider of inheritances and properties is not a king in temporal matters, for those things are known to pertain to the office of a king; but Christ was not a judge of litigation or a divider of inheritances and earthly properties; therefore Christ was not a king in temporal or secular and earthly matters. The major [premise] is known, the minor is manifestly proved by the authority of Christ and of blessed Ambrose. For, as we read in Luke 12[:13], when someone from the crowd said to Christ, "Master, tell my brother to divide the inheritance with me," Christ answered, "Man, who has appointed me judge or divider over you?" – as if to say, "No one"; therefore Christ was not a judge of litigation or a divider of inheritances. Blessed Ambrose, commenting on the same passage, asserts this manifestly: "Well, therefore, does he avoid earthly things, who had come down for the sake of divine; neither does he deign to be a judge of litigation and an arbiter of property, being judge of the living and dead and arbiter of merits . . . Thus the brother who wished to occupy with corruptible things the dispenser of heavenly things is here deservedly repulsed." It could not be said more clearly than this that Christ was by no means a judge of secular litigation or arbiter of earthly property, and consequently he was not to be regarded as a king in secular matters.

The second argument for the same assertion is this. No one who teaches us by word and example to despise temporal kingdoms should be thought to be a king in temporal matters. But by word and example Christ taught that temporal kingdoms should be despised. That by word he taught that rulerships and temporal kingships should be despised is quite clear from the text of Matthew 20[:2–6], "But Jesus called them to him and said, 'You know that the rulers of the peoples lord it over them, and the great men exercise power over them; it will not be so among you. But whoever wishes to be the greater among you, let him be your servant,'" etc. From these words it is plainly inferred that by word Christ taught that rulerships and temporal power over others – and consequently temporal kingdoms – should be despised. That he also taught by example that temporal kingdoms should be despised is clearly apparent from the text of John 6[:15], "When Jesus, therefore, knew that they would come to seize him and make him king, he fled again to the mountain." Commenting on this text Chrysostom says: "He," i.e., Christ, "was already a prophet among them, and they wished to enthrone him as king," because of greed, namely because he had fed them. "But Christ fled, teaching us to despise earthly offices," and consequently he instructed us by example to despise worldly kingdoms. Therefore Christ was by no means a king in temporal matters, for otherwise he would have been in conflict with himself in both words and deeds, teaching one thing by word and example and doing another.

The third argument is this. Anyone who undertakes to govern a kingdom but does not in any way involve himself in its government, though he could do so, deserves blame for malice, wickedness, or negligence; for such a person wishes to have the name of king but not at all to perform the duty and functions of a king, and this must be attributed altogether to malice or negligence. But Christ in no way involved himself in the secular government of any kingdom whatever; therefore either he did not undertake to govern a kingdom, and consequently was not a king, or he deserved blame for malice or negligence. But neither malice nor negligence should be attributed to him; therefore it must be held that, as mortal man, he did not undertake to rule any kingdom, and consequently did not possess either the reality or the name of secular king.

The fourth argument is this. There cannot be in the same secular kingdom several true kings, not holding the kingdom jointly, none of whom acknowledges the kingdom as being from another. But in Christ's time the Emperor of the Romans was true king of Judaea, though he was king of other kingdoms; and it is certain that Christ and the emperor did not hold the kingdom of Judaea jointly, and neither did Christ acknowledge the kingdom of Judaea as being from the emperor, nor the emperor from Christ. Therefore Christ was not true secular king of Judaea; and consequently, by like reasoning, he was not a secular king of any other kingdom whatever.

Here three things seem to require proof. The first is that Caesar or the emperor was king of Judaea. This is drawn evidently from the Gospel, where Christ says, "Give to Caesar the things that are Caesar's": from these words we gather that the things that Caesar claimed in Judaea were truly his. But Caesar claimed tribute as being king of Judaea and lord; therefore tribute was truly his as being king and lord; therefore he was truly king. The second thing to be proved here is that Caesar did not acknowledge the kingdom as being from Christ and was not obliged to acknowledge it. For before Christ's birth Caesar was true king; but by Christ's birth Caesar's kingship was in no respect diminished or changed or brought into any subjection; therefore, just as before Christ's birth he was not obliged to acknowledge any kingdom whatever as being from any man, so after Christ's birth he was not obliged to acknowledge the kingdom as being from any man, as man; and so he was not obliged to acknowledge the kingdom as being from Christ as man. The third thing that seems to require proof is that Christ did not acknowledge the kingdom as being from Caesar. But this needs no proof, since he never claimed any kingdom, but refused to be made king and fled so as not to be made king, as is clear in John 6.

The fifth argument is this. If Christ was king of any temporal kingdom, and there is no more reason why he was king of one temporal kingdom more than another, unless one says that because he was the son of David he was king particularly of Judaea, then it follows that he was king of all kingdoms, or particularly of Judaea. But neither can be said. For, whether he had been king of all kingdoms or particularly of Judaea, all the Jews, at least those living in Judaea, would have belonged to his kingdom; but it is not the case that all Jews living in Judaea belonged to his kingdom; therefore he was not temporal king of Judaea; and consequently, *a fortiori*, he was not temporal king of another kingdom.

Here it must be proved that not all the Jews, even those living in Judaea, belonged to Christ's kingdom insofar as he was a mortal man, though all belong to his kingdom insofar as he is God. This is clearly proved by the gloss on the text of John 19, "Jesus of Nazareth, king of the Jews," which says, "In the heart, not in the flesh." By these words it is established that Christ was king only of those Jews who were Jews in heart, such as the faithful were, and not only in the flesh, such as the unfaithful were; therefore Jews who did not believe in Christ did not belong to Christ's kingdom insofar as he was a man. This is also clear because Christ's kingdom was the Church of Christ, since according to Gregory, as quoted above, "the kingdom of heaven," which is the kingdom of Christ, is "the Church of the present time." But the Jews who did not believe in Christ did not belong to the Church of Christ; therefore they also did not belong to the kingdom of Christ. This is also clear, third, because just as the same Christ was, and is, bridegroom, king and shepherd, so the same congregation was Christ's bride, kingdom and flock. But the Jews who did not and would not believe in Christ did not belong to Christ's flock, as Christ himself testifies when he says in John 10[:14], "I am the good shepherd, and I know mine, and mine know me." From these words we gather that all Christ's sheep recognized Christ by faith. Therefore the Jews who did not believe were not Christ's sheep, and consequently did not belong to Christ's flock; from this it follows that they did not belong to Christ's kingdom. This is also quite clear from the many texts quoted above that assert that the believers were the kingdom of Christ. And thus Christ was not king in secular matters.

The sixth argument is this. The kingdom of Christ was the kingdom about which the prophets prophesied. But the prophets prophesying Christ's future kingdom did not prophesy concerning any temporal kingdom; and therefore no temporal kingdom was the kingdom of Christ. The major [premise] is clear; the minor is proved. For the kingdom of Christ concerning which the prophets prophesied was to be renewed and restored by Christ, on the testimony of Isaias, who in chapter 9[:6–7] says: "For a child is born to us, and a son is given to us; and the government is upon his shoulder; and his name will be called, Wonderful, God, Mighty, Father of the world to come, Prince of Peace. His empire shall be multiplied, and of peace there shall be no end; he will sit upon the throne of David and upon his kingdom, to confirm and strengthen it in judgment and justice, from now and for ever." From these words we gather clearly that the kingdom of Christ concerning which Isaias prophesied was to be confirmed and strengthened by him, and consequently renewed and restored. Similarly in Jeremias 23[:5–6] Jeremias prophesied concerning Christ, saying: "Behold the days come, says the Lord, and I will raise to David a just shoot, and a king will reign, and he will be wise, and he will execute judgment and justice upon the earth. In those days Juda will be saved, and Israel will dwell confidently; and this is the name they will call him: The Lord our Just One." From these words we gather that those who were to be of Christ's kingdom were to be saved and would dwell confidently; therefore the kingdom of heaven concerning which Jeremias prophesied in the foregoing words was to be renewed by Christ. But the temporal kingdom of Judaea was not renewed by Christ, neither was it restored by him, but rather it was scattered, since because of the sins they committed against Christ it was destroyed. And thus, as we read in Luke 19[:41–4], he foretold the overthrow of Jerusalem, which was the metropolis of the kingdom of Judaea: "When he drew near, seeing the city he wept over it, saying: 'If you also had known, and that in this your day, the things that are for your peace; but now they are hidden from your eyes. For the days shall come upon you, and your enemies will carry a trench around you, and compass you round, and hem you in on every side; and they will throw you down to the ground, and your children within you, and they will not leave in you a stone upon a stone because you did not know the time of your visitation.' " From these words we gather evidently that the kingdom of Judaea was not renewed temporally by Christ; but afterwards, because it did not know the time of its spiritual visitation but persecuted Christ to death, it was scattered. The kingdom of Christ about which the prophets made predictions was therefore not a temporal kingdom, and the prosperity the prophets then prophesied would come should not be understood as temporal, but as spiritual, because of the abundance of graces and spiritual gifts with which Christ most richly honored, affirmed, strengthened, and saved those who believed in him – who were his kingdom – and made them confident and secure amid the adversities of the world.

The seventh argument is as follows. Without distinguishing between the one office entrusted to him and another, Christ appointed blessed Peter as his vicar, saying, "Feed my sheep"; therefore Christ appointed blessed Peter as his vicar regarding his subjects in respect of every office that he had as man. But blessed Peter was not Christ's vicar in respect of the office of temporal king. Therefore Christ also did not have the office of temporal king, and consequently the kingdom of Christ was not temporal, but spiritual. Such a kingdom he entrusted to blessed Peter when he said, "Feed my sheep," and had previously promised to him when he said, "I will give you the keys of the kingdom of heaven."

Here it is necessary to prove that blessed Peter was not Christ's vicar in respect of the office of temporal king, nor even in any temporal matters whatever. This is proved first as follows. If blessed Peter had been Christ's vicar in respect of the office of temporal king in any temporal kingdom, blessed Peter would have had power to judge all, and concerning all, who lived in the kingdom subjected to him, not only believers but also non-believers. But blessed Peter did not at all have power to judge concerning unbelievers who had never accepted the faith of Christ, as the Apostle testifies. In 1 Corinthians 5[:12] he said, in the person of all the prelates of the Church, "What business is it of mine to judge those who are outside?" Therefore it did not pertain to blessed Peter to judge concerning those who were "outside" in any kingdom whatever; and thus he was not Christ's vicar in any temporal kingdom whatever.

Second, as follows. One who in any kingdom is general vicar of any temporal king who does not have a superior has temporal jurisdiction over all those living in the kingdom who have never been exempted by the king. But in appointing blessed Peter as his vicar, Christ exempted no one from blessed Peter's jurisdiction; therefore blessed Peter had temporal jurisdiction over everyone living in the kingdom; and so, since the kingdom of Christ was not one [kingdom] rather than another, it follows that blessed Peter had temporal jurisdiction over the [Roman] emperor and all other kings. From this it follows that, since the Roman pontiff is blessed Peter's successor, equal to him in the power granted to him by Christ, each and every Roman pontiff has had temporal jurisdiction over the Roman emperor and all other kings in the world: which plainly conflicts with the sacred canons. For Pope Nicholas, as we read in dist. 96, c. *Cum ad verum*, says: "Since [the world] has come to the truth, no longer has the emperor seized for himself the rights of the pontificate, nor has the pontiff usurped the name of emperor. For the same mediator between God and men, the man Christ Jesus, distinguished the duties of both powers by their own acts and distinct offices." By these words we are given to understand that the Roman bishop does not have from succession to blessed Peter temporal jurisdiction over the emperor. That the pope also does not have jurisdiction over other kings Innocent III seems to testify. As we read in *Extra, De iudiciis*, c. *Novit*, he says, "Let no one think that we mean to disturb or lessen the jurisdiction of the illustrious king of the French," etc.; therefore the pope does not hold temporal jurisdiction over the king of France. Also, if the pope had by succession from blessed Peter temporal jurisdiction over kings, much more would he have by the same succession temporal jurisdiction over their possessions and over those of others. Bernard plainly asserts the contrary. Writing to Eugenius, *On Consideration*, Book I, chapter 5, he says: "Therefore your power is in criminal matters, not over possessions; because it is on account of the former, not the latter, that you have received the keys of the kingdom of heaven, to shut out sinners and not possessors – 'That you may know' (he says) 'that the Son of Man has power on earth to forgive sins' [Matthew 9:6] . . . Which seems to you the greater dignity and power, to forgive sins or to divide estates? These lowest and earthly things have their own judges, the kings and rulers of the earth. Why do you invade the territory of others? Why do you put your scythe into another's crop?" From these words it is clear that by the power given him by Christ the pope does not hold temporal jurisdiction over possessions. From these and a great many other [authorities] it is clear that blessed Peter did not have temporal jurisdiction over the emperor and kings, and thus was not Christ's vicar in any temporal kingdom.

But perhaps someone will object to the foregoing. First, by a text of Pope Nicholas, included in dist. 22, c. 1, where we read: "He alone founded it, and erected it on the rock of a faith soon

arising, who gave blessed Peter, the bearer of the keys of eternal
life, the rights of both earthly and heavenly empire." From these
words it is clear that blessed Peter held the rights of the earthly
empire and consequently held jurisdiction over the earthly emperor.
That blessed Peter's successors also had jurisdiction over emperors
and kings is proved: First, because the pope deposes emperors and
kings, as is clear in 15, q. 6, c. *Alius*. Also, he transfers the Roman
Empire, *Extra, De electione*, c. *Venerabilem*; therefore he is known
to have jurisdiction over the Empire. Also, the emperor takes an
oath of fidelity to him, and is therefore subject to him in temporal
matters. Also, we see with our eyes that the Roman pope has
temporal jurisdiction; but the pope does not have more authority
than blessed Peter had; therefore blessed Peter also had temporal
jurisdiction. But he did not have a temporal jurisdiction that was
limited; therefore kings and others were subject to him temporally.

To the first of these arguments some of the attackers say that
by "earthly and heavenly empire" Pope Nicholas means good and
bad people in the Church militant; and thus by "earthly empire"
he does not mean an earthly imperial office. They explain this as
follows. By "heavenly empire" Pope Nicholas cannot mean anything
but good people in the Church militant, because by "heavenly
empire" he cannot mean good people who are in the Church
triumphant, since over them Peter had no jurisdiction. Therefore,
similarly, by "earthly empire" Nicholas means bad people in the
Church militant. And thus it cannot be inferred from the above
text that blessed Peter had temporal jurisdiction over the emperor,
but that he had spiritual jurisdiction over good and bad people in
the Church militant.

To the second argument they reply in two ways. In one way,
that the Christian emperor is subject to the pope by reason of
crime, and they say the same of other kings; and so, by reason of
crime, the pope has spiritual jurisdiction over emperors and kings,
not temporal. In another way, they say that although the pope does
not have temporal jurisdiction over the emperor and other kings,
nevertheless to have such temporal jurisdiction is not repugnant to
him. And therefore a people, both the Roman people and another,
can transfer to the person of the pope the jurisdiction they are
known to have on occasion both over the emperor and over a king
without any person superior to him, and then the pope can depose

the emperor or king by the authority of the people. And in this way we read in 15, q. 6, c. *Alius* that he deposed a king of France; on the word "deposed" the gloss there says, "He is said to have deposed because he consented with those who deposed," that is, by the authority of the people, who thought the king should be deposed, he deposed that king. And in that way an archbishop or bishop could depose some king, not by reason of their spiritual office, but by the authority of the people who conferred such power on them.

To the third some say that the pope transfers the Roman Empire not as the successor of blessed Peter, but by the authority of the Romans, who granted him such power.

To the fourth some say that the emperor who first swore an oath to the pope swore it to him out of devotion or humility, or by an ordinance of the Romans; and therefore his predecessors, who did not swear to the pope, did not in any way withhold anything due to him because of his succession from blessed Peter, because they were not at all obliged to swear to him.

To the fifth they say that the Roman pope does not have the temporal jurisdiction he is known to have by succession from blessed Peter, because then he would not have greater temporal jurisdiction in one region than in another, just as blessed Peter did not: yet this is known to be false. The pope therefore has temporal jurisdiction in various regions, not by reason of succession, but by grant of the faithful. This is Bernard's opinion, as is said elsewhere. And when it is said that the pope does not have more power than blessed Peter had, they say that in respect of spiritual things the pope does not have more power than blessed Peter had, but in respect of temporal things he has more power, just as he is richer than blessed Peter was.

From the above it is gathered that blessed Peter did not receive from Christ any temporal kingdom. Therefore neither did Christ have any temporal kingdom.

The eighth argument for the above assertion is as follows. Christ was the model and exemplar of all Christian perfection; therefore, whatever belongs to perfection and was advantageous to the faithful, Christ practiced. But it belongs to perfection to abandon a temporal kingdom, just as it belongs to perfection to avoid ecclesiastical offices; for to seek secular or ecclesiastical offices is known to belong to imperfection. Now it was advantageous to the faithful that Christ should despise every secular office. Therefore Christ did not have any secular office, either royal or other; therefore Christ was not a king in temporal matters.

But perhaps someone will object against the foregoing argument that Christ did not practice all the things that belong to perfection. For (as has been mentioned) to avoid ecclesiastical offices is known to belong to the perfection of humility to this extent, that only those who avoid ecclesiastical offices are regarded as worthy of those very ecclesiastical offices, as blessed Gregory testifies. As we read in 8, q. 1, c. *In scripturis*, he says, "Just as a position of rule should be denied to those who desire it, so it should be offered to those who avoid it." And yet Christ did not refuse a position of rule; therefore Christ did not practice all the things that belong to perfection. Therefore from the premise that it belongs to perfection to abandon temporal kingdoms it cannot be inferred that Christ was not a secular king, or a king in secular matters.

But this objection is excluded, since in the second premise it is added, "and was advantageous to the faithful." For Christ did do the things that belong to perfection and advantage that he taught to others. But for Christ to abandon a position of spiritual rule was of no advantage, but would have harmed the faithful, and for Christ to keep a position of spiritual rule was of great advantage. And for Christ to have a temporal kingdom but in no way involve himself in the temporal kingdom would have been of no advantage. It was therefore fitting that Christ should keep a position of spiritual rule and not have a temporal kingdom; and thus it is clear that Christ did not have a temporal kingdom.

[ii] However, since a difference is found between ruling and being lord (or having lordship and ownership) of temporal things, now that it has been shown that Christ was not a king in temporal matters in the sense that someone is called "king" from the supreme mode of ruling temporally, the attackers try, secondly, to show that Christ as mortal man was not a lord having lordship and ownership of all temporal things, [a] first by authoritative texts and [b] second by arguments.

[ii.a] First, therefore, they show this by the authority of Christ himself, who says in Matthew 8[:20], "Foxes have holes, and the birds of the air have nests, but the Son of Man has nowhere to lay his head." From these words we gather evidently that Christ did not have his own lodging, and consequently did not have ownership and lordship of all things.

But perhaps someone will say that it cannot be inferred from the above words that Christ did not have a lodging in respect of lordship and ownership. This is shown as follows. Christ uses "have" in the same way when he says affirmatively, "Foxes have holes," etc., and when he says negatively, "But the Son of Man has nowhere to lay his head": otherwise Christ would be using the same word in the same sentence equivocally. But when he says, "The foxes have holes," "have" is not used for the mode of having in respect of ownership and lordship, but for the mode of having in respect of a custom of staying or remaining or resting. Therefore, when he says, "The Son of Man has nowhere to lay his head," "have" is not used for having in respect of lordship or ownership, but in respect of a custom of remaining or resting; that is, "The Son of Man does not have a lodging in which he customarily dwells, as foxes have holes in which they customarily dwell."

But this objection does not succeed, according to them. For according to the tradition of the saints, and especially of Saint Clement, as we read in dist. 23, c. *Relatum*, divine Scripture must be understood as it is expounded by the holy Fathers. But according to the exposition of the saints, when Christ said, "But the Son of Man has nowhere to lay his head," he was speaking of the mode of having in respect of lordship or ownership, as the gloss attests. It says there, in the person of Christ, "I am so poor that I do not have even a lodging, and I do not use my own shelter." From these words we gather clearly that it was because of poverty that he did not have a lodging. But not to have a lodging in respect of the custom of living there does not necessarily result from poverty, just as rich men traveling do not while they travel have a lodging in respect of the custom of living there, since they move around, and yet they have great riches. Since, therefore, Christ said the above words by reason of poverty, it follows that he meant that he did not have a lodging in respect of lordship or ownership.

Again, although a king who customarily travels around his kingdom, going from place to place, could say that he did not have a lodging in respect of a custom of living there, he nevertheless could not say that he used another's shelter. But according to the gloss, Christ used another's shelter; therefore the shelter Christ used was not his in respect of lordship or ownership.

And when it is said that then in the same sentence Christ would have used the same word equivocally, they say that Scripture often does this, as Innocent III proves, *Extra, De summa Trinitate et fide catholica*, c. *Dampnamus*, by these two texts: "I wish that they should be one in us, just as we are one," and "Be perfect, just as your heavenly Father is perfect." In the first of these "one" used twice is taken equivocally, and in the second the word "perfect" used twice is taken in the first and second occurrences in different meanings.

The second text by which the same assertion is proved is taken from the prophet Zacharias. In chapter 9[:9], speaking of Christ, he says, "Rejoice greatly, daughter of Sion, shout for joy, daughter of Jerusalem. Behold, your king will come to you, just and a savior; he is poor, and riding upon an ass, and upon a colt, the foal of an ass." These words establish that although Christ was a king (not indeed in temporal matters but in spiritual), yet he was poor, and consequently he did not have lordship and ownership of all temporal things; for if he had had particular lordship and ownership of all temporal things he would have been a richer man than ever existed.

The third text is taken from the second letter of blessed Paul to the Corinthians, chapter 8 [2 Corinthians 8:9–10]. He writes to them thus: "For you know the grace of our Lord Jesus Christ, that, whereas he was rich, he became needy for your sakes, that through his poverty you might be rich. And in this I give some advice," etc. These words clearly establish that for our sakes Christ became poor and needy. But someone who is lord of all temporal things by right of particular ownership is not poor and needy; therefore Christ was not lord of all temporal things. Augustine also manifestly asserts this, commenting on the Apostle's text; he says, "He was made needy, he says, to this extent, that he did not have what foxes have." And Bernard, treating of the above words in his "Letter to the Brothers of the Mount of God," says, "Whereas he was rich, he became a poor man for our sakes, and he who gave the commandment of voluntary poverty condescended to demonstrate the model in himself." From these words it is clear that Christ demonstrated in himself the model of that voluntary poverty of which he gave the commandment. But he gave a commandment of voluntary poverty through lack of lordship and ownership; therefore he demonstrated in himself the model of voluntary poverty through lack of lordship and ownership. From this it follows evidently that he was not lord of all temporal things by right of ownership.

The fourth text is taken from the Psalmist, who says [Psalm 39:18] in the person of Christ, "But I am a beggar, and a poor man." The gloss here says, "Christ says this of himself in the form of a servant, so that no one will arrogate to himself the glory of that rejoicing." Therefore Christ as man was a poor man, and consequently did not have universal lordship of temporal things.

The fifth text is taken from Lamentations 3[:1], where Jeremias says in the person of Christ, "I am a man seeing my own poverty." From these words it is clear that Christ was a poor man, and consequently he did not have universal lordship of things. And that Jeremias did say these words in the person of Christ is clear from the gloss in that place, which says: "Although it seems to befit all, nevertheless it is understood more excellently of Christ, in whom, just as all things excel, so also that seeing ... Just as the poverty of Christ is more glorious, so this seeing of poverty is more profound." Jeremias therefore said the above words in the person of Christ, showing his very great poverty.

The sixth text is taken from a decision of the Church, included in the decretal *Exiit*, in which the pope writes by way of definition: "We say that such renunciation of ownership of all things, both individually and also in common, for God's sake, is meritorious and holy; Christ, also, showing the way of perfection, taught it by word and confirmed it by example." By these words it is most clearly asserted that Christ confirmed by example the renunciation of ownership of all things, and thus he renounced ownership of all things; and consequently he did not have universal lordship of all things. And from these [words] the attackers infer (as was touched on above, chapter 9) that either he [John] is a heretic or Nicholas III is a heretic. And if he is a heretic he is not a true pope; and if Nicholas III was a heretic, he [John] was never a true pope; and consequently, whether he is a heretic or a Catholic, he is not now a true pope.

The seventh text is taken from a letter of blessed Jerome to Nepotian. He says, "It is disgraceful for the lictors of consuls and soldiers to keep watch before the doors of a priest of the crucified and poor Lord, who ate others' bread." From these words it is quite clear that Christ was a poor man and ate others' bread, and consequently he did not have universal lordship of all temporal things.

The eighth is also from Jerome, writing to Heliodorus. He says, "He who is poor with Christ is rich enough"; therefore Christ was a poor man.

The ninth is from Gregory Nazienzen, who says, "I will follow the footsteps of him who for our sakes became poor, whereas he was rich"; therefore Christ, since he was a poor man, did not have universal lordship of temporal things.

The tenth is from Chrysostom, who says, commenting on the epistle to the Hebrews: "Let no one argue about poverty as the cause of many evils or make reproaches of Christ, who called it a perfection – 'If you wish to be perfect' etc. For this he himself said in words, showed in deeds, and taught through his disciples." Therefore, according to him, Christ was a poor man.

The eleventh is also from Chrysostom, in the place cited above. He says: "Do you wish to hear the praises of poverty? Christ professed it and said, 'The Son of Man has nowhere to lay his head.'" From these words it is clear that Christ did not have lordship of all things.

The twelfth is also from Chrysostom. Commenting on Christ's words in Matthew 8, "The Son of Man has nowhere," etc., he says: "See how the Lord demonstrated in deeds the poverty he had taught. He did not have table, candlestick, house, or any other thing of that kind." From these words it is clear that Christ was so poor that he did not have table or candlestick or house, etc. From this it follows evidently that he did not have universal lordship of all temporal things.

The thirteenth is from Bernard, commenting on the text of Luke [2:42], "When Jesus was twelve years old." He says, "So that you would conform, O Lord, to our poverty in every way, you begged alms from door to door, like one of the crowd of paupers." Christ therefore begged alms from door to door, out of voluntary poverty; and consequently he did not have universal lordship of all things.

The fourteenth is from Anselm, *On the Sacraments*. He says, "Christ was so poor that when he came into the world he was born not in his own but in another's house, and when born was put, because of the poverty of the place, into the brute animals' manger, and living in the world had nowhere to lay his head, and dying had nothing to cover his nakedness, and dead had no winding sheet and no tomb or place where his dead body might be laid." These [words] establish evidently that Christ did not have lordship and ownership of all temporal things; for if he had had such lordship, he would have been born in his own home, and living in the world he would have had as his own many lodgings – indeed all lodgings – where he could have laid his head, and dying he would have had something of his own to cover his nakedness, and when he was dead his body would have been laid nowhere else than in a sepulcher and place of Christ's own.

By these texts, therefore, and by others almost beyond counting, which for brevity's sake I omit, it is shown evidently that Christ as mortal man did not have from the instant of his conception universal lordship of all the things of this world.

[ii.b] Second this same assertion is plainly proved by arguments based on the divine Scriptures and authoritative texts of the holy fathers. The first argument is as follows. All things relating to perfection and to the advantage of the faithful that Christ taught, he himself did. But to renounce lordship and ownership of temporal riches pertains to perfection and to the advantage of the faithful, and Christ taught this renunciation; therefore he himself observed this renunciation; and consequently he did not have lordship and ownership of all riches. The major [premise] is proved in many ways. First by the authority of Luke in Acts 1[:1]. He says, "The first discourse I made, O Theophilus, concerning all things that Jesus began to do and to teach"; therefore Christ did the things he taught. Also, in Matthew 5[:19] Christ himself says, "Therefore anyone who has weakened one of the least of these commandments, and has taught men to do so, will be called the least in the kingdom of heaven." But Christ was not the least in the kingdom of heaven but the greatest; therefore he did not weaken the things he taught. Also, Christ did not do anything for which he reproached others; otherwise it would have been fitting to apply to him the text of the wise man that says, "It is shameful to a teacher when his fault contradicts him." But Christ reproached the Pharisees because they did not do the things they taught; he says, to their reproach, "For they say, and do not do" [Matthew 23:3]. Therefore Christ did the things he taught. Also, Chrysostom clearly asserts in the tenth and twelfth texts quoted above that Christ did in particular the things he taught about poverty. Bernard also testifies to this same point, as is clear above in the sequel to the third text. Thus, therefore, the major [premise] is proved.

The minor includes three parts. The first is that to renounce lordship and ownership of riches pertains to perfection; the second is that it was advantageous to the faithful that Christ should renounce ownership and lordship of riches; the third is that Christ taught such renunciation of riches.

The first part is clear. First, because Christ said, "If you wish to be perfect, go, sell all you have, and give to the poor" [Matthew, 19:21]; therefore to renounce lordship of riches for God's sake pertains to perfection. Also, because every one of the essential vows of perfect religious orders pertains to perfection; therefore the vow of poverty pertains to perfection; and consequently to renounce lordship of riches for God's sake pertains to perfection.

The second part, namely that it was advantageous to the faithful that Christ should renounce lordship and ownership of riches, is quite clear. For by this means he gave an effective example to the faithful of contempt for temporal things, and the faithful would have gained no spiritual advantage from his retaining of riches; therefore it was advantageous and exemplary to the faithful that Christ should renounce the lordship of riches. And by this the objection is resolved, if someone should object that Christ did not renounce or avoid prelacy and the highest priesthood, and yet the avoidance of ecclesiastical offices, even the papacy, pertains to perfection, and Christ taught that one should avoid such offices when he said, in Matthew 18[:3], "Unless you are converted and become like little children, you will not enter into the kingdom of heaven," and in Matthew 23[:12], "Whoever humbles himself will be exalted"; therefore Christ did not do all that he taught that pertains to perfection – this objection, I say, is easily answered: for just as Christ came for the sake of our salvation, so he did those things that were advantageous for our salvation; but it was advantageous for our salvation that Christ should renounce lordship of all riches, and it was not advantageous that he should renounce every prelacy and the highest priesthood; and therefore he did the one and not the other.

The third part, namely that Christ taught abdication of lordship and ownership of riches, is quite clear, when Christ said to a young man, Matthew 19[:21], "If you wish to be perfect, go, sell all you have, and give to the poor, and come, and follow me." From these words we gather evidently that Christ taught us to sell riches and give to the poor. But when riches are sold and given to the poor they are renounced in respect of ownership and lordship; therefore Christ taught renunciation of the lordship of riches. Also, in the same place Christ said to the apostles, "Amen, I say to you, that in the regeneration, when the Son of Man will sit on the throne of his majesty, you who have left all things and followed me will also sit," etc. There, by approving and praising the apostles' mode of abandoning everything, Christ explicitly taught that same mode of abandoning everything. But the apostles abandoned the things they abandoned in respect of lordship and ownership; therefore Christ taught renunciation of the ownership and lordship of temporal things. Also, in Matthew 10[:9] Christ said to the apostles, "Do not possess gold or silver," etc.; there he expressly taught renunciation of lordship of gold and silver, and of money. Also, in Matthew 6[:19] Christ said to his disciples, "Do not lay up treasure for yourselves on earth"; there he taught renunciation of the lordship of treasures. In many other places also Christ taught contempt of the world and renunciation of the lordship of riches. Therefore, even if (which, however, is not true) Christ had not taught renunciation of the lordship, both particular and common, of all temporal things, nevertheless it is certain that he taught renunciation of the lordship of treasures, of gold and silver, and of great riches. From this and [the premise] taken as the major it follows evidently that Christ renounced the lordship and ownership of at least great riches, and consequently did not have universal lordship of all temporal things.

The second argument for the same assertion is this. The poverty of religious is not greater or higher or more perfect than the poverty of Christ. But religious renounce ownership and lordship of riches, at least particular lordship; therefore Christ also renounced at least particular lordship of riches. And it is certain that no one other than Christ had a lordship of all temporal things in common with Christ; therefore Christ did not have either particular or common universal lordship of temporal things. The major [premise] is manifest: for all religious imitate Christ in poverty; therefore no religious are poorer than Christ. And the minor premise needs no proof.

The third argument is this. In appointing blessed Peter as his vicar, when he said, "Feed my sheep," Christ entrusted to blessed Peter all things pertaining to Christ that were necessary for feeding the sheep. Therefore since temporal things are useful for feeding the sheep, if Christ had lordship and ownership of all temporal things, it follows that Christ entrusted all temporal things to the control and ordering of blessed Peter; from this it follows that all temporal things belonged to blessed Peter's control and ordering: which is absurd. For then all temporal things would belong to the Roman pontiff, blessed Peter's successor, which is known to be false.

Here it remains to prove two things. The first is that not all temporal things belonged to the control or ordering of blessed Peter; the second is that not all temporal things belong to the control or ordering of blessed Peter's successors. The first is clearly proved, first, by the text of Ambrose in his book *De Officiis*, "He who sent the apostles without gold, gathered the churches without gold." By this we are given to understand that gold did not at all belong to those who with the assistance of divine power first gathered the churches; and consequently gold did not belong to blessed Peter, who was the principal gatherer of the churches. Peter himself testifies to this, saying, "Silver and gold have I none"; these words plainly imply that the control of all things did not at all belong to him. Also, if by Christ's commission all temporal things had belonged to blessed Peter, and (according to him [John]) after the conversion of the Jews related in Acts 2 the apostles shared all they had with the Jewish converts, and vice versa, and thus all things became common: therefore blessed Peter shared all temporal things with the Jews and others; and consequently all temporal things, even those of the unbelievers, were then common to them: which is absurd. Again, if all temporal things were entrusted by Christ to Peter, therefore Peter was either, as to temporal matters, superior to Caesar and other kings and rulers and also to anyone else at all who had property, or he was inferior, or he was equal. If he was superior in temporal matters, therefore all who did not acknowledge their temporal things as being from blessed Peter were unjust detainers of temporal things, and thus Caesar and all men in the world who had property and did not acknowledge their temporal things [as being] from blessed Peter would have been unjust detainers: which is absurd, especially in reference to the faithful, who were subject to blessed Peter in spiritual matters and yet did not acknowledge their temporal things [as being] from blessed Peter. Nor can it be said that blessed Peter was inferior in temporal matters to all who had property, because then either Christ would have been inferior to all in temporal matters or he would have subjected blessed Peter in temporal matters to all those who had property: each of which is absurd. Nor can it be said that blessed Peter was equal in temporal matters to all who had property, because then no one would have had a licit power to sell and alienate his things without the explicit consent of blessed Peter, and vice versa, because if two have some kind of right in some thing, one does not licitly sell the thing without the other's consent. It is clear, therefore, that temporal things did not by any means all pertain to the control or management of blessed Peter.

The second, namely that temporal things do not by any means all pertain to the control or management of blessed Peter's successors – that is, insofar as they are blessed Peter's successors – is proved. For blessed Bernard expressly testifies to this effect in his book *On Consideration, to Pope Eugenius*. He says: "What else did the holy Apostle bequeath to you? 'What I have, that I give to you.' What is that? I know one thing: it is not gold or silver, since he himself says, 'Gold and silver have I none' [Acts 3:6] ... You may perhaps claim these things on some other grounds, but not by apostolic right." These words clearly establish that the pope does not have control of gold, silver and other riches by apostolic right, that is, insofar as he is blessed Peter's successor.

Whom the pope had abundant riches from, Bernard explains in the same book. He says: "This is Peter, who is not known ever to have appeared bedecked with jewels or silks, or covered with gold, or riding a white horse, or attended by a knight, or hedged round by shouting servants. Yet he thought it quite possible without these things to fulfill the salutary command, 'If you love me, feed my sheep' [John 21:15]. For in these things you are the successor not of Peter but of Constantine." From these words we gather that in abundance of riches the pope has succeeded, not blessed Peter, but Constantine. This implies that the pope is not Christ's vicar in any temporal matters whatever. For no temporal matters can be found in which he can more be called Christ's vicar than in others, and thus he is Christ's vicar either in all temporal matters or in none; but he is not Christ's vicar in all temporal matters, as has been shown; therefore he is Christ's vicar in no temporal matters. From this it follows that Christ, as man, did not have ownership and lordship of all temporal things. And let these arguments for the above assertion suffice at present, because afterwards it will be shown that Christ as man did not have lordship and ownership of *any* temporal thing.

[On the letter] It remains, therefore, to run through the letter and answer each of the texts quoted in favor of the contrary assertion. *That he did have lordship of temporal things*: Here he takes "lordship" for the lordship that is ownership, the ownership introduced after the sin of our first parents; for he does not take "lordship" for the lordship conferred on the human race, because then Christ would not have been lord of all temporal things in another way than anyone besides Christ – which he means to deny. *Testifies in many places*: Rather, it does so in no place. *For instance, many prophets prophesied that he would be the king of the Israelite people*: It is true that many prophesied that he would be king, not only of the Israelite people according to the flesh but also of all peoples who would believe in him. And thus David said, "Say to the peoples, that the Lord has reigned." Thus they say that it must be known that Christ was king of all, both of the good and of the bad, according to his divinity, but according to his humanity he was king of the believers, whether these believers were Jews according to the flesh or gentiles: all of these believers, however, and they alone, were Jews according to the spirit. *And consequently would have lordship of a kingdom*: They prophesied that he would have lordship of a kingdom in some way, namely in a spiritual, not a secular or temporal way.

"See, the Lord is our judge, the Lord is our lawgiver, the Lord is our king; he will come and will save us": This text is against him [John], because it cannot be understood of a secular or temporal judge, or of a secular or temporal lawgiver, or of temporal salvation; therefore, similarly, it should not be understood of a temporal

kingdom. That it cannot be understood of a temporal or secular judge when it says, "The Lord is our judge," has been clearly proved above by the text of Luke 12[:14], when Christ said, "Who appointed me judge or divider over you?" For we nowhere read that Christ judged concerning temporal matters; therefore he was not a judge in temporal matters. Also, when Isaias said, "The Lord is our lawgiver," it cannot be understood of a temporal lawgiver, for we nowhere read that he enacted laws concerning any temporal matters whatever: unless perhaps you say that he enacted a law concerning temporal matters when he taught that such things should be altogether despised; but such a law should be regarded not as temporal but as spiritual. Also, when it is said, "He will come and will save us," this cannot be understood of temporal salvation, since he said to his followers, as we read in Matthew 24[:9], "They will hand you over to tribulation and will kill you." Christ therefore did not come to save the Jews, whether believers or non-believers, temporally: not the believers, since believers underwent "every tribulation," and many underwent temporal death with him; and not the non-believers, since because of sins committed against him they were destroyed by the Romans. Since, therefore, the text of Isaias cannot be understood either of a temporal judge or of a temporal lawgiver or of temporal salvation, it can in no way be shown through it that Isaias prophesied that Christ would be a temporal king; but, just as Christ was a judge spiritually, and a lawgiver spiritually, and will save believers spiritually, so also spiritually he was king over those who believed in him.

"*And a king will reign*": These words of Jeremias also should not be understood of a temporal king, just as Jeremias also did not mean that Christ would reign temporally when he said, "will reign." For no reason is apparent why Jeremias, in saying "a king will reign," any more meant that Christ would be a temporal king than that he would reign temporally. "*And this is the name they will call him, The Lord our Just One*": Here "lord" is taken, speaking of Christ insofar as he was a mortal man, not for a lord of temporal things, but for a lord on account of the prerogative of the union of his human nature to a divine subject, and of spiritual authority, sanctity, and other graces. *To whom "the God of heaven" gave "a kingdom that will forever not be scattered*": These words of Daniel cannot be understood of a temporal kingdom, because every such kingdom will be scattered; but they should be understood of a spiritual kingdom – that is, of the Church of Christ, which will never be scattered, but, with all harmful influences excluded, will be perfected, confirmed, strengthened, and established at the end of the world. *"Behold, your king will come to you, just,"* etc.: Here Zacharias speaks of a king spiritually. He shows this when he adds, "He is poor," etc., from which it is quite clear that he was not a king in temporal matters, because a temporal kingdom cannot be well ruled without riches. *"I am made king by him"*: David spoke this in the person of Christ, speaking of a king spiritually. He shows this well, making clear the mode of ruling, when he adds, "Preaching his commandment." Christ reigned, therefore, by preaching and teaching and establishing sacraments, not temporally; and thus he was a king spiritually, not in temporal matters.

In the whole of the psalm "Eructavit" he speaks of that king. It is certain that that psalm cannot be understood literally of Christ insofar as he was a man. For when it says, "Gird your sword upon your thigh, O most mighty one. Set out, go forward prosperously, and reign . . . your arrows are sharp, under you peoples will fall . . . Your throne, O God, is for ever and ever . . . God, your God, has anointed you . . . with myrrh and aloes and cassia, your garments, from the ivory houses, out of which the daughters of kings have delighted you in your honor. The queen has stood at your right hand, in gilded clothing . . . In place of your fathers, sons are born to you; you will appoint them rulers over all the earth," etc. [Psalm 44] – this cannot be expounded literally, so that the foregoing words should be understood of a material sword, temporal prosperity and a temporal mode of reigning, of material arrows, a material throne, a bodily anointing, material garments, of flesh-and-blood daughters of kings, a flesh-and-blood queen and flesh-and-blood sons, and temporal princes; and consequently that psalm does not speak of a temporal king. And when the psalm speaks of his bride, the Church, it does not speak of a flesh-and-blood bride of Christ but of a spiritual; therefore similarly, it speaks of a spiritual king, not a temporal one. Also, here he [John] says that the Church is the bride of which the foregoing psalm speaks; but that bride is a queen, but is not a queen temporally; therefore she is queen only spiritually; therefore, the king of which it speaks must also be regarded as king, not temporally, but spiritually.

And many other psalms speak . . . of such a king: Just as other psalms speak of Christ the king, so they speak of his rule, saying that he reigns. But the other psalms do not speak of a temporal rule of Christ but of a spiritual, and they do not say that he reigns temporally but spiritually; therefore from those psalms it cannot be inferred that Christ was a temporal king. This could be shown by running through the psalms that speak of Christ the king. But he concedes that Christ did not reign temporally except over very few; this will be discussed below, and therefore nothing will be said of it at present.

"See King Solomon," etc.: Those words as applied to Christ should be understood of a king spiritually, just as the words that follow – when there is reference to "the diadem with which his mother crowned him on the day of his betrothal, and in the day of his heart's joy" – should not be understood of a material diadem, a material coronation, a carnal betrothal, or a worldly joy. *"The Lord God will give him the throne of David his father, and he will reign,"* etc.: Just as these words are not understood of a material throne, because Christ never sat on the material throne of David, so they should not be understood of a temporal kingdom or of a temporal mode of reigning. Thus they say that it follows from the interpretation given by the attacked of the foregoing words that some temporal kingdom will last in perpetuity, since it says there explicitly, "He will reign in Jacob's house forever, and his kingdom will have no end": if, therefore, Christ's kingdom was temporal, and his kingdom will have no end, therefore some temporal kingdom will have no end, and consequently there will never be a general resurrection of the dead. The foregoing words should therefore be understood of a spiritual kingdom, which is the Church, which will never have an end but will be crowned on the day of judgment and will continue happily in perpetuity.

"This day is born to you a savior, who is Christ the Lord," that is, *king and lord:* This is conceded of a king spiritually understood, and of a lord on account of his very great prerogatives, not on account of temporal lordship. *"Where is he who has been born king of the Jews?":* Although the three wise men, not having been, as it were, instructed fully and explicitly concerning Christ's manner of reigning, may have meant a temporal king, nevertheless those words should be understood, according to the truth of the matter,

of a spiritual king. *"You are the son of God, you are the king of Israel"*: The first clause is understood of Christ according to his divinity, and the second can also be understood of Christ according to his divinity; and equally it can be understood of him according to his humanity, but then it is said of a king understood spiritually, not temporally.

"Jesus of Nazareth, king of the Jews": Just as these words, inasmuch as they have truth, should be understood of those who were Jews not carnally but spiritually (according to the gloss), so they should be understood of a spiritual, not a temporal king. *This our Savior also confessed, in John 18*: They say that the Savior did not confess absolutely that he was king but with a certain qualification, namely: not in the way the Jews meant but in another way. Therefore Christ, answering Pilate, said, "You say that I am a king. For this I was born, and for this I came into the world, to bear testimony to the truth": there he declared that he was a king in another way than the accusers meant. They prove this by a text of Augustine, who seems plainly to assert the above opinion in commenting on the text of John, "You say that I am a king." He says, "Not that he was afraid to confess that he was a king, but it is balanced in such a way that he neither denies that he is a king nor confesses that he is a king of such a kind that his kingdom is thought to be of this world."

"My kingdom is not of this world": According to them these words should be understood in the same way as Christ's words in John 15[:19], when he said to the apostles, "You are not of this world, but I have chosen you from the world," and in chapter 17 [John 17:16] he says of them, "They are not of the world": these words should not be interpreted as if the apostles were not begotten by men of this world; but just as the apostles are said to be not of the world because they are not worldly, living in a worldly way, so Christ's kingdom was not of this world, that is, was not worldly, to be ruled in a worldly way. *Making an inference from this, Pilate said, "You are a king, then?"*: They say that Pilate did not infer this from "My kingdom is not of this world," as will be seen below. *And Jesus answered, "My kingdom is not from hence"*: They say that here he reports the Evangelist's words falsely. For Jesus did not, because of Pilate's conclusion stated above ("You are a king, then?"), answer, "My kingdom is not from hence"; rather,

he answered, "You say that I am a king; for this I was born," etc. Thus, so that it may be known that he reports the Evangelist's words falsely, they quote the words of the text, as follows: " 'What have you done?' Jesus answered, 'My kingdom is not of this world. For if my kingdom were of this world my servants would certainly fight so that I would not be handed over to the Jews. But as it is my kingdom is not from hence.' Pilate therefore said to him 'You are a king, then?' Jesus answered, 'You say that I am a king. For this I was born,' " etc. It is clear, then, that from the words, "My kingdom is not from hence," Pilate drew the conclusion, "You are a king, then?" And therefore, by the words "My kingdom is not of this world, my kingdom is not from hence," Pilate was not fully satisfied concerning the accusation of the Jews who said that Christ made himself a king to Caesar's injury; as Augustine says (in the same place): "It was said, 'You say . . .,' as if to say: 'Being carnal, you speak carnally.' " Accordingly, after Pilate said, drawing his conclusion, "You are a king, then?" understanding carnally, Christ informed Pilate more fully how he was not a king to Caesar's injury, saying: "You say," understanding carnally, "that I am a king. For this I was born," etc., as if to say: "It is true that I am a king, but not carnally, as you carnally understand; because I am not a king temporally to Caesar's injury, as the Jews falsely impose on me, but I am a king spiritually, because for this I was born and for this I have come into the world, to bear testimony to the truth" – as if to say, "I have not come to reign temporally, but I have come to bear testimony to the truth, teaching men to turn to the truth." On account of this answer of Christ, Pilate, asking "What is truth?" and not waiting for Christ's answer, "went out to the Jews, and said to them, 'I find no case against him,' " as if to say (questioning and diligently examining him): "He denies that he is a king temporally to Caesar's injury, but he says that he is a king in another way; and you cannot prove that he has made himself a temporal king to Caesar's injury. Therefore I say to you that I find no case against him."

"My kingdom is not from hence": That is, "My kingdom does not relate to worldly persons." *He did not say, "It is not here"*: This is true, because physically his kingdom was here, but in the mind it was in the heavens. *As if to say, "I do not have my kingdom from the world"* – *as indeed he did not have it, but rather from God*: That

seems to have been Pilate's understanding, which he had from the foregoing words, "My kingdom is not of this world, my kingdom is not from hence"; and therefore he still doubted whether Christ had made himself king to Caesar's injury. For if Christ had made himself a temporal king, even if he had said that he had his kingdom from God, Pilate would have thought no less – indeed perhaps more strongly – that Christ had injured Caesar than if he had said that he had a temporal kingdom from the world; and therefore, wishing to be informed more fully of what Christ intended, he drew the conclusion, "You are a king, then?" as if to say, "What does it matter to me from whom you say you had the kingdom? Tell me whether you think that you have a temporal kingdom to Caesar's prejudice (whether from God, or from another); because, if you confess that you are a king temporally and that you have a temporal kingdom (whether from God or from anyone else at all), since you do not have a kingdom from Caesar, I will condemn you as being Caesar's enemy." Accordingly, Christ said, explaining more fully in what way he was a king, "For this was I born," etc.; and from that moment Pilate did not interpret those words in that way. The meaning, therefore, that he [the attacked] devises for Christ's words is not, they say, the meaning of Christ's words; that is what was stated before.

"*As the angel had foretold to his mother*": Here also, they say, he interprets wrongly the angel's words to the mother of Christ, as has been explained before. "*God has made him both Lord and Christ, this Jesus*": Peter calls him Lord on account of the prerogative of union, holiness, and spiritual authority and other graces; and he calls him "Christ" on account of a spiritual, not a bodily, anointing. *That he did not have his kingdom from the world, but from God*: This is true – of a spiritual kingdom, not of a temporal one. God *made Jesus "Christ", that is, "king"*: This can be conceded of a king understood spiritually and not temporally. *For by "christ" we understand "king"*: By "christ" in Scripture we understand not only a temporal king, but also a king spiritually, and also priests; thus, when the Psalmist says, in the person of God, "Do not touch my christs" [Psalm 104:15], by "christs" is meant there not only temporal kings but also other saints of God. *Since it was the custom to anoint kings*: It is true that it was the custom to anoint temporal kings bodily; and therefore, since Christ was not anointed bodily, it cannot be inferred from the premise that he is called "anointed" that he was a temporal king. It was the custom also to anoint priests and prophets. We read of the anointing of priests in many places in the divine Scriptures; we read of the anointing of prophets in 3 Kings 19[:16], where the Lord says to Elias, "And you will anoint Eliseus, the son of Saphat, of Abelmeula, to be prophet in your place." From the fact, therefore, that it was the custom to anoint kings, and that Jesus was anointed, it cannot be inferred that he was a temporal king.

"*Shows . . . that Christ's kingdom is not earthly but heavenly*": Here Rabanus calls a heavenly kingdom those who believe in Christ – believers in heavenly things. *Also, Peter implies by the words above that Christ was made lord and king as man subsisting in a divine subject*: This can be conceded, understanding that he is lord on account of the prerogative of graces, and a king spiritually, not temporally. *Since he was made king and lord as crucified*: Here he is inconsistent with himself. For afterwards he will say that Christ had kingdom and universal lordship from the instant of his conception, but here he says that he was made king and lord as crucified; these two plainly conflict. For if he was made king and lord as crucified, therefore before he was crucified he was not king and lord; just as it follows, "Christ was made man as incarnate, therefore before incarnation he was not man"; so also it follows, "Peter as man was made rational, therefore before he was a man he was not rational." *God granted him both kingship and lordship also as man*: This can be conceded, understanding kingdom spiritually and lordship on account of the prerogative of graces. "*Christ the Lord,*" *that is, king and lord*: Although it can be conceded in accordance with a correct interpretation that Christ was king and lord, nevertheless it cannot be inferred from the premise that anyone is "christ" [anointed] that he is a king, especially a temporal king, because many have been "christs" who were not kings: this does not need proof because it is evident. *What the archangel Gabriel had said*, etc.: The whole of this can be conceded if it is correctly understood, namely of a spiritual kingdom. "*The Lord Jesus Christ is a true king and a true priest*": Augustine meant this statement speaking spiritually of a king. "*As man, indeed, Christ was made both king and priest, to whom 'God gave the throne of David his father, and his reign will have no end'*": Just as the angel does not speak here of a material throne of David and does not mean that some temporal kingdom will have no end, so he does not refer to a temporal king. *Also, it seems that the Savior was lord of all temporal things*: This can be conceded, taking it according to his divinity and not according to his humanity, as he [the attacked] takes it. *"Send forth, O Lord, the Lamb, the dominator of the earth"*: These words of Isaias cannot be understood of Christ according to his humanity according as "dominator" is said from dominating temporally. For just as God is not called creator before he created, so no one is called dominator before he dominates. But it is manifest – and he [the attacked] concedes it, as will appear later – that Christ according to his humanity did not dominate the earth; therefore he was not dominator of the earth, though, according to him [John], he did behave as a lord in a certain few matters. These words must therefore be understood of Christ according to his divinity. *"For from you will go forth he who will be the dominator in Israel"*: These words of Micheas must be understood of Christ according to his divinity, just as the words that follow, when it is said, "And his going forth is from the beginning, from the days of eternity," cannot be understood of Christ except according to his divinity. *"The Dominator, whom you seek"*: These words must also be understood of Christ according to the form of divinity. *"You call me Master, and Lord"*: He is called Lord not only according to his divinity, but also according to his humanity: not on account of a lordship of temporal things before the passion, but on account of a prerogative of very many graces. So also knights and others often call the Friars Minor lords on account of the prerogative of religion, though they do not have lordship of any temporal thing. *"The Lord has need of them"*: Here he is called "lord" according to his divinity. Hence the gloss on this text: "Lord simply of all things, whom the creature should serve." He can also be called "lord" according to his humanity on account of the prerogative of graces. *"King of kings and lord of lords"*: These words can be understood of Christ according to his divinity; or according to some, they are understood of Christ according to his humanity after the resurrection, when "all power was given" to him "in heaven and on earth" [Matthew 28:18], as they show by means of the words of the text. *"And in Jesus Christ, his only son, our Lord"*: These words are understood of Christ according to his divinity; or they are understood according to his humanity on account of the prerogative of graces. The same thing is said of the words of the creed sung at mass. *But the foregoing, namely kingship and universal lordship, Jesus had as God from eternity:* These words are erroneous, since from them it follows that Christ as God would have been king and lord from eternity, and so the world would have existed from eternity, which is heretical. It must be said, therefore, that, just as God the Father did not have a slave from eternity, so he was not lord or, also, king from eternity, but, from a time, without mutability on his part, he became king and lord through the creation of things; so also Jesus as God did not have kingship and universal lordship from eternity, but from a time, on account of his being one in substance with the Father. *And as man from a time, namely from the moment of his conception, by God's gift:* This was disproved above.

A Dialogue, Part III, Tract I, on the
Power of the Pope and Clergy

A Dialogue, Part III, Tract 1, On the Power of the Pope and Clergy

Book 2. Is it beneficial for the whole community of the faithful to be subject to and to be under one faithful head, leader, and prelate under Christ? What sort of person should a single ruler of the Church be? Is it beneficial for the community of the faithful to have the power to change an aristocratic regime into a regime similar to a royal regime and vice versa?

Book 2

Chapter 1

Student Since this fifth assertion, taking a middle way among the other four, agrees with each of the others in some respects and is understood to disagree in others, I propose to discuss it carefully in some of its parts and to treat of others to some extent.[1] Let us therefore make some inquiry about it, beginning with its first part: namely, whether Christ made blessed Peter the head, leader, and prelate of the other apostles and of all the faithful. For a fuller understanding of this, let us first of all examine by discussion whether it is beneficial for the whole community of the faithful to be subject to and to be under one faithful head, leader, and prelate under Christ. Try to argue first for the affirmative side.

Master That it is beneficial for the whole congregation of the faithful to be under one faithful head under Christ seems provable in many ways.

For [1] it is beneficial for one body to have one head, because a body without a head is, obviously, imperfect, since it has been

---

[1] The five positions discussed in Book 1 are: (1) That in both spiritual and temporal matters the pope has by Christ's ordinance such fullness of power that he can do, regularly and in every case, everything not expressly forbidden by divine or natural law; (2) that he has such fullness of power in spiritual matters but not in temporal; (3) that he has such fullness of power partly by Christ's ordinance and partly by human law; (4) that he does not have such fullness of power, either regularly or occasionally; (5) that he does not have such fullness of power regularly but has it on occasion by divine law. In chapter 16 the positive part of the fifth opinion is stated thus: "Christ made blessed Peter the head (*caput*), leader (*princeps*), and prelate (*praelatus*) of the other apostles and of all the faithful, giving him – regularly, in spiritual matters, in respect of everything that must of necessity be done or omitted for the sake of ruling the community of the faithful in respect of good morals and all spiritual necessities whatever of the faithful – all power, in those things that would be entrusted to one man without danger but prudently and to the common advantage, and liberty and jurisdiction, even coercive – without any detriment and notable and enormous cost to the temporal rights of emperors, kings, princes, and other laypersons or clerics whomsoever that belonged to them by natural law, the law of nations, or civil law, before or after the establishment of the gospel law. And in temporal matters he gave him regularly only the right of asking for temporal things for his sustenance and for the performance of his office. And this power, whether in spiritual matters or in temporal, the successors of blessed Peter, namely the Roman pontiffs, now have regularly by divine law. And every power which the supreme pontiffs regularly had or have beyond this they held or hold from human ordinance, concession, spontaneous submission, or by express or tacit consent, or because of the weakness, negligence, or wickedness of other men, or from custom, or in some way from human law."

deprived of its principal member, whereas a body with two or more heads seems monstrous. And all the faithful are one body, as the Apostle testifies in Romans 12[:5]: "So we, being many, are, I say, one body in Christ." It is therefore beneficial for all the faithful to be under one head. That head should not, however, be an unbeliever, because he would try to infect all the other members, especially in matters relating to the salvation of the soul; he should therefore be a believer.

Student That argument seems to fail, since it does not prove that the head should be "under Christ." Indeed it seems to show that all the faithful should *not* be under one head under Christ. For Christ is the head of the whole Church, as the Apostle says in Ephesians 1[:22] and manifestly asserts in many other places. It follows from this that, since a body with two or more heads should be regarded as monstrous (as the above argument suggests), the whole congregation of the faithful should not be under one head under Christ, but must venerate Christ alone as its head.

Master It appears to some that this objection can easily be excluded. Although Christ is the head of the Church, there must be under Christ another head of the same Church to take care of it under Christ, since the Church should have a delegate to direct it, someone physically present to it, visibly ruling it and physically accessible to the faithful, when necessary, for various necessities. Christ does not rule the Church in that way, since (except sometimes on occasion) he rules it only invisibly. Therefore, although Christ is the head, a mortal faithful man should be the head, though under the head. Yet neither should the body be thought for this reason monstrous, for it is certain that a bishop is the head of his subjects and a king is the head of his subjects, and yet they all have one head, God; therefore, although a natural body would be monstrous if it had two or more physical heads, because one is not the head of the other, nevertheless one mystical body can have many spiritual heads, one under another: and this is not monstrous, but natural, and in many respects beneficial and fitting.

Student Bring forward other arguments for the same conclusion.

Master The same [conclusion] is proved thus. [2] It is beneficial for one fold to be ruled and fed by one shepherd. The Savior himself seems to suggest this when he says (as we read in John 10[:16]), "There will be one fold and one shepherd." But the whole congregation of the faithful is one fold, as the supreme shepherd himself testifies. In the same place he says, "I have other sheep who are not of this fold; I must bring them in, and they will hear my voice, and there will be one fold," etc.[2] Therefore it is beneficial for the whole congregation of the faithful to be under one shepherd: not only Christ, who feeds the Church invisibly, but also a believer (not an unbeliever, because he would be a wolf and a thief, scattering, afflicting, and destroying Christ's sheep) who would feed and govern all the faithful perceptibly to the senses.

[3] Further, it is beneficial for every people to be under one rector, as Solomon testifies. In Proverbs 11[:14] he says, "Where there is no governor the people will be ruined." In saying "Where there is no governor," not "Where there are no governors," he seems also to suggest plainly that where there is not *one* governor the people will be ruined. But the whole congregation of the faithful is one people (though it includes many particular peoples), as John testifies. In the Apocalypse 21:[3] he says, "Behold the dwelling of God with men; he will dwell with them, and they will be his people." Therefore it is beneficial for the whole body of the faithful to be under one head and governor.

[4] Again, it is beneficial for a community that cannot be best ruled without a multitude of judges, who can vary among themselves concerning cases and proceedings and also disagree to the peril of the whole community, to be under one supreme rector and head, who can make known to all the truth of judgment. God himself seems to have ordained this among his own people. As we read in Deuteronomy 17[:8], He commanded: "If you perceive that there is among you a difficult and doubtful judgment, between blood and blood, case and case, leprosy and non-leprosy, and you see that the words of the judges within your gates vary, arise, go up to the place that the Lord your God will choose, and you will come to the priests of the levitical race and to the judge who is [in office] at that time, and you will ask of them, and they will make known to you the truth of judgment." But the community of the faithful, also, with respect to matters peculiar to the Christian religion, which do not at all pertain to unbelieving judges and rectors, cannot suitably be ruled without a multitude of judges,

---

[2] John 10:16.

since different judges and teachers must be appointed in various provinces, dioceses, and cities, and they can disagree about such cases and proceedings to the peril of the community. It is therefore beneficial for the whole community of the faithful that for such cases it should be under one believing head and rector – and not an unbeliever, who would in such cases quite overturn judgment and by no means make known the truth of judgment.

Student The text quoted in that argument seems to militate against the opinion. We gather from it that in such a case recourse must not be had to one head or judge but to many, since it says explicitly, "You will come to the priests of the levitical race and to the judge": therefore in the Old Law recourse was to be had in such a case to many. This seems to be proved by the words that follow, when it says, "And you will do whatever they say who preside in the place the Lord will choose ... But anyone who is proud and refuses to obey the command of the priest who ministers at that time to your Lord and the decree of the judge, that man will die."[3] By these words we are given to understand, it seems, that in such a case the final decision of the case pertained to many.

Master You are answered that by God's commandment there should have been among the Jewish people one supreme judge, head of all and rector, whether a priest or some other; however, he was obliged to decide major cases with the advice of the priests. And thus at that time recourse was to be had to one as head and supreme judge and to many as counselors of the head and judge.

Student Bring forward still other arguments for the same conclusion.

Master Another possible argument is as follows. [5] It is beneficial for those obliged to agree in one faith and in certain identical rites and observances to have one head who (saving the right of others) may compel, or at least lead, transgressors to such truth; for without such a head they would easily divide into diverse sects and heresies and impermissible observances and rites. But the whole community of Christians is obliged to agree in one faith and in certain identical rites and observances, since, as the Apostle testifies, Ephesians 4[:5], there is "One faith, one baptism." Therefore it is beneficial for the whole community of the faithful to have one believing

---

[3] Deut. 17:10–12.

head – not an unbeliever, who would lead all the faithful to a contrary faith and impermissible observances and rites.

[6] Besides, it is beneficial for those who are under different judges capable of erring about major cases to have one head to whom those major cases may be referred, by whom they may be judged justly and properly. Moses seems to have done this wisely among the people entrusted to him, on the advice of his kinsman Jethro, who was moved by right reason. We read about this in Exodus 18[:24–6]: "Having heard all this, Moses did everything that he," namely Jethro, "had suggested; choosing able men out of all Israel he appointed them rulers of the people, over thousands, over hundreds, over fifties, and over tens, and they judged the people at all times; more serious cases they referred to him, and they judged the easier cases only." As we read in Deuteronomy 1[:17] he also said to the inferior judges, "If something seems difficult to you, refer it to me and I will hear it." But in matters pertaining to the Christian religion the faithful scattered over the breadth of the earth are under various judges and prelates, many of whom often do not have enough skill in major cases. It is therefore beneficial for the community of the faithful to have one head to whom such major cases may be referred.

Student A twofold answer can be made to those two arguments[4] together: first, that both for compelling transgressors or the unwilling to the unity of faith and of observances and ecclesiastical rites, and for major cases, recourse must be had to a general council, not to some one person; second, that recourse should be had to the supreme secular judge, who must judge concerning both spiritual and temporal matters.

Master Some attack the first of these answers as follows. Since the faithful are divided throughout the breadth of many provinces, it is difficult and takes a long time and very heavy labor and expense to assemble a general council; therefore, since such cases can occur even many times every year, it is not beneficial for the community of the faithful that a general council should be assembled for every such case. Therefore, so as to forestall dangers in such cases more easily, it is beneficial for the community of the faithful to have one head and prelate with power in such matters,

---

[4] That is, arguments 5 and 6.

to whom recourse may be had to punish the excesses of the highest prelates and settle other major cases for which the skill and powers of one man are enough. The second answer is repulsed as follows. Before Christ's ascension and for some time afterwards, there was no secular, lay believer with secular power or jurisdiction, and this could happen again; yet it would be beneficial for the community of the faithful that such cases should be provided for. It is therefore beneficial for the community of the faithful to have, besides lay powers and judges, one head with power in such cases. For the emperor or king or other secular ruler does not have such power over the faithful by virtue of his office, since the emperor and all kings and secular rulers were once unbelievers, and they could be again. Otherwise an unbeliever could have power over the faithful in such matters and would in all such matters judge wrongly.

Student Bring forward still other arguments.

Master Another possible argument is as follows. [7] It is not beneficial for the community of the faithful that many among them, and especially many with power over others, should be able to do wrong insolently without any fear of correction and temporal punishment, because as we read in 6, q. 1, *Ex merito*, "When the head becomes weak the other members become corrupt." Therefore, since the prelates of the faithful, like everyone else, are inclined to evil – because, as the Council of Toledo says (as we read in 12, q. 1, c. 1), "Every age from adolescence is inclined to evil" – it is highly beneficial for the faithful that prelates "whom divine fear does not call back from evil, temporal punishment, at least, should restrain from sin," *Extra, De vita et honestate clericorum*, c. *Ut clericorum*. Therefore it is beneficial for the congregation of the faithful to have one head able to correct all prelates if they do wrong to the peril of the Christian religion. Nor does it avail to say that (as it seems to some) such correction pertains to a lay judge, because, as was mentioned earlier, before the Lord's ascension there was no lay believer who had any jurisdiction over anyone, and it would still be possible for all lay believers to be subjected to the power of unbelievers. Therefore it is beneficial that there should be, besides the lay judge, some believing prelate with power in such matters over other prelates.

[8] Also, the same thing is beneficial to the whole and to the part, in little matters and great, just as the same right exists in the

whole and in the part, in little matters and great, *Extra, De Appellationibus*, c. *De appellationibus*; *Extra, De praebendis et dignitatibus*, c. *Maioribus*;[5] and 14, q. ult., c. ult. But it is beneficial for each and every part of the faithful people to have one bishop as head of all in spiritual matters and not many: 7, q. 1, *In apibus*, where Jerome says, "Single are the bishops of churches, single the archpriests, single the archdeacons; and every ecclesiastical order rests upon its rectors." Therefore it is beneficial for the whole community of the faithful to have one head.

[9] Moreover, it is beneficial for the community of the faithful to be governed in matters relating to the Christian religion under the form of government that most resembles the best secular constitution. But the best secular constitution is kingship, as Aristotle testifies. In *Ethics*, Book VII[6] he says: "There are three kinds of constitutions and the same number of perversions, i.e., corruptions of these. The constitutions are kingship and aristocracy, thirdly that which is based on wealth, which it seems appropriate to call timocracy, though many are accustomed to call it 'constitution.' The best of these is kingship." Afterwards, speaking of tyranny, he says, "It is clearer in this case that it is the worst, and the worst is the opposite of the best." These words plainly establish that of all the constitutions kingship is the best. But one kingdom has one king, who is over all. Therefore it is also beneficial for the whole multitude of the faithful that one should be over all.

[10] Further, no less unity of head is required in the whole community of the faithful than in the whole totality of mortals; but it is beneficial for the whole totality of mortals that one should rule all; therefore it is also beneficial for the whole community of the faithful to have one head to be over the totality of the faithful.

Chapter 2

Student From that argument[7] I infer that I can easily work out how this question can be argued on both sides from what I will

---

[5] See gloss to the decretals, col. 1028, v. *In minimis*: "An argument that the same right exists in small matters as in great matters, 14, q. ult., c. ult.; supra *De appell.* c. *De appellationibus* ... Also, it is an argument that the same right exists in the part as in the whole, argued 1, q. 1, *Si quis episcopus*."

[6] 1160 a32.

[7] That is, argument 10.

be able to find in the first book of the second tract of this third part of our dialogue, which discusses whether it is beneficial for the whole world to be under one secular ruler, since all those arguments,[8] or many of them, can be applied to this matter. So do not argue further for the above assertion, but bestir yourself and pass quickly to the opposite assertion, and bring on a few arguments, short ones, in its favor.

Master That it is not beneficial for the community of the faithful to be under one head under Christ seems provable as follows.

[1] Nothing unjust is beneficial to the community of the faithful. But for one man to be head and to rule all the faithful is unjust. For many among the faithful are equal, or are not known to be unequal, in prudence and virtue and all conditions requisite to a good head and ruler; but it is unjust for someone to rule his similars and equals. Aristotle seems to testify to this in *Politics*, Book III, chapter 15,[9] where he says: "Those who are by nature similars must have by nature the same right and the same rank. If, therefore, it is indeed harmful to their bodies for unequals to have equal food or clothing, so it is also with anything relating to offices, and similarly for equals to have what is unequal; and therefore [for equals it is] by no means just to rule rather than be subject." From these words we gather that it is unjust for someone to rule his similars and equals, since anyone who has the same virtue and capacity should have equal office and rank, just as in natural things those who do not have an equal digestive power should not receive equal food. Therefore it is not beneficial that one person should be the head of the whole community of the faithful.

[2] Further, nothing useless is beneficial to the congregation of the faithful; but for one head to be over the congregation of the faithful is useless. A head who cannot perform his due function must be regarded as useless; but the due function of a head who rules the other members is to attack iniquities by coercing the wrongdoer with fitting punishments; therefore anyone who cannot coerce the wicked rules uselessly. The wise man in Ecclesiasticus 7[:6] seems to suggest this when he says, "Do not seek to be

---

[8] That is, in Tract II, Book I; translated below, pp. 231 ff.

[9] Chapter 16, 1287 a12.

made a judge, unless you have the strength to attack iniquities, lest perhaps you fear the person of the powerful and lay a stumbling-block for your integrity." But no one who was over the congregation of the faithful would have power to inflict due punishment on wrongdoers, since such punishment, especially of a multitude and of the powerful, cannot be carried out without temporal power, which is usually not had without ample riches. Thus a king, whose business it is to repress crimes (according to the testimony of blessed Cyprian, as we read in 23, q. 5, c. *Rex debet*), should abound in power and riches, as Aristotle testifies: in *Ethics*, Book VIII, chapter 10,[10] he says, "For a man is not a king unless he is by himself sufficient and excels in all good things; and such a man needs nothing." But no one who was over the congregation of the faithful would on that account abound in riches: First, because in the time of the apostles, when the congregation of the faithful was governed best, no believer placed over the others abounded in riches. Also, because Christ ordered no riches for any prelate of the faithful, but rather seems to have advised the leaders among the faithful to be content with food and clothing; thus the Apostle, in 1 Timothy 6[:8], says, for himself and for others who were over the faithful, "Having food and clothing, with these we are content." Also, because if the head of the faithful abounded in riches, since emperors and kings and secular rulers abound in riches, dissensions and very dangerous wars could easily arise between them and the head of the faithful, since they communicate with one another in many matters and live together; for among rich men who dwell together disputes and quarrels are easily begotten, from which follow fights and wars. We find an example of this in Genesis 13[:6ff], where a quarrel came about between the herdsmen of Abraham and Lot because of riches, and Abraham feared that if they remained together dangerous dissension would arise between himself and Lot, though they were holy and kin, because of the abundance of their wealth. In that place we read: "For their property was great, and they could not dwell together. And thus a quarrel arose between the herdsmen of Abraham and Lot ... Therefore Abraham said to Lot, 'Let there be no quarrel, I beseech you, between me and you and between my herdsmen and your

[10] 1160 b3.

129

herdsmen, for we are brothers. Behold, the whole land is before you: go away from me, I pray you.' " Between rich men, therefore, discords easily arise. And thus some believe that all the dissensions, wars, fights, and battles and the destructions and devastations of cities and regions and the countless other evils which have occurred in Italy for many years past, and still do not cease, have resulted from the riches of the Roman Church; it would have been beneficial for the whole Church of God if the Roman Church had in fact and deed imitated the apostles' poverty and their way of living, putting at a distance all display in respect of vessels, clothes and furnishings generally, guards and every other kind of servant, and all sorts of other things. It is, therefore, as it seems to some, in no way beneficial for the community of the faithful to have one head.

[3] Again, it is beneficial for the community of the faithful to be ruled by many; therefore it is not beneficial for it to be under one head and prelate. The premise seems provable by means of arguments like those which Aristotle brings forward in *Politics*, Book III, to show that it is better for a city to be ruled by the best laws than by the best men, and by many best rather than by the one best man. Some of these arguments can be applied to the present matter as follows. It is beneficial that the whole congregation of the faithful should be ruled by him (or those) whose judgment is more certain and better in judging and deciding what should be sought as useful to the whole community of the faithful and what should be altogether rejected as useless and harmful, and by him (or those) who can weigh carefully and see many such things. For without certain skill concerning all such things no community can be governed properly, because, as the Savior himself testifies in Matthew 15[:14], "If the blind lead the blind, both fall into the pit." But many judge and discern better and more certainly in such matters, and weigh carefully and see more such things, than one alone. And thus, in the *Politics*, Book III, chapter 13,[11] Aristotle says: "Meeting together, they discuss and consult and judge, and all these judgments are about particular cases. Compared individually, therefore, each may perhaps be worse, but a state is made up of many, just as a feast to which the guests contribute is finer than

---

[11] Chapter 15, 1286 a27.

a single and simple one; for this reason also a crowd judges many matters better than one person, whoever he may be." And in chapter 14[12] he says: "It will perhaps seem especially strange if a person sensed better with two eyes and two ears and acted better with two feet and hands than many with many." For it is strange to say that one senses better or more things with two eyes and two ears than many with many eyes and many ears; similarly it is strange that one would do better and more things with two feet and two hands than many with many feet and many hands. Many, therefore, see more certainly, and see more things, than one. Thus also in Acts 15[:6] we read that "The apostles and elders met to see about this doctrine," namely about the question concerning the observance of circumcision that was controverted between Paul and Barnabas and certain other Christians. The apostle Paul also, as he himself testifies in Galatians [2:2], consulted with the other apostles about the Gospel, lest perhaps he should be running, or had run, in vain. From these passages we gather that many see more things and more certainly than one, even the best, as Pope Innocent testifies. As we read in dist. 20, c. *De quibus*, he says, "What is sought by many elders is found more easily," and by the same reason more certainly. Thus it is that a general council is assembled for more difficult and important ecclesiastical cases, when they are pending. It is beneficial, therefore, for the whole congregation of the faithful to be ruled by many, rather than by one.

[4] Further, it is beneficial for the community of the faithful to be ruled by one (or several) whose appetite or will is less corruptible and pervertible by evil desires, wishes, and wicked passions; for a ruler must be virtuous and good, and not a follower of his passions. The wicked and those who follow wicked feelings and wishes are not in any way worthy to rule, as Solomon testifies. In Proverbs 28[:12] he says, "When the wicked reign, men are ruined," and in chapter 29[:2] he says, "When the wicked take over government, the people will groan." Thus that wise man Jethro, assenting to right reason, advised Moses that he should set over the people only good men; he says, "And provide out of all the people able men who fear God, in whom there is truth, who hate avarice, and

---

[12] Chapter 16, 1287 b26.

appoint from them rulers," etc.[13] And Aristotle in *Politics*, Book
III, chapter 2[14] says, "The equitable," i.e., the virtuous, "should
rule." But the many are less pervertible and corruptible by evil
desires, wishes, and wicked feelings than is one man. Therefore
it is more beneficial for the community of the faithful to be ruled
by many than by one. The major premise of this argument could
also be shown by countless authoritative texts of both philosophers
and believers, but it seems so well-known that it is not necessary
to prove it further. The minor premise seems provable in many
ways. For in *Politics*, Book III, chapter 8[15] Aristotle says: "It is,
however, possible that, when they meet together, the many, each
of whom is not an educated man, may be better than those," i.e.,
better than the few, and consequently much better than one, "not
individually but all together – just as a feast to which the guests
contribute is better than feasts provided from one purse; for when
there are many, each one may have a part of virtue and wisdom,
and when gathered together they may become as it were one man
having a multitude of many feet and many hands and many senses;
and it is thus with things concerning character and understanding."
From these words we gather that it is better for the whole multitude
to rule than for a few, even if they are virtuous; from this it follows
that it is better for many to rule than for one alone. Also, in
chapter 14[16] he asks whether one leader can be perverted and
corrupted with more difficulty than many, even good men. He says:
"If the many are good men and citizens, is the one a more
incorruptible ruler?" And he answers: "Or rather the many in
number, and good men." By these words we are given to understand
that the many are less corruptible and pervertible by wicked passions
than one. And thus he seems to conclude that it is better for a
city to be ruled by many than by one. He says, "Is it not clear
that it is the many?" [ibid.] – i.e., that the many rule better than
one. Thus, also, in the same place,[17] Aristotle seems to conclude
that aristocracy, which is government by many good men, is more
choice-worthy and better than kingship, which is government by

---

[13] Exodus 18:21.
[14] Chapter 10, 1281 a30.
[15] Chapter 11, 1281 a41.
[16] Chapter 15, 1286 a38.
[17] 1286 b5.

one. He says: "If, therefore, we should call government by many men who are all good aristocracy and government by one man kingship, then aristocracy will be indeed more choice-worthy for cities than kingship, both when the government is supported by force and when it is without force, if the many are available." From all the foregoing it follows that it is better for the community of the faithful to be ruled by many, rather than by one who is the head, leader, and prelate of all the others.

Chapter 3

Student Above you have quoted Aristotle from his *Politics* and also his *Ethics*, and perhaps you are going to quote him often below. He uses many Greek terms the meanings of which are unknown to specialist jurists and others who have not studied moral philosophy. Bestir yourself, therefore, and explain the meanings of some of these terms, so that such people may better understand the matters to be treated. At the same time explain, in brief summary, who should rule others and how, according to Aristotle's intentions in the *Politics* and *Ethics* (as some understand him).[18] Since he treated this matter at length and is thought to have argued reasonably in many respects, no little opportunity will be given to scholars for understanding who among Catholics should govern others, and how, in both spiritual and temporal matters.

Master Although I do not think that what you ask is easy, I will try to satisfy your wish. I will report to you Aristotle's meaning in this matter according to the opinion of some (with whom, however, not everyone agrees at all points). It is said, therefore, that in the *Politics*, Book I, Aristotle puts forward three communities in which some person or persons should rule others. The first of these, according to him, is the **household**, which includes three combinations, communities, or conjunctions, namely of husband with wife, of father with child, and of lord with slaves. The first combination Aristotle calls marital, the second can be called paternal (Aristotle calls it celmostine, i.e., likely to produce children), and the third Aristotle calls despotic, i.e., dominative, for [Greek] *despotes* is the same as *dominus* [lord], and despotic rule is dominative rule.

---

[18] This occupies chapters 3–8.

(So that this may be better understood, it is said that it must be known that such terms as *dominus, dominans, dominari,* and terms of like meaning are taken in different writings and sciences equivocally. Because of ignorance of their equivocation the meaning of authors who use such terms in contrary senses is often not understood. Setting aside various meanings of such words as *dominus, dominans, praedominans, dominium, dominantium,* and the like, which are sometimes used in different ways in natural and moral philosophy, the legal sciences, and common speech (which the divine Scriptures often use), the meanings that seem to need explaining for the present purpose are of only two kinds. It must be known, therefore, according to them,[19] that in one way *dominus,* "lord," is said in respect of subjects who are indeed free, namely those over whom someone is lord not mainly for his own advantage but mainly for the advantage of the subjects. Such a lord is not called by Aristotle a despot, and the government by which such a lord rules he does not call despotic. In another way "lord" is said in respect of subjects who are not free but slaves, who are the lord's possession in the same way as other temporal things are said to be someone's possession. Such a lord is called by Aristotle a despot and his rule is called despotic. Just as this despot possesses other temporal things for his own advantage and not for their advantage, so he rules slaves mainly for his own advantage and not mainly for the advantage of the slaves – though, according to Aristotle, often the same thing is beneficial for the slaves and for the lord. Therefore, although we find that Aristotle says in the *Politics* that the king is the lord of his subjects, he never says that he should be called a despot or that kingly government should be called despotic. Sometimes, however, tyrannical rule is called despotic, because of the great similarity between despotic and tyrannical rule. Properly speaking despotic rule is not tyrannical: for just as, according to Aristotle, some are justly slaves – namely, both those who are deficient in reason, so that they do not know how to rule themselves, though they are robust in body so that they are able to serve others (and these, according to Aristotle, are called natural slaves), and those who are slaves according to just law, because they are captured in a just war or in some other way become the

---

[19] That is, those whose exposition of Aristotle the Master is presenting.

slaves of others – so despotic rule, which is over such slaves only, is just and permissible and good; but tyrannical rule is unjust, impermissible, and evil – and thus, according to Aristotle, tyranny is the worst constitution.)

Besides the despotic rule by which the head of the household rules the slaves in the household, there is the paternal rule by which he rules the children as free persons. According to Aristotle they are ruled royally and not despotically: not that paternal rule *is* a royal government, because royal government exists only over a city or a kingdom (which is greater than a city and commonly includes many cities); but the father is said to rule his children royally, not indeed when the household in which he rules is part of a village or city or kingdom, but when he rules in a household that is not part of a more perfect community: as Adam ruled his children, and Noah his, before the children had different households. Although such paternal rule is not called royal strictly speaking, it can, however, be called royal because of its great similarity to royal government in the strict sense: for just as in a kingdom with a king most properly and authentically called a king there is one who rules all free persons mainly for his subjects' advantage according to his will and not according to law, according to Aristotle, *Politics*, Book III, chapter 15[20] (how this should be understood is explained afterwards), so in a household that is not part of a more perfect community, whenever there is such a father, he rules the children mainly for their advantage according to his will and not according to law, in such a way that he is able to chastise children who do wrong with every beneficial punishment and can do concerning them and to them whatever redounds to their advantage. Because he does not rule them mainly for his own advantage, he can be said to rule, not despotically, but, in a way, royally. But in a household that is part of a village or city the father does not rule the children royally, because his power over the children is not so great that he rules them according to his will and not according to law, even in many things which would be to their advantage; and for many crimes he cannot coerce them with beneficial punishment, but such punishment must be reserved to the ruler of the village or city or kingdom.

[20] 1287 a1–5.

The head of the household rules his wife in the household neither despotically nor royally: not despotically, because she is not a slave, and not royally, because he should rule her not according to his will but according to the law of marriage, for the man does not have as much power over his wife as a father has over the children. When his house is not part of a more perfect community, therefore, the man rules his wife by a constitutional government. This rule of man over wife is likened to constitutional government in this respect, that just as the rulers in a constitutional government excel their subjects in virtue and wisdom, so a man naturally surpasses his wife in wisdom and virtue – unless something happens apart from nature, according to Aristotle in *Politics* Book I,[21] as happens in effeminate men. (We must understand in this way the statements made above about despotic and paternal rule – namely, [subject to the qualification:] when nature is not deficient in the despot or father. If for some reason nature were deficient in the father or despot it would not be natural justice for the despot or father to rule the slaves or children. However, the governments over them are natural – i.e., arising by natural reason and not from human establishment – when nature is not deficient in the father or despot.)

The three rulerships spoken of above relate to "economy," i.e., to the government of a household. (Aristotle takes "economy" in that sense in moral philosophy, though in the law *economus* is the name for him to whom church property is entrusted for management (for example the administrator of the property of canons); in some churches he is called the Provost.)

Chapter 4

The second community, which is more perfect than the household, is called the **village**; it is made up of many households as parts, and yet it does not attain so much perfection that it is and should be called a city. If this community is not part of a more perfect community (namely, of a city, or of some other comprising many villages or districts or cities), and if the multitude of households in it has come from one surviving parent, then, just as children

---

[21] 1259 b1–3.

are ruled by their father, it is reasonable (if nature is not deficient in him) that it should be ruled by him according to his will and not according to law, as far as concerns those who have come from him. But as far as concerns the wives, of whom he is not the parent, it is reasonable that he should rule constitutionally, since reason demands that he should observe the law of marriage, according to which man and wife are in many things judged to be on equal terms. But if the multitude of households in the village has not come from one surviving parent, it is reasonable that it be governed by some government like the government by which a city is ruled.

Chapter 5

The third community, which is made up of many villages, is called a **city**. Aristotle says, in *Politics*, Book I, that this is the most principal of all communities. (This is said to be true of communities of people living together, not of a community of people living in separate places and in many cities. Such a community is a kingdom or dukedom; this can also be called a community [*communitas*], because it consists of people who share together [*communicant*] in many things and are ruled by one ruler; and many things said about the city must be understood *mutatis mutandis* of a kingdom and of any community that embraces several cities.) A city, then, is the multitude of citizens living in the city. Their order is called a constitution; without order there is no city, for unless it has a ruler or rulers and subjects it must not be called a city. In a city there are (often, at least, and in a most perfect city) different kinds of subjects subject in different ways. Some are found to be subject as slaves or hirelings or *banausi* (those who, working with their hands or bodies, spoil their bodies by their work are called *banausi*, and in a city with a tempered and rational constitution they are not citizens, properly speaking). Others in the city are subject in such a way that they somehow share in rulership; although they do not rule, yet in some way they attain rulership, because they are called to court and council or elect the ruler or the electors of the ruler. The ruler in a city Aristotle sometimes calls the *policernia*. *Policernia* has, according to some, three meanings: first it means the imposition of the order of the constitution, second the imposer of it, and third it signifies the order itself that is imposed, which is the constitution. In one meaning *policernia* is thus the same as the lord and ruler in the city.[22]

Chapter 6

There are two primary kinds of constitutions, just as there are two primary kinds of governments or prelacies and of rulers or prelates or rectors. Every government is either ordered chiefly to the common good or benefit (i.e. the good of the ruler or rulers and also of the subjects) or not ordered to the common good. If it is ordered to the common good the regime is tempered and right; if it is not ordered to the common good the regime is defective and perverted, because it is a corruption and perversion of a regime that is tempered and right and just. Every constitution, therefore, is either tempered and right, or defective and perverted.

There are three principal and unmixed kinds of tempered and right constitutions. The first is when the ruler is one person; this is called **royal monarchy**, in which one alone rules for the sake of the common good, and not principally on account of his own will and benefit.[23] According to Aristotle, *Ethics*, Book VIII, such a constitution is the best, when it takes its best form. It has several forms, according to Aristotle, *Politics*, Book III, chapter 16. [1] Its most powerful form seems to be when someone reigns and rules in the kingdom not according to law but according to his will. Some understand this as follows. Someone is said to rule and reign according to his will and not according to law if he reigns for the common good of all and is not bound by any purely positive human laws or customs but is above all such laws, though he is

---

[22] The English word "government" has a comparable range of meanings. *Policernia* seems to be a corruption of *politeuma*. See Aristotle, *Politics* III.6, 1278 b9–12, and III.7, 1279 a23.

[23] It should be remembered that in the middle ages kings were not always hereditary; sometimes they were elected, though not by the whole population. The medieval Roman emperor and the pope were elected monarchs. "Monarchy" means simply "rule by one," however that one is selected and for whatever term of office. Prime-ministerial government, even in a republic, is a form of monarchy (one of the "less powerful" forms). The tyrannical or despotic rule of one person is also monarchy in this sense, but is not kingship. Kingship and tyranny are opposed species of monarchy.

bound by the natural laws. And therefore such a king does not have to swear or even promise that he will observe any laws or customs whatever introduced by human beings, though it is beneficial for him to swear that he will observe the natural laws for the common benefit and that in all things relating to the government he has undertaken he will aim at the common good, not at private good. Such a king can be said to have fullness of power, namely in respect of things relating to the common good and not private good. Such government differs from tyrannical rule because it exists for the common good, whereas tyrannical rule does not exist for the common good. It differs also from despotic rule because despotic rule is chiefly for the ruler's own good, in the same way as lordship over beasts and other temporal things is for the good of the possessor, whereas royal government is for the common good; and therefore it is not properly called despotic rule. Yet such a king is, in a way, the lord of all, but in another way than in a despotic regime. For in a despotic regime the ruler has so great a lordship that he can use his slaves and any other property whatever that belongs to his rulership of this kind not only for the sake of the common good but also for his own good, as long as he attempts nothing contrary to divine or natural law; but the ruler in the royal government mentioned above can use subjects and their property however he pleases for the common good but cannot use them however he pleases for his own good, and they are therefore not his slaves but enjoy natural liberty. It belongs to natural liberty that no one can use free persons for the user's advantage, but it is not contrary to natural liberty that someone should use free persons reasonably for the sake of the common good, since everyone is obliged to prefer common to private good.

Student According to these [ideas] a despotic rulership would be greater and more perfect than such royal rulership, since it would include greater power. For one who rules despotically can use slaves and their goods for both common and private advantage and a king only for the common advantage; therefore it is greater and more perfect.

Master It is answered that despotic rule is in a way greater, because in a way it extends to more things; but by this very fact it is more imperfect, either because the good of many is better than the good of one or because detriment to the good of many implies no perfection, but rather imperfection. In despotic rule there is detriment to the many from the very fact that the despot can use his subjects and their goods for his own advantage, and therefore such greater power includes the imperfection of a better good, namely of the good of the many. Accordingly despotic rule – not only of a father in a household, but of a king in a kingdom, and consequently of an emperor in the whole world – would be simply more imperfect than such royal rule.

[2] Besides that royal rule[24] there are other royal rulerships that fall short of it in various ways but agree in being kinds of monarchy. For a certain rulership of one monarch falls short of that one in respect of *aiming at the common good*, namely because it was not established wholly on account of the common good but also for the ruler's own good. Such royal government has something of tyrannical or despotic rule and is in some way a mixture of despotic, tyrannical, and royal rule. For inasmuch as in certain respects it aims at the ruler's own good and not the common good it has something of tyranny or despotic rule, but inasmuch as in many things it aims at the common good it has something of tempered and right government – and therefore, since one man rules by himself, it has something of royal government; and therefore it is in a way a mixture of those kinds of rule. And thus some royal rule is called tyrannical by Aristotle. And [3] rule by one man sometimes falls short of the oft-mentioned royal government in respect of *power*, namely because it does not have the fullness of power that the above-mentioned royal government has. Such royal government is said to be "according to law," because, although one man rules, he does not rule according to his will but is bound by certain laws and customs introduced by human beings, which he is obliged to observe, and he is obliged to swear or promise that he will observe them; and the more he is obliged to observe many such laws and customs the more he recedes from the above-mentioned royal government – perhaps these days such royal government does not exist in the whole world.

According to Aristotle no one is worthy of such kingship unless he excels in wisdom and virtue and all good things both of body and soul, and also in external goods, namely in friends and wealth.

[24] That is, the most powerful form.

Otherwise it is to be feared that he may turn to tyranny. And thus he should have his own property, either from himself or by an allocation made by those he is over, so that he will never appropriate to himself the property of free persons or even accept it in any way, unless evident benefit or manifest necessity demands it.

To this royal government is opposed – even in the highest degree – tyranny, which is its perversion and corruption; this is the first kind, and the worst, of defective constitutions. Tyranny does not aim at the good of subjects except accidentally, but aims chiefly at the tyrant's own good, whether his own good is also the good of others or their ill. According to Aristotle, *Politics*, Book v, chapter 8,[25] tyrants often develop from demagogues. (Demagogues are those who lead the people according to their own will by the people's favor, not as kings or lords or tyrants or as having a right to rule the people or command them; but they urge the people, as agents or speakers or advisers, to the things that please the people – i.e., the things the people believe in; and therefore Aristotle, in *Politics*, Book iv, chapter 3,[26] calls them flatterers.) After they have united the people to themselves, such men, because of their power, often begin to tyrannize and to dominate even the unwilling. Tyrants also develop sometimes from kings; as Aristotle says, *Ethics*, Book viii,[27] a bad king becomes a tyrant. Whether someone is at first a king according to his will, or according to law, if he begins to rule the unwilling for the sake of his own good he becomes a tyrant. If he begins to rule willing subjects for his own good he becomes properly speaking a despot, whose rule Aristotle sometimes calls tyranny because of its great similarity to despotism, though tyranny is not properly despotism, as can be made clear from what is said above.

From the above it can be gathered that royal government, especially the most powerful, is opposed in some way not only to tyranny in the proper sense, but also to despotic rule – or they are regimes so disparate that no one government can be both royal and despotic with respect to the same persons (though it does not seem inconsistent that one government should rule over some royally and others despotically).

[25] Chapter 5, 1305 a10; chapter 10, 1310 b14.
[26] Chapter 4, 1292 a17.
[27] Chapter 10, 1160 b10–11; cf. *Politics*, Book v, chapter 10, 1310 b18.

Chapter 7

The second kind of tempered, right, and just constitution is called **aristocracy**, namely that in which some few men, and the best, rule for the common good of the multitude, and not for their own good. It has several kinds, as Aristotle teaches, *Politics*, Book IV, chapter 5.[28] The first and best kind is when, in appointing some to aristocratic rule, only the virtues, namely the intellectual and moral virtues, can be considered and are considered, and not wealth, power, friends, or anything else whatever that could be found without goodness and wisdom. The untempered, defective, and perverted constitution directly opposite to aristocracy is called oligarchy: when some, namely rich or powerful men, or men remarkable in whatever way, rule for their own good – indeed, if even the best men ruled for their own good and did not rule for the good of the multitude, they would have to be said to rule oligarchically, and their government would have to be regarded as an oligarchy. And therefore whatever is done in the choice or appointment of rulers in view of some prerogative besides wisdom and virtue (for example, wealth, power, family, friends, office, rank, age, following, or any other way of excelling at all) must be regarded as oligarchical. However, this need not always be regarded as reprehensible, since in such matters it is permissible, for a reason, for the sake of a good end, to have regard to some other prerogative or way of excelling. Both aristocracy and oligarchy are of various kinds, which are not to be discussed at present.

Chapter 8

The third kind of tempered, right and just constitution is called by various names. By one name it is called by the common name **"constitution."** In one meaning this name is common to every constitution, right and not right. In another meaning it means a certain kind of constitution only, which by another name is called timocracy.[29] About this there are various opinions. One is that timocracy – or, called by the common name, "constitution" – is that in which many rule for the common good, whether they are

---

[28] See *Politics*, Book IV, chapter 7, 1293 b14–21.
[29] See *Nicomachean Ethics*, 1160 a35, *Politics* 1289 a37.

the best or not the best, whether they are rich or poor, so that "constitution" is distinguished from aristocracy essentially by multitude. Another opinion is that "constitution" is that in which some poor virtuous men rule for the common good. Another is that "constitution" is that in which some, neither best nor bad but middling, rule for the sake of virtue and the common good, so that it is distinguished from aristocracy by a falling short in virtue and goodness. But whatever constitution should be called timocracy or, by the common name, "constitution," the defective and perverted constitution is called democracy: namely, when the people rule, or determine and appoint the ruler, not for the sake of the common good. This includes several kinds. Just as the best of all the tempered constitutions is kingship, and after it aristocracy, and last of all timocracy, so the worst of the untempered and defective constitutions is tyranny, and after it oligarchy; but the least perversion is found in democracy, according to Aristotle, *Ethics*, Book VIII.[30]

Chapter 9

Student You have explained, I think, according to the opinion of some, the meanings of the foreign terms that occur more often in the texts of Aristotle quoted and to be quoted, so do not explain any further, but go back to the main inquiry. Bestir yourself and describe how the arguments advanced above in the first and second chapters of this second book in favor of the various conflicting opinions can be answered in accordance with those opinions. But before you relate answers to them, I ask you to bring forward some arguments to prove that it is more beneficial to the whole community of the faithful to be ruled by one than by many.[31]

Master What you ask for can be understood in two ways, because it is possible for many to rule their subjects in two ways: in one way, so that the many have different persons subject to them, so that the government of many does not extend to the same persons, as several archbishops rule all who live in some extensive region,

---

[30] *Nicomachean Ethics*, VIII.10, 1160 b20.

[31] This was already argued in chapter 1. The case is now made again with fuller use of Aristotle, as an argument for monarchy in preference to aristocracy. This occupies chapters 9 and 10.

and different kingdoms are ruled by different kings none of whom is under another (and sometimes no one is over them). In the other way many rule over their subjects in such a way that they all have the same persons as subjects, whom they rule by common counsel, as is found in aristocracy and "constitution" in the narrow sense and in the defective and perverse constitutions opposed to these, namely oligarchy and democracy. Whether you mean it in the first way or in the second, you can find some arguments for what you ask above, in the first chapter of this second book. Some of those not only prove that it is beneficial for the community of the faithful to be ruled by one and not by many in the first way, but also seem to show that it is beneficial for it to be governed by one and not by many in the second way. It therefore does not seem necessary to bring forward many arguments in relation to your question.

Student Although some of the arguments brought forward above can be advanced in relation to my question (and there are also some concerning a similar matter stated in this dialogue, [Part III], Tract II, Book III, from which I will be able to perceive more things concerning this question), nevertheless, I would like you to bring forward some specific arguments to prove that it is more beneficial for the community of the faithful to be ruled by one than by many in the second way.[32]

Master This seems provable as follows. It is more beneficial for the community of the faithful to be ruled by the government that is more like natural government and rule; for just as art, if it is right, imitates nature, so rule, if it is right, imitates and is like natural rule; and consequently the rule that is more like natural rule is more right and more perfect, and consequently more beneficial. But the government or rule of one person, namely when one alone governs many and presides over them, is more like natural rule than the government or rule of many. For such a government is like royal rule, which is rule of one, and royal rule is more like natural rule than aristocratic rule or "constitutional" rule in the narrow sense, and it is more like the household, in which one head of household rules; and thus the rule of the head of the household seems in a way to be royal, as Aristotle testifies.

---

[32] On the first, see below, chapter 28.

In *Politics*, Book I, chapter 10,[33] he says that the head of the household rules the offspring royally, and in the same chapter[34] he says, "Rule over the children is royal, for because he begot them he rules by virtue of both love and age, which is indeed a royal kind of rule." From these words we gather that royal government is like the household community, in which one rules and not many (either in the first way or in the second). And the household community is natural, according to Aristotle. In *Politics*, Book I, in the prologue,[35] he says, "The household, therefore, is the community established according to nature for everyday life." These words establish that the household community is in accordance with nature and natural. Royal government, therefore, is more like natural government than aristocracy and "constitution" in the narrow sense, and consequently the government that is more like royal, namely that in which one rules and not many, is more like natural government, and consequently more perfect and better and more beneficial. From this it follows that it is more beneficial for the community of the faithful to be ruled by one than by many, even in the second way.

Student It seems that that argument is not conclusive, because royal government does not more resemble the household community than does constitutional government in which many rule. According to Aristotle, *Politics*, Book I, chapters 2 and 10, the household community, which is the "economic" community, has three parts, of which one is despotic, another marital, and the third paternal; and therefore there are in the household three rulerships of different kinds, namely despotic, by which the head of the household rules the slaves, constitutional, by which the head of the household rules the wife, and royal, by which the head of the household rules the children or offspring. Aristotle says: "There were three parts of the economic, one indeed despotic, which we have spoken of above, and one paternal, and the third marital. For he also rules over the wife and offspring as free persons; but he does not rule both in the same way, but the wife 'constitutionally' and the offspring royally."[36] From these words we gather the things that have been

---

[33] 1259 a40.
[34] 1259 b10.
[35] 1252 b13.
[36] 1259 a37.

said, and it follows that royal government is not more similar than "constitutional" government is to the household community, because just as royal government is like one part, so is "constitutional" government like the other part. Therefore, it seems, royal government is not more like natural government than is "constitutional" government, since the rule by which the head of the household rules his wife in the household, which "constitutional" government resembles, is natural, just as the rule is by which he rules the offspring, which royal government resembles. As Aristotle testifies in the same chapter, "*By nature* the male is more ruler-like than the female, unless there is something out of the ordinary course of nature, and the elder and fully developed is" – is, namely, more ruler-like – "than the younger and less developed."[37] This implies that the male naturally rules the wife and the father the offspring. Aristotle plainly says this of the male in respect of the wife in *Politics*, Book I, chapter 3: "And again, the male and the female, the one is *by nature* better and the other worse, the one ruling and the other ruled."[38] These [passages] imply that from the fact that royal government is like natural government it cannot be proved that it is better and more perfect than aristocratic government and "constitutional" government in the narrow sense. **Master** Some try to void that answer, saying that although both royal and "constitutional" government, and also aristocratic and indeed every right rule, is similar in some way to natural government, royal government is, nevertheless, more like the more perfect and better natural government than is "constitutional" government in the narrow sense. For the rule of the head of a household over the offspring is more rule-like, and more perfect and better, than the rule by which he rules his wife: First, because rule over children is better than rule over a wife, for among the children there are males, who are better than females, as has been proved above from Aristotle, and rule of better subjects is always better, according to Aristotle, *Politics*, Book I, chapter 3. Also, because the rule by which the head of the household rules his wife is for the sake of the rule by which he rules his offspring, for a wife should be married mainly for having children. Also, because the father naturally loves

---

[37] 1259 b2.
[38] Chapter 5, 1254 b12.

146

his children more than his wife, because they are joined to him by natural conjunction and more perfectly than is his wife. And thus in the community of the household the most rule-like and most suitable and most natural rule is that by which the head of the household rules the offspring, and royal government resembles this; royal government is therefore more perfect than the other rulerships in the community of the household.

Further, royal government is more like the natural rule by which the head of the household rules his offspring than "constitutional" rule is like the rule by which the head of the household rules his wife. Royal rule is like paternal rule both as to the unity of the ruler and as to fullness of power, because in each regime there is one ruler with fullness of power over his subjects. But although "constitutional" government is like the rule by which the head of the household rules his wife in that neither ruler has fullness of power, they differ in that the ruler in "constitutional" government is not one but many, whereas in the natural rule by which the head of a household rules his wife the ruler is one, whether he has several wives or one. And so royal government is more like natural government than is the rule of the head of a household over his wife. From this it follows that it is more beneficial for the community of the faithful to be ruled by one than by many.

Chapter 10

Student Here we could examine many things about royal government and fullness of power, both the father's over offspring and the king's over subjects. But these will perhaps have their place later; so, passing over them, bring forward another argument to prove that it is more beneficial for the community of the faithful to be ruled by one than by many.

Master Again, some prove this as follows. That form of government is most of all beneficial to the community of the faithful by which friendship and harmony are most of all preserved and sedition, which is the corruption of any community, warded off, as Aristotle testifies. In *Politics*, Book II, chapter 3,[39] he says, "We believe that friendship is the greatest of goods for cities, for thus

---

[39] Chapter 4, 1262 b7.

they never make seditions." And in [*Ethics*], Book VIII, chapter 1, he says, "And it seems also that friendship holds cities together, and legislators care more about it than justice: for concord seems to be something like friendship, and they seek this most of all."[40] Also, truth himself seems to suggest this in Matthew 12[:25], when he says, "Every kingdom divided against itself shall be made desolate, and every city or household divided against itself" by discord and hatred "will not stand," etc.

Chapter 11[41]

Student Now you have indeed sufficiently proved by many arguments, though you could bring forward many more, that there should be one person in the rulership of the Church because greater unity and harmony are thereby produced and fostered. I would, however, very much like to know what sort of person he should be.

Master Concerning the question you want explained there are two modes of speaking. Some say [1] that no one should rule everyone else unless he surpasses all the rest in wisdom and virtue. Others say [2] that someone can rule all the rest even if he does not excel them all in wisdom and virtue; and this mode of speaking is again diversified, since some say [2ai] that if among the Christian people no one is found more excellent than the rest, yet someone good is found, then such a person should be chosen pope, but [2aii] if no one good and suitable is found no one should be elevated to so great an office; according to others, [2b] whether someone good is found or not, nevertheless someone should be chosen as highest pontiff, and to prove this they rely on the argument that it is better to have a head of any kind than not to have a head at all.

Chapter 12

Student Since I regard as rather unreasonable the second mode of those who say that sometimes the Church should be without a

---

[40] 1155 a23.
[41] According to a note in each of the manuscripts, chapter 10 is incomplete. Chapters 11 and 12 are not in the manuscripts and may not be authentic.

ruler and shepherd,[42] since it destroys the whole constitution and
hierarchy, I therefore do not want you to bring forward any arguments for it; let us leave it as being vacuous. But the other mode
of this second mode[43] – that someone may be elected as highest
pontiff, whatever kind of person he may be, if no one else is found
better and more worthy – this conflicts altogether with the first
mode of speaking.[44] Therefore bring forward some arguments and
authorities to the contrary,[45] for by them the first mode will be
the more confirmed.

Master Against that mode of speaking, and in confirmation of the
first, some argue first as follows. That person should be elected
as shepherd in relation to whom the rest can be called a flock;[46]
but they are called a flock in relation to no one except one who
surpasses each of them in knowledge and holiness; therefore no
one should be elected as highest pontiff who is equal to the rest.
The major premise seems to need no proof, but the minor is
proved: A shepherd should offer to everyone guidance in knowledge,
as we read in dist. 63, *Ephesios*,[47] and in 8, q. 1, *Audacter*, at the
end;[48] similarly also in holiness of life, as is written in 11, q. 3
Praecipue;[49] and consequently he should surpass each of them in
such qualities. Also, the same is clear from a text of Pope Sym-
machus included in 1, q. 1, *Ubi sit*.[50] He says, "He who is more
outstanding in honor must be regarded as most contemptible unless
he excels in knowledge and holiness." Moreover, "the more outstanding" and "more holy" should be chosen for the priesthood
and should be preferred to everyone, as Jerome says.[51] And, as we
read in dist. 63, *Si forte*, Pope Leo says this: "By the judgment
of the metropolitan let that person be preferred who is supported

---

[42] That is, 2aii.
[43] That is, 2b.
[44] That is, with [1].
[45] That is, arguments for [1], the proposition that no one should be pope unless he
surpasses all other Christians. This occupies chapters 12 and 13.
[46] See dist. 25, dictum post c. 3, para 2.
[47] There is no c. *Ephesios*. According to 43 dist. c. *Ephesiis*, a pastor who does not
correct his flock kills them by his silence.
[48] It speaks of the hunger of the people to hear the word of God.
[49] Prelates who do something wrong should know that they deserve as many deaths
as they transmit to their subjects by their example.
[50] Rather, c. *Vilissimus*.
[51] See 8, q. 1, c. 15.

by greater learning and merits."[52] And Ambrose [says], "Deacons and priests should in behavior and speech lead all of the people living a wholly secular life";[53] therefore, also, he who should be over everyone should lead others, however holy, in life and behavior. Many other arguments and authorities could be brought forward which for the sake of brevity we must pass over.

Chapter 13

Student If any other arguments occur to you to prove that no one should be over all the faithful unless he surpasses all in wisdom and virtue, bring them forward.

Master This is again proved as follows. No less wisdom or virtue is needed in one who rules the whole congregation of the faithful in spiritual matters than in a king who presides over his subjects in temporal matters, as Aristotle seems to maintain in *Politics*, Book VII, chapter 13. According to him (in the same place) it is not just for some to rule always (as kings do, and also highest pontiffs) and the others always to be subject unless they differ from their subjects as much as gods and heroes differ from men. (Gods and heroes, according to him, simply excel all men.) He says this: "If, therefore, some men differed from others as much as we think gods and heroes differ from men, having simply great superiority, first of body and then of soul, so that the superiority of the rulers in respect of their subjects were undoubted and manifest, it is clear that it would be better for those to rule always for life," etc.[54] For what is more excellent and more perfect, while it remains such, is fit to rule whatever lacks such great excellence. When, however, men are not found who differ from others as gods and heroes differ from men, then it is not just that some of them should rule the others for the whole of their lives, but it is just that all should in some way share in the rulership, namely so that all of those who are equals in wisdom and virtue should rule by

---

[52] The Latin is ambiguous. Pope Leo probably meant: "by those who are greater in zeal and merits."

[53] Not found in Ambrose. Jerome: "Bishops, priests and deacons should earnestly ensure that in behavior and speech they lead the whole people over whom they preside"; 8, q. 1, c. *Qualis.*

[54] 1332 b17.

turns, first some and then others, as Aristotle in the same place seems to maintain. He says, "But since this is not easily found, and there are no kings (as Scylax says there are in India) who differ so much from their subjects, it is manifest that for many reasons all must share, and must rule and be subject in turn" – namely, so that no one should rule through the whole period of his life, but instead they should sometimes rule and sometimes be subject. He gives a reason for this, saying, "For fairness is: the same for similars."[55] From these words the following argument is drawn. It is unjust that someone should always rule his equals and similars; therefore, when some are similar, it is unjust that some of them should always rule and others always be subject. Therefore it follows that, if among the faithful there are many who are like one another in wisdom and virtue, it is unjust that one of them should rule always, for the whole time of his life, and the others always be subject. Therefore, since the pope should be over all the faithful for the whole time of his life, it is unjust that someone should be made pope if others are found like him in wisdom and virtue. It is therefore unjust that someone should be made pope unless he surpasses all the faithful in wisdom and virtue.

Further, papal government is more perfect than royal government, as Gregory Nazienzen testifies. As we read in dist. 10, c. *Suscipitis*, he says, writing to the emperors of Constantinople, "He also gave power to us; he gave a rulership much more perfect than your rulerships." But no one is worthy of royal rulership unless he surpasses others in wisdom and virtue, in fact in all good things, as Aristotle seems to assert in *Ethics*, Book VIII, quoted above in chapter 2 of this second book. This is also proved from the fact that "kingship is established in accordance with aristocracy," according to Aristotle, *Politics*, Book V, chapter 8.[56] But in aristocracy those rule who are better than the rest, according to Aristotle, *Politics*, Book IV, chapter 5.[57] Therefore in a kingdom, also, no one should rule royally unless he surpasses the rest. And thus when God first appointed a king over his people, he chose the best man of the whole people, as Samuel testifies. In 1 Kings 10[:24] he said of him, i.e., of Saul, as he was at that time, "Surely you see

[55] 1332 b23.
[56] Chapter 10, 1310 b33.
[57] Chapter 7.

him whom the Lord has chosen, that there is none like him among all the people." Therefore, *a fortiori*, no one is worthy of papal rulership unless he excels all in wisdom and virtue. Therefore when there is not found anyone whose excellence is without doubt and manifestly so great (since the excellence of rulers should be undoubted and manifest, according to Aristotle, as was said above in the first chapter[58]), then no one should be chosen as highest pontiff, but instead several should be appointed who are more excellent than others, who should rule all others aristocratically or "constitutionally."

Chapter 14

Student By those arguments you have given me occasion to think of a great many things both in favor of the conclusion for which they are brought forward and against it, and also concerning the whole matter we began to treat of at the beginning of this second book: namely, whether it is beneficial for the congregation of the faithful to be under one prelate. So I intend to probe that matter, and things already touched on, more thoroughly than I proposed and to investigate the force of the arguments brought forward for one side and for the other. In the first place bring forward some arguments to prove that even if no one among the whole Christian people surpassed all the others in virtue and wisdom, it would be better for the Christian people to be ruled by one than by many, as is held by the second mode of assertion related above in chapter 11 of the second book.[59]

Master This seems provable as follows. The form of government most of all beneficial to the whole congregation of the faithful is the same kind as the one that God in both the Old Testament and the New wanted his people to be governed by, since he is himself the best and wisest establisher of every virtuous and useful form of government. But in both Old and New Testaments God wanted his whole people to be governed by one man who would be the governor of all through the whole of his life, even if he

---

[58] Not in the first chapter, but in the beginning of this chapter.

[59] The case made in chapters 1, 9, and 10 is made again: even if the monarch is not outstandingly good, monarchy is better for the Church than aristocracy.

did not surpass all others in wisdom and virtue. For it is not found that any judge or king in the Old Testament excelled all others in wisdom and virtue. Saint Peter also does not seem to have been holier and wiser than all the apostles and other orthodox believers, for Saint John the apostle seems to have outdistanced him in love of Christ and consequently in holiness and virtue; he seems also to have been inferior in wisdom to Saint Paul. Therefore, even if no Christian is found who excels all others in wisdom and virtue, someone should be elected as highest pontiff to be the prelate of all Christians.

Chapter 15

Student To give me and others occasion to find the truth about the above matters more clearly, bestir yourself and report some answers to all the things brought forward in favor of the conflicting assertions. First, however, tell how answer is made to the things reported above in chapter 2, which seem to militate against the second mode of assertion reported above in chapter 11, for which you have now argued in the last chapter. That mode of assertion seems to me to have some plausibility.

Master That mode of assertion is twofold. In one way it is said that if no one is found among the Christian people who is more excellent than all the others, yet there is found someone suitable and good, then such a person should be elected as pope; but if no one is found who is good and suitable, then no one should be elevated to so great an office. In the other way it is said that whether a suitable person is found or not, someone should be elected to the highest pontificate, because it is better to have any sort of person as head than not to have a head at all.

Student First describe how answer is given according to the first of those ways.

Master To the first argument[60] brought forward above in chapter 2 of this second book, which seems to be based on a text of Aristotle, who seems to assert that it is unjust that someone should rule his similars and equals, it is answered that if in some com-

---

[60] This chapter answers argument [1] of chapter 2 (p. 128 above); arguments [3] and [4] are answered in chapter 19, and argument [2] in chapter 29.

munity all were good and not at all pervertible by wickedness, actual or potential, it would be unjust that someone should rule those similar and equal to himself in wisdom and virtue, because in that case there would seem to be no reason why one should rule rather than another. But when in some community there are many or several who have been or can be perverted, and when the greater and more powerful part willingly accepts the rule of one, so that they cannot be diverted from such will, then it is beneficial that one should accept rulership over all, provided a person is found who is worthy to rule over the worse members (since otherwise he could not be regarded as good or suitable). If, however, there is some party so powerful that it can raise an irrepressible sedition dangerous to the whole community, a party that would by no means be willing to accept the rule of one person, then no one should be promoted over all those like himself and over others, but the appointment of such a ruler should be deferred to another time; for just as sometimes it is permissible for a bishop to desert his subjects because of their wickedness, even renouncing rule altogether (*Extra, De renunciatione, Nisi cum pridem*;[61] 7, q. 1, *Hoc tamen servandum*[62]), so it is sometimes permissible to defer the appointment of a ruler because of the wickedness of some. And therefore, although as a rule it is beneficial for the whole community of the faithful that some one person should be elected to the highest priesthood to be over all the others, nevertheless, if there were so much wickedness in some party of Christians that it could expose the whole of Christianity to danger, and they would in no way obey one high priest, no one should then be elected to that office, but his election should be deferred; for as lesser evils are often permitted to avert greater ones, dist. 3, c. *Omnis*,[63] so sometimes certain good things, even great ones, are not done so that the greatest dangers may be avoided. Aristotle means, therefore, that it is unjust that someone should rule others similar in virtue and equal *unless* it is beneficial, because of some advantage or

---

[61] Para. *Propter malitiam*: "And because of the wickedness of the people, a prelate is sometimes compelled to decline to govern them, when the people are so stiff necked that he can get nowhere with them." The gloss to the decretals, col. 234, v. *Plebis*, refers to 7, q. 1, c. *Adversitas*, para. *Hoc tunc servandum* [*sic*].

[62] 7, q. 1, c. *Adversitas*, para. *Hoc tunc observandum*.

[63] Not in text but in gloss, col. 9, v. *Permittit*.

necessity, to determine that someone should rule over his similars and equals also, and not only over unequals and dissimilars.

To the argument by which Aristotle seems to prove absolutely and without distinction or qualification that it is unjust that someone should rule his similars and equals because equal office and rank is due to equals in virtue, it is answered that when it can come about suitably and usefully that equal office and rank is given to equals, then this should be done, and Aristotle is speaking with reference to this case. But when it is not possible or not useful or less useful, especially to the common good, for equal office and rank to be conferred on equals, then, without any injustice, indeed justly, by election or lot or in any other permissible way, someone can be promoted in rank and offices over his similars and equals. If others were disturbed by this and were provoked into making a sedition, they would become dissimilar and unequal in virtue to the other to whom they had before been equal and similar, as being ambitious and envious, preferring their own honor to the common good, since they would rather want the common good to be endangered or not cared for than that someone should be promoted over them to the common advantage.

As for Aristotle's example of those who have equal or unequal digestive power and of those who have an equal or unequal body (that it is beneficial for those equal in digestive power or body to have equal food or clothing, which harms those unequal in digestive power and body), it does not prove universally and without any exception that the same office and rank should be given to those who are equal and similar in virtue, because in the provision of food and clothing to equals or unequals in digestive power or body notice is taken only of each one's own strength and own body – namely, of what benefits or harms each of them separately. In distributing offices and ranks, however, notice is sometimes taken only of the merit and worth of those to whom they should be distributed, because it is then unjust that unequal office or rank should be given to equals, and then Aristotle's example has its place; but notice is sometimes taken not only of the merit and worth of those to be honored but also of the public advantage, which is better cared for governmentally by one than by many; and then, because more regard should be had to the common good than to the merit and worth of those to be honored, it is just that unequal offices and rank should be given to those who are equals and similars in virtue.

Chapter 16

Student The arguments above in chapters 12 and 13 seem to militate especially against this mode.[64] It is shown there that no one should be promoted over all the faithful unless he excels them all in virtue and wisdom, and the opposite of this is held by this mode of assertion. So relate how those arguments are answered.

Master To the arguments brought forward in chapter 12 it is answered that, as a rule, when someone is found who surpasses and excels all others in virtue and wisdom, he should be promoted to be highest pontiff, and, as a rule, those who knowingly pass over such a person commit sin and would deserve to be deprived of the power of electing; the texts brought forward speak with reference to this case. But when no such person is found but many are similar and equal in virtue and wisdom, then such a person should not be elected, since there is no one such, and yet the election should not for this reason be deferred until such a person is found; it is enough then to elect one of those who are equal or similar in wisdom and virtue, having regard to something else that in some way recommends him.

Student I think I understand that answer. However, I do not know how that opinion explains the texts advanced above in chapter 12, which seem to militate strongly against it. So run briefly through them and say how they interpret them.

Master To the text that says that someone should be elected in relation to whom the rest are called a flock, it is answered that it can have a true sense in two ways. One is that when someone is elected, such a person should be elected in relation to whom the others, good and bad, can rightly be called a flock. The other is that (because bad people are always found in the Church) such a person should always be elected in relation to whom the rest, i.e., the bad, are called a flock; however, it is not always possible to elect someone in relation to whom those who are outstanding in wisdom and virtue can be called a flock.

[64] That is, [2] in chapter 11 (p. 148 above).

To the text quoted in 1, q. 1, c. *Vilissimus*, it is answered that a prelate must be thought most contemptible, i.e. very base, unless he greatly excels the bad and unworthy in honor, knowledge, and holiness, but he should not be thought most contemptible if he does not excel in knowledge, and holiness even those who are outstanding in wisdom and virtue.[65]

To the third, which is by Jerome, it is answered that when there is someone more outstanding, holier, etc., he should be elected to the priesthood; when, however, there is no such person, it is enough to elect someone more outstanding, holier, more learned, and more eminent in every virtue than all the bad and foolish among the people.

To the text of Pope Leo it is said likewise that when there is someone who is best he should be elected, when there is not someone who is best a good man should be elected.

To the text of Ambrose it is said that priests and deacons should in behavior and speech lead all of the people living a wholly secular life, but they need not lead those of the people who live an especially holy life.

Other texts are answered in a similar way.

Student I think I am not ignorant how that opinion interprets all the sacred canons which seem in this matter to militate against it. But say whether it holds that an election should be quashed if the best man is not elected, when there is found someone best and more excellent than all.

Master It holds that because on account of scandals, disturbances, disagreements, and also seditions, lesser evils are often tolerated to avoid greater ones; so the election of a good man who is not the best, when a best is found, can licitly not be quashed and would often be most dangerous to quash.

Student Even though such an election should not be quashed, is the good man elected obliged not to consent to the election made of himself, or to withdraw if he has already consented, when someone who is best has been passed over?

Master It is answered that if such a man, when some other, best, man is found, is able not to consent without danger or notable

---

[65] See gloss, col. 518, v. *Nisi praecellat*: "That is, unless he has the discretion required in a prelate – if not outstanding, yet sufficient ... For it suffices if he

disturbance, or can withdraw if he has consented, he is obliged, of necessity for salvation, not to consent, or to withdraw, especially if he can do so with good example and edification to the whole community of the faithful. Otherwise he would reprehensibly prefer his own good or honor to the common good.

Chapter 17

Student Say now how the arguments brought forward above in chapter 13 are answered.

Master They are all based, it seems, on the premise that no one is worthy of royal rulership unless he surpasses all others in wisdom and virtue, as Aristotle seems to think in the *Politics* and also in the *Ethics*, so that no one should be king unless he is the best, and better in wisdom and virtue than all his subjects. To which it is said that this is not, according to Aristotle, true universally, without any exception. To make this clear, it is said, it must be known that royal rulership can be obtained in many ways, of which it is enough for the present to enumerate two. One of these is when someone is voluntarily made king by subjects. The other is when someone voluntarily transfers himself from a despotic rule that he has justly obtained to a royal rule. If someone should (as a rule) be appointed to royal government in the first way, then the best man in wisdom and virtue should be appointed, if such a one is found and no just impediment impedes his advancement. If a family is found that in this way excels all others, then (as a rule) it is just that this family should reign. This is what Aristotle means in *Politics*, Book III, chapter 16,[66] when he says, "When, therefore, it happens that either a whole family or one individual differs in virtue so much that his virtue exceeds that of all others, then it is just that this family should be royal and rule over all, and this one man be king, as was said above." If, however, [such a family or man] is not found, yet many good men are found, then one of them should be appointed, and the others similar and equal to him in wisdom and virtue are obliged to bear his government

is good ... What then if all are very expert? He will not be 'most contemptible' because he is not like Solomon."

[66] Chapter 17, 1288 a15.

patiently and willingly for the common good. How he should be appointed you can inquire afterwards, if you like.

If, however, someone comes to royal rulership in the second way (for example, because he first held lordship of the whole region and of all those living there, whether by occupation, by gift, by purchase, by just war, or in any other just way, and afterwards, renouncing despotic rule, is content with royal rulership only – that is, so that he chiefly wishes to rule his subjects for their good and advantage and not, as a despot rules, for his own good), he can justly take possession of a royal rulership even if he is not the best of men, because from the fact that he is giving up part of his right and keeping a part he should not be regarded as unjust, even if he is not the best man.

And Aristotle's suggestion in *Politics*, Book VII, chapter 13, that it is not just for some always to rule unless they differ as much from their subjects as gods and heroes differ from men, is answered in many ways. In one way, that this is true if account is taken only of the merit and worth of the ruler, but not if account is taken of advantage to the common good.

In another way it is said that this is true of natural justice in particular, i.e. that it is not natural justice that they should rule over all others unless they differ in such a way from all the others whom they rule; in this way it is just that the husband should rule over his wife or wives, a father over his children, and the lord over slaves that are naturally slaves, according to Aristotle, *Politics*, Book I. But it is not true of positive justice. For since it is often just (and natural)[67] that someone should be lord over many who are similar and equal to himself in a perfect community (because those who are similar and equal in virtue are so many that they cannot usefully all rule together, and yet such a community cannot stand without a ruler, according to Aristotle), and yet it is not natural justice that these should rule rather than those, it must therefore be determined by positive justice that these should rule, either simply for the whole of their life or for a time; and thus,

---

[67] "And natural" is an anticipation of what is to be said in the next two paragraphs. The position the Master is explaining seems to be this: It is not natural justice for any *given* individual to rule his equals, but under some circumstances it may be natural justice for *one or another* of the equals to rule the rest; and positive law will determine which.

though, as Aristotle thinks, it is not natural justice that this man should rule for his whole life those who are his similars and equals, nevertheless it can become, for a reason, positive justice. Aristotle did not intend to deny this.

Student How can it be natural justice that someone should rule those who are similar to himself, and yet not natural justice that *this* man should rule those who are similar to himself, and not natural justice that *this* [other] man should rule those who are similar to himself, and so on of each man?

Master It is answered that your question arises from an ignorance of elementary matters (namely, of logic) which no one working in any science whatever should fail to know, for otherwise he will argue sophistically when he thinks he is arguing demonstratively. It is said, therefore, that just as, often, both the universal and the particular [proposition] are necessary though each of their singulars is contingent,[68] so it is possible that the particular is in accordance with natural justice and yet no singular will be in accordance with natural justice.[69] It is therefore possible that it is natural justice that *someone* should rule those who are similar to himself, and yet not natural justice that *this* man should rule those who are similar to himself, and not natural justice that *this* [other] man should rule those who are similar to himself, and so on of each man. And just as it is possible that a categorical proposition about a disjunct term, having as its subject discrete terms contained under some common term,[70] is necessary, and that the corresponding disjunctive with

---

[68] In Aristotle's terminology (which Ockham says may be improper, *Summa logicae*, II, 9.47–66, pp. 274–5, or *Theory of Propositions*, p. 110), "Every red thing is colored" is a universal in respect of the singular propositions "This red thing is colored," "That red thing is colored," etc. "That every red thing is colored is necessary" may be true, but "This red thing is colored" is contingent (because, according to Aristotle, it will cease to be true when this thing perishes). See *Summa logicae*, II, 9.30–8, p. 274 (or *Ockham's Theory of Propositions*, p. 109), *Summa logicae*, III-3, 34.30–42, pp. 717–18.

[69] According to Ockham there are other modes besides the four famous ones (necessary, contingent, possible, impossible); see *Summa logicae*, II, 1.36–68, pp. 242–3 (or *Ockham's Theory of Propositions*, p. 80). "In a broad sense, every proposition is called modal in which occurs some term that can belong to a whole proposition"; Ockham, *Expositio in librum Perihermeneias Aristotelis*, II, 5.87–8, *Opera philosophica*, vol. II, p. 462. "In accordance with natural justice" fits this definition of a mode.

[70] E.g., "This man or that man or ..." – "this" makes the term discrete (i.e., a term referring to an individual), "man" is a common term.

the mode of necessity is nevertheless false, and that therefore none of those singulars is necessary,[71] so it can happen that this is true: "It is natural justice for this man or that man," and so on of each man, "to rule over those who are similar to himself," which is a categorical statement about a disjunct subject, and yet the disjunctive is false, and consequently each singular is false. Therefore, according to them, so that we may reason without any deception in such matters, we must learn most diligently the difference between a disjunctive proposition and one about a disjunct term,[72] and between a proposition of the same terms taken in the sense of composition and in the sense of division (according to some), or between the different senses of such propositions according to amphiboly (according to others).[73] For often, because of ignorance of the difference between such propositions and senses, the meaning of authors is in many matters not known, when they are thought to have had one sense and sometimes have had another, indeed sometimes the opposite. In such matters various kinds of sophisms are committed (though by many in ignorance) when one sense or equivalent proposition is sophistically inferred from the other, or the converse; or from a proposition taken in one sense, or from one sense, are inferred things that follow not from it but from the other sense – or, conversely, one sense is sophistically inferred from things from which the other sense can by a true argument be inferred. In many other ways also sophisms are committed in such matters because of ignorance of this distinction in sense of propositions that are the same verbally.

Student You have related two ways of answering Aristotle. Now relate another, if it occurs to you.

Master In another way it is said that for some men (or man) to rule always is not just, unless they differ (or he differs) from the

---

[71] " 'This man or that man or ... is P' is necessary" may be true, and yet "This man is necessarily P, or that man is necessarily P ..." may be false.

[72] See *Summa logicae*, III-4, 5.136–143, pp. 768–9; cf. II, 37.11–18, p. 355 (*Ockham's Theory of Propositions*, p. 194).

[73] Amphiboly and "composition and division" are fallacies arising not from the ambiguities of terms but from ambiguities of construction: "composition and division" from uncertainty of punctuation or grouping of words (*Summa logicae*, III-4, 8.3–6, p. 786), amphiboly from ambiguities of syntax. Ockham thinks that some ambiguities commonly classed under "composition and division" cannot easily be exhibited by difference of punctuation and would be better classed under

subjects as much as gods and heroes differ from men, if it is feared with probability that the equals will bring about dangerous dissensions and seditions if they are not honored equally.

Student In accordance with those [answers], run through the texts brought forward above in chapter 13.

Master This opinion concedes the first text of Aristotle just as it sounds. To the second it is said that when there are many equals in some perfect community, Aristotle maintains that it is beneficial that all should share in rulership "in part" – i.e., sometimes to rule, sometimes to be subject – when it is feared with probability that otherwise, unless each who is equally worthy sometimes rules, dangerous seditions will arise. If, however, there is no fear of such sedition, it is beneficial, if some suitable man is found, that one man should rule all as king, even during his whole life, unless it is presumed that he would wish to convert royal rule into tyranny or there is fear of some other evil that could happen because of some wickedness.

And to the other argument from Aristotle, that fairness is "the same for similars," the answer was given earlier.

To the other, when it is taken from Aristotle that no one is worthy to rule unless he surpasses all others in all goods, the answer given is that this is true if only the merit and the personal worth of him who should be king are taken into account, not having regard for the common good.

To the other, when it is taken [as premise] that kingship is established in accordance with aristocracy, in which only those rule who are better than the rest, it is answered that if in some community willing to be ruled aristocratically some few are found who are better than the rest, then it is just that, unless there is some other obstacle, these should rule the rest. If, however, there are not found some few who are better than the rest, but there are many equal in wisdom and virtue, and so many that it would not be beneficial for all of them to rule, then it cannot happen that aristocratic rulers are better than the rest; yet aristocratic government is beneficial for the whole community, if they are not willing to tolerate royal government; and then to appoint some few

amphiboly (*Summa logicae*, III-4, 5.76–93, 174–99, pp. 766–7, 770; 8.36–43, pp. 787–8).

of the equals to rule all will be more useful than to establish a "constitutional," oligarchic, or democratic regime.

To the statement that God chose as first king of Israel the best man from the whole people, namely Saul, it is answered that Saul was not better in virtue and wisdom than all the others, for Samuel was much better than him, and perhaps many others excelled him in virtue and wisdom. However, it was said that there was no one like him in the whole people on account of his tall stature, because (as we read in that place), "he was taller among all the people by head and shoulders."[74] Many infer from this that it is not universally and without exception necessary always to choose the better man as king, because Samuel was not chosen as king and yet he was much better than Saul.

Student Applying the above to the pope, say briefly how what was written before is answered insofar as it seems to prove that no one should be over all the faithful as pope unless he surpasses all in wisdom and virtue.

Master It is said that if some Catholic were found of whom such excellence were known, then, unless some circumstance particularly impeded it, he should be set over the whole community of the faithful; so that if someone else, less perfect, were elected, or even were presiding already, by love of the common good that person would be bound of necessity for salvation to resign in his favor, unless some special reason stood in the way of such resignation. If, however, no one were found who excelled in that way, someone should be appointed from among the equals. For although it is not natural or divine justice that this man should be appointed, it is natural justice that someone should be appointed; and because not all the equals should rule, it is therefore beneficial that someone from among the equals should be promoted by lot, if it cannot reasonably be done otherwise than by lot; just as the apostles, because they judged Matthias and Joseph called Barsabbas to be equal in all respects, gave them lots, and appointed him upon whom the lot fell to the office of apostle.[75] If, however, some are perceived to be in some ways unequal, though not in wisdom and virtue, then it is possible to take notice of the inequalities, in

---

[74] 1 Kings 11:23.
[75] Acts 1:24.

accordance with the quality of the time: at one time notice can justly be taken of one thing and at another time of the opposite, for at one time notice could justly be taken of the power of friends and at another time of lack of friends. And thus some think it should likewise be said of other things besides wisdom and virtue.

Chapter 18

Student I have heard how the arguments are answered that seemed to prove that no one should be made highest pontiff and head of all the faithful unless he excelled all others in wisdom and virtue. Now relate how answer is made to those by which it is shown in chapter 2 of this second book that it is not beneficial for the community of the faithful to be subject to one head and prelate because it is beneficial for it to be ruled by many. I ask you first of all to say what advantage, according to them,[76] makes it more beneficial for the community of the faithful to be ruled by one than by many.

Master They say that it has many advantages. One is that it is easier to get access to one than to many, because the many are not always found in the same place, and it is of no little benefit to subjects to be able to have easy access to the ruler for various necessities; for this reason rulers, both secular and ecclesiastical, must be regarded as blameworthy if they make themselves inaccessible to their subjects. Another advantage is that, as a rule, one ruler can, when the need arises, hold court and do justice and ward off dangers more easily than many. If one man is ruler, he need not wait for another whenever it is necessary to hold court and do justice and to ward off some danger, but if there were many rulers, one would have to wait for another or the others, even if it were necessary to expedite such matters quickly and they could not be deferred without danger. A third advantage is that one, if he strays, is corrected more easily than many, because many would have more defenders than the one would have. A fourth is that no great community can be well ruled without the advice of

---

[76] That is, according to those who wish to answer the arguments presented in chapter 2, i.e., advocates of monarchy.

many, according to that text of Solomon in Proverbs 24[:6], "There will be safety where there is much advice"; and thus in 1 Machabees 8[:15] it is said in praise of the Romans that "three hundred and twenty men used to deliberate every day, giving advice always about the multitude, that they might act worthily." Their community will therefore be better ruled if one rules the others and can decide the time and place of meetings and all other things (for example which counselors should be admitted or turned away and the like) than if many ruled, one of whom could not easily exclude another from the council and from whatever else has to be done, even if he were plotting evil to the state. A fifth advantage is that one can expedite many matters both in more ways and with less labor than many, for in many ways something can happen to prevent many persons from deciding the same affairs together.

Because of these and many other advantages, they say that it is beneficial for the community of the faithful to be ruled by one best man rather than by many best men, and similarly it is beneficial for it to be ruled by a good and wise man willing to act with the advice of wise men, rather than by many good and wise men. Thus it is said (in the place cited above) in praise of the Romans, "They entrust their magistracy to one man each year, to rule over the whole earth, and they all obey the one," and yet, as was quoted, there were three hundred and twenty counselors giving advice every day. Thus Abimelech, as we read in Judges 9[:1 ff], speaking through his mother's brothers, cleverly persuaded the men of Sichem to accept him as lord, holding out what was more advantageous to them (if he had been good), saying, "Say to all the men of Sichem, 'Is it better for you that seventy men, all the sons of Jerobaal, should rule over you, or that one man should rule over you?'"

Chapter 19

Student I have heard some advantages which they say make it beneficial for the community of the faithful to be ruled by one believer rather than by many. Now tell how the arguments brought forward in chapter 2 of this second book, which seem to prove the opposite, are answered.

Master To the first of them,[77] when it is advanced that it is most of all beneficial for the whole congregation of the faithful to be ruled by him (or by those) whose judgment is more certain and better in judging and deciding which things should be sought as useful and which should be rejected altogether as useless or harmful, it is answered that this is not universally true, though it is true on occasion. For it is certain that the judgment of a general council, in which the better and wiser from every province and region of Christians should meet, is more certain and better than the judgment of one, or of a few who can conveniently remain continuously in some one place, and yet it is not beneficial that there should always be a general council to govern the community of the faithful – though, indeed, on occasion, for certain particular affairs that cannot be dispatched suitably by one or a few, it is beneficial for a general council to be called and its decision followed. But for matters that can usefully be dispatched by one or a few it is not beneficial for a general council to be assembled, and thus it is as a rule beneficial that the community of the faithful should be ruled by one or a few rather than by a general council. So, also, it is beneficial, as a rule, for the community of the faithful to be ruled by one best or good man making use of sufficiently good advice rather than by many ruling together, because it is better that the many, without whose advice the community of the faithful would not be ruled well, should be only the advisers of the one best or good man (who can, when it is beneficial, invite them and call them all, or certain of them, and entrust various matters to various of them), rather than that all of these should be rulers or rectors. For it would often be necessary to call them all together for matters that could be dispatched by a few; also, many other difficulties and inconveniences would occur that are avoided if one best or good man rules with advisers who are sufficient and as good as many rulers would be (for rulership imparts neither wisdom nor goodness).

And to Aristotle – who seems to prove in *Politics* that it is beneficial for a community to be ruled by many best men rather than by one because the crowd judges better than any one person –

---

[77] That is, to argument [3] of chapter 2 (p. 130 above), which is the first argument in that chapter to prove that it is more advantageous to the Christian community to be ruled by many.

it is answered that many often judge better and more certainly than one and a crowd better than one, and therefore there is indeed a need for discussion, taking advice, and the judgment of many: not necessarily as rulers, however; often it is enough if they are present only as advisers. Someone who is only an adviser (if he has a good intention) discusses, advises, and judges, deciding between good and evil, the just and the unjust, just as if he were a ruler. Often, also, the deliberation and judgment of one alone is enough for the things that have to be done. And therefore it is more beneficial for the whole community of the faithful if one supreme ruler rules, dispatching by himself matters for which he is sufficient by himself and dispatching other matters for which his own skill alone is not enough with the advice of others, than if many such persons rule, who must meet for all matters, small and large, easy and difficult.

To the other text of Aristotle – which seems to assert that many, with many eyes and many ears, perceive more things and perceive them better than one, with two eyes and two ears, and similarly, many can do more things with many hands and many feet than one with two hands and two feet, and thus rule by many is more beneficial than rule by one – it is answered that if one good and wise man rules the community of the faithful, he does not use only two eyes and two ears and also two hands and two feet, but sometimes he uses many such instruments. It is beneficial that he should sometimes use only two eyes and two hands rather than many, but sometimes it is beneficial that he should use many rather than only two. It is therefore beneficial for the whole community of the faithful to be ruled by one who sometimes, as it is beneficial, uses his own sufficiency, and sometimes another's, rather than by many who meet unnecessarily to deal with everything.

To the text from Acts 15[:6], that "The apostles and elders met to see about this doctrine," which is taken there as if it is always beneficial for matters to be concluded and decided by many rather than by one, it is answered that sometimes it is beneficial for matters to be concluded by many rather than by one, and sometimes it is more beneficial that they be dealt with by one. Therefore it is beneficial for the community of the faithful to be ruled by one best man, or at least by a good man, who deals with and decides some matters and questions by himself but deals with some together with others – many others or few, as is beneficial – and decides. In the case spoken of in Acts 15, it was therefore beneficial for, not one by himself, but many, to inquire about that doctrine. The apostles and elders met, not indeed as all being rulers of the community of the faithful, but as being necessary and useful to the one ruler and head of all in providing support or advice. For sometimes some are called to deliberations in which the wisdom of one is enough more for support against those resisting or disobeying than to seek advice.

To Pope Innocent, when he says that what is investigated by many elders is more easily discovered [dist. 20, c. *De quibus*], it is answered that concerning many doubtful matters this is true; however, when one is enough to discover something by himself and does not then need the support or help or advice of many, it is better that the investigation and discovery be by one rather than by many.

To the other argument[78] – based on this, that many are less pervertible and corruptible by vices, desires, and wicked passions than one person is, and consequently it is beneficial for the community of the faithful to be ruled by many rather than by one, because it is more beneficial for it to be ruled by him or those whose will is less pervertible and corruptible by wicked passions – it is answered that in some way the will of one is less pervertible and corruptible by wicked passions and feelings than the will of many. To make this clear, it is said, it must be known that for the will of many or of a multitude to be pervertible can be understood in two ways: that it is pervertible either in the whole of it, understanding "whole" syncategorematically,[79] or in part. In the first way, the will of many is less pervertible than the will of one.[80] In the second way, the will of many is more pervertible than the will of one given person, for example the will of this person or that person. A multitude can be perverted and corrupted in part more quickly and easily than can one by himself, because upon the corruption of any one of that multitude the multitude itself is

---

[78] That is, to argument [4] of chapter 2 (p. 131 above).
[79] See *Ockham's Theory of Propositions*, pp. 103–4. If "whole" is taken syncategorematically, then "The whole of X is Y" is equivalent to "Every part of X is Y."
[80] That is, that the will of every individual should become perverted is less likely than that the will of any given individual should become perverted.

in that way [i.e., in part] corrupted and perverted, because, though each one is not perverted, some perversion is found in that multitude. It is necessary to the goodness and suitability of the ruler not to be perverted even in part, and it is therefore more beneficial for the community of the faithful to be ruled by the ruler that is less pervertible even in part; and such is one man and not many. It is therefore beneficial for the community of the faithful to be ruled by one rather than by many.

To the text of Aristotle taken from *Politics*, Book III, chapter 8, it is answered that on occasion, when a few are not enough to see perfectly what should be done and what omitted (though in some way they imperfectly understand the matter), then it is beneficial on that occasion for the multitude to meet, not indeed to rule, but to deliberate and discover what is beneficial for the whole community and to advise what the ruler ought to do; and if the ruler were not willing to follow their advice and some serious damage threatened, they would have to correct him. In such a case it would therefore be beneficial for the multitude to meet in that way, because all together are something better than a few and can see more things concerning both character and understanding. But when a few are enough for seeing perfectly what should be done and what omitted, it is not beneficial for the multitude to meet to deal with the matter, but it is better that a few should meet, yet enough. When one is enough it is therefore not necessary for many to meet. If one is not enough to discover what should be done, it is beneficial that he should be able to call together as many as are enough (many or few), and to proceed with their advice, in such a way that they do not rule with him.

From the above it is clear how the text of Aristotle is answered when he suggests that many are more impervertible than one. They say that in one way they are more impervertible, and in another way they are more pervertible: not indeed that all are perverted together more easily than is any one given person, but because perversity is more easily found among them than in one given person, because when any of them is perverted perversity is found among all, though not necessarily in some one given person. The goodness and suitability of the ruler [or ruling body] requires, however, that there should be in it no perversity. Therefore, whenever perversity is found in some multitude, even in only one of that multitude, by that fact that multitude is not suited to rule, according to the text of the Apostle in Galatians 5[:9], "A little yeast ferments the whole mass." It is therefore beneficial for the community of the faithful to be ruled by one, rather than by many ruling together and acting in place of one, because perversity is not as easily found in one as in any multitude, however small, of which that one is a part together with another who can be perverted just as he can.

Student According to that, many should never be called to give advice and neither should the multitude – and not only Aristotle and others, but also this opinion, holds the opposite. For perversity is more easily found in the multitude, and in any group whatever of many persons, than in one alone; but perversity is most of all to be avoided.

Master It is answered that whenever one is enough, so that he does not need either the advice or the support of others, many should not be called, because what can just as well be done by one is done in vain by many. But when one by himself is not enough to see or do perfectly what should be done, then it is beneficial to call many, for advice or help or support, because just as among the many and in the multitude perversity can be found, so among the many and in the multitude greater knowledge, wisdom, and goodness are found. And therefore when one is not enough many should meet – though this can be indifferent to good and to evil, since many meeting together sometimes act well, sometimes badly. Therefore, when it is believed with probability, because of the goodness of those who have to meet, that they will advise and act rightly, action should be taken for them to meet, if one is not enough. When, however, it is found with probability that they will stray from the right paths, they should be prevented from meeting, because it is better to do nothing than to do evil. Thus when some are called to a general council, if it is believed with probability that they will not hold the council rightly, they should be prevented from meeting; if, however, it is believed with probability that they will hold the council rightly, action should be taken for them to meet, unless it is believed that they would do less good than the disadvantage they will incur from their labors and expenses.

Student Now tell how Aristotle's statements which seem to conclude that aristocracy is better and more choice-worthy than kingship are answered.

Master It is answered that Aristotle did not mean to conclude
that aristocracy is simply and always better and more choice-worthy
than kingship even when it is ruled by one best or good man, but
he meant to conclude that aristocracy is sometimes better and more
choice-worthy than kingship. For since the whole multitude of
rulers in an aristocracy is not, in its entirety, as pervertible as any
one who would belong to that multitude, and the prudence and
also the virtue or goodness is greater in the whole multitude than
in one, it can happen that it is better for many to rule aristocratically
than one royally. The one who ruled royally could be perverted
when the others were not perverted, and it is worse for someone
to be perverted when he rules by himself than when he rules with
others; for if he is perverted when he rules with others he can as
a rule do fewer and lesser evils than if he is perverted ruling by
himself; and therefore aristocracy is sometimes better and more
choice-worthy than kingship. Often, however, and more commonly,
and therefore in a way simply, kingship is better than aristocracy,
because of the advantages spoken of above in chapter 18 and many
others. And thus it is that the ancients sometimes reasonably
changed an aristocracy into a kingship and sometimes a kingship
into an aristocracy. Many examples could be given from the Romans
and many other nations, for sometimes kings have ruled and sometimes many together; and many nations, both the Romans and
others, have made such changes.

Chapter 20

Student On the occasion of what you have just related I have
decided that it should be asked whether, according to that opinion,
it is beneficial for the community of the faithful to have the power
to change an aristocratic regime into a regime similar to a royal
regime and vice versa,[81] so that it has power to appoint one highest
pontiff who is over all others and power also to appoint or elect

---

[81] This question occupies chapters 20–7.

many highest pontiffs at the same time who, with equal power, would together rule aristocratically and be over all the other faithful, so that it can change one regime into another indifferently as seems beneficial, as nations have reasonably changed aristocratic rule into royal rule and vice versa.

Master About this there are various opinions. Keeping to the opinion that asserts that sometimes aristocratic government is better for some than royal government and sometimes royal government is better for the same people, one opinion is that it is beneficial for the community of the faithful to have such power to change aristocratic government into the rule of one highest pontiff and vice versa, according as necessity and the quality of the time demands and requires one regime or the other.

Student Bring forward some arguments for that opinion.

Master In favor of this opinion [1] the following argument can be given. Just as it is beneficial that human enactments should change with the change of the times (*Extra, De consanguinitate et affinitate, Non debet reprehensibile*), so it is beneficial that human regimes should change with the change of the times. But Christ's Church chiefly has power over human rulerships in respect of all things that are beneficial to it; therefore it has power to change such rulerships.

Student It could be said that the rulership by which the highest priest rules all the faithful is not human but divine, because it was established by God alone; therefore it is not decent, and consequently not beneficial, that the Church should have power over the papal rulership.

Master This answer is attacked. Although papal rule is divine in that Christ decided that it should exist in the Church, in many respects it seems to be human. For it is for men to decide who should be appointed to it, and who should elect, and who should correct the one appointed if he needs correction, and the like. Therefore, similarly, it will be human in this respect, that it should be decided by men whether one only, or, when beneficial, many, should be appointed to such rulership.

[2] Further, in respect of everything necessary for the things that are special to Christians, provision has been made for the community of the faithful in the best way, and not less well than for any other community or nation; so that in all such matters it

has power in respect of all things that are beneficial and as they are beneficial. But if the Church had power to change a regime that began to be less beneficial into another, more beneficial, regime, it would be better provided for than if it did not have such power; therefore, since in such matters it has been provided for in the best way, it has power to change rule by one into rule by many, if it notices that it is more beneficial to be ruled by many in an aristocratic regime than by one alone.

[3] Again, it is not less beneficial for the community of the faithful to have power to abolish regimes that begin to be burdensome or less useful than to have power to abolish burdensome customs, since nothing can do more harm to the Church than a burdensome and useless regime, according to the opinion of Augustine. As we read in dist. 81, *Nemo*, he says: "No one indeed does more harm in the Church than he who, though acting perversely, has the name or order of holiness and priesthood." From this we gather that nothing does more harm to the Church than a perverse ruler and a perverse regime. Therefore, if the Church notices that the Church is ruled perversely or less usefully because of the fact that one by himself rules over all, it is beneficial for it to have power to change such a regime into another that will be more useful for the time.

[4] Besides, it is not beneficial for the Church to be tied to a regime that can be changed into the worst regime; but the regime in which one rules by himself can be changed into the worst regime, as royal government, even though it is the best, can, so far as it depends on the nature of the rulership, be changed into tyranny, which is the worst regime, as Aristotle in the *Ethics* and the *Politics* asserts and plainly proves. Therefore it is not beneficial for the Church for it to be so restricted to the regime in which one rules by himself that it cannot change it into another regime, namely aristocracy, more useful for the time.

[5] Moreover, as the civil law also testifies, "In new matters for decision, to depart from a law that has seemed fair for a long time, the advantage ought to be evident." We gather from this that innovation should be made for the sake of evident advantage, even so as to depart from a law that has seemed fair for a long time. But a law should not be departed from more than a form of government, because in every community nothing can be more necessary to observe than law; for what is incongruous with the

law should in no way be observed. Therefore, for the sake of evident advantage, innovation should be made, so as to depart from a form of government that has seemed reasonable and fair for a long time. Therefore, if it appears evident to the Church that for some particular time a greater advantage will come to the Church from an aristocratic regime in which many rule the community of the faithful together than from the rule of one, such innovation should be made, so as to depart from the rule of one which has seemed fair and useful for a long time.

[6] Also, what has been introduced for the support and advantage of certain persons should not be turned to their damage and loss. But the regime to which all the faithful should be subject was introduced for the support and advantage of all the faithful; therefore, if a certain kind of regime begins to be damaging to the faithful, or less useful, it is beneficial that that kind of regime should be changed into another more useful for the time. Therefore the Church has power to establish aristocratic government over all the faithful, if they consider that government by one man is beginning to harm the faithful.

[7] Further, according to Pope Leo, as we read in dist. 45, c. *Licet enim*,[82] "A provision made for concord" should not "tend to harm." This implies that whatever was provided for the sake of concord should be abolished if it tends toward harm. But rule by one highest pontiff was provided for the concord of all the faithful, namely that one should be over others "lest schism occur," according to the gloss in the same place;[83] therefore if rule by one highest pontiff tends toward harm, i.e., toward love of dominating or ruling tyrannically, or even to a dangerous schism among Christians – that is, if a greater and temporally more powerful, or equal, part of Christians will in no way tolerate the rule of one highest pontiff and yet will tolerate the aristocratic rule of many ruling at the same time, each of whom is highest pontiff, as sometimes there have been several emperors at the same time, and sometimes there are several judges with equal power in the same case – the rule of the one, similar to royal government, should be abolished at

---

[82] Rather, *Licet nonnunquam.*

[83] See gloss, col. 216, v. *concordiam*: "Namely, that one should rule over others, lest schism occur."

least for the time, and an aristocratic regime should be established, at least until those evils or dangers and others like them cease.

[8] Again, when the reason ceases the effect should cease, *Extra, De appellationibus, Cum cessante*. But the common advantage is the reason why one highest pontiff should be over all the faithful. Therefore, if there comes from the rule of one, not common advantage, but common loss, such rule should cease for then. Therefore the community of the faithful then has power to establish another regime.

[9] Further, in all churches what the greater part judges should be observed ought to be observed: *Extra, De his quae fiunt a maiori parte capituli*, c. 1;[84] dist. 65, c. 1, 2, and 3; *Extra, De electione, Licet*. Therefore, if the greater part of the faithful think that an aristocratic regime should be established over the whole community of the faithful, such a regime ought to be established. From this it follows that the Church or community of the faithful has power to establish such a regime.

Student As the gloss notes upon the quoted chapter, *Extra, De his quae fiunt a maiori parte capituli*, "We do not always conform to the greater part, or the plurality: as here, and in dist. 31, *Nicena*, and above, *De electione, Ecclesia vestra* . . . It is the rule that we conform to the greater part, but the greater part is that which relies on the greater piety and reason: dist. 9, *Sana quippe*; dist. 40, *Multi* at the end; 4, q. 3, para. *Iurisiurandi*." The gloss on dist. 40, upon the last chapter, also seems to take this view. It says: "Not the more distinguished rank, but the action of a better life, is approved, 23, q. 4, *Sicut*, and 16, q. 1, *Sunt nonnulli*. There is here an argument that the party that relies on the juster reason is called the greater, even if it is the smaller: dist. 31, *Nicena*, 19, *In canonicis*; 4, q. 3, para. 2; and *Extra, De testibus, In nostra*." By these it is plainly established that we must *not* always conform to the greater part. Therefore even if the greater part of Christians were to judge that the rule of one should be changed into an aristocratic rule, this should nevertheless not be done.

Master That answer is attacked. Although we should not always conform to the greater part but sometimes to the lesser, nevertheless

---

[84] The remaining references are in the gloss to this chapter of the decretals, col. 1100, v. *Pluribus*.

we should always conform to the greater part unless it is plainly proved by the lesser that we should not conform to the greater part. This is gathered from the gloss on the above-quoted chapter of *De his quae fiunt a maiori parte capituli*, which says, after the words quoted above: "The presumption is in favor of the plurality, dist. 61, *Nullus*, at the end, unless the contrary is proved, as is clear here and in dist. 23, *Illud*, and above, *De electione, Dudum.*" In the same place, on the word *Ostensum*, it says: "It is not enough to object, unless it is proved." Since, therefore, it cannot be proved that we must not conform to the greater part of Christians if, for the common utility, they wish to change the rule of one highest pontiff into aristocratic rule, it follows that in this matter we must conform to the greater part of the faithful.

Student It seems that it *could* reasonably be shown that in this matter we must not conform to the greater part of Christians if it decides to establish aristocratic government over all the faithful. For in contradicting the greater part the lesser part would rely on a juster argument; for the lesser part would then rely on an ordinance of Christ, which prevails over every human ordinance.

Master To some it seems that, even if Christ had ordained that one highest pontiff should rule over all the faithful, the Church could, for the common utility, establish another regime. This is proved as follows. Necessity and utility are of equal force, as Alexander III seems to suggest, *Extra, De qualitate et aetate praeficiendorum, Quaeris.*[85] But for the sake of necessity it is permissible to act against a divine commandment, even one that is explicit, in things not evil in themselves but evil only because they are prohibited. Therefore, also, for the sake of the common utility it is permissible to act against a commandment of God and an ordinance of Christ. Therefore, even if Christ had ordained that one highest pontiff should be set over all the faithful, it would be permissible for the faithful, for the sake of the common utility, to establish some other regime, at least for the time. The major premise seems to have been proved manifestly, and it is also proved from the premise that necessity and piety have equal force, as Gregory IX suggests *Extra, De feriis*, last chapter;[86] but piety includes usefulness;

---

[85] " . . . and the utility of the Church or usefulness persuades."
[86] " . . . unless necessity urges, or piety persuades."

therefore, necessity and utility have equal force, and consequently whatever necessity makes permissible utility also makes permissible. The minor premise is shown in many ways. Bede seems clearly to assert this in his *Commentary on Mark*, quoted in *Extra, De regulis iuris*, c. *Quod non est*. He says, "What is not permissible in the law, necessity makes permissible; for it is also a commandment to observe the sabbath, but the Machabees fought on the sabbath without fault." It seems to be clearly established by these words that the Machabees acted licitly, out of necessity, against an explicit divine command. Christ himself also seems to teach this explicitly in Matthew 12[:4] and Luke 6[:4] when he says that David and those who were with him licitly ate the loaves of offering against a divine commandment, for God explicitly commanded that no one except a priest should eat that bread. From these and a great many other [texts] we gather that the rule, "Necessity has no law," which is asserted in *Extra, De consuetudine, Quanto*, and the rule, "Necessity does not submit to law," *Extra, De observatione ieiuniorum*, c. 2, and the rule, "In the laws necessity is excepted," *Extra, De iureiurando, Querelam*, and the like, should be understood not only of positive human laws, but also of positive divine laws, unless in those divine laws the opposite is laid down expressly, so that "necessity does not submit to" *positive divine* "law." (It is otherwise with natural law, because to that law necessity does submit, and neither can any necessity excuse.)

[10] Further, it is shown that such an ordinance would not conflict with an ordinance of Christ. Christians in the New Law do not have less power to change the regime of priests than those had who were living under the Old Law. But notwithstanding the commandment of God concerning the appointment of one highest pontiff in Exodus 29[:29–30], also found in the *Decreta*, dist. 21, para. 1, David afterwards appointed several highest pontiffs, as we gather from 1 Paralipomenon 24[:5]; and thus the evangelist Luke, in chapter 2,[87] seems to testify that in Christ's time there were several chief priests at the same time. Therefore Christians also have power to appoint several highest pontiffs, even though Christ ordained that some one person should be appointed as highest pontiff.

---

[87] Luke 3:2.

Chapter 21

Student I think you have brought forward rather strong reasons in favor of the above opinion. Try to argue, therefore, in favor of the contrary opinion.

Master That the Church does not have power to change the highest pontificate into an aristocratic regime or into any other whatever seems provable: [1] For as Christ testifies, Matthew 10[:24], the disciple is not above the master, nor the slave above his lord. But all Christians are disciples and slaves of Christ; therefore all Christians do not have power to take away an ordinance of Christ. But Christ ordained and willed that one man should be highest pontiff and head of all Christians. He showed this in his action, when he appointed blessed Peter alone as highest priest. And thus Pope Anacletus, who was alive in the time of the apostles, testifies to this, as we read in dist. 21, c. *In novo*. He says, "In the New Testament the priestly order began, after Christ, from Peter, because to him was first given the pontificate in the Church, when the Lord said to him, 'You are Peter,' etc." Therefore all Christians do not have power to do away with the highest priesthood and establish any other regime whatever.

[2] Further, no Christians, neither the greater part nor the lesser, have power to do away with the oneness of the Church. Anyone who divides the Church must be regarded as a schismatic, and it is not permissible for any multitude of Christians, however great, to bring about a schism in the Church. But the oneness of the Church seems to be based on this, that it has one head under Christ, who rules all, as blessed Cyprian testifies. As we read in 24, q. 1, c. *Loquitur*, he says: "The Lord says to Peter, 'I say to you that you are Peter, and upon this rock I will build my Church.' He builds the Church upon one man; and although after the resurrection he gives equal power to all the apostles and says, 'As the Father has sent me I also send you; receive the Holy Spirit,' yet, to manifest oneness, he determined by his own authority the origin of that oneness beginning from one man. Certainly, the other apostles were what Peter was, endowed in equal fellowship with honor and power, but the beginning proceeds from oneness, to show that the Church of Christ is one ... This oneness we should hold firmly and defend, especially we bishops who preside

in the Church of God, to show that the episcopate itself also is one and undivided; let no one deceive the brotherhood, let no one by faithless duplicity corrupt the truth of the faith. The episcopate is one, and each holds his part of it firmly." From these words we gather that the oneness of the Church, which must be held firmly, proceeds from one, and requires one episcopate; it is therefore not permissible for any multitude of Christians to change the one episcopate into an aristocratic or other regime.

[3] Again, just as there is not, nor can there be, any true Church except the apostolic, so in the Church there is not, nor can there be, any true and permissible first rulership (namely, an episcopate or pontificate) except the apostolic. [Pope] Pelagius, quoting blessed Augustine, seems to testify clearly to this. He says, in 24, q. 1, c. *Pudenda*: "It is certain that there is no other," i.e., no other Church, "except that which is founded on the apostolic root, by whom," i.e., by the apostles, "there can be no doubt the faith itself was spread to the whole world. Although this is very well known to you, let us confirm it by the testimony of blessed Augustine. Hear what this most famous doctor of the Church says in one of his works. He says: 'And if that can in no way rightly be called the Church in which there is schism, it remains that since the Church cannot not exist, it is that which, based through successions of bishops on the root of the Apostolic See, no men's wickedness (even if it is well-known and cannot be excluded, but is judged to be something that must be tolerated by reason of the times) can in any way extinguish.'" From these words we gather that there is in the Church no true rulership except the one which through successions of bishops is continued in the Apostolic See. But if an aristocratic regime, or any other whatever, were established, it would not be apostolic, and would not be based on the Apostolic See through successions of bishops; therefore it would have to be regarded as impermissible.

[4] Moreover, the pope has fullness of power in the Church of God; therefore what the pope cannot do, *a fortiori* neither can any multitude of Christians. But the pope would not be able to decide or enact that after his death, or with his consent and will, there should be in the Church of God a regime other than the highest pontificate, since for all Christians to be ruled by one highest pontiff pertains to the general state of the Church, against which

the pope can make no dispensation, as the gloss seems to testify, 25, q. 1, on the chapter *Quae ad perpetuam*.[88] Therefore, neither can any multitude establish another regime.

[5] Further, no multitude of Christians has power to do anything through which they can fall into the wickedness of heresy. But if any multitude whatever established another regime to which all Christians were subjected, by that act itself they would fall into the wickedness of heresy. They would be trying to take away a privilege of the Roman Church; and, as Pope Nicholas testifies in 22, q. 1,[89] "Anyone who tries to take away a privilege of the Roman Church given by the highest Head of all the churches undoubtedly falls into heresy." Therefore no multitude of Christians can establish a first rulership other than the rulership of the Roman Church, which is based on the fact that one highest pontiff rules over all Christians.

[6] Moreover, in one bishopric there cannot be two bishops, or in one archdiaconate two archdeacons, 7, q. 1, *In Apibus*; therefore, *a fortiori*, in the Church of God there cannot be two or more highest pontiffs. But it is certain that the Church of God should not be entirely without a highest pontiff. Therefore the Church does not have power to establish a principal rulership other than the highest pontificate of one man who rules all others.

[7] Further, it is not permissible for any Christians whatever to make the condition of the Church worse in respect of temporal matters, although it is permissible to improve it, *Extra, De donationibus, Fraternitatem*; *Extra, De restitutione in integrum*, c. 1. Therefore, *a fortiori*, it is not permissible for anyone whatever to make the condition of the Church worse in respect of spiritual matters. But for one highest pontiff to rule all Christians relates to spiritual matters, because such government is spiritual, dist. 10, *Suscipitis*. Therefore it is not permissible for any Christians whatever to change this regime in any way into one that is worse or less good. But an aristocratic regime (and any other) is less good than

---

[88] See gloss, col. 1438, v. *Nulla commutatione*: "From this it is clear that the pope cannot dispense against the general state of the Church or against the articles of faith; for even if all assented to it, the statute would not be valid, but all would be heretics ... But against a state of the Church that is not so general (such as the continence of the priesthood) he can indeed dispense."

[89] Rather, dist. 22, c. 1.

a regime in which one rules by himself, since such a regime is royal or similar to royal. Therefore it is not permissible for any Christians whatever to establish in any way an aristocratic (or other) regime in place of the regime of one highest pontiff.

Chapter 22

Student Because of the great plausibility that the arguments brought forward for both opinions seem to have, I desire to probe them further and to hear how they are answered in accordance with the different opinions. So first relate how the first opinion[90] tries to answer the arguments brought forward in the last chapter. **Master** The first – which is based on the premise that all Christians cannot do anything contrary to an ordinance of Christ – is answered by means of what was laid down in chapter 20,[91] namely that necessity and utility make permissible what would otherwise be impermissible as being contrary to an ordinance of Christ. And therefore, although all Christians are Christ's disciples and slaves and are not above him, nevertheless, from necessity or utility they can do something contrary to an ordinance of his – that is, against his words and deeds according to what at first they seem to express, though not against his intention; for he means that in his words, where he ordains or does something the opposite of which is not at all opposed to the natural law and he does not make explicit that necessity and utility should by no means be excepted, urgent necessity and evident utility are excepted.

An attempt is made to prove this in another way than before. As we read in Matthew 5[:39] Christ commanded his apostles not to resist evil, but if someone struck them on one cheek they should offer the other also; and yet it was permissible for the apostle Paul when he was struck to say to the chief priest, "God will strike you, you whitened wall,"[92] as Augustine testifies in his sermon on the centurion's son, quoted in 23, q. 1, c. *Paratus*. Therefore, just as, according to Augustine in the same place, Christ's commandments concerning patience were "rather to the preparation of the

---

[90] That is, the opinion presented in chapter 20.
[91] See pp. 76–7 above.
[92] Acts 23:3.

heart than to the work done in the open, so that patience with benevolence should be held in the secrecy of the mind, but outwardly we should do what seems beneficial to those to whom we should wish well," so, concerning Christ's ordinance about appointing one highest pontiff, we should do what is more beneficial to his Church, for whose utility he ordained that one highest pontiff should be appointed: namely, so that when it is beneficial for the Church that there should be several, then let there be several to rule the Church aristocratically.

It seems possible to confirm this answer as follows. If it is permissible to act contrary to the words of a more express commandment, then it will be permissible to act contrary to the words of a less express commandment. But the commandments concerning patience that Christ gave to the apostles in Matthew 5[:39–41] were more express than the commandment about appointing one highest pontiff after Peter: because he said expressly, without any condition, qualification, exception, or specification, "But I say to you, do not resist evil," etc.; nowhere, however, is it found that he said, "I say to you that you should appoint a highest pontiff after Peter," or similar words. Therefore, if it is permissible to contravene the express words of Christ about patience but not his intention (just as Christ himself also did, as Augustine attests in the place cited above, where he says: "This is clearly shown, because when the Lord Jesus himself, who was a singular example of patience, was struck in the face, he answered, 'If I have spoken evil charge me with the evil, but if well why do you strike me?' He therefore by no means fulfilled his own commandment if we look to his words, for he did not offer the other cheek to the one who struck him, but rather forbade him to do it"), much more is it permissible for Christians to act against the *not* express words of Christ about appointing a highest pontiff, i.e. so that they appoint not one but several highest pontiffs, when this is beneficial to the Church of Christ.

Christ commanded in express words, not excepting any case, that one should not swear. In Matthew 5[:34] he says, "But I say to you do not swear at all, either by heaven" etc., and afterwards, "Let your speech be 'Yes, Yes, No, No' – what is more than these is from evil." Yet notwithstanding that express commandment of

Christ, it is permissible on occasion to swear: *Extra, De electione, Significasti*; *Extra, De iureiurando, Etsi Christus*; and 22, q. 1, *Non est*, where Augustine asserts that to swear is permissible on account of the weakness or incredulity of those not otherwise moved to belief. Therefore, *a fortiori*, even though Christ made blessed Peter highest pontiff and head of all Christians, it is permissible for Christians, for the sake of the common utility of the whole Church, to appoint several at the same time as highest pontiffs, if this is at some time beneficial.

Again, in Matthew 10[:9–10], Christ expressly commanded the apostles not to possess gold or silver or money and not to have two cloaks or to wear shoes, and yet, when manifest necessity compelled it, it was permissible for them to contravene those commandments – fulfilling, that is, Christ's intention and not his words. He seems himself to suggest this clearly enough when he says to his apostles in Luke 22[:35]: " 'When I sent you without wallet and bag and shoes, was anything lacking to you?' And they said, 'Nothing.' He therefore said to them, 'But now, he who has a wallet, let him take it, and similarly a bag, and he who does not have a sword, let him sell his cloak and buy one.' " From these words Bede draws out a certain general rule, namely, that notwithstanding Christ's commandment, there is one rule of living in a time of peace and another in a time of persecution. From Bede's rule another more general rule can be gathered, namely, that for the sake of necessity and utility it is permissible to contravene an ordinance of Christ. For if, notwithstanding Christ's commandment, there is one rule of living in a time of peace and another in a time of persecution, then, by similar reasoning, notwithstanding Christ's commandment, there is one rule of living in a case of necessity and utility and another outside the case of necessity and utility, since it is only on account of necessity and utility that there is one rule of living in a time of peace and another in a time of persecution; for if there appears no necessity or utility because of persecution, a rule of living – especially one [to which obedience has been] promised – must by no means be abandoned. Because of necessity, therefore, and utility, it is permissible not to fulfill the words of Christ. Therefore, notwithstanding any ordinance whatever of Christ concerning the appointment of one highest pontiff, it will be permissible, if evident utility demands it, to appoint several highest pontiffs to govern the whole body of the faithful aristocratically.

Further, it is permissible for a reason to defer the election of the highest pontiff; therefore it is permissible for a time to appoint others to govern the community of the faithful.

Chapter 23

Student The arguments above and some others brought forward earlier are based on the premise that it is permissible to contravene the words of a commandment of God and of Christ, though not the purpose or intention of the giver of the commandment. These statements seem to have some plausibility. I will therefore make objections against their basis, so that I may better understand both the basis and the above arguments and others like them and so that I can perceive whether they contain anything of truth.[93]

It seems, therefore, that it is in no way permissible to contravene the words of a commandment of God or Christ, either on account of necessity or on account of utility. Of similars the same judgment must be held; therefore we must think the same way of any divine commandment whatever and of them all. But the divine commandment not to dissolve a marriage between man and wife obliges in such a way that in no case except the case expressed by Christ, namely the case of fornication, is it permissible to send away a wife for any necessity or utility whatever, as Christ himself testifies in Matthew 5[:32] and 19[:9], and in Mark 10[:11]. Therefore every commandment of God and of Christ obliges in such a way that in no case not expressed by God or by Christ would it be permissible to contravene the divine commandment on account of necessity and utility.

Further, if it were permissible to contravene a divine commandment on account of necessity and utility, it would be permissible to change all the sacraments of Christ on account of necessity and utility. For no one is obliged to any sacraments whatever except because of a divine commandment; it would therefore be permiss-

---

[93] On this topic see above, chapters 20 (at the end) and 21, and chapters 23 and 24; see also *Short Discourse*, pp. 45–7, 59.

ible, on account of necessity and utility, not to baptize, or to baptize in another way than was established by Christ, for example in wine or some other liquid, if water could not be had and baptism could not be deferred; it would be permissible also to make the body of Christ of some other bread besides wheaten, when wheaten bread could not be had; it would also be permissible, when wine could not be had, to make the blood of Christ of water or some other liquid. And thus it would be permissible to change all the sacraments on account of necessity and utility.

Again, no one is permitted to contravene the words of any commandment unless he has power to dispense against such a commandment or to interpret that commandment. But no one can dispense against divine commandments or interpret those commandments; therefore, no one is permitted to contravene the words of a divine commandment.

From these [arguments] it follows that if Christ ordained that one highest pontiff should be set over all the faithful, it will in no way be permissible for any Christians whatever to appoint several at the same time as highest pontiffs. Those are the arguments that seem to me rather effectively to disprove the above assertion. So relate how they are answered, and begin with the last, because perhaps some answers to the others will depend on it.

Chapter 24

Master That objection mentions two things, a power to dispense against a commandment of God or of Christ, and a power to interpret a commandment of God or of Christ. As to the [1] first, it is said that no Christians whatever have power to dispense against a commandment of God or of Christ, unless interpretation or declaration of the law is called dispensation. This is how the gloss upon 25, q. 1, c. *Sunt quidam* seems to speak. It says that "the pope dispenses from the gospel by interpreting it."[94] The assertion of some jurists seems to harmonize with this. They say, "Declaration or commutation is called dispensation; thus he," i.e., the pope, "can dispense from a vow, and from things which are done by

---

[94] See gloss, col. 1439, v. *Apostoli.*

divine and natural law, provided there is necessity or utility and compensability."[95]

[2] Concerning the power to interpret a commandment of God or of Christ and, consequently, to dispense in the above way, the studious can perceive what should be said (according to a certain opinion) from our extensive disputation concerning the power to interpret the statements and enactments of others in the first part of our dialogue, Book VI.[96] I will relate a few things from it, adding some. It is said, therefore, that interpretation of some statement or commandment or statute, divine or natural or human, is necessary only because of the ignorance of some one for whom an interpretation is necessary, because "where the words are not doubtful there is no room for interpretation," as the gloss notes, *Extra, De consuetudine*, upon the chapter *Cum dilectus*.[97] Interpretation therefore pertains to anyone who knows the true meaning of what has to be interpreted, that is, when someone else is in doubt about its true meaning. But many experts know the true meaning of the commandments of God and Christ. They can interpret those commandments to those who do not know, because such interpretation is nothing but an exposition, clarification, or making manifest of the true meaning of God's commandments. And thus Christians have power sometimes to interpret a divine commandment, namely when they know its true meaning. If, however, the true meaning of some commandment of God were not known, because God's intention in making the commandment was not known and could not be known through reasoning or through other Scriptures but only by a revelation of God – as, according to some, the true literal meaning of many of the prophecies included in the Book of the Apocalypse and in other prophetic writings cannot be known except through a new revelation – then the interpretation of such a commandment must be awaited from God alone. But the meaning of God's commandments or ordinances about preserving patience, not making oaths, not carrying a wallet or a bag, and about appointing a highest pontiff, and of many other commandments, is known by many Christians, and can be known through reasoning and the Scriptures; Christian experts can therefore interpret such com-

---

[95] The source has not been found.
[96] See I *Dial.*, 6.100.
[97] See gloss to the decretals, col. 94, v. *iuri communi*.

mandments or ordinances, and they ought to be observed according to the true interpretation. And "we must not always stick to the words," even of Christ, "but to the intention," according to the gloss, 23, q. 1, on the chapter *Paratus*, which in that place speaks specifically of the words of Christ.[98]

Student According to these ideas it would be no more permissible for the pope to interpret the words of God and Christ than for anyone else wise and learned in sacred literature, and we would not have to believe the pope in such matters more than any other wise man.

Master It is answered that it is not permissible for the pope to interpret the words of God or Christ otherwise than it is for another, nor do we have to believe him in such matters more than any other wise man – indeed, in such matters those more expert than the pope should be preferred to the pope himself, as we read in dist. 20, para. 1, where we read that in explaining the sacred Scriptures those who treat of the divine Scriptures are preferred to the highest pontiffs. However, if the pope's exposition or interpretation is Catholic, containing no error, it is in some way more authoritative than the interpretation of another learned man, because from then on it will not be permissible for anyone knowingly to opine and hold the opposite in public. This is not true of the same interpretation if it were only that of another learned man, because if it were not about something that one was obliged to believe explicitly, it would be permissible, despite this interpretation, for another, expressing an opinion in public, to hold the opposite, though not pertinaciously. If, however, the pope's interpretation were erroneous and not in harmony with the truth, it would be permissible for anyone knowing that it is not in harmony with the truth to reject it openly and publicly, and anyone knowing this would be obliged, of necessity for salvation, to attack it, according to place and time.

Student According to these ideas the pope could in no way dispense against the Apostle or against sacred Scripture. The gloss to 25, q. 1, on the chapter *Sunt quidam*,[99] seems to hold the opposite of this. It says, "It can be maintained that the pope

---

[98] See gloss, col. 1285, v. *Si verba*.
[99] See gloss, col. 1439, v. *Apostoli*.

dispenses against the Apostle, but not in matters that pertain to the articles of faith."

Master It is said that the gloss here takes "dispense" for interpreting or clarifying the Apostle's meaning; this the pope can do.

Student In this way the pope can dispense in matters that pertain to the articles of faith, which, however, the gloss denies. For he can clarify the true meaning of things that pertain to the articles of faith, as also of other things.

Master It is answered that he cannot interpret the articles of faith included in the Creed, of which the gloss speaks, otherwise than as they have been interpreted, because in respect of their literal sense they have been sufficiently interpreted and clarified. But the pope can, if he is an expert, interpret in a new interpretation [the sense] of many other things found in the sacred Scriptures, because they are not found in particular to have been interpreted by earlier interpreters in such a way that they do not need, for many simple people, and indeed for experts, a new and explicit interpretation, which many, even learned men, do not know how to gather from all the writings of highest pontiffs and of those who treat of the divine Scriptures; and none of the highest pontiffs or doctors is, or was, so expert that he has not been and could not be able, continually and always, even if he lived a thousand years or more, to advance in the understanding of divine Scripture, by newly finding Catholic literal senses (which are the foundation of all other senses) by studying the sacred Scriptures; this is because of the difficulty of understanding sacred Scripture in various places.

Student You have said enough about this objection. Now relate how the first objection I brought forward in the last chapter is answered.

Master To that argument it is said that we should hold a similar judgment about similars when it is not prohibited, either explicitly or implicitly, to hold a similar judgment. However, where it is explicitly or implicitly prohibited to hold a similar judgment about similars, there we should not hold a similar judgment about similars. Because Abraham received the command about sacrificing his son, he was obliged to prepare himself to kill his innocent son; and yet he was obliged to take care not to kill other innocents, because it was commanded to him simply to sacrifice his son, and not others, and he could therefore not have drawn any other meaning from the words of the commandment except that which they first expressed. And they were so explicit, being free from all ambiguity, that there was there no room for interpretation, and he could not have drawn any other meaning. And by reasoning, also, he could have drawn no other meaning from these words of God, since he was not ignorant that God was the lord of life and death. Therefore, even if there were a similarity between God's commandment not to dissolve a marriage or not to send away a wife and any other commandment of God, nevertheless, a similar judgment does not and would not have to be held in all respects concerning that commandment and any other commandment of God whatever, because in excepting one special case in which it is permissible to send away a wife Christ prohibited other cases, because "what is conceded of one is denied of the others" (dist. 25, c. *Qualis*;[100] 15, q. 3, *De crimine*; dist. 45, c. *Disciplina*; 1, q. 1, *Per Esaiam*); this rule holds where the argument from the opposite sense holds, which is very strong in the law, as the laws say.[101] But in many other commandments of God and Christ special cases are not excepted explicitly. Therefore in them one case should not be understood to be excepted more than another. We must therefore gather from other places of divine Scripture whether some case should be excepted though it is not expressed, whether there is the same reason for excepting such a case in one commandment and in another, and whether the commandments are similar in kind (for example, whether they are natural commandments or positive commandments or one natural and the other positive). If they are simply commandments of natural law, no case should be excepted for any necessity or utility whatever, unless God specially excepted some case (as, notwithstanding the commandment of purely natural law about not knowingly killing the innocent, God made a special exception in commanding Abraham to sacrifice his son). If, however, they are purely positive commandments, a case of necessity and utility should be excepted in the same way in one as in another, unless it can be especially gathered from the Scriptures that in some such commandment a case of necessity and

---

[100] See gloss, col. 126, *Casus* (which mentions the argument from the opposite sense), and v. *Negatur*, which seems to be the source of the other references.

[101] See gloss to *Digest*, 1.21.1, v. *Fortissimum*, col. 114.

utility should not be excepted. And in that way similar judgment can be held concerning similar commandments.

To the argument following it is answered that it does not follow from the foregoing that it is permissible to change all the sacraments. To change a commandment is one thing, to omit a commandment is another, and similarly to change sacraments is one thing and to omit sacraments is another. Therefore, although it is sometimes permissible to omit some sacraments, it is not permissible to change them. Consequently it is not permissible for anyone to baptize in wine or in a liquid other than water, or to make the body of Christ except in wheaten bread and in wine; on occasion, however, it is permissible because of necessity or utility to omit some sacraments.

Chapter 25

Student Now explain how it is maintained that it is permissible for Christians, on account of utility or necessity, to appoint several highest pontiffs, even though it is not permissible for them to divide the oneness of the Church, which is based on this, that one head under Christ rules all. On this was based the second argument brought forward above in chapter 21.

Master It is answered that it is not permissible for any Christians to divide the oneness of the Church, but the oneness of the Church can continue without the oneness of a highest pontiff; for while the Apostolic See is vacant the oneness of the Church remains, and thus while a highest pontiff does not exist the oneness of the Church can persist. Neither is the Church divided because it has no highest pontiff; otherwise the Church would often be divided, since there is often no highest pontiff. And thus the Church is free from all division without one highest pontiff, and consequently from the fact that several highest pontiffs ruled the Church at the same time it could not be inferred that the Church had been divided.

To the text of blessed Cyprian it is answered that he speaks with reference to a case in which several presented themselves in discord as highest pontiff in such a way that each of them said that the pontificate and the Church was with him alone, as happened in the time of blessed Cyprian with Cornelius and Novatian; because of their discord Cyprian spoke the words quoted above, knowing that Cornelius was the true highest pontiff and not Novatian. If, however, for necessity or utility, without discord, and with the consent of the faithful, several at the same time occupied the Apostolic See and ruled God's Church in concord, from such a plurality of highest pontiffs no danger of division would result, because there would be no division either among the highest pontiffs themselves or among their subjects: just as, if there were in the same bishopric several bishops mutually helping one another, there would not on this account be any division in that bishopric.

From this an argument is taken to prove that, without any separation and division in the Church, there could, for necessity or utility, be several highest pontiffs at the same time. For the same right exists in the part as in the whole and in small matters as in great; but in the same bishopric there can be two bishops at the same time, 7, q. 1, c. *Non autem*, c. *Petisti*, and c. *Quia vero*;[102] similarly, therefore, there could be, because of necessity or utility, several highest pontiffs at the same time. Although it has never happened, it could happen, just as neither before Augustine's time nor afterwards do we read that while there was a bishop existing in good health another was appointed bishop in the same bishopric, and yet we read that this was done in the case of blessed Augustine. In 7, q. 1, c. *Non autem* we read: "But we have not written only this as a matter for thankfulness, that Augustine obtained a bishopric, but that by God's grace the African Church merited this care, that it should receive heavenly words from Augustine's lips; having been advanced in a new way to the greater grace of an office of the Lord's, he was consecrated in such a way that he did not succeed a bishop in the chair, but, acceding to the church while Valerius, bishop of the Church of Hippo, was in good health, Augustine was made co-bishop." If, therefore, for the utility of the Church of Hippo there were several bishops at the same time in the Church of Hippo, *a fortiori* for the utility of the whole Church there can be at the same time several apostolics.[103]

Student Against this is the gloss on the same chapter *Non autem*, which says in these words: "Could there be in the same way two

---

[102] 7, q. 1, c. 42, para. *Qui vero.*

[103] The pope was sometimes called "the Apostolic", presumably because of the tradition that the see of Rome was founded by the apostles Peter and Paul.

apostolics? An argument that there could not: above, the same [question], c. *Factus*. And the Lord appointed only one: 24, q.1, *Loquitur*, and c. *Quicunque*. Dispensation from this is not possible, 25, q.1, *Sunt quidam*. Moreover, because the Catholic Church is one and has one head. However, we read that there have been several emperors. But here it is not thus, because the rule 'One holy Church' would be violated." From these words we gather that for there to be several apostolics at the same time conflicts with an article of faith, namely the article "One holy Catholic Church." **Master** It is answered that the gloss does not speak there assertively but only argumentatively; thus it says, "An argument that there could not"; and therefore it does not decide for that side but only argues for it. These arguments do imply that there cannot be two opposed and discordant apostolics of whom both or either says and asserts that he alone is the apostolic and not the other, or of whom either was not lawfully appointed as apostolic.

The cited chapter *Factus* speaks in reference to such a case, because it speaks of Cornelius and Novatian, of whom Cornelius had been elected correctly and lawfully, as the same chapter asserts and testifies. And Novatian usurped the apostolic rank not for the necessity or utility of the Church but out of ambition, with scandal and division of the Church, as the following chapter testifies. In it we read: "Novatian is not a bishop. While Cornelius was bishop in the church, made bishop by twenty-six bishops, he [Novatian], an adulterer and an outsider, tries through ambition to be made a bishop by deserters." Concerning this we read in *Ecclesiastical History*, Book VI, chapter 35, as follows: "Novatus, a priest of the Roman Church, puffed up by a certain pride, quite took from them [the lapsed] the hope of salvation, even if they had repented worthily. From that time also he was the leader of the heresy of the 'Novatians,' who, having separated from the Church, called themselves by the proud name of 'Cathars,' i.e., 'the pure.' Because of this affair a very well attended priestly council, of sixty bishops and the same number of priests also together with very many deacons, was assembled in the city of Rome. Further, also, after great deliberation about this matter, what must be done is made known by decrees throughout every single province. It is enacted, therefore, that Novatus is outside the Church, together with those who were following this man puffed up with pride of mind and turned toward that inhuman opinion preserving nothing of fraternal charity." And below: "There is extant also another letter of Cornelius written to Fabian, bishop of Antioch, relating every particular about Novatus – who he was, and what sort of a person in life or character, and how he turned away from the Church – in which he [Cornelius] reports that he fell into all these evils from a desire he bore secretly within himself for a bishopric ... Sidonius and Celerinus were regarded as very famous among confessors because they overcame all kinds of torments. 'But,' he says, 'when they had seen more carefully that he,' " i.e., Novatus, " 'did everything by frauds and deception, lies and perjuries, and that he only pretended goodness so as to deceive the ignorant, they left, or rather execrated, him and went back with great satisfaction to the Church, and in the presence of the priests and bishops, and also of laymen, they confess first indeed their own error and then also his frauds and deceptions.' He added, moreover, in this letter, that 'whereas he was accustomed to swear to his brethren that he did not at all desire a bishopric, suddenly and unexpectedly, as if he were a new creature, he appeared as a bishop – indeed, the man who championed discipline and church customs presumptuously took to himself a bishopric he had not got from God. When three bishops, very simple men and ignorant of everything, had been invited (rather, deceived by his subtle snares) from a remote part of Italy, he extorted from them an imaginary, rather than a lawful, imposition of hands' ... And he added also that Novatus was in his youth troubled by an unclean spirit, and after he had wasted a considerable time with exorcists he fell into a serious illness, so that he was despaired of; and because of necessity, he was sprinkled while lying on a bed, and the remaining things that customarily follow baptism were in his case not ceremoniously completed, and the signing with chrism was not completed; hence he was never worthy of the Holy Spirit." From these words we gather that Novatus was unworthy of the supreme bishopric and that he usurped the priesthood unlawfully and practised many frauds and deceptions; he therefore divided the Church. But if, being worthy, he had been appointed by the unanimous consent of Catholics, the Church would not on this account have been divided.

Neither does a plurality of apostolics governing the Church in concord conflict with the oneness of the Church, just as a plurality of bishops does not conflict with the oneness of the episcopate, nor a plurality ruling aristocratically in a city destroy the oneness of the city. Neither on this account would there be a violation of the article of faith, "one, holy, catholic Church"; a plurality of apostolics appointed for necessity or utility with the unanimous consent of the faithful would not make several Churches, but the Church would remain one, because of the oneness of faith and the concord "in the same mind and in one judgment"[104] of the apostolics ruling over the rest of the orthodox.

Therefore, when Cyprian says, as was quoted,[105] that "the beginning proceeds from oneness, to show that the Church of Christ is one," it is answered that when necessity or utility does not require a plurality of apostolics – and it is with reference to this case that Cyprian was speaking – one man should be the apostolic, so that Christ's Church is shown to be one not only by the oneness of faith, of baptism, and of the other things the Apostle enumerates in Ephesians 4[:3–6], but also by the oneness of the apostolic in whom Catholics unanimously agree. But when necessity or utility demands several apostolics, it is enough that the Church be one by the oneness of the things the Apostle enumerates in Ephesians 4; by the oneness of these things it is one when, while the Apostolic See is vacant, the Church is subject neither to one nor to several apostolics. Among these things he [Paul] does not include "one apostolic" when he speaks of the oneness of the Church. He says, "Careful to preserve the oneness of the spirit in the bond of peace, one body and one spirit, just as you have been called in one hope of your calling: one Lord, one faith, one baptism, one God and father of all, who is above all and throughout all things and in us all." In these things the faithful must preserve oneness, whether they have some apostolic or none: whether, also, they have one apostolic or several. However, whenever it is beneficial, the Church should have one apostolic, and the oneness of the Church would not be shown unless, when it was beneficial and possible, the Church was subject to one apostolic.

Cyprian means the above words in that way. This is shown by his words following (also quoted above), when he says: "This

---

[104] 1 Corinthians 1:10.
[105] See above, chapter 21.

oneness we should hold firmly and defend, especially we bishops who preside in the Church of God, to show that the episcopate itself also is one and undivided." From these words we gather that, according to blessed Cyprian, not only the apostolate but also the episcopate should be one and undivided, and yet, as was proved above, in the same bishopric there can be for necessity or utility several bishops at the same time: and, consequently, in the apostolic office there can be several apostolics, for otherwise less provision would have been made in necessities for the apostolic office than for the episcopate. Therefore, just as there can be several bishops in the same bishopric, so there can be several apostolics in the apostolic office, and yet both the episcopate and the apostolic office will remain one and undivided because of the oneness of wills and the other things the Apostle enumerates (just as, because of the oneness of the wills of the many ruling aristocratically in the same city, the city remains one, its oneness being sometimes better preserved by many than if one ruled alone); though if nothing particular stood in the way, it would be better ruled by one.

Chapter 26

Student Turn to the other arguments brought forward above in chapter 21 and relate briefly how they are answered.

Master To the argument [3] based on the premise that there is no true rulership in the Church except the apostolic, such as government by several presiding over the orthodox would not be, it is answered that even if there were several ruling over Catholics because of necessity or utility, their government would nevertheless be apostolic and each of them would truly be a successor of blessed Peter and a vicar of Christ, just as, if there were several emperors, each of these would be a true emperor. So even if there were several apostolics at the same time, if several of one mind, for the common utility, and by willing concord of the faithful, occupied the Apostolic See at the same time, the Church would truly be based on the apostolic root, and the regime would be the apostolic regime truly continued through the successions of bishops without any division: just as the empire of the Romans was one and the same continued through successions of emperors both when there were several emperors at the same time and when there was one alone. Thus also there have sometimes been in various kingdoms several kings at the same time, namely father and son, and yet the kingdom was the same and was continued through successions of kings.

Student If, however, there were several apostolics at the same time, they would rule the totality of the faithful aristocratically, and their government would have to be regarded as aristocratic. But the apostolic regime is not aristocratic but royal, according to the text of 1 Peter 2[:9], "You are a chosen race, a royal priesthood," and in Apocalypse [1:6] blessed John says that he has made us a priestly kingdom. Therefore, if there were several apostolics the royal regime would have been changed to aristocratic and consequently would not be apostolic.

Master It is answered that the apostolic regime would not have been changed into another, because there would not be in the regime any variation of power but merely a plurality of rulers, not by a necessity of the rulership but because of another utility or necessity. But aristocratic government differs from royal government more through different power than through the unity and plurality of ruler and rulers, because aristocratic government differs from royal government at least in this respect, that one of those ruling aristocratically cannot perform the things that pertain to aristocratic government without special commission from another;[106] this is not so in royal government, and would not be so in government by several apostolics, if there were several at the same time.

Student Say how [4] the next argument is answered.

Master It is answered in many ways. In one way that the pope does not have power to appoint another to be highest pontiff because the highest pontiff ought to be appointed by the faithful; and the pope therefore does not have complete fullness of power. In another way it is said that the pope does not have as a rule, but [would have] on occasion, power to appoint another to be highest pontiff, namely when he saw some danger threatening the faithful or the faith if another were not appointed, or saw some singular utility if another were appointed, and he could not conveniently seek the consent of the faithful and there were danger

---

[106] That is, the other members of the regime have to commission one to act on their behalf.

in delay. But when it is said that the pope cannot dispense against the general state of the Church, it is answered that regularly the pope cannot dispense against things explicitly or implicitly contained in the sacred Scriptures, and also not against things that pertain to the rights of others; on occasion, however, and for a just and reasonable cause, he can bring in novelties that do not conflict with the faith. And therefore, for reasonable cause, he could appoint another as highest pontiff, in the same way as blessed Peter, according to some, made another man highest pontiff while he himself was still alive; as a rule, however, the pope cannot do this, and if he does so it does not hold good.

[5] To the next argument it is said that in appointing for a reason several highest pontiffs the faithful would by no means fall into heretical wickedness, because they would not take from the Roman Church a privilege given it by Christ: because it would remain the same Roman Church, with power to appoint for itself and for the totality of the faithful one highest pontiff – and also, when beneficial, several.

[6] To the next it is said that there can be two bishops in one bishopric, as happened in the time of blessed Jerome concerning Augustine and Valerius, who were at the same time bishops of the Church of Hippo, as was shown above.

Student The gloss on that chapter (7, q. 1, *Non autem*) seems to say that Valerius and Augustine did not rule the same bishopric at the same time.

Master It is said that if such a gloss existed it would manifestly corrupt the text. The text says explicitly that "While Valerius, bishop of the Church of Hippo, was in good health, Augustine was made co-bishop"; but if Valerius had resigned, Augustine would not have been made co-bishop; therefore they ruled the same bishopric at the same time. The gloss does not assert the contrary but speaks as raising a doubt, saying that "perhaps" Valerius resigned the administration to Augustine.

To Jerome it is said that he meant that as a rule and without some just reason there should not be several bishops in the same bishopric; for a reason, however, there can be.

[7] To the last, it is answered that if the faithful, for a sufficiently moving and persuasive necessity or utility, appointed several highest pontiffs, they would not worsen the condition of the Church in

respect of spiritual matters but would improve it, because in such a case it would be beneficial for the Church to be ruled by many rather than by one. When it is said that aristocratic government, and any other, is less good than royal government, it is answered that as regards the nature of the rulership it is less good, yet sometimes it is in some way better than royal government, just as many medicines are in themselves worse than the food that is suitable to healthy people and yet are sometimes better for certain sick people. And therefore, although as regards the nature of the thing it is better that one should rule by himself because, as the gloss says on the oft-quoted chapter 7, q. 1, *Non autem*, "Administration is dispatched by one more easily than by many, *ff.*, *De administratione*, *Tutor*, l. 3, last para.," and this commonly has truth: yet not always, because on occasion it can be better that many should rule, and sometimes administration is dispatched by many more easily than by one.

Chapter 27

Student You have reported how, according to one opinion, the arguments showing that the faithful cannot appoint several apostolics at the same time are answered. Now relate how answer is made according to the contrary opinion to the contrary arguments brought forward above in chapter 20 of this second book, by which it is shown that it is permissible for the faithful to appoint several rulers over the community of the faithful: either that they can establish another regime than the apostolic, or merely that they can promote several at the same time to apostolic status.

Master According to those who hold that there can in no way be several apostolics at the same time, [1] the answer made to the first argument is that human enactments that do not conflict with divine commandments can be changed, and so also it is permissible to interchange regimes that are not at all opposed to a divine ordinance, but not regimes one of which would be in conflict with a divine ordinance. For there to be several apostolics at the same time would conflict with the ordinance of Christ, who appointed one, and therefore it is not permissible to appoint several apostolics at the same time.

[2] To the second it is said that in respect of all necessary things the best provision has been made for the community of the faithful, in that by loving and obeying God all things work together for the good of the faithful, according to the Apostle;[107] and therefore, although sometimes it would be better and more beneficial for several apostolics (rather than one) to preside if it were not against the ordinance of Christ, it is, nevertheless, better and more beneficial for Christians to be subject to and to obey one apostolic rather than several, because of Christ's ordinance.

[3] To the other it is answered that customs that are in harmony with Christ's ordinance, however much they began to be burdensome, could not be abolished by Christians. Just as divine laws given to the Jewish people, though they were burdensome (according to words of Peter that we read in Acts 15[:10]), could not be abolished by that people, so even if government by one apostolic alone began to be burdensome, it could not be abolished but would have to be borne with, just as bad prelates must be borne with.

[4] To the next it is answered that it is beneficial for the Church, because of the good of obedience, to be bound, if it is God's will, to a regime that can be changed into the worst, just as because of the good of obedience it is beneficial for a church, because of God's commandment, to obey even the worst prelate; and therefore, although the rule of one highest pontiff could be changed by his wickedness into the worst, because he can become a tyrant, nevertheless, because of the good of obedience, it is beneficial for the Church to endure it.

[5] To the next argument it is answered that for the sake of evident utility innovation should be made so as to depart from that human law which has seemed just for a long time, but for no utility should any departure be made from a divine law that has seemed just for a long time. So, also, a departure should be made for the sake of evident utility from a regime humanly established, but not from the regime established by Christ, just as it was not permissible for the Jews for any utility to depart from the levitical priesthood. But the apostolic regime was divinely instituted in such a way that one alone should rule. This regime must therefore not

---

[107] Romans 8:28.

be transformed for the sake of any utility into an aristocratic or other regime, and in no way will it be permissible for the faithful to appoint several apostolics.

[6] To the next it is answered that government by a highest pontiff can be damaging to Christians only because of the wickedness of the ruling highest pontiff or because of the wickedness of subjects; that regime must therefore not be changed into another, but those because of whom it tends to harm, or because of whom damage happens to Christians, should be corrected.

[7] Through the same [argument] it is answered to the other, that sometimes when something provided for harmony tends to harm because of the wickedness of some, it must not be abolished, but those because of whom it tends to harm must be corrected.

[8] To the next it is said that the effect does not always cease when the cause ceases, as is clear in many cases.

[9] To the next it is answered (as it was answered)[108] that it is not true that we must always conform to the greater part or to the plurality; and therefore, even if the greater part of Christians wished to appoint several apostolics at the same time, we would not be obliged to conform to them, because the lesser part would rely on the greater reason: namely, the ordinance of Christ, who appointed one apostolic alone. To the arguments on the other side it is said that it is *not* permissible to act against an explicit divine commandment for the sake of necessity, except when it can be gathered from the Scriptures that in the divine laws necessity is excepted. But it cannot be established from the Scriptures that any necessity was excepted in Christ's ordinance about appointing one apostolic, and therefore neither because of necessity nor because of utility should several apostolics be appointed.

[10] To the last it is answered that David made that division of the priests by divine inspiration; and therefore, if God ordered it, several apostolics could be appointed, but without a divine commandment this could never lawfully be done.

Chapter 28

Student You have related, according to one opinion, that it would be permissible for Christians, when it was beneficial, to appoint

---

[108] By the Student in chapter 20.

several apostolics. Now indicate whether, according to the same opinion,[109] it is permissible in any case to appoint several patriarchs or primates having no superior, none of whom should be regarded as an apostolic.

Master According to one mode of asserting the above opinion, it would be permissible to appoint several such patriarchs or primates if it were beneficial to the community of the faithful. It asserts this because of several circumstances which were brought forward above in chapter 20 of this second book to prove that it would be permissible to have several apostolics at the same time. According to the other mode of assertion this would in no way be permissible.[110]

Student Explain according to the first mode of assertion other possible cases in which it would be permissible to have several such patriarchs or primates.

Master It is said that one case would be if the pope and cardinals became heretics and the Romans supported them or would not elect a Catholic as highest pontiff. Then it would be permissible for any province, and for as many provinces and regions as agreed in wishing it, to elect for themselves one primate to preside over everyone else in spiritual cases; and therefore, if some provinces agreed on one and others on another, several such primates not having a superior, none of whom would be an apostolic, could be over Christians until the whole body of the faithful was cared for by an apostolic.

Another case would be if, because of the heresy of the pope or discord among the electors, the Apostolic See were vacant for a long time, so that the common affairs of the Church could not be dispatched by it (as it sometimes has been vacant for six years). Then it would be permissible for the provinces that wished to do so to appoint themselves a primate in the above way to dispatch the common affairs of those provinces.

Another case would be if all Catholics except a few were oppressed in such a way by internal war or by unbelievers or schismatics, or in some other way, that they could not have recourse to a true apostolic, yet different provinces could meet to set up

---

[109] That is, the opinion presented in chapter 20.

[110] For the two modes see above, chapter 9. The second mode postulates that the many rulers rule together over the same subjects at the same time, which excludes the hypothesis considered in the present chapter.

one head for themselves. Then it would be permissible for any province, and for as many provinces as were able and willing, to appoint for themselves one primate who would have power over them all. Thus some provinces in one part of the world could appoint for themselves one primate and others in another part of the world another, and therefore several such patriarchs or primates could licitly come into being.

Student Bring forward some arguments to show that in those cases, or others, several such primates or patriarchs could be appointed.

Master This seems provable. For as we read in dist. 1, c. *Ius civile*, each city and people can, for a divine and human reason, establish its own law. The gloss there on the word "city" says, "Thus any church enacts law for itself, as below, dist. 11, *Catholicam*, and *De consecratione*, dist. 3, *Pronunciandum*." And on the word "human" it says, "That is, in contemplation of God and men" (that is, because of reverence for God and the advantage of men). From these [words] we gather that each church and each Christian people can by its own authority enact its own law for its advantage; therefore, by analogy, or *a fortiori*, it can appoint itself a head and prelate because of reverence for God and the advantage of men, because the existence of law in a city is of little importance unless there are some who can delimit and secure rights, *ff.*, *De origine iuris*, l. 11.[111]

Further, anyone permitted to resign his right is permitted to accept a superior over himself. But patriarchs, and primates are permitted to resign their right for the common advantage; therefore much more are they permitted to accept a superior over themselves for the common advantage. But if it is permitted to bishops, patriarchs and primates, much more is this permitted to inferiors; and consequently they can if they wish appoint over themselves one head whom all would be under.

Student This opinion seems to conflict with the sacred canons, which enact and assert that a new office cannot be established without permission of the pope: *Extra, De constitutionibus, Cum accessisset*; dist. 22, c. 1; *Extra, De consuetudine, Cum olim*.

Master It is answered that when it is possible to have recourse to the pope no new office should be established without the pope's

---

[111] *Digest*, 1.2.13.

permission, and the sacred canons speak in reference to this case. But when it is not possible to have recourse to a Catholic pope, then, for the common advantage, it is permissible in some way to establish a new office, to last at least until it is possible to have recourse to a pope. For just as "difficulty" admits or "permits something that otherwise would be prohibited" (as the gloss notes, *Extra, De ecclesiis aedificandis,* on the chapter *Ad audientiam*), so also impossibility admits or permits something that would otherwise be prohibited; therefore, it is permissible, because of an impossibility of having recourse to the pope, to appoint such patriarchs or primates, even though this is prohibited by the sacred canons. These must be understood to speak with reference to a time when it is possible to have recourse to the pope. Just as canons that prohibit certain excommunicates to be absolved by anyone but the pope must be understood [to apply] when the excommunicate can have recourse to the pope, not when he is prevented from having recourse to the highest pontiff, *Extra, De sententia excommunicationis, Quamvis* (and the same is found in many other sacred canons), so also, when it is impossible or inexpedient to have recourse to the pope, a new primate can be appointed without the pope's permission, if it is beneficial and necessary to some nation or region or regions or provinces; and he will have authority and power, at least until the pope lawfully and usefully decides otherwise.

Chapter 29

Student You have reported answers to several arguments brought forward above in chapter 2 of this book to prove that it is not beneficial for the community of the faithful to be under one head under Christ.[112] On the occasion of these answers we have treated of some other annexed matters, concerning which you have reported certain opinions and certain modes of assertion, which I do not want dealt with further at present. Leaving those to another time, therefore, relate how answer is made to the second argument brought forward in chapter 2 of this second book – but briefly, because I intend to discuss its basis with you more thoroughly at another time.[113]

---

[112] See above, chapters 15 and 19.
[113] See above, p. 128, and below, p. 280.

Master That argument seems to be based on the premise that without riches, which the head of the faithful should not have, no one can effectively and usefully rule subjects. To this it is answered that the power of ruling Christians in the matters that pertain to the Christian law was established by God alone in such a way that Christians have by no means been exempted by the Christian law and by Christ's ordinance alone from secular power and jurisdiction; thus from the time of the apostles and long afterwards Christians were subject, in secular crimes and other matters that in no way pertained specifically to the Christian law, to the power and jurisdiction even of unbelievers. For this reason the head of Christians does not as a rule have power to punish secular wrongs with a capital penalty and other bodily penalties, and it is for thus punishing such wrongs that temporal power and riches are chiefly necessary; such punishment is granted chiefly and as a rule to the secular power. The pope, therefore, can as a rule correct wrongdoers only with a spiritual penalty. It is therefore not necessary that he should excel in temporal power or abound in temporal riches, but it is enough that Christians should willingly obey him.

Chapter 30

Student I will hold disputation with you about this matter later; therefore pass over it, and relate carefully how answer is made, according to the opinion holding that it is not beneficial for the community of the faithful to be under one head under Christ, to the arguments brought forward above in the first chapter of this second book.

Master [1] To the first of them it is answered, as was touched on in the same place,[114] that Christ is the head of the faithful, and therefore Christians are not under one head under Christ. To the argument to the contrary it is answered that it is not necessary that there should be under Christ one rector of the whole Church, but it is enough if there are several ruling various provinces, just as there are several kings governing several kingdoms.

[2] To the next it is said that it is beneficial for one fold in which the sheep live together to be ruled and fed by one mortal

---

[114] Student's objection, above, p. 122.

shepherd, but for one fold in which all the sheep do not live together it is enough to be ruled by the chief of the shepherds, namely Christ.

[3] To the third it is answered by the same [distinction] that it is beneficial for a whole people living together to be under one mortal rector, but not for one people that includes many peoples living in separate places. For such a people it is enough to be under Christ.

[4] To the fourth it is answered that to be under one supreme rector is not beneficial for every community that cannot be ruled without a multitude of judges who can have conflicting opinions about causes and cases, because such a community can be so great that no one man, mortal and in many things deficient, is equal to conducting and deciding all cases about which the other judges can disagree. Therefore, since the community of the faithful can be in that way so great that no mortal man can carry all such cases, it is beneficial for the community of the faithful to be ruled by several, not by one.

[5] To the fifth it is answered in a similar way that because one man is not enough to compel the whole of the faithful to preserve unity of faith and of the rites and observances that all Christians are obliged to observe, it is therefore beneficial for the community of the faithful to be ruled by several who may compel all to such unity.

[6] To the sixth it is answered that it is beneficial for those able to err about major cases to have one head when one man is enough to settle all such cases. But no one is enough for the settling of all such cases as can arise among worshippers of Christ; it is therefore beneficial for them not to have one head under Christ, but many.

[7] To the seventh it is answered that it is not beneficial for the community of the faithful that many among them, and especially prelates, should be able to do wrong insolently when a remedy can be furnished against such a danger without a greater danger. But a greater danger would threaten the community of the faithful if it had one head than if it had several, because, since one is more easily infected by evil than several, it is more to be feared that one man ruling the whole of the faithful may be infected by evil than that several ruling it may be. But according to the opinion

of the wise man in Ecclesiasticus 10[:2], "As the judge of the people is himself, so also is his minister: and what kind of man the ruler of a city is, such also are those who live in it." Pope Anterus agrees with this. As we read in 6, q. 1, c. *Ex merito*, he says, "When the head becomes weak the other members of the body are infected." The gloss there says, "The king's realm conforms to his example"; and consequently, when the head of any body of Christians is corrupted, it is reasonable to fear the corruption of his subjects. Therefore, the general, or almost general, corruption or infection of Christians should more be feared if they all have one head than if they have several, although some particular corruption of one or other part of Christians is more to be feared if Christians have many heads; therefore the greater danger threatens Christians if they all have one head, who can infect all or nearly all Christians, than if they have several, none of whom can infect all or nearly all but only those subject to them; for the simultaneous corruption of several heads is not so much to be feared as the corruption of one only.

Student Why does this opinion add "almost," when it says that "general or almost general corruption" should more be feared?

Master "Almost" is added because of Christ's promise, when he said, in Matthew, last chapter, "I am with you all days, until the end of the world."[115] Because of this it is not at all to be feared that because of the wickedness of one head there will ever be a general corruption or infection of all Christians, because such a corruption of Christians would conflict with that promise of Christ; but an almost general corruption of Christians would in no way conflict with that promise. Christ's promise would stand if, under one perverted or infected head of all Christians, all were infected except two or three. Therefore, it need not in any way be feared that one head of all Christians would infect all Christians, but it must be feared that, if he were infected, he would infect *almost* all. Accordingly, if a pope became a heretic, especially a pope with temporal power or temporally powerful adherents, it must be feared that he would infect almost all Christians with heretical wickedness. But if there were several heads of Christians, all would not so easily be infected at the same time, but when one had been infected in morals or by heretical wickedness, often another would remain sound in morals and in faith, together with his subjects.

---

[115] Matthew 28:20.

Student Pursue the other arguments which follow.

Master [8] To the eighth it is answered that the same things are not always beneficial to the whole and to the part, in great matters and in small, and there is not the same right (either never or [only] with exceptions) in the whole and in the part, in great matters and in small: though this is true when there is the same reason concerning the whole and the part, concerning great matters and small.[116] And therefore, although it will be beneficial for one bishop to be over one particular faithful people, it is, however, not beneficial that one person alone should be over the whole faithful people: first, because one man by himself can carry all the affairs of one particular people, but no one man can carry all the affairs, even the greater affairs, of all Christians; also, because it is less evil for a particular people, and a small one, to be infected by one bishop than for the whole (or almost the whole) Christian people to be infected by one head who is over all.

[9] To the ninth it is said that although kingship is the best constitution in one city, according to Aristotle (who speaks only of the constitutions that are observed in cities, as we gather from very many of his statements in the books of *Politics*), kingship is nevertheless not the best constitution for the whole world or for every part of the world, because the whole world and various kingdoms are better ruled by several, none of whom is superior to another, than by one man alone, for the reasons touched on above.

[10] Through this [argument] the last argument is answered: it is not beneficial for the totality of mortals to be ruled by one monarch of the whole world, but it is, as a rule, beneficial for it to be ruled by several none of whom is superior to another; although in some case that can happen it would be more beneficial for the whole world to be ruled by one rather than by many. So much for the second book.

Book 3

Chapter 8

Student I think I perceive the meaning of the above opinion, which in many respects is based on the premise that a general

---

[116] See below, III *Dial.*, II.1.9, first answer, pp. 257–8.

council can err against the faith. The first opinion reported in chapter 1 above holds and tries to prove the contrary of this.[117] Relate how the last opinion tries to answer its arguments.

Master To the first argument, when it suggests that we should piously hold that the interpretations of a general council have been revealed to us by the same spirit as revealed the divine Scriptures,[118] it is answered that it is not necessary, nor must all Christians always believe this. A general council often relies, or can rely, on human wisdom, which can deviate from what is true. Therefore it is not obligatory, of necessity for salvation, to believe that whatever a general council defines as necessary to hold concerning the faith, it defines as having been revealed to it by God, and that it is then relying on a spiritual revelation.

This seems provable in many ways. [1] For when it is hoped that something will be revealed by God, it is necessary to apply oneself, not to study and human thought, but only to prayer or other good works – or at least it is less necessary to apply oneself to study than to other good works. Thus when Daniel was hoping that Nabuchodonosor's dream and its interpretation would be revealed to him by God, he exhorted his companions to seek such a great mystery, not through study, though they were learned men, but through prayer and supplication from God. Afterwards Daniel asserted that he had obtained it through prayer, when he says in chapter 2, "To thee, O God of my fathers, I give thanks, and I praise you, because you have given wisdom and strength: and now you have shown me what we asked of you, for you have made known to us the king's discourse" [Daniel 2:23]. Thus also, because Christ promised his apostles that he would reveal to them what they ought to say when they were led before kings and governors, he forbade them to occupy themselves then in study. He said to them, as we read in Matthew 10[:19], "And when they deliver you up, think not how or what to speak, for what to speak will be given to you in that hour; for it is not you that speak, but the Spirit of my Father who speaks in you." When, therefore, something is to be hoped for only through revelation, one must not devote oneself to study and human thought, but to prayer. But when there

---

[117] Chapter 1 is drawn from Marsilius, II.19, pp. 274 ff.
[118] Cf. Marsilius, p. 274.

is a question of faith to be decided in a general council, effort is given to meditation on the Scriptures. It is therefore not necessarily through revelation that a question of faith should be decided in a general council, but such a question can be decided by a wisdom that is had, and can be had, through study and human meditation; although God can by a special grace reveal it, it must not be held as certain that it is had through revelation, unless God reveals this miraculously and openly.

[2] Further, when it should be held as certain that something is to be had through revelation, recourse must reasonably be had, in order to obtain it, not to those who are wiser, but to those who are better – whether they are learned or unlearned, clergy or laity, men or women – or to prophets, because commonly God reveals his secrets not to the wiser but to the better. Truth himself seems to testify to this, when he says in Matthew 11[:25], "I give thanks to you, O Father, Lord of heaven and earth, because you have hidden these things from the wise and prudent and revealed them to little ones." Thus, as we read in 4 Kings 22[:14], when that holy king Josias wished to know through revelation God's will concerning the words of the book found in the temple, he sent even the priests and experts in the divine law themselves to Holda the prophetess, the wife of Sellum; he did not seek the truth from those priests and experts in the law, even though it is said, in Malachias 2[:7], "The lips of the priest keep knowledge, and they seek the law at his mouth." For in respect of things in the law that can be had through effort and thought, the law of God must be sought from the mouth of the priest, who is obliged to know the science and law of God explicitly, but in respect of things that must be had through revelation, recourse must be had chiefly to those who have the spirit of prophecy, if there are any, and to those who are more holy, whose prayers are more accepted by God. In respect of such things, the law is not necessarily to be sought from the mouth of a priest and the highest pontiff more than from the mouth of a widow or of a layman ignorant of letters. But for deciding a question of faith in a general council, recourse is had, even according to the common opinion of men, to the wiser [and] more learned, whether they are better or not. Therefore it should not be held necessarily that a question of faith is always settled by divine revelation.

From these [arguments] we gather that it is not necessary to hold that a question of faith is always settled in a general council by revelation, but it must be held, unless the opposite is revealed miraculously by God, that God permits those assembled in a general council, in defining a question of faith and in other matters, to proceed according to their own intelligence, assisted by the general divine influence. It is therefore conceded that it is not impossible for a general council to err.

This[119] is further proved in accordance with the above as follows. [1] Those present in a general council discussing, deliberating on, and deciding a question of faith rely either on divine revelation by itself or on human wisdom and virtue. The first cannot be said, because then, in accordance with the above, it would not be necessary in deciding a question of faith to consult those who are expert in sacred Scripture or to turn the divine book over in the mind, nor would it be necessary to think how the question of faith should be settled, but instead it would be appropriate to commit the whole to God, only calling on him through prayer who can alone reveal any Catholic truth whatever. However, this is not done when there is a question of faith to be decided in a general council, because the wise men in the general council deliberate about it and try to draw out the truth from sacred literature, to decide it in accordance with the divine Scriptures. We know that general councils so far have done this, because they have decided questions of faith arising out of the Scriptures by means of the sacred Scriptures. Therefore, those present in a general council who wish to decide a question of faith do not commit the whole to God and ask him through prayer alone for the definition of the question of faith, but instead they rely on human wisdom and virtue, because they rely on the expertise concerning the Scriptures that they have and can have by careful thought. But error can be found in all things that rely on human wisdom and virtue; therefore members of a general council can err in deciding a question of faith.

It is not necessary to hold that those assembled in a general council always and in all their discussions, even when they discuss a question of faith that has to be decided, are guided by the Holy Spirit in any other way than the pope is when he discusses business

---

[119] That a general council can err.

with the cardinals in his consistory, or than the patriarchs, primates, archbishops, or metropolitans are when they hold provincial councils, or in any other way than bishops and other prelates are when they settle church business; though it has sometimes happened, and can still happen, that those who come to a general council are especially guided by the Holy Spirit and that some truths are revealed to them miraculously and that God miraculously preserves them from every error and by manifest miracles confirms their definition concerning the faith and other things enacted by them. But without the working of a miracle it is not necessary to hold that something is revealed by the Holy Spirit to those called to a general council in any other way than to provincial councils and other gatherings of Christians, of which it is certain that they are not directed by the Holy Spirit in such a way that they cannot err both in morals and in faith; therefore it is not necessary to assert the contrary of every general council.

[2] Also, an assembly that can proceed in business badly and conclude with a bad result can err against the faith. But these things can happen with a general council; for, as we read in 1, q. 1, c. *Principatus*, "It is difficult to complete with a good outcome things begun with a bad beginning." Every assembly that can begin with a bad beginning can conclude with a result that is not good. And a general council can begin with a bad beginning: a general council must be assembled by the pope, as we read in dist. 7, throughout; but since the pope can sin and be damned and can err against the faith with a bad and corrupt purpose – indeed, he can assemble a general council with the purpose of defining something contrary to Catholic truth – therefore a general council assembled with a bad beginning and a corrupt purpose can be completed with a bad result, and consequently it can err against the faith.

Chapter 9

Student Point out how the above opinion tries to answer other arguments brought forward above in chapter 1 of this third book. **Master** To that which is based on Christ's promise in the last chapter of Matthew, it is answered that Christ is going to be with the universal Church until the end of the world, and therefore (as

Rabanus says, as has been quoted), "Until the end of the world there will not be lacking in the world some who are worthy of the divine presence and indwelling."[120] From these words of Rabanus we gather that that promise of Christ should not be understood of a general council: First, because he says "there will not be lacking in the world," and does not say that there will not be lacking in a general council; also, because seldom is there a general council in the world, but the universal Church will always be in the world until the end of the world. Therefore, according to Rabanus, that promise of Christ should not be understood of a general council but of the universal Church, so that it should be held piously and without doubt that the Holy Spirit is always present to the universal Church. Thus also Jerome refers to the universal Church when he says that Christ "will never depart from believers,"[121] because until the end of the world there will always be some who believe in Christ, whether a general council is taking place or not.

The argument based on Acts 15[:28][122] is answered in two ways: in one way that the decision made by the apostles and elders related in Acts 15 was made by a miraculous revelation of the Holy Spirit, such as can still be made in a general council; but it is not necessary that a revelation be made, neither was it always made, nor, perhaps, will it always be made whenever a general council is held. And it is not unsuitable to say that some revelations were made to the apostles, yet such are not made in every general council. In another way it is said that, without a revelation of the Holy Spirit made to them then, the apostles and elders inferred that decision from words they had heard from Christ's lips and from his deeds that they had seen. They had seen that he did not observe many legal and ceremonial [commandments of the Old Law], and he had also taught them that it was not necessary to observe them; without a special revelation, therefore, they were able to know that the faithful converted from the gentiles were not at all bound to observe such things. And thus the apostle Paul steadfastly asserted this before that assembly took place, which he would not have done unless he had been certain of it beforehand.

---

[120] Quoted by Marsilius, p. 274.
[121] Quoted by Marsilius, pp. 274–5.
[122] Marsilius p. 275.

And even if all the others had contradicted him, he would never have retreated from his opinion. He testifies to this when he says to the Galatians 1[:8], "Though we, or an angel from heaven," etc.;[123] and yet he would not have been pertinacious even if he had been resisting all other men, because pertinacity cannot be found concerning a truth knowingly asserted. When, therefore, the apostles and elders said "For it has seemed good to the Holy Spirit and to us" etc.,[124] they said it under the same sort of interpretation as that under which the Apostle said in 1 Corinthians 12[:3], "No one can say 'Jesus is Lord' except in the Holy Spirit": because all good things are from the Holy Spirit, though God does not in all such speech work a new miracle.

In the same way answer is made to a great many texts that assert in substance that whatever the holy fathers assembled in general councils defined, enacted, and did, they did under the inspiration of the Holy Spirit, and consequently that the interpretations they made to decide doubtful points of faith were revealed to them. For they are not said to have been inspired by the Holy Spirit because the Holy Spirit breathed something to them at that time in some special and unaccustomed way, beyond the influence of the Holy Spirit required for every work pleasing to God, but because the Holy Spirit moved them to make a right definition of the faith just as he moves everyone to the performance of all meritorious works whatever. Therefore, according to the opinion of the holy fathers, general councils that were held rightly, justly, in a holy way, canonically, and in a Catholic way, must be most devoutly received, embraced, and venerated by all Catholics. If, however, they had not been held in a Catholic way, even if all the bishops of the world had been present, they should be, not received, but absolutely rejected by the faithful. If it is asked who is to judge whether they were held in a Catholic way, it is answered that because they did not define anything except what can be drawn out from the divine Scriptures, therefore it is for experts in the Scriptures, and those having sufficient understanding of the other written sources, to judge in the manner of firm assertion that the things defined by them are defined in a Catholic way. If the highest

---

[123] " . . . preach a gospel, besides that which you have received, let him be anathema."
[124] Acts 15:28.

pontiffs were not present, but the councils were held only by their authority with their legates present, it is for them to judge authoritatively that they were held in a Catholic way; but if the highest pontiff was present, it is enough that he should authenticate them.

Student According to that opinion, is someone who is not certain that a general council was held rightly and in a Catholic way permitted to deny what has been defined by that council, or at least to doubt it?

Master This is answered by means of a distinction, because your question is general and does not specify whether the general council defines in a Catholic way or erroneously. A general council defines that something is to be believed either in a Catholic way or erroneously. If in a Catholic way, it is not permissible for anyone to deny publicly, or even to doubt publicly, the thing so defined, and it is also not permissible for anyone in private, or even mentally, to doubt pertinaciously concerning a thing so defined. But no one is obliged, even if he is certain that the general council did define in a Catholic way, to believe the thing so defined explicitly and absolutely without any contradiction, explicit, implicit, or tacitly understood; it is enough that he should believe implicitly.[125] However, if something is erroneously defined by a general council or by an assembly that is regarded by the multitude of the faithful as a general council, anyone who does not know that the general council or such assembly errs ought to presume in favor of such council or assembly – not, however, with a presumption so violent that no proof to the contrary may be admitted: just as a presumption must be made in favor of a judge's sentence, even if in truth it was unjust and wicked, until the contrary is proved or becomes certain. And therefore, after it is certain through the sacred Scriptures that such a general council has erred, whether it is approved or rejected by the pope, such a general council must in no way be believed, but it must be rejected, even publicly, at [the appropriate] time and place, by all who know.

Student Say how the next argument is answered.

Master To the argument based on the premise that the congregation of the faithful, or a general council, truly represents by

---

[125] Because the contradictory belief may not be held pertinaciously. See *Short Discourse*, p. 6, n. 9.

succession the congregation of the apostles, elders, and the rest of the faithful,[126] it is answered that only the whole Church represents that congregation quite perfectly and alone succeeds it properly and primarily and therefore alone cannot err. But a general council by no means represents it quite perfectly and does not succeed to it primarily; neither does the succession that Christ promised cease because of the fact that a general council is often not in session. But it can be conceded that imperfectly and in some way a general council represents the congregation of the apostles and the others and in a way succeeds to it, just as the pope with the college of cardinals in a way represents that same congregation and in some way succeeds to it: yet they can err, both in matters pertaining to the faith and in morals; and thus it cannot be proved by means of such representation and succession that a general council cannot err.

Chapter 10

Student Relate how answer is made to the final argument brought forward to prove that a council cannot err, which is based on the premise that Christ would have given the law of eternal salvation in vain if he did not reveal its true meaning to inquirers.[127]

Master It is answered by two distinctions. The first of these is that among things that are decided and can be decided in general councils (and, similarly, that can be doubted about the faith), there are some that can be inferred from the divine Scriptures by infallible deduction, so that although neither what is inferred nor the thing or things from which it is inferred can be known by natural reason, yet the inference can be known naturally (since even an inference of false from false can be known naturally and infallibly); and there are some that cannot be inferred from the divine Scriptures by an infallible deduction – as according to blessed Jerome it cannot be established certainly from the Scriptures that the Blessed Virgin is bodily in heaven; as also, concerning those of whom it is said in Matthew 10,[128] "Many bodies of the saints arose" with him, etc.,

---

[126] See Marsilius, p. 275.
[127] See Marsilius, p. 275.
[128] Matthew 27:52.

it cannot be deduced infallibly from the divine Scriptures either that they did ascend bodily into heaven, or that they did not ascend bodily.

The second [distinction] is that a doubt about the faith or about divine matters and matters that relate to salvation can be twofold: for of some things explicit knowledge is necessary to salvation, and of other things explicit knowledge is not necessary to salvation.

Through this the above argument is answered. For in a general council either some doubt is put forward for decision that can be inferred from the divine Scriptures by a deduction that is infallible and naturally known, at least to the wise and to experts, or something is put forward for decision that cannot be inferred in such a way from the divine Scriptures but can be had by divine revelation alone; again, knowledge of what is put forward for decision in the general council either is necessary to the faithful, or it is not necessary to the faithful. If what is put forward for decision in the general council can be inferred from the divine Scriptures by an infallible deduction, and knowledge of it is necessary to the faithful, then the wise men assembled in the general council should, not without prayer and other good works, most diligently search the sacred Scriptures, following the example of those of whom it is said in Acts 17[:11] "They received the word eagerly, daily searching the Scriptures." In such a case, because the general council and any Catholic, when something must be done, should, so as not to be seen to tempt God, do whatever reasonably and prudently can be done (following the example of Abraham, who, according to Augustine in *Questions on Genesis*, quoted in 22, q. 2, c. *Quaeritur*, when he went into Egypt, fearing the Egyptians because of his wife's beauty, "did what he could, and what he could not do he entrusted to God, in whom he hoped") . . . [129]

Chapter 11

Student Relate how, through the foregoing, the argument for the contrary opinion is answered.

Master It is answered that when they take [as a premise the proposition] that "Christ would have given the law of eternal

---

[129] According to a note in two of the manuscripts, the rest of chapter 10 is missing.

salvation in vain if he did not make plain its true meaning – the meaning it is necessary for salvation for the faithful to believe – to those who seek it and call on him for it together but instead allowed the majority of the faithful to err about it,"[130] if [1] by the majority of the faithful (i.e., of Christians rightly believing) they mean the *whole* Church (or congregation of the faithful), [2] speaking (as their words suggest) of the true meaning of everything contained in divine law that is *necessary to salvation* and [3] of making such meaning plain by means of the Scriptures or by revelation to those assembled in a general council *or to others* who were outside a general council (for both when a general council is being held and when it is not being held many things necessary to salvation are made plain, or can be made plain, both through the Scriptures and through miraculous revelation, to those who are not in a general council, through whom they can come to those present in a general council, if they are worthy or if it is necessary to the Christian people for salvation): and thus[131] it cannot be proved from this that it is necessary to believe that the decisions of general councils on doubtful senses of Scripture derive their truth from the Holy Spirit in the way the divine Scriptures were breathed into the writers. For an understanding of a law that is necessary to salvation can be made plain to other persons, either through the Scriptures or through a miraculous operation; this should not be regarded as remarkable or incredible, since often many wiser and better persons than are there assembled are not called to a general council. And a general council can be called with a corrupt intention; and even if it was assembled with a right intention, it can afterwards be held not rightly, since those assembled there are not confirmed in faith, grace, or good morals, but sometimes, perhaps, all or many will have been, or could be, involved in serious sins.

And the law of Christ is not for that reason useless or given to harm men, because, whether its true meaning is revealed or otherwise manifested to those present in a general council or to those not called to that general council, it can be useful for eternal salvation to those who seek it piously and rightly. God has revealed

---

[130] See Marsilius, p. 275.
[131] That is, under this interpretation of their premise.

and in other ways manifested many things regarding the meaning
of the divine law to experts, to saints, and to the inexpert who
have not been called to a general council (and not only because a
general council was not being held but in the time of a general
council), and God is still able to do the same: because the meaning
of the law can be made plain in many respects through consideration
of the Scriptures, without the Holy Spirit's making their meaning
plain to anyone whatever in a special way; also, because in a general
council many doubts about faith can be clarified that are not
necessary to salvation;[132] also, because it has been shown earlier
that a general council, or what is thought to be a general council
by the greater part of Christians, can err against the faith.

If, however, those who hold this opinion [1] mean by the majority
of Christians the greater *part* of the faithful or of Christians, and
if [2] by the meaning of the law they mean the understanding of
whatever is contained in the divine law without any exception, and
[3] mean to speak of those who seek that understanding for *every*
time, as often as they seek such understanding and have called
[on God] for it, they err in many ways: First, because the law of
eternal salvation given by Christ would not be in vain even if the
great part of the faithful – indeed, all except a very few, or except
one – erred, not damnably but detestably, about it, even about an
understanding necessary to salvation; nor would the law have been
given in vain even if all Christians except a few or one erred about
it damnably, because the whole Christian faith could be preserved
in one alone (as during the three days[133] the whole faith remained
in the mother of our redeemer alone) without its being true that
the law of eternal salvation had been given in vain. Second, because
many things are contained in the divine Scriptures whose true first
and literal meaning is not at all times necessary to salvation, even
if a solution is sought by those present in a general council both
by earnest meditation on the Scriptures and by prayer, so that they
quite intend to define it. It is not necessary to believe that God
makes such a true understanding plain to them through the Scriptures or through miraculous revelation, because although God does
not fail his Church (that is, the congregation of the faithful) in

[132] It would be implausible to say that not even such minor truths can become
manifest to believers not present in a general council.
[133] That is, between Christ's crucifixion and his resurrection.

necessary matters, he does not always make himself available for things not necessary to salvation, without which there can be salvation, even though they try to obtain them with continual prayers.

Book 4

Chapter 8

Student Examine the second answer asserted by those holding the opinion often mentioned.[134]

Master That answer is based on this, that by the words "Feed my sheep" [John 21:17], the people of Israel, who were stiff-necked toward God, were especially entrusted to blessed Peter, because of his constancy. But it seems to some that this answer plainly implies the opposite of what it holds. If by the words "Feed my sheep" the care of the people of Israel was entrusted to Peter, and Christ in these words did not distinguish between some sheep and other sheep of the people of Israel and did not except any sheep, therefore the care entrusted to blessed Peter was of all the sheep of Israel. But the sheep of Israel included especially the apostles; therefore those words entrusted to blessed Peter the care of all the apostles.

Student Perhaps the holders of this opinion would reply that although in the words "Feed my sheep" Christ did not distinguish between these sheep and those and did not then exempt some, yet elsewhere he did distinguish and did manifestly exempt some, namely the apostles. For he seems to have exempted the apostles when he sent them just as he sent Peter and gave them the same power as he gave to Peter: when he said to them all, as we read in Matthew 18[:18], "Whatsoever you shall bind upon earth," etc.; and when he said to them, as we read in John 20[:21], "As the Father has sent me, I also send you ... Receive the Holy Spirit; whose sins you shall forgive they are forgiven them, and whose sins you shall retain, they are retained"; and when he said to them

---

[134] See Marsilius, pp. 379–80. Marsilius is answering objections to his thesis (argued for pp. 241 ff.) that Christ did not give Peter any authority over the other apostles.

all in Matthew, last chapter [28:19], "Going therefore teach all nations, baptizing them in the name of the Father," etc.; and when he said to them all, as we read in Matthew,[135] last chapter, "Go into the whole world and preach the gospel to every creature; he who believes and is baptized shall be saved," etc.; in all these Christ seems to have distinguished the apostles from the other faithful sheep and to have exempted them altogether from the power of Peter. Since those words "Feed," etc., said to Peter were general, and the special derogates from the general, *Extra, De Rescriptis*, c. 1, it follows that from those general words said to Peter a derogation has been specially made in respect of the apostles, to whom Christ specially gave the same power as he gave to Peter – as is clear, it seems, from the above.

Master This reply is attacked. Although Christ gave the rest of the apostles some special power, he never granted them a general power or a power equal to the power of Peter. For in appointing Peter he used a word more general than those he used in granting the apostles power over others, namely the word "Feed," which is more general than the word "teach," or "baptize," or any other such. And therefore, although Christ sometimes distinguished between the apostles and his other sheep and in a certain respect exempted them in some way from Peter's power, yet when he said to Peter, "Feed," etc., setting him over all, he did not distinguish between them and others. He therefore did not exempt them, and did not wish them to remain exempt or free from Peter's power, except in respect of the things he expressed in granting them a specific power; therefore they were not exempted from Peter's power except in respect of the office of preaching, baptizing, binding and loosing from sins, and anything else, if there was anything, that Christ expressed when he granted them some power. When you say, therefore, that a special command derogates from what is granted in the general, that is conceded in respect of things explicit in the special command, but not in respect of other things. The command given to the apostles concerning baptizing, preaching, teaching, loosing, and binding therefore derogated from the command given to Peter, "Feed my sheep," in respect only of those things that Christ enjoined on the apostles. (And yet not in every

---

[135] Mark 16:15.

case; for if they had committed excesses in such things, then by reason of wrongdoing they would have been subject to Peter even in respect of those things, because by reason of wrongdoing those who are exempt receive a court,[136] and "he deserves to lose a privilege who misuses the power permitted to him," *Extra, De regularibus*, c. *Licet*, and 11, q. 3, *Privilegium*.)

Student This attack seems to militate against the truth, because the apostles were not only preachers and teachers with power to baptize, bind, and loose, but they were also appointed by God as shepherds, as the Apostle testifies in Ephesians chapter 3.[137] Speaking of Christ, he says, "And he gave some to be apostles and some prophets and others evangelists, and others shepherds and teachers." From these words we gather that Christ appointed the other apostles as shepherds in the same way as he appointed Peter, and consequently, in so many words or in substance, he said "Feed my sheep" to every other apostle just as he did to Peter. From this it is inferred that he gave the others, like Peter, every power implied by the word "Feed," because he did not give such power more to anyone than to the apostles; therefore the apostles had the same authority in all things as Peter had.

Master To this objection of yours it is answered that Christ (who even now does not cease to govern the Church invisibly, according to the Apostle) appointed certain men as shepherds, using Peter as intermediary. The Apostle does not say that Christ gave some to be shepherds *without the ministry of Peter*, but that "he gave ... shepherds," because he gave them by means of the ministry and authority of Peter. This is true.

Chapter 9

Student Say now, briefly, how answer is made to the text of the Apostle and the gloss which were brought forward to prove the equality in particular of blessed Paul to Peter.[138]

Master All those texts are answered by means of the things said above. Although the other apostles besides blessed Peter were not

---

[136] That is, subject themselves to a court from which they had been exempt.
[137] Ephesians 4:11.
[138] See Marsilius, p. 379.

appointed by Christ as shepherds of the universal Church and did not have the same power over the universal Church as Peter had, blessed Paul had the office of preaching immediately from Christ and exercised this office before he had seen Peter or Peter knew that he had been converted. For in Acts 9[:18–20] it is written of him, "Rising up, he was baptized, and when he had taken food he was strengthened; and he was with the disciples who were in Damascus for some days. And immediately Paul went into the synagogues and preached Jesus, that he was the Son of God." That he had then no authority to preach from Peter is seen from the things that follow, when it is said, "And when he had come to Jerusalem he tried to join himself to the disciples, and they were all afraid of him, not believing that he was a disciple. But Barnabas took him and brought him to the apostles and told them how he had seen the Lord on the road and spoken to him and how in Damascus he had acted confidently in the name of Jesus."

As for the Apostle's statement[139] that the evangelization of the uncircumcised had been entrusted to himself, as to Peter that of the circumcised, some say that it was not said by the Apostle because Paul was teacher and preacher only to the gentiles and Peter only to the Jews, since this seems to conflict very plainly with canonical Scripture: both had authority and power to preach both to the uncircumcised and to the circumcised, that is, to both gentiles and Jews, and sometimes both did preach to both. (Of Paul, indeed, it is manifestly clear in Acts 9[:20], 13[:5], and 14[:1] that he preached to the Jews, and he himself asserts in his epistles that he was also teacher of the gentiles, and the apostolic history [Acts] also testifies this of him; concerning Peter the same is also clear, for he preached to the Jews, as is clear from many places, and he preached to gentiles, namely to Cornelius and others, as is clear in Acts 10.) Rather, the Apostle says that the evangelization of the uncircumcised was entrusted to him and that of the circumcised to Peter because Paul was more intent upon the conversion of the gentiles and Peter on the conversion of the Jews, so that often and in various provinces Peter preached to Jews alone, as Eusebius testifies in his *Ecclesiastical History*. In Book III, chapter

---

[139] Galatians 2:9.

2, he says: "Peter is found to have gone around Pontus, Galatia, Bithynia, Cappadocia, and other bordering provinces, preaching to Jews alone." And yet it was permissible for him to preach to gentiles, just as it was permissible for Paul to preach to Jews. The gloss that the holders of the above opinion quote[140] in the answer we are now discussing manifestly asserts this. It says: "However, the dispensing was distributed to them in such a way that Peter also preached to the gentiles, if some reason demanded it, and Paul to the Jews." This is also gathered evidently from the *Ecclesiastical History*, when it asserts that Peter and Paul founded the church in Rome (as will be said later).

When that gloss says that the evangelization of the uncircumcised was in that way chiefly entrusted to Paul, as the evangelization of the circumcised was to Peter, it is answered that the gloss says this because Christ entrusted the office of preaching to Paul directly and without Peter, so that he did not have the office of preaching from Peter. And yet Paul was in some way subject to Peter even in respect of the office of preaching, for if in the office entrusted to him by Christ he had committed some excess, he would have had to be corrected by Peter.

When it is taken [as a premise] in the above answer[141] that neither Paul nor any other saint could have assumed that the Jewish people had been entrusted especially and chiefly to Peter from anything else except that Christ said to him, "Feed my sheep," it is answered that Paul said many things about Christ and the apostles that he did not get from the canonical Scriptures of the New Testament. For he says in 1 Corinthians 15[:6], "Then he," namely Christ, "was seen by more than five hundred at the same time," and, as we read in Acts 20[:35], "[the word of the Lord Jesus, how he said:] It is more blessed to give than to receive"; and yet those things are not contained in the earlier writings of the New Testament. So also he could have said, as one who for the great part had knowledge of Peter's deeds, that the evangelization of the circumcised had been entrusted to blessed Peter, even though he did not take this from the statement, "Feed my sheep," or from any thing else that anyone wrote before him.

---

[140] See Marsilius, pp. 379–80.
[141] See Marsilius, p. 380.

Chapter 10

Student Because, as I said before, many or all who hold that Christ appointed blessed Peter as head and ruler of the other apostles try to prove it chiefly by means of those words of Christ, "Feed my sheep," I would therefore like those words to be still further examined, so that I may better understand their truth. It seems, therefore, first, that it cannot be proved (as others[142] suggest) by those words that blessed Peter was appointed ruler and prelate of any persons whatever. For someone can feed others with words and examples, and also by physical support, even though he has over them no authority at all. Therefore by saying to Peter, "Feed," etc., Christ committed to him no authority at all over the others who had to be fed.[143]

Master It seems to very many that that answer is not at all satisfactory. Just as the grant of a benefice or privilege made indefinitely and simply is understood generally, *Extra, De privilegiis, Quia circa,* so also the entrusting of power or of an office made indefinitely and simply should be understood universally – namely so that all things are understood to have been granted or entrusted that are not prohibited, concerning which there is the same reason for entrusting or granting and concerning which it is not likely or probable that the one entrusting or granting specifically did *not* entrust or grant those things; for "he who excepts nothing" and could have made exceptions "seems to have granted or entrusted the whole," as the sacred canons testify.[144] But in the words, "Feed my sheep," Christ entrusted to blessed Peter and enjoined on him something conveyed by the word "Feed," and that entrusting or enjoining was done indefinitely and simply; therefore all things are understood to have been entrusted that are not found prohibited, concerning which there is the same reason for entrusting, and concerning which it is not likely or probable that the one entrusting specifically did not entrust them.

But by the word "Feed" is conveyed not only feeding others with word and example and bodily maintenance, but also [feeding them] by way of power and with authority – especially as the word "Feed" is

---

[142] The people Marsilius is answering.
[143] See Marsilius, p. 378.
[144] The quotation marks are guesswork; the source has not been found.

taken in the sacred Scriptures and in the expositions of the holy fathers. This can be proved abundantly, but let it suffice to bring forward a few [passages]. Ezechiel, therefore, says – indeed, the Lord says through the prophet Ezechiel – in chapter 34[:2]: "Woe to you shepherds of Israel, who have been feeding yourselves . . . That which was weak you have not strengthened, and that which was sick you have not healed, that which was broken you have not bound up, and that which was driven away you have not brought again, what was lost you have not sought." But to lead straying sheep back to the flock, to seek lost sheep, and to carry back again those found belongs to him who has power over the sheep. And truth himself, as we read in John 10[:2], says, "He who enters by the door is the shepherd of the sheep, the door keeper opens for him, and the sheep hear his voice, and he calls his own sheep by name and leads them out; and when he has let out his own sheep he goes before them, and the sheep follow him." From these words of Christ, and from others that follow, we gather that in respect of his office the shepherd of Christ's faithful is like the shepherd of irrational sheep. But by his office he [the latter] has some superiority and power over his lord's sheep; therefore the shepherd also of Christ's sheep, who are the faithful, has by his office power and authority over them. This is found so plainly in the expositions and assertions of the holy fathers that it seems that to prove it from them is quite superfluous.

Therefore Christ through his words to him, "Feed my sheep," entrusted to blessed Peter some power over his sheep; especially since he is not found to have forbidden him absolutely all power and authority. There was, also, the same reason for granting him some authority and power over all as for entrusting to him the feeding of Christ's sheep by good words and examples, because they needed a guide and one with power over them just as they needed someone to build them up by means of good words and examples; it is therefore not likely or probable that he would specifically not have granted him such power. From these points it follows that by those words Christ granted and entrusted to blessed Peter some power.

Chapter 11

Student Here I could, by arguing from what has been said, undermine [the statement] that Christ entrusted to Peter all power over his sheep, even the fullness of power that the first opinion of the first chapter of the first book attributes to the pope, on the grounds that the entrusting was done indefinitely and simply. But I will discuss this with you later. Therefore I turn to another argument to prove that by the words, "Feed," etc. Christ did not appoint Peter as superior to the other apostles. It seems, therefore, that often an indefinite statement is not equivalent to a universal but can be verified even of a singular. Since, therefore, Christ said, "Feed," etc. indefinitely, this can be understood of some sheep without being understood of them all, and consequently without being understood of the apostles. It therefore cannot be shown by those words that blessed Peter was superior to the rest of the apostles.

Master Some think that this argument can be answered easily. Although both in things judged and in other matters it is not always the case that a statement uttered indefinitely should be understood generally, nevertheless, when power over some is entrusted to someone, a statement uttered indefinitely should be understood generally, in such a way that no one is then understood to be exempt unless he can be proved exempt by something else. The reason for this is given:[145] Just as "judges should not be uncertain," therefore – because "similar judgment must be made of similar cases" – when power or prelacy is entrusted to someone over others by a statement uttered indefinitely, just as "neither procurators nor tutors nor arbitrators" (as both the canon and civil laws testify and reason recommends), so also prelates and subjects, "should not be uncertain." Indeed "all should be understood who have the same thing in common," unless it can be shown from elsewhere that some must be excepted; otherwise subjects would in that case be uncertain. Therefore by the words, "Feed my sheep," all Christ's faithful should be understood, lest the sheep to be fed by Peter should be uncertain, unless it can be shown from elsewhere that some are excepted. This cannot be shown of the apostles, as many say who answer all the arguments by which it is shown that the apostles were excepted from Peter's power.

Chapter 22

Student Bring forward still other arguments, but only a few, to prove Peter's superiority in respect of the other apostles.

---

[145] The quotation marks in the rest of this paragraph are guesswork; the sources have not been found.

Master It is proved in the following way. What has been believed from the times of the apostles until our own time by prelates and doctors of the Church succeeding one another in a continuous series and by the peoples subject to them should be held firmly by all Catholics. It seems possible to prove this clearly by a text of Augustine in his book *Against the Manicheans*, quoted in *Decretum*, dist. 11, c. *Palam*, when he says: "It is clear that in a doubtful matter the authority of the Catholic Church, which is confirmed by those very well established sees of the apostles in a series of bishops succeeding one another down to our own day and by the consent of so many peoples avails to faith." Nevertheless, because some say (as is clear above) that texts other than those of the writers of canonical Scripture and of general councils should not be accepted,[146] this is proved by reason. Even according to the opponents, the universal Church cannot err, therefore what the universal Church has thought and does think should be held firmly. But the universal Church includes only the prelates of the Church and the peoples subject to them; therefore what the prelates of the Church succeeding one another in a continuous series and the peoples subject to them have believed from the times of the apostles to our own times must be believed firmly. But the prelates of the Church from the apostles themselves to these times, with the peoples subject to them, have held and thought that Peter was superior to the other apostles. Pope Anacletus held this (as quoted above[147]), and he could not have been ignorant of the truth in this matter. Also blessed Pope Clement, a disciple of the apostles, thought the same; as we read in dist. 80, c. *In illis*, he said, "Among the apostles themselves the appointment was not equal, but one was above all," and none other than Peter. Eusebius of Caesarea also thought this. Because he was steeped in the teachings, traditions and writings of those who were disciples of the apostles and of those educated by those disciples, he was not ignorant of what preceding [generations] thought, and it must in no way be presumed that he knowingly taught falsehood; none of the prelates of the Church or doctors afterwards contradicted him, and consequently by being silent they all consented to him. He says, therefore, in the *Ecclesiastical History*, which blessed Jerome[148] translated, in

---

[146] See Marsilius, pp. 274–5, 371.
[147] In chapter 15 (not translated).
[148] Rufinus.

Book II, chapter 14: "In the times of Claudius, the mercy of divine providence led Peter, the most approved of all the apostles and the greatest, by the greatness of his faith and virtue deservedly the chief of the leaders, to the city of Rome as if to fight against the common destruction of the human race: a leader and general of his army, knowing how to wage the divine battles and how to command the camp of the virtues." Blessed Jerome thinks this, and blessed Ambrose, blessed Augustine, blessed Pope Marcellus, and blessed Cyprian, as is explicitly clear in their texts quoted in various places above. But it seems far from all likelihood that those men – most careful students of the canonical Scriptures, of histories, of chronicles, of records of deeds, of the customs and traditions of the universal Church – did not know what the apostles and their disciples thought concerning something so necessary to the whole Church of Christ, and it must by no means be presumed about them that they knowingly taught falsehood; it must therefore be held that the above assertion came down to them from the apostles themselves through chronicles and histories worthy of belief, some of which we perhaps do not have, and through the tradition and custom of the universal Church continued down to them. All other prelates and doctors of the Church from the time of blessed Sylvester down to our own times have held the above assertion, as could be shown in many ways. And Catholic peoples have agreed with the above prelates and doctors in the same assertion, because no Catholic people has been found to contradict them. Therefore this assertion must be attributed to the universal Church and consequently must be held firmly.

Student Perhaps some will say that not all Christian peoples have thought this. It is said that the Greeks, who were Christians and Catholics before the Romans, do not hold this, and so not all Christian peoples have believed this down to our own times.

Master This answer is attacked by others. While the Greeks were Catholics they agreed in this, following the teaching of Catholic doctors. We do not read, and it does not seem probable, that before they divided from the Roman Church the people of the Greeks did not follow the teaching of Catholic Greek doctors, and their doctors taught the above assertion publicly and left it in writings. For Eusebius of Caesarea, who was a Greek and expert in the writings of all the Greek doctors (as is limpidly clear from the *Ecclesiastical History* which he wrote), taught this and wrote it, as is clear from what was said above. While the Greeks were Catholics, therefore, they held the above opinion. Their errors after they divided themselves from the Roman Church are in no way an obstacle to the above argument; it must therefore be held, following the Latins, that Peter was superior to all the others.

Student Some might perhaps answer the above argument in another way, by saying that although all the Christian peoples agreed with their prelates and doctors in that assertion, not all from among the people did, and the truth of faith can be preserved in a few of the people; therefore the above argument does not succeed.

Master That answer is refuted by this, that according to the Apostle, in Romans chapter 8,[149] "With the heart we believe unto justice, but with the mouth confession is made unto salvation," namely, when the faith is endangered. It would not have been enough, therefore, for some few of the people to have held the contrary assertion in their hearts, if it were Catholic, unless they had also confessed it with their mouths, publicly contradicting those who were in error. Since, therefore, we do not read that, from the times of the apostles and their disciples up to the time of our fathers, any, even a few, from the Christian peoples, publicly contradicted the assertion we have been speaking of, it must be held that this assertion should be ascribed to the universal Church. But the universal Church cannot at any time, even for a short time, err against the faith and in matters of right belonging to the faith or to good morals (though according to some it can err in matters of fact, namely in regarding someone as pope or as a good man, though he is not, and in similar matters). The above assertion must therefore be believed firmly.

[149] Romans 10:10.

A Dialogue, Part III Tract II, On the Rights of the Roman Empire

A Dialogue, Part III, Tract II, On the Rights of the Roman Empire

Prologue

Student The divine Scriptures, as we know, praise the Romans, at the time when they were working to acquire world empire, with many great expressions of praise, as we clearly read in the book of Machabees.[1] After the tract about the power of the pope and clergy, therefore, let there be added a tract on the rights of the Roman Empire, which some of the learned try to derive from sacred literature: especially since it was on the occasion of the Roman Empire that disagreement about the orthodox faith began among some, whose deeds (as also those of many others) we will try to discuss in the tracts to follow, to which these first two tracts of the third part of our dialogue are preparations and preambles. And let the present tract contain five books. Let the first inquire whether it is beneficial to the whole human race for one emperor to be over the whole world; by what excellences or graces, characteristics, and virtues the emperor of the world should be conspicuous; from whom the Roman Empire has proceeded; and whether it can by right be destroyed or annulled, diminished, divided, or transferred. Let the second investigate what rights the Emperor of the Romans has over temporal matters. Let the third examine whether the Emperor of the Romans has any power over spiritual matters, or is capable of power over spiritual matters. Let the fourth explore whether an emperor of the Romans is obliged, of necessity for salvation, to defend the rights of the Roman Empire (and, if they have been disturbed, to restore them), by arms and power if he cannot do so otherwise, against any attacker, invader, or anyone who in any way impedes them – even against the pope, cardinals, and clergy, if they attack, invade, or impede the rights of the Roman Empire – notwithstanding any sentence, ordinance, constitution, or process whatever of pope or cardinals or of anyone else whatever. Let the fifth treat of rebels, traitors, destroyers, dividers, and usurpers of the Roman Empire or of any part of it.

Master Perfect knowledge of the things you mention as needing treatment could be more clearly drawn and more solidly defended from books of sacred theology, of both laws (that is, canon and civil), and of moral philosophy, and from the histories of the Romans, of emperors and highest pontiffs, and of other nations.

[1] Machabees chapter 8.

Of these I have hope of obtaining only the Bible, the *Decretum*, and the five books of the *Decretals*. Therefore, lest perhaps we make a work that is imperfect and even ridiculous, it seems wiser to desist altogether.

Student Although at present we cannot make a perfect work, yet since (as I believe) others have not so far at all attempted a special work on a matter so necessary (seeing that it touches the whole human race), it will be useful not to be completely silent, so as to summon those who have plenty of books to make perfect works. For from the disputation we are about to have those who are zealous for truth, justice, and the commonwealth will, I think, see plainly that a great many truths about the above matters are hidden (to the detriment of the common good) from those who direct others by ruling, advising, informing, or teaching; and experts who are lovers of what is just and useful will be stirred up to produce thoroughly researched works on the above matters – works effectively disproving the false things we will report and supporting with undeniable arguments and authorities the true things we will relate: for in this tract, as in the whole of this dialogue, we will not say anything except in reporting. Accordingly, concerning the matters to be investigated you will report judgments or opinions that are true and false, solid and fantastical, and you should try to defend them pretty strongly. For often not only the assertion and explanation of truths, but also persuasive though sophistical arguments for false and fantastical judgments occasion advance in manifesting, publishing, and exalting the truth, both because they[2] exercise the abilities of the studious, and because their unreasonableness makes the contrary truth shine out more clearly, since opposites placed side by side appear more clearly and truth hard pressed shines more into light, and truth is made bright by questioning, opposing, disputing, and answering conflicting arguments.

Such a useful work, therefore, must by no means be given up because of shortage of books, especially since you can find in the above-named books, which you can obtain, many things relating to the matters to be discussed, and you can, when appropriate, cite many things you have read that I think you have not altogether forgotten, reporting them either verbatim or in substance.

---

[2] That is, sophistical arguments.

Master Your insistence conquers me, so I will go on to the tract with you. I do not doubt that if I explained in it what I think about the matters to be investigated, it would suffer the excessive calumnies of the malignant, to the prejudice of truth and to the detriment of justice. In this tract, therefore, just as you wish, I will not indicate at all which of the reported opinions I think should be approved. Truth will not thereby incur danger but avoid it, since I do not believe that anyone would adhere to the truth more firmly because of my approval, but I fear that, from the malice of hatred, envy and rancor, many would attack it more sharply and more wickedly by both words and deeds – which I am not ignorant is done in connection with other matters by some, prompted by envy against me. However, if ever I notice that the truth can be advanced by the expression of what I hold, I will not delay to publish it in express words. Therefore, since you quite wish this tract to be written, move on quickly to begin it.

Book I

Chapter I

Student If it were not at all beneficial that one emperor or ruler should govern all the provinces of the world, then, since the Romans took for themselves government over the whole world, the rights of the Empire would have to be regarded, deservedly, not as rights, but as injuries and injustices and cruel tyrannies. Since I am about to investigate many aspects of the rights of the Roman Empire, I have therefore decided to ask, first of all, whether it belongs to the advantage and utility of the whole human race for the whole world to be under one emperor or secular ruler in temporal matters. Relate the diverse and opposing opinions about this.

Master One opinion on the question you propose is that the world would be best ruled in temporal matters by one secular ruler, not inappropriately called emperor, and that the peace and quiet of the whole of human society cannot be well enough provided for by any other form of government.

Student Try to argue for that opinion.

Master That opinion seems provable in many ways. [1] The form of government most beneficial to the whole world is that by which the bad are restrained more easily, more justly, more severely, more effectively, and more salutarily, and the good live more quietly among the bad. For it is chiefly on this account that rulers and princes are appointed, as blessed Peter testifies. In his first epistle, chapter 2[:14], he asserts that governors have been sent by kings to punish evil doers and to praise the good. Blessed Paul agrees with him, teaching in Romans 13[:3–4] that the secular powers are from God for the terror of the wrongdoers and the security of the good. He says: "Do you wish, then, not to be afraid of the power? Do what is good, and you will have praise from him. For he is God's minister to you for good. But if you do what is evil, be afraid, for he does not bear the sword without reason." Blessed Augustine followed the opinion of those holy apostles. As we read in 23, q. 5, c. *Non frustra*, he says: "Not in vain have been established the power of the king, the law of the judge, the tongs of the torturer, the weapons of the soldier, the discipline of the ruler, the severity also of the good father. All these have their modes, causes, reasons and uses. Since all these are feared, the bad are restrained and the good live more quietly among the bad." With these[3] reason seems not at all to disagree. For secular rulers are established for the same reason as laws are made, and thus rulers are the ministers of the law and the emperor is called "the living law." But laws are made so that the audacity of the bad may be restrained and the good live safely, dist. 4, *Factae sunt leges*, and *Extra*, in the prologue, at *Ideoque lex proditur*. The government of rulers has been established, therefore, so that the bad may be restrained and the good live quietly. But by the government of one secular ruler with power over the whole world the bad are restrained more easily, more justly, more severely, more effectively, and more salutarily, and the good live more quietly among the bad: First, because such a world ruler would have greater and surer power for repressing the bad more strongly and defending the good more powerfully; without power the bad are in most cases not restrained and the good are not safe. Also, because there would be fewer oppressors of the good and encouragers of the bad. Also, because if there were not one world ruler but several with no superior, very many would be readier and more daring to raise rebellions

---

[3] That is, Peter, Paul, and Augustine.

and wars than if all obeyed one ruler. And thus we see that wars between kings, princes, and communities who refuse to obey one ruler are, as a rule, more dangerous, more difficult to moderate, and crueler than wars between subjects obedient to one secular ruler. And in times of rebellion and war the bad grow insolent and the good are disturbed in many ways. It is therefore beneficial to the whole world that there be one ruler and prince of the world, with power over all mortals.

[2] Further, just as spiritual matters are controlled by priests and ecclesiastics, so are temporal matters by secular rulers and laymen, as blessed Peter testifies. In appointing Clement, as we read in 11, q. 1, c. *Sicut enim*, he says: "For just as it is a fault of impiety for you, Clement, to neglect study of the word of God to undertake secular cares, so for any of the laity it is a fault if, for their part, they do not faithfully attend to the things that belong to the practice of the common life." And he says the same to the same Clement, as we read in the same *causa* and question, c. *Te quidem*: "Christ does not wish today to appoint you judge or arbiter of secular cases, lest, being suffocated by the present cares of men, you be unable to devote yourself to the word of God. Let the laity, for their part, show themselves devoted to these works which we have said are less appropriate for you." Blessed Paul seems to confirm this teaching of blessed Peter, saying in 1 Corinthians 6[:4], "If therefore you have secular matters for judgment, appoint as judges those who are more despised in the Church." By these words he seems to suggest that secular matters for judgment should be dealt with by those who are "more despised in the Church," who are the laity,[4] just as spiritual matters should be controlled by the clergy. The holy fathers and teachers who lived soon afterwards maintained this apostolic teaching in their writings. As we read in the *Decreta*, dist. 96, c. *Cum ad verum*, Pope Nicholas says: "Since [the world] has come to the truth, let the emperor no longer seize for himself the rights of the pontificate, and let the pontiff not usurp for himself the name of emperor. For the same mediator between God and men, the man Christ Jesus, distinguished the duties of both powers by their own distinct activities [. . .] so that

---

[4] According to Marsilius, this is the interpretation of the glosses. See Marsilius, pp. 128–9.

Christian emperors would need the pontiffs for eternal life and the pontiffs would use the imperial laws only for the course of temporal affairs. In this way spiritual activity would be distanced from carnal interruptions, and those on God's service would not at all involve themselves in secular affairs; and, in turn, someone involved in secular affairs would not seem to be over divine matters." Blessed Cyprian asserts this same opinion in almost all the same words, as we read in dist. 10, c. *Quoniam idem*. Pope Nicholas, as we read in the same distinction, c. *Imperium*, also says, "Your empire should be content with its daily administration of public affairs, and not usurp things that befit priests alone." From these and countless other assertions of the saints, and from sacred canons that we read in the *Decreta* – at dist. 10, c. *Certum* and c. *Suscipitis*, dist. 96, c. *Denique*, c. *Duo sunt*, and c. *Si imperator*, and dist. 88, c. *Episcopus*, and in a great many other places – we gather that, just as spiritual matters are to be controlled by the clergy, so temporal matters are to be controlled by the laity. But even if the whole world were converted to the faith, it would be beneficial to the totality of the faithful to be under one highest pontiff in spiritual matters, not only inasmuch as spiritual matters involve the clergy, but also inasmuch as they involve the laity and secular rulers: therefore in temporal matters also, not only inasmuch as temporal matters involve the laity, but also inasmuch as they involve clerics and the highest pontiff, it is beneficial to the totality of mortals to be under one secular ruler.

[3] Again, a similar judgment must be held concerning whole and part, concerning great matters and small, just as the same right exists in the whole and in the part, in great matters and in small: *Extra, De Appellationibus*, c. *De appellationibus*; 14, q. ult., c. ult., and *Extra, De praebendis et dignitatibus*, c. *Maioribus*. But it is beneficial to every particular kingdom, as part of the world, to be subject to one secular ruler; otherwise all the kingdoms of the world would have to be regarded as wicked or useless or harmful. Therefore, similarly, it is beneficial for the whole world to be subject to one secular ruler.

[4] Besides, all who have, or can have, community with one another in temporal matters, so that each can alike help and harm the other, are not best governed unless they are subject in temporal matters to one highest ruler: First, because all who are such

constitute one people; but according to Solomon, in Proverbs, chapter 11[:14], "Where there is no governor the people will be ruined"; therefore unless there is one governor set over all who have such community, there must be a probable fear of their ruin and loss. For in saying, "where there is no governor" – not "where there are no governors," – "the people will be ruined," Solomon seems to suggest that no one people, however great, can stand without one governor. Also, because all who have community with one another are compared with a sheepfold and a flock, and where there is one sheepfold and one flock there should be one shepherd: as truth himself testifies in John 10[:16], where he says, "There will be one fold and one shepherd," and as truth himself also testifies in Matthew 26[:31], where he says, "I will strike the shepherd, and the sheep of the flock will be scattered." In saying "shepherd" and not "shepherds" he seems to suggest that one flock or fold should have one chief shepherd, not several. Also, because all who have, or can have, community with one another, become, or can become, one body, one city, one college,[5] one nation, one kingdom, and unless they are well unified they are not at all well ordered; but a body that has no head or several is a monstrous body (and also city, and college, nation, and kingdom). Therefore all who can have community with one another in temporal matters should be subject to one secular ruler, and otherwise they cannot be best governed. But all mortals, however much they are distant from one another geographically, can have community with one another, so that they become, or should become, unless wickedness separates them, one people, one fold, one flock, one body, one city, one college, one nation, one kingdom. Thus the Apostle says, in Romans 12[:5], "We are one body in Christ, and all members one of another," manifestly suggesting that just as all mortals, not only the faithful but also unbelievers, should, renouncing the devil, cling the more firmly to Christ through faith and love, so all, if they are well ordered, should be one body. Thus also Solomon, in Proverbs, chapter 18[:19], says, "Brother helped by brother is like a firm city," suggesting that just as all mortals are brothers, so, unless wickedness obstructs, they should form one

---

[5] *Collegium* had no particular reference to an educational institution. Like *universitas*, it was a term applicable to any body of people: a corporation.

city. Thus also in Wisdom 6[:3] the wise man, rebuking wicked kings, says, "Power has been given to you by the Lord and strength by the most high, who will examine your works and search out your thoughts, because being ministers of his kingdom you have not judged rightly." By these words we are given to understand that although because of the sins of the bad many kings are appointed by the Lord – "who" also, as we read in Job 34[:30] "makes a hypocrite reign because of the sins of the people" – the whole world is nevertheless one kingdom; therefore it should have one secular ruler in temporal things.

[5] Also, that form of government is best by which discord is removed and taken away from the totality of mortals most effectively and most perfectly, as far as is possible for the present life, and concord and justice chiefly preserved. But if the totality of mortals is subject to one secular ruler, discord among mortals will be taken away more effectively than if there are several rulers without a superior: First, because where there is plurality there is discord. Also, because just as – on the testimony of truth himself, in Matthew 12[:25] – one particular kingdom divided against itself by discord will be made desolate, so if by having many rulers not at all subject to one they are divided against themselves by discord, the totality of mortals will incur desolation. It is therefore beneficial to the totality of mortals to obey one secular ruler.

[6] Also, that form of government is beneficial to the totality of mortals by which quarrels and litigations, to which the nature of mortals is inclined, are decided more equitably and more suitably. But quarrels and litigations are decided more suitably among litigants if they have one judge, lord, or ruler than if they have several in no case subject to one. For if litigants, one of whom has inflicted damage or harm on the other and has denied his right, are subject to several kings or rulers without a superior, justice can easily be endangered, and it is not clear under which judge it is safe for both parties to litigate. For the party offended will litigate either under his own lord or a judge appointed by his own lord, or he will litigate under the offender's own king or a judge deputed by him. If the party offended litigates before his own lord or king or a judge appointed by him, he [the judge] may deservedly be suspect to the offender, *Extra, De officio iudicis delegati*, c. *Causam quae*, and c. *Insinuante*. But it is dangerous to litigate under a suspect judge.

Thus also "it is in a way natural to avoid the snares of suspect judges," 3, q. 5, *Quia suspecti.* It is therefore not safe for both parties to litigate under the king or lord of the offended party or a judge appointed by him. And it is also not safe for both parties to litigate under the king or lord of the offender or a judge appointed by him, because, by the above laws, he may be suspect to the offended party. And thus, if the litigants have several lords with no superior, justice can easily be endangered. It is beneficial to the totality of mortals, therefore, to have one highest ruler to whom, as to a common judge, any litigants whatever can have recourse, in whom the equal lordship over both the offended and offending parties will not unreasonably remove suspicion.

[7] Moreover, that form of government or lordship is beneficial to the totality of mortals by which not only inferiors, but also superiors, if they do wrong, can justly be corrected. Otherwise the peace of human society – which is so sweet that for its sake even wars are waged, according to Augustine, as we read in 23, q. 1, c. *Noli* – cannot be preserved, and justice – and "to cultivate justice is the highest good in things," according to Gregory, as we read in 12, q. 2, c. *Devotissimam*[6] – will not be maintained, unless care is taken, as far as possible, that superiors cannot do wrong insolently: as can be gathered, it seems, from the words of Innocent III quoted *Extra, De accusationibus, Qualiter et quando.*[7] For if there are many kings or rulers in different parts of the world who have no superior, they will be able freely and with impunity to disturb the peace and rights of lesser people. But if all kings and rulers are subject to one emperor, then not only inferiors, but also superiors, can lawfully be corrected if they do wrong. It is therefore beneficial to the whole world that one emperor should preside over all kings and rulers and have coercive jurisdiction over all mortals.

[8] Further, there should be such connection among all mortals that any of them, in relation to another, is an inferior or a superior, or both of them are inferiors in relation to the same person, so that true harmony may come about among all and each may devote reverence or love to each. This is gathered from a text of Popes

---

[6] Rather, c. *Si saeculi.*

[7] "However, they wished to provide for superiors so that they should not be accused of crimes unjustly: in such a way, nevertheless, that they should take care not to transgress insolently"; c. 24, col. 1598.

Gregory and Boniface included in dist. 89, c. *Ad hoc*, where we read: "To this [end] the foresight of divine providence appointed that there be different grades and distinct orders, so that while lesser persons showed reverence to the more important, and the more important devoted love to the lesser, a true concord should come about and connection from diversity and the administration of every office be carried on correctly; for the whole could not have lasted on any other plan." But such a connection does not exist among all mortals unless one presides over all the others. It is therefore beneficial to the totality of mortals for the world to be governed by one ruler.

[9] Again, the form of government that God does not permit among mortals, but takes away, because of the sins of the multitude is better than that which God introduces to punish the sins of the multitude. But God ordains that not one but many should have lordship over the totality of mortals to punish the sins of mortals, as Solomon testifies. In Proverbs 28[:2] he says: "For the sins of the land, many are its princes." Simply, therefore, it would be beneficial to the totality of mortals for all to be subject to one.

[10] Also, if it is not beneficial to the totality of mortals to be under one emperor, this will be either on account of human inadequacy, because no one can be found who is adequate to ruling the whole world, or on account of the excessive temporal power of one lord of the whole world by which he could run riot at will over his subjects. But inadequacy is no objection: just as human inadequacy is also no objection why one man should not preside in spiritual matters over the whole world, even if the totality of mortals were converted to the faith. And excessive power is no objection, because the whole world can, in proportion, resist the cruelty of one emperor of the whole world just as one particular kingdom can resist a king. And the emperor of the whole world would not have greater power over the whole world than a king has over a particular kingdom; but the power of the king is no objection why one king should not be over one kingdom, therefore neither is the emperor's power an objection why he should not be over the whole world.

[11] Moreover, if it is not beneficial for there to be one emperor over the whole world, then it is not just for one to have lordship over all. But if it is not just and not beneficial it is wicked. But it is not wicked for one to rule over all others, because if it were wicked it

would be against law, therefore either against natural law or against positive law. But it is not against natural law, because then it would always have been wicked, and thus no one would ever have been a true emperor of the world, since empire usurped against natural law is not a true empire. And it is also not against positive law, because a positive law by which it is decreed that no one should be emperor of the whole world could not be established except by the totality of mortals; but the totality of mortals never established this, but rather the opposite. Therefore it is not wicked for one to have empire over the whole world; it must therefore be regarded as beneficial.

Chapter 2

Student I think you have touched on rather strong arguments for the above assertion, and those who have plenty of books can strengthen them in many ways with the opinions of the fathers. So relate another opinion concerning my question.

Master Another opinion is the opposite, that it is not beneficial to the world for the totality of mortals to be subject to one emperor or secular ruler.

Student I would like to hear the arguments for this opinion.

Master This opinion can be argued for in many ways. [1] Nothing of which the opposite was ordained by God is beneficial to the world, for everything contrary to a divine ordinance must be regarded as pernicious and bad and not beneficial. But a division of kingdoms so that they are under different kings with no superior is from God; for, as is clear in 3 Kings, 12 and 13, God wished the children of Israel to have two kings who would neither of them be subject to the other and would not have a superior king. Therefore it must not be judged beneficial for one secular ruler to have lordship over all mortals.

[2] Further, the same right exists in great and in little, in whole and in part, as was shown above by means of many sacred canons. But that any one king or secular ruler, no matter who, should preside over a part of mortals, even the part that uses the justest laws, is not beneficial. For what displeases God is not beneficial; but that the Israelite people, which was a part of mortals and used the justest (because divine) laws, should be subject to a king or secular ruler was displeasing to God, so that, when that people asked for a king,

he said to Samuel, as we read in 1 Kings 8[:7]: "Listen to the voice of the people in all they say to you. They have not rejected you, but me, that I should not reign over them." Therefore, *a fortiori*, for one secular ruler to reign over the whole world, even if the whole were converted to the faith, is not beneficial.

[3] Besides, that form of government is more beneficial to the totality of mortals in the state of fault that is more like the form of government that would have existed if mankind had remained in the state of innocence, because that which is more like the better is more beneficial. But if mankind had remained in the state of innocence, one man would not have been the emperor of all the others. Therefore neither is it beneficial in the state of fault that one should have lordship over all others.

[4] Again, what conflicts with and is repugnant with the law of nations must not be regarded as beneficial, since the law of nations is natural law. For as we read in dist. 1, *Ius gentium*, the law of nations is the same among all nations; and natural law alone is such – no custom or multitude or positive law can derogate from it in any way, *Extra, De consuetudine, Cum tanto*. But for the totality of mortals to be under one ruler or emperor conflicts with and is repugnant with the law of nations: First, because "wars and captivities" belong to the law of nations, dist. 1, *Ius gentium*; these would cease if one emperor powerfully commanded the totality of mortals. Also, because by the law of nations intermarriage with foreigners is prohibited (same distinction, same chapter). This cannot be understood of all foreigners whatever, for then intermarriages between anyone at all of different provinces would be prohibited; therefore it is understood of foreigners who should have no community with one another; all those subject to one emperor or lord are not such, for all who are subject to the one lord can have, and in many cases should have, community with one another, helping each other and defending one another. Therefore it is not beneficial or fair that the totality of mortals should obey one emperor or ruler.

[5] Also, those who should neither bear the same yoke, nor have community or peaceful society with one another, nor licitly have recourse to the same judge to undergo judgment, should not obey one ruler or emperor. Now some mortals are believers and some are unbelievers. But believers should not bear the same yoke with

unbelievers, because the Apostle prohibits it. In 2 Corinthians 6[:14], he says, "Bear not the yoke with unbelievers." Nor should they have community or peaceful society with them, by the testimony of the King of Kings and Lord of Lords himself, who says in Matthew 10[:34]: "Do not think that I have come to bring peace to the earth; I came not to bring peace, but the sword. I have come to divide a man against his father," etc. In Deuteronomy 7[:2] believers are explicitly commanded to strike unbelievers even to death and not enter into any treaty with them, and not to have mercy on them. The Apostle also teaches this in 2 Corinthians 6[:14], saying: "For what share has justice with injustice? Or what fellowship has light with darkness? And what concord has Christ with Belial? Or what part has the believer with the unbeliever?" The wise man speaks in agreement with these: in Ecclesiasticus 13[:22] he says, "What fellowship has a holy man with a dog?" Nor, also, should believers have recourse to the court of unbelievers to undergo judgment, as the Apostle testifies. As we read in 1 Corinthians 6[:5], he sharply rebukes believers who were litigating before unbelievers, saying: "I speak thus to your shame: is there not among you any wise man who can judge between a brother and his brother? But brother contends with brother in court, and this before unbelievers." From these [texts] we gather that believers should be altogether separated from unbelievers both in respect of litigation in court and in respect of all peaceful sharing. Therefore the totality of mortals should not be subject to one emperor or secular ruler.

[6] Moreover, no one who cannot take due care of them should preside over the totality of mortals; but no one man can take due care of the totality of mortals, since no one is adequate of himself to have the care of even one small kingdom (small in relation to the whole world), as Solomon testifies. As we read in 2 Paralipomenon 1[:10], he says, speaking to God, "For who can judge worthily this people of yours, which is so great?" – as if to say, "No one." Therefore, *a fortiori*, no one will be able to judge worthily the totality of mortals.

Chapter 3

Student Report another opinion on this question.

Master Another opinion is that it would be beneficial for one ruler, not a secular but an ecclesiastic, to preside over the totality of mortals.

Student We can find many things in favor of this opinion in the tract concerning the power of the pope and clergy, so bring forward a few for its confirmation.

Master In favor of this opinion it can be argued thus. Wisdom seems to be chief among all the excellences by which a ruler should excel his subjects, even one who presides over subjects in temporal matters. And thus we read that Solomon, who asked for wisdom from God so that he could worthily rule God's people in temporal matters, was magnificently commended by God. The Lord said to him, as we read in 2 Paralipomenon 1[:11]: "Because this has pleased your heart more, and you have not asked for riches and wealth and glory, nor for the lives of those who hate you, nor for many days of life, but for knowledge and wisdom to be able to judge my people over whom I have appointed you king, wisdom and knowledge have been granted to you; I will give you moreover riches and wealth and glory." And the same Solomon says, Proverbs 1[:5], "He who understands will possess governments." By these [texts] we are given to understand that for a ruler wisdom is especially necessary. But greater wisdom is found in ecclesiastics than in seculars. Therefore not a secular ruler, but an ecclesiastic, is worthy to be over the whole world.

Student This argument does not seem to follow. He who is over others in temporal matters should excel others in worldly wisdom and skill in secular business, not in divine wisdom. But although ecclesiastics excel in divine wisdom, seculars excel in worldly wisdom. He who presides in temporal matters should therefore be a secular and not an ecclesiastic, a layman and not a cleric.

Master Some try to disprove this answer. As we gather from the divine Scriptures, he who is over others in temporal matters should be more expert not only in worldly wisdom but also in divine wisdom and in God's law, since a king who rules in temporal matters should meditate continually on the law of God, as God says. In Deuteronomy 17[:18], speaking of the king, He says, "And after he sits on the throne of his kingdom, he will write out for himself the Deuteronomy of this law in a volume, and, taking the exemplar from the priests of the levitical tribe, he will have it with him and will read it all the days of his life." And the Lord also instructed Joshua, who presided in temporal matters, saying, "Let not the volume of this law depart from your mouth, but you will meditate on it by day and by night, so that you may keep and do all the things written in it" [Joshua 1:8]. We gather from these [passages] that a temporal president should surpass others not only in worldly wisdom and skill in secular business but also in divine wisdom.

Chapter 4

Student I would like to hear yet another opinion about my question.

Master There are some who say that it is not beneficial that one ruler, either a secular or an ecclesiastic, should preside over the totality of mortals, and it is also not beneficial that several seculars or ecclesiastics with no superior should be the lord of different mortals in different provinces or kingdoms; but the world would be ruled best if many held lordship of the world together, just as in many cities and communities, as we know, not one only but many rule.

Student Bring forward some argument for this opinion.

Master It seems possible to support this opinion as follows. That form of government or lordship is more useful to the whole world in which fewer errors and sins occur, because through such a lordship or government justice, peace, and the concord of all is better achieved and also preserved. But if many wise and virtuous persons were lords over the totality of mortals, fewer errors and sins in ruling would occur than if one person alone governed all; for just as the truth of justice that is sought by many is found more easily,[8] so it is more difficult for many to err than one alone. Thus Solomon in Proverbs 13 and 24[:6] asserts that "there will be safety where there is much advice." Thus also in 1 Machabees 8[:15] it is said in praise of the Romans that "they made themselves a senate-house, and three hundred and twenty men used to deliberate every day, giving advice about the multitude, that they might act worthily." It is more beneficial to the totality of mortals, there-

---

[8] The manuscripts do not give any source. See dist. 20, *De quibus* ("What is sought by many elders is found more easily"), and gloss to the decretals, *Extra*, 1.29.21, col. 344, v. *Plurimorum* ("What is sought by many wise persons is found more easily"). The phrase "the truth of justice" comes from Deut. 17:9.

fore, that several together should preside over all, rather than one
alone.

Chapter 5

Student Relate another opinion about my question, if there is one.
Master Another opinion is that it is beneficial that the governments
and lordships of mortals should vary according to the diversity,
quality, and necessity of the times, so that sometimes it is beneficial
that one ruler, a secular or an ecclesiastic, should be over all
mortals, but sometimes it is beneficial that many together, seculars
or ecclesiastics, should govern all others, and sometimes it is useful
that several rulers without a superior should preside over different
regions of the world.
Student Try to support this opinion with some arguments.
Master It seems possible to support this opinion in several ways.
[1] Just as laws should be established for the common advantage,
dist. 4, *Erit autem*, so rulers, rectors and lords, both seculars and
ecclesiastics, should be placed over others for the common advantage, which, also, they are obliged to take care of more than their
own; for if they put their own ahead of the common advantage,
they should be regarded not as rectors or princes or lords but as
tyrants. But sometimes the common advantage would be taken care
of better by one ruler, a secular or an ecclesiastic, ruling over all,
than by several with no superior, whether ruling together or presiding in different provinces, because sometimes the multitude of
mortals would bear the lordship of one secular or ecclesiastical
ruler conspicuous in wisdom, justice, and the other virtues required
in a ruler with more equanimity than they would the lordship of
many. Sometimes, however, the great multitude of mortals would
not bear the lordship of one but would willingly subject themselves
to the lordship of many (either ruling together or having care of
different provinces), and consequently the common advantage would
then be taken care of better by many than by one alone. It is
beneficial, therefore, for one or several to rule mortals, according
to the diversity and necessity of the times.
[2] Further, the totality of mortals is best ruled in the way that
is more like the way of ruling in which God ordained that the
people should be ruled who were subject to himself by the true
faith. But God ordained that the Israelite people subject to himself

should be ruled sometimes by one secular ruler (for David and also Solomon ruled over the whole people of God), sometimes by one priest (for Hely the priest judged the whole Israelite people), sometimes by several kings none of whom was subject to another (for Roboam and Jeroboam reigned over the Israelite people in different regions). It is therefore beneficial that the totality of mortals be subject to one or to many rulers or rectors according to the diversity and necessity of the times.

[3] Again, the way of ruling the totality of mortals that was once just and permissible must be regarded as beneficial, for everything just and permissible should be judged beneficial. But sometimes the world was justly and permissibly subjected to government by one ruler and sometimes to government by many. Such a varied way of ruling the totality of mortals according to the diversity, quality, and necessity of the times must therefore still be reckoned beneficial.

Chapter 6

Student That opinion is understood to agree in some respects with the other contrary opinions, and it also seems to disagree with them in some things – or perhaps it does not disagree in any way with the first as interpreted by some, though verbally it seems to conflict with it. Therefore, whether it is altogether the same as the first opinion as some understand it or is in conflict with it in some way, I wish to know how those who hold that last opinion try to answer the arguments brought forward for the other opinions insofar as they are, or seem to be, against that one. Let us therefore discuss thoroughly the first argument for the first opinion, which is based on the premise that if one secular ruler were lord over all the provinces of the world the bad would be restrained more severely and the good would live more quietly. Say, therefore, how it is answered.

Master The answer made to it is that although it is the rule, and happens more often, that when one secular ruler is lord over all mortals the bad are restrained more strictly and the good live more quietly among the bad, yet this fails in particular cases.

Student Explain some cases (but only a few) in which they say this fails; for perhaps when a few have been explained I will be able to think of others by myself.

Master One case in which they say that under one ruler of the world the bad are not more strictly restrained and the good do not live more quietly among the bad is when some multitude of those who from wickedness refuse to obey the one is so great and so strong that they dare to stir up seditious and dangerous wars against the monarch of the world, with notable loss to the commonwealth and to good people, from which they would cease if different secular rulers with no superior governed the different provinces of the world.

Student[9] So that I may understand this case more explicitly and more manifestly I would like you to bring forward some examples of it.

Master Although a manifest matter needs no proof, to satisfy your wishes I will bring forward an example from Roman history concerning Julius Caesar. Because he wished to take sole possession of the Roman Empire, which was previously in the power of the senate and consuls, there resulted numberless seditions, factions, and massacres. The whole city of Rome was divided in intestine and civil war; so much slaughter therefore arose that there scarcely survived farmers to till the fields. And thus many of the very best citizens and defenders of the commonwealth were murdered by a cruel death, and the bad were carried to insolence and unbearable pride. Thus it was necessary that the Roman Empire, which by the advice and foresight of many, namely of the whole Senate, grew to an immense size, should little by little decrease, reduced to the lordship of one man. Also, in other factions and civil wars, both Roman and other, it is manifestly seen how when one man wishes to predominate over many powerful men he often stirs up the greatest disturbance of the commonwealth and the exile or killing of good men. In a case in which many would not be willing to endure the dominance of one man, therefore, it would be beneficial to the commonwealth for several to be over different [subjects] in concord.

Student I believe I understand this case now, for I do not doubt that it has often happened and can happen every day. So in a few words relate to me one case more.

---

[9] The next four paragraphs are not found in the manuscripts and may not be authentic.

Master Another case is when the ruler of the whole world has through temporal force raged with tyrannical cruelty against good men who are lovers of the commonwealth and has advanced the bad who support and help him in his tyranny, as we can read in the histories of many tyrants – for example, Nero, the cruelest of the Roman emperors, who committed many murders against wives, in-laws, and kin and did such great evils that he incited the other kingdoms to rebellion and at length, having been condemned as an enemy by the Senate, turned his hand against himself also and was his own executioner. Similarly, it is sufficiently manifest how pernicious to good men was the emperor Domitian, who could not have inflicted such murder on good citizens and the best among the nobles if he had not held the empire alone. The same could be shown of many others. But let these suffice.

In these two cases, therefore, under one monarch of the world the bad would grow insolent and the good would be very greatly troubled. For this reason, if the world were neither in fact nor of right subject to one secular ruler, and it were feared with probability that if someone assumed the monarchy of the world the bad would grow insolent and the good would be troubled – whether because of the malice of the multitude refusing to obey one man or because of the malice of the one to be appointed – no one should for that time be appointed to the lordship of the whole world.

Student From the things you have just said I understand better the mode of asserting that opinion, and from those things I also conjecture that all cases in which they say that the bad can become insolent and the good be troubled under one monarch of the whole world can be reduced to the two foregoing cases; for, according to them, as I understand it, it never happens that the bad are less restrained and the good live less quietly under one ruler than under many except [1] because of a dangerous rebellion or the particular wickedness of some powerful and large multitude able to stir up dangerous wars, or else [2] because of the wickedness, ignorance, or negligence of the ruler: and in these cases, according to them, if there *had never been* by right any ruler of the whole world, then no one should be appointed to lordship of the whole world. Do not, therefore, explain more cases in which according to them the bad are less restrained and the good live less quietly under one lord of the whole world than under several. But I wish to know whether, according to them, *after* someone had been of right lord of the whole world (whether by election or by succession), someone should be appointed to the imperial majesty, notwithstanding the wickedness of any multitude unwilling to obey one [ruler] and notwithstanding that it seemed probable that none of those who could be appointed to world empire would wish, and know how, to use such an office justly and lawfully.

Master You will have an opportunity to ask about this afterwards if you wish, when we investigate whether the Roman Empire can be destroyed or annulled or can cease.[10]

Student All the same, say briefly what answer they make to this.

Master Some of them say that in the above cases the appointment of anyone whatever to world empire should be deferred, because nothing detrimental to the commonwealth should be done, especially if it proceeded from human ordinance and not from divine law or the law of nature; and therefore, as long as the appointment of someone to world empire would be detrimental to the commonwealth, whether because of the wickedness of subjects or because of the inadequacy of the one to be appointed, such appointment should not be attempted, because "a provision made for concord" should not "tend to harm," dist. 45, *Licet*.

Chapter 7

Student I understand how they say that the bad can grow insolent and the good be troubled more under one ruler of all than under several. Therefore say how the proofs brought up on the opposite side are answered.

Master To the first – which is based on the premise that if one man were ruler and lord of the totality of living persons, he would have the greatest power to restrain the bad and protect the good – it is answered that because sometimes someone is lord of the whole world by right and not in fact (because many rebel against him), it can therefore happen that the lord and ruler of the whole world has less power to restrain the bad and protect the good than many against whom none, or not as many, try to rebel.

---

[10] See III *Dial.*, II, 1.31; also *OQ*, III.11 (translated below).

And to the second proof and the third – which are based on the premise that if the totality of mortals were subject to one [ruler] there would be fewer oppressors of the good, and men would be less inclined to wars than if there were several without a superior having lordship in different regions – it is answered that these things could and would happen if *in fact* one wise and just man powerfully ruled all, but it need not always be true that the multitude of those oppressing the good is reduced and audacity in stirring up wars restrained by one man's lordship *by right*. For when one man is lord of all by right it can happen – both from the particular wickedness of some great multitude of wicked men seeking their own good, and not the common good, and from the wickedness, ignorance, and negligence of the one man commanding all – that the multitude of oppressors of the good and audacity in stirring up wars (and troubling the good in other ways) both increase: from which, also, they would sometimes cease if many presided with no superior. For it is possible sometimes for even a few, resenting the fact that someone is placed over them, to incite many peoples to rebel with them against their superior and to oppress the good by causing wars and battles. It can also happen that, while one who is foolish or idle or rages tyrannically against the good is lord of the whole world, the bad are more bold to oppress the good and to stir up wars than if several wise and just [men] presided over different regions. It can therefore happen that the bad grow more insolent and the good live less quietly if one man rules over the totality of mortals than if many without a superior rule different regions.

Chapter 8

Student Say how, according to them, it can be maintained that it is not always beneficial to the totality of living persons for one secular ruler to rule, even though temporal things are controlled by the laity just as spiritual things are controlled by the clergy – from which the second argument advanced above in chapter I tries to infer that, just as one ecclesiastical ruler is over all others in spiritual matters, so it is always beneficial for one secular ruler to preside over all in temporal matters.

Master To this a twofold answer is made: [1] In one way, that the cases of a president in spiritual matters and a president in temporal matters are not altogether similar, because for one man to preside in spiritual matters over all the faithful (even if the whole world were converted to the faith) is immediately from a particular divine ordinance, and not from human ordinance. This can be gathered from sacred canons included in the *Decreta*, dist. 21, c. *Quamvis*, and dist. 22, c. *Omnes* and c. *Sacrosancta*, and in a great many other places; therefore, unless God ordained otherwise and revealed this to the faithful, all the faithful (even if all mortals had received the faith) should obey one highest pontiff in spiritual matters, because it is not in the power of men to change a divine ordinance in any way. But that one secular ruler should preside over the whole world in temporal matters is from human ordinance, which (because it is not of divine law or natural law) can licitly be changed by men, because everything is dissolved by the same causes as gave it birth, *Extra, De regulis iuris, Omnis*. Therefore, before one secular ruler presided over all mortals, those who wished, for a just and reasonable cause, could licitly not consent that someone should be appointed to empire of the whole world: for when there is a loss to the liberty or power or right of some, "the consent of all must be sought" and had, dist. 54, c. 1.[11] Similarly, if for some reason it would be to the notable detriment of the common good for one ruler to be appointed to world monarchy, then for that time no one should be promoted to empire.

[2] In another way it could be said that although Christ ordained that all the faithful should obey one highest pontiff, nevertheless, because that ordinance of Christ was affirmative and not negative and therefore obliges always but not for always, it is not necessary that all the faithful should at all times obey one pope; since, also, this is not possible, because that see must often be vacant. And therefore, although all the faithful should always be ready, according to place and time and due manner, to obey one highest pontiff, yet the election of a highest pontiff when the see is vacant can, for a reasonable and manifest cause, be deferred for a time, and not only for a short time but also for a long time; so that just as

---

[11] In the gloss, col. 274, v. *Qui aliquid*.

such an election has, for a reason, sometimes been delayed for several days, sometimes for several months, sometimes indeed for several years (and thus that see has sometimes been vacant for six years), so, for a reason, it could licitly be deferred for a hundred years, or two hundred, or more; and the like could be said of appointment to world empire.

Student I perceive that in some respects this last answer treats appointment to the supreme priesthood and promotion to empire as analogous, because elevation to the one, as to the other, can be deferred for a reason. But I would like to know whether, just as the faithful cannot enact that no one should ever be elected highest pontiff, so mortals cannot ordain that no one should ever be raised up to world empire.

Master It is answered that it is not and never will be permissible for mortals to enact that no one should ever be elevated to empire of the whole world, because it is not permissible to make any permanent enactment against something that is beneficial to the common good as a rule though it can harm the common good occasionally. But for one ruler to preside over all mortals is beneficial to the common good of all mortals as a rule, though it can do harm occasionally. Therefore it can never be enacted absolutely that no one should ever be promoted to the empire, although it would be permissible to ordain with some qualifications or specifications or conditions that for the time being no one should be promoted to such an office.

Chapter 9

Student Relate how it is beneficial as a rule, though not in every case, for all mortals to be subject to one secular ruler, even though it is beneficial for each single particular kingdom to have one king and the same judgment should be made of the whole and of the part, just as the same judgment must be made in small matters and in great; upon these things is based the third argument above for the first opinion reported in the first chapter.

Master It is answered in two ways. [1] In one way, that a like judgment need not always be made of the whole and of the part, just as the same right does not always exist in great matters and in small. For often the quantity of the thing brings about a difference of right, *Extra, De simonia, Etsi questiones*,[12] 12, q. 2, c. *Terrulas*, and c. *Bona rei*, and 1, q. 1, *Iudices*.[13] And thus sometimes great things do harm but not small; for also "a moderate amount does no harm," as is noted in the gloss on the prologue to the *Decretals*,[14] and *Extra, De rescriptis, Si proponente*.[15] But when there is *the same reason* concerning whole and part and concerning great matters and small, then a similar judgment must be made of them and the same right exists in them, since "where there is the same reason there ought to be the same right," *Extra, De constitutionibus, Translato*.[16] But there is never, or not always, the same reason concerning the whole world and one particular kingdom, because, as was suggested before, it can happen, because of the particular and unusual wickedness of some multitude that has great power or because of the inadequacy of the person to be appointed, that to set one ruler over all will be detrimental to the common good, whereas to set one ruler over one particular kingdom will be to the advantage of the inhabitants of that kingdom; and therefore in such a case a similar judgment should not be made concerning the whole world and concerning one particular kingdom.

[2] In another way it is said that it is also often not beneficial that one king should be set over one kingdom. Indeed, just as sometimes different bishoprics should be united, 16, q. 1, *Et temporis qualitas*, so it would sometimes be beneficial to the commonwealth for different kingdoms to be united and for one person to reign over several kingdoms. And when there did not exist one world ruler, the more several kingdoms were united the more usefully they would be ruled, if some just man were to govern them for the common advantage and not for his own benefit.

Chapter 10

Student Lengthy treatment of the remaining arguments advanced for the first opinion above in chapter 1 would perhaps be tedious

---

[12] See gloss to the decretals, col. 1617, v. *Modici pretii*.
[13] Rather, 11, q. 1, *Iudices*. See gloss, col. 506, v. *Quinque sunt oboli*.
[14] See gloss to the decretals, col. 5, v. *In iudiciis*.
[15] See gloss to the decretals, col. 82, v. *Minus competens*.
[16] See gloss to the decretals, col. 16, v. *Quod de uno*.

to the reader, so if one answer can be given to them I would like to hear it.

Master It appears to some that they are refuted by a single answer, since they all infer that it is true as a rule that it would be beneficial for the whole world to be under one secular ruler; this fails in some cases, however, and for these cases those arguments do not prove their point.

Student To me that answer seems too general, and therefore it will in no way appear reasonable unless it is applied particularly to those arguments. So try to apply it briefly to those arguments.

Master The fourth argument adduced above in chapter I – which is based on the premise that since all mortals can have community with one another in temporal matters they will not be governed best unless they are subject to one secular ruler, and therefore it is beneficial for all to be subject to one emperor – seems to be ruled out by this: By no means will all who can have community with one another not be governed best unless they are subject to one ruler; therefore on occasion it is not beneficial for all to be subject to one emperor. For on occasion the best way of governing mortals is wrongly blocked, and therefore, because of the particular wickedness of subjects or because of the iniquity or inadequacy of the one to be appointed to empire, the totality of mortals sometimes cannot be governed in the best way. In some cases, therefore, it is better – abandoning the best form of government, because it cannot be had – for different provinces to be subject to different rulers than for one ruler to claim for himself, to the ruin of many, lordship of the world: even if he is elected by those who, if the community of mortals had been well disposed, by right and in fact should have promoted to world empire someone worthy and suitable.

And the fifth argument – which is based on the premise that if the totality of mortals were subject to one secular ruler, discord among mortals would be abolished more effectively than if there were several rulers with no superior – is broken by this: although it is true as a rule that discords are taken away more effectively by the government of one man than by several, yet this fails in the cases spoken of before.

The sixth argument – which seems to have its force from the premise that conflicts and litigations are decided more fairly if all mortals have one supreme judge than if there are several supreme judges – is overturned by this: as a rule this [premise] has truth when all obey one both by right and in fact, yet it fails in the cases often mentioned before.

The seventh argument – which is founded on the premise that if the totality of mortals were subject to one, not only inferiors but also superiors, even kings, if they do wrong, can be lawfully corrected, which would not happen if there were several rulers with no superior – is answered by this: this [premise] is true as a rule, if no multitude powerfully rebels against a ruler of the world reigning powerfully and justly; it fails, however, when he who is by right lord of the world would not reign thus.

The eighth argument – which is founded on the premise that among all mortals there should be such a connection that each in respect of another is a superior or an inferior, as is gathered from the text of Popes Gregory and Boniface – is refuted by this,[17] that without such a connection of all mortals the totality of mortals will not be governed by the best form of government, and therefore there should be such a connection among all mortals, and consequently all mortals (if they were disposed in the best way, so far as the condition of mortals permits) should be subject to one ruler: but because such a connection is in fact obstructed by wickedness, it can therefore happen on occasion that such a connection of all mortals also does not exist, even by right.

The ninth argument – which is based on the premise that God ordained that many rulers should be lords over mortals to punish the sins of men, and consequently such lordship of many rulers is not best – does indeed prove that the lordship of one ruler over the whole world is better than the lordship of many rulers with no superior: however, because such lordship cannot be had in fact, due to the unworthiness of men and by the just judgment of God, it is therefore on occasion beneficial that such lordship should cease for a time, even by right, so that no one is in fact raised to such lordship.

The tenth argument – which is based on the premise that if it is not beneficial to the totality of mortals to be under one emperor, this would be either because of human inadequacy or because of

---

[17] The refutation comes after various points have been conceded, after the colon.

the excessive temporal power of such an emperor – argues from an inadequate division: for it might not happen for either of those reasons, but because of the unusual and particular wickedness of subjects, or because for some determinate time it is not certain that someone suited to such an office could be found.

To the eleventh argument – which is based on the premise that if it were not always beneficial that one emperor should be lord over all mortals, this would be because it is against natural law or against positive law – it is answered that since natural law is a natural commandment, as can be gathered from the gloss included in dist. 1, *Ius naturale*, then, just as there can be a twofold division of natural commandments, so there can be found a twofold division of the natural law. Some natural commandments are absolute and without any condition, qualification, specification, or determination, such as "Do not worship strange gods," "Do not commit adultery," "Do not bear false witness," "Do not lie," and the like. And some are not absolute but are subject to some condition, qualification, specification or determination, such as "Use something of another's even against the owner's will – if you are in a situation of extreme necessity," "Cut off one of your members – to preserve the health of the body," and the like. Thus there is a twofold natural law: some absolute and some with some condition, qualification or specification or determination. It cannot be against natural law in the first sense for one emperor to preside over all mortals, because then in no case could any emperor ever rule licitly over all mortals. But it can be against natural law in the second sense for one emperor to preside over all mortals, because natural reason says that one emperor should *not* rule over all mortals – when such lordship would be to the detriment and ruin of the commonwealth and of the common good. And therefore such lordship is as a rule just and expedient and in harmony with natural law, but on occasion it can be wicked and contrary to natural law in the second sense.

Chapter 11

Student I have heard how answer is made to the arguments by which it seems possible to prove that it is always and in every case beneficial for one secular ruler to preside over all mortals in temporal matters. Now I wish to hear how the arguments are dissolved which were brought forward in chapter 2 above, by which it seems possible to show that it is never beneficial for the totality of mortals to be under one secular ruler in temporal matters.

Master To the first of those reasons – which is based on the premise that the division of kingdoms proceeded from God, who rules all things in the best way – it is answered that God does some things to punish the sins of the bad, and those things are beneficial when the bad should be punished; but often, when the bad are not to be punished, they are not beneficial but the contrary. And the division of kingdoms was from God to punish the sin of the bad; and therefore, when kings were not to be appointed to punish the sins the wicked have committed, but for the advantage of the good and to preserve them from evil deeds, it would be beneficial for all kingdoms to be subject to one supreme ruler.

The second argument – which is founded on the premise that God was displeased by the request of the Israelite people, who were using the justest laws, when they requested that a king be given to them – is answered in many ways. In one way, that the people's request displeased God, not because they requested something bad, but because they asked with a bad will and a bad intention. They did indeed ask with a bad intention, because they asked for a king over themselves so as to be in this respect like the unbelievers. And thus they said, as we read in 1 Kings 8[:5,19,20]: "Make us a king to judge us, as all nations have." And afterwards in the same chapter we read as follows: "But the people would not hear the voice of Samuel, but they said, 'Nay: for there shall be a king over us, and we also will be like all peoples.' " They were asking for a king also with a bad will, because, being ignorant and stupid, they asked for a king so as to avoid thereby the rule of Samuel, who had ruled them most justly. God himself, who saw their hearts, testified to this, it seems, when he said to Samuel: "According to all their works that they have done from the day when I brought them out of Egypt until this day, as they have forsaken me and served strange Gods, so do they also unto thee."[18] From these words we gather that they wickedly wished to avoid Samuel's rule.

Student It seems that they did not desire to throw off Samuel's rule but that of his sons, who were unjust and wicked and therefore

---

[18] 1 Kings 8:8.

were rightly to be driven away. In the same place we read: "And it came to pass when Samuel was old, that he appointed his sons to be judges over Israel ... And his sons walked not in his ways: but they turned aside after lucre and took bribes and perverted judgment. Then all the ancients of Israel, being assembled, came to Samuel at Ramatha. And they said to him, 'Behold, you are old, and your sons walk not in your ways: make us a king, to judge us.' "[19] From these words we gather that they were content with Samuel's rule, but the rule of his sons displeased them.

Master It is answered that although they were not willing to say explicitly that Samuel's rule displeased them, they implied that it displeased them when they said, "Behold, you are old," as if to say, "Now you are not fit to rule"; and they alleged the wickedness of his sons only to hide their bad will, because they intended chiefly to throw off Samuel. We are given to understand this by God's words quoted above.

Student I have heard one answer to that argument; now relate another.

Master In another way it is answered that although, as has often been said above, it is beneficial as a rule that a king should be lord in temporal matters, on occasion it is not beneficial. When it is beneficial and when not, though often hidden from men, and especially from the inexpert and the bad, is never hidden from God, to whom all things are naked and open. And therefore, when it was hidden from those petitioners that it was not beneficial to them to have a king, their request displeased God because, without questioning him who had ordained that they should not be ruled by a king because he knew it would not be beneficial to them to have a king, they unwisely and impudently and unseasonably asked for a king. They should not have asked for a change in the way of ruling ordained by God before questioning the mouth of the Lord; though having a king is not as a rule bad – indeed, it is good as a rule and bad on occasion.

The third argument – which is founded on the premise that that form of government is better which is more like the form of government that would have existed if men had remained in the state of innocence, who would never have had one emperor of

---

[19] I Kings 8:1–5.

all – is excluded by this: because of the difference between the state of innocence and the state of fallen nature, the form of government more like the form of government that would have existed in the state of innocence is not always better in the state of fallen nature – just as the form of government more like the form of government that will exist in the state of glory is also not better in the state of fallen nature, because then it would be better for each to rule himself and no one to have rule or prelacy over others (because in the state of glory rule or prelacy will not exist).

The fourth argument – which is based on the premise that for one emperor to be lord over all mortals is against the law of nations, which is the natural law, and is consequently never beneficial or permissible – it seems possible to refute by the things said in the preceding chapter. Although what is against the law of nations is sometimes wicked, it is not always wicked: sometimes, indeed, it is equitable as a rule and wicked on occasion. For (at least in respect of many things) the law of nations is not the absolute natural law without any condition, qualification, determination, or specification, but is the natural law conditioned, qualified, or with some specification or determination. For as we read in the *Decreta*, dist. 1, *Ius gentium*, "To the law of nations belong wars, captivities, enslavements"; these, however, do not exist by natural law absolutely, without any condition, qualification, specification, or determination, because then the opposites would never be permissible, because what is against the absolute natural law is never permissible but always impermissible and beyond dispensation, *Extra*, *De consuetudine*, c. *Cum tanto*, and dist. 9, para. 1.[20] Therefore, even if one emperor is lord over all, wars, captivities, and intermarriages between foreigners may sometimes be in accordance with the law of nations and can therefore pertain to the natural law that is conditioned or qualified or with some specification or determination. However, they are not always wicked,[21] because they do not belong to the absolute natural law that does not vary but remains unchange-

---

[20] Rather, dist. 5, para. 1. See gloss to dist. 5, col. 13, v. *Haec, quae*: "Against natural law no dispensation is made."

[21] *Iniqua*; but the argument seems to require *aequa*, "right." The objection is that a world emperor would prevent war, which is in accordance with the law of nations; the answer is that the law of nature does not *require* war.

able and immovable,[22] dist. 5, para. 1, and dist. 6, para. *His itaque.*
The fifth argument – which is founded on the premise that some mortals are believers and some unbelievers, who should not bear the same yoke or have community or peaceful society with one another or have recourse to the same judge to receive judgment and consequently should not be under one emperor – it seems can be broken in many ways. First, because even if it were true that believers should not bear the yoke of unbelievers with unbelievers and should not have community or peaceful society with unbelievers when the unbelievers attack believers or do anything in contempt of the creator or try to draw believers to mortal sin, and that believers should not have recourse to an unbelieving judge to receive judgment, it would, nevertheless, be permissible for believers to bear the yoke of *believers* with unbelievers and to have community and peaceful fellowship with them if they attempt nothing bad, and to have recourse with them to a believing judge to receive judgment; and therefore, even if it were not permissible for believers to be under one unbelieving emperor of all mortals, it would, nevertheless, be permissible for both unbelievers and believers to be under one believing emperor. Second, because even if believers should not bear the same spiritual yoke with unbelievers, they can licitly bear with unbelievers the same temporal yoke. And thus there were many believers in both the New and Old Testaments who bore the same temporal yoke with unbelievers, obeying an unbelieving ruler. Believers can also licitly have community and peaceful society with unbelievers, as many saints did have, though not in sin and against God's honor. It is permissible also on occasion for believers to have recourse to an unbelieving judge to undergo judgment, on the example of many saints who did this. And thus it could on occasion be beneficial that even an unbelieving emperor should preside over all mortals. Third, because it is accidental that some are believers and some unbelievers, for all mortals were believers once, and it could happen still.
The sixth argument – which is based on the premise that no one is adequate to caring for all mortals – is refuted by this:

---

[22] See gloss to the decretals, *Extra, De consuetudine*, c. *Cum tanto*, col. 95, v. *Naturali iuri*: "Which remains unmovable."

Although no one is adequate to the care of all without any danger, loss, and inconvenience to any subject, nevertheless many have a sufficiency for this [care] as much as the condition of fallen nature permits. For this reason it is more useful to the totality of mortals to be under one than under many. And thus, although no one is adequate to rule one kingdom, even a small one, without any shortcoming, it is more useful to a particular kingdom to be subject to one lord than to several. Thus, also, although he perceived that no one could judge the Israelite people worthily and without any shortcoming, deficient in nothing, Solomon nevertheless did not refuse government but asked for wisdom to rule more perfectly and more worthily.

Chapter 12

Student Answer the argument for the third opinion reported in chapter 3 above, namely that it would be beneficial to the world for one ruler to preside, namely an ecclesiastic, not a secular.

Master That argument is based on the premise that wisdom, which is most of all necessary to a president, is found more in ecclesiastics, in both temporal and spiritual matters, than in seculars. To this you answered[23] that in ecclesiastics greater wisdom is found concerning divine matters, not concerning human matters. Some try to disprove that answer by asserting that according to divine law a king should be more expert than others even in matters that relate to the divine law, on which he should continually meditate. Others try to exclude this objection, asserting that, although by the commandment found in Deuteronomy 17[:19], as quoted, the king should read God's law "all the days of his life" – that is, at suitable times – yet priests are by God's commandment more obliged to such reading; and therefore, although the king should not have been completely ignorant of divine wisdom, he was not obliged to excel the priests in divine wisdom: especially since he should not teach divine wisdom publicly, because no king should take to himself the office of preaching; this office, however, does pertain to priests.

---

[23] See above, chapter 3 (p. 248).

Student It seems that that answer can still be blocked and that the main argument proves its point. For that person is more suitable to preside in temporal matters who should excel others not only in divine wisdom but also in human wisdom and skill in secular affairs, because to preside pertains especially to the wise, as Solomon testifies. In Proverbs 1[:5] he says, "He who understands will possess government." Also, in chapter 17[:2] he says, "A wise servant shall rule over foolish sons." But prelates of the Church should excel others not only in divine wisdom but also in human wisdom and skill in secular affairs, dist. 39, para. 1, and c. 1. There Gregory, speaking about appointing a bishop, says, "At this time there should be appointed in the stronghold of government one who knows how to be solicitous, not only concerning the welfare of souls, but also concerning outward benefit and security." And in 16, q. 1, c. *Nulli episcoporum* we read: "Concerning the bishop, since he is the best at taking care, let him take care in such a way that all of the sheep entrusted to him are nourished especially by him and helped in their necessities." We gather from these [passages] that prelates of the Church should excel others in skill in secular affairs. Therefore, not a secular ruler, but an ecclesiastic, should – not improperly, because of a greater skill even in temporal matters – preside over all mortals.

Master You are answered that although it has often been appropriate, because of the wickedness or negligence of laymen, for prelates of the Church to undertake the management of certain temporal things, and they are therefore then obliged to have knowledge of secular affairs, yet they should not have the highest degree of skill in such affairs; middling skill is enough for them. For this reason, as the law testifies, and it is noted in the gloss to dist. 37, c. 1, "it is a reproach" to prelates of the Church "if they wish to be experts in the forensic disciplines"; and thus they are forbidden to hear [lectures on] the civil laws, *Extra, Ne clerici vel monachi secularibus se negotiis immisceant, Super specula.* For since no one can acquire the most complete knowledge of the civil laws and secular affairs together with the most complete knowledge of sacred literature, and monks and clergy are forbidden to hear [lectures on] the laws so that they may apply themselves more fully to the sacred page, it follows that prelates of the Church should not surpass others in skill in secular affairs, since they should excel everyone in knowledge of sacred writings. Therefore, as a rule, a prelate of the Church should not be set over all mortals in temporal matters, "lest," as blessed Peter testifies (as we read in the *Decreta*, 11, q. 1, c. *Te quidem*), "being suffocated by the present cares of men," he be "not able to devote" himself "to the word of God." Therefore, although on occasion, when a suitable layman is not found, an ecclesiastic could for a time undertake the care of all in temporal matters, this should not be tolerated as a rule, since according to the apostolic doctrine ecclesiastics should not involve themselves in such care and solicitude concerning temporal matters, except for an unusual reason and as little as possible. Blessed Peter agrees with this; as we read in the *Decreta*, 11, q. 1, c. *Te quidem*, in appointing Clement he says: "Indeed, you must live beyond reproach, and try your utmost to shun all the occupations of this life: do not be a guarantor, do not become an advocate in disputes, lest you be found in some occupation entangled by the circumstances of some worldly affair."

Chapter 13

Student Those who read the tract "Concerning the power of the pope and clergy" can find in it many things on this matter, so turn to the argument brought forward in chapter 4 above for the fourth opinion and relate how it is answered.

Master That argument, to prove that government of the world by many wise men together is the best, is based on the premise that when many rule together fewer errors and faults occur. To this it is answered that the argument might seem to have probability if errors and faults in ruling came about solely from lack of skill, or solely from lack of sound advice, and if the one secular ruler ought to govern his subjects without the advice of the wise. But because errors and faults in ruling come about not only from lack of skill but also from bad will and negligence, and a ruler ought to rule his subjects with the advice of the wise, and no one should be promoted to rulership unless he is better and more prudent than others and it is believed of him with probability that he will wish, when it is necessary and beneficial, to seek the advice of the wise, therefore, as a rule, government by one virtuous and prudent man is superior to government by many virtuous and wise men. For mortals are inclined to conflict and to seeking their own interests and not what belongs to the common good, and hence come disturbance of tranquility and peace, corruption of justice, and an infinity of other evils, especially from those who have power over others; and when there were several rulers none of whom was superior to another, conflict would happen more easily than if one were superior to the others, since no one is in conflict with himself; also, many who could not be restrained by a superior would seek their own advantage more easily than if one were lord over the others. Therefore, if one were the ruler, there would be, as a rule, less reason to fear disturbance of peace and corruption of justice and other evils known to come from lack of good government than if several were rulers together and none of them was superior to another: especially since it is easier for the people to correct one ruler, if he goes astray in such a way that he should be corrected or even removed, than several. And it is no objection that the truth of justice that is sought by many is found more easily, and that "there is safety where there is much advice," because, as has been said, a virtuous and wise ruler, when it is beneficial, seeks the advice of wise men and causes the truth to be sought by many; he can rule the advisers seeking the truth and impose on them the due manner (in respect of time and place) of seeking and disclosing it that for each seems best, much better than those advisers could themselves if none of them had power over another, especially since one ruler with power over all the advisers concerning the manner of ruling the advisers can inquire of each of them and accept whichever advice seems sounder. Therefore, however much it is beneficial in difficult cases for the truth to be sought by many, it is useful that one should have power over all the other advisers seeking the truth. Hence it is that, although, as was quoted above in chapter 4, the Romans made themselves a senate-house and 320 men used to deliberate every day giving advice about the multitude, as we read in 1 Machabees 8, yet, as we read in the same place, they entrusted their magistracy to one man, and as a rule all obeyed one man; it is therefore better that one virtuous and prudent man should have world empire than that many should.

Chapter 14

Student So far we have inquired whether it is beneficial for the whole human race for one emperor or secular ruler to be over the whole world, and we have treated at some length the opinion which says that as a rule it is beneficial for all mortals to be subject in temporal matters to one secular ruler. But now I intend to investigate with you, though briefly, what excellences or graces, virtues, and characteristics the emperor of the world should be outstanding in. Now I believe that faith, skill, justice, truth, power, riches, liberality, and courage are most of all required in an emperor of the world, and so I propose to ask briefly some questions concerning these. First, therefore, I ask whether an emperor of the world is obliged to have the true and Catholic faith?

Master It seems to some that your question admits of no doubt, since every adult mortal who has the use of reason is obliged to have the faith, especially if he has been able to be informed of the faith. But perhaps you meant to ask whether someone can be a true emperor who does not have the true and Catholic faith. About this there are different and conflicting opinions.

Chapter 15

Student Concerning the second [version of the question] I will afterwards inquire somewhat at length,[24] so I pass to the skill necessary to an emperor. And first I wish to know whether an emperor of the world, if he is a Catholic, is obliged to have skill in divine Scripture?

Master There are various opinions about this. One is that a Catholic emperor of the world should have skill in the divine law and in sacred literature. For a Catholic emperor in the New Testament should not be less perfect than a king was in the Old Testament. But a king in the Old Testament was obliged to have skill in sacred literature and to meditate on the divine law continually; therefore a Catholic emperor should have these things more perfectly. Also, it pertains to a Catholic emperor to defend the Christian faith, which is contained in sacred literature, and to chastise its attackers with due punishment; but no one is obliged to defend what he does not know; therefore a Catholic emperor should have skill in sacred literature.

---

[24] See III *Dial.*, II, 1.25; also *Short Discourse*, pp. 74 ff.

There is another opinion, that although it befits a Catholic emperor to have knowledge of some sacred literature, so that he knows at least how to read the sacred Scriptures and, in reading them, how to understand them literally, it is not simply necessary for him to have such skill, since without such skill he can usefully and justly control temporal matters, which alone, as we know, pertain to the emperor.

Student Should the emperor be skilled in the civil laws?

Master One opinion is that he should. For since the emperor is the supreme judge in temporal matters, he should have no less skill than inferior judges in the laws according to which sentence is to be passed. But inferior judges are obliged to have knowledge of the civil laws, according to which they are obliged to judge. Therefore, much more should the emperor have skill in the civil laws.

There is another opinion, that the emperor is not obliged of necessity to have skill in the civil laws, though it is very suitable and useful that he should not lack such skill. For there have been many emperors and kings who were just, and even saints, who did not at all have skill in the civil laws, who yet would have become quite learned in the laws if they had been obliged of necessity to know them. And the case of the emperor or king is not similar to that of other, inferior, judges, for the emperor of the world and the king in his kingdom are not tied by the laws, and are not obliged of necessity to judge according to the laws in the way inferior judges are obliged of necessity to judge in accordance with the laws; as much knowledge of the laws is therefore not required in an emperor or king as in inferior judges.

Student From the foregoing it seems to me probable that it befits someone who is to be made emperor (and king) to have deep knowledge of both the sacred Scriptures and the civil laws and that such a person, if he were found, should, other things being equal, be promoted before all others to be emperor (and also to be king, when someone should receive government of a kingdom through election and not through succession). But if the person promoted to be emperor or king were not deep in the knowledge of the sacred Scriptures and the civil laws, would it be fitting for him to apply himself to study, to acquire outstanding knowledge of such things? Or if he were outstanding in such knowledge, would it be fitting for him to be occupied constantly in meditation on such things?

Master It is answered that it would be praiseworthy in an emperor and in a king to devote himself to such study as far as he could – with discretion, however, so that he is not kept by such study from the care entrusted to him. But to neglect his subjects or entrust the government of the empire or kingdom to another so that he may apply himself to such study must be regarded as reprehensible and deserving of condemnation in an emperor and a king, because such a ruler does not expend due care on his subjects; the Apostle's statement is verified of him, that "he who does not take care of his own people, and especially of members of his household, has denied the faith and is worse than an unbeliever."[25] For if a prelate of the Church should for the sake of his subjects' advantage sometimes interrupt the contemplative life and direct himself to the active life, as we gather from the sacred canons, 8, q. 1, c. *Olim*, c. *In scripturis*, and c. *Qui episcopatum*, much more should an emperor or king omit such study so as to devote due governance to his subjects, not only through others but in person.

Student Should an emperor have outstanding knowledge of secular affairs?

Master It is answered that he who outdoes others in skill in secular affairs, and who exceeds others in natural sense, discretion, natural activity, and judgment of reason, should, other things being equal, be promoted ahead of others to be emperor (or a king who is appointed to the government of a kingdom by election). For it seems that in a person to be promoted in such a way natural sense and excellent judgment of reason should be preferred to all learning, command of language, eloquence, experience, and memory, however excellent; though in promoting someone to a temporal office, especially one to last a short time, both learning and experience should sometimes be preferred to excellent judgment of reason. But after someone has been appointed to empire or to the government of a kingdom, he should apply himself to skill in secular affairs and to knowledge of natural law (especially of natural law about which it is possible for even the learned to err or doubt), knowledge of which chiefly pertains to his office, more than to knowledge of the

[25] 1 Tim. 5:8.

sacred Scriptures or of secular sciences or of any laws whatever, unless he can by their means more than in any other way acquire skill in secular affairs.

Student Why is it said that he must apply himself to knowledge of the natural law "about which it is possible for even the learned to err or doubt"? For it seems that there is no such natural law, since any ignorance of a law about which it is possible for experts to err seems to excuse anyone who acts against it; because the reason why ignorance of fact excuses is that it deceives even experts, as the gloss notes, dist. 38, c. 1;[26] therefore, if it is possible for experts to err about natural law, ignorance of such law could excuse. Again, probable ignorance always excuses; but ignorance that can be found in experts can be probable; therefore some ignorance of natural law would excuse. But the gloss notes the contrary of this, dist. 38, c. 1,[27] and Gratian, 1, q. 4, para. *Notandum*, says that in all adults ignorance of natural law deserves condemnation. From these [texts] it seems possible to gather that there is no natural law about which it is possible for experts to err or even doubt.

Master It is answered that there are found to be three kinds of natural laws. [1] Some are self-evident principles, or follow or are taken from such self-evident principles of morals; and about such natural laws no one can err or even doubt. One can, however, be ignorant of them, because it is possible not to think and never to have thought of them; and such ignorance excuses no one, because even if we have never before thought of them, such natural laws occur [to us] immediately when we are obliged to do or omit something in accordance with them, unless we will to proceed to the act, or to omit such act, without any deliberation and rule of reason. Ignorance of such a law in such a case therefore proceeds from negligence or contempt deserving of condemnation and there-fore does not excuse. For if, on some occasion, someone is tempted to kill an innocent person who never did harm, then immediately, if he wills to deliberate, even briefly, about whether he should kill him, it will occur [to him] that he should not kill him; and therefore, if without any deliberation he kills him, such ignorance does not

---

[26] See gloss, v. *Cum itaque*, col. 188.
[27] "Ignorance of natural law excuses no one, if he is an adult and of sound mind."

excuse him. [2] There are other natural laws that are drawn plainly and without great consideration from the first principles of the law, just as in knowable things certain conclusions are inferred from first principles plainly and without great consideration even by the less learned; and such ignorance of natural law does not excuse, because anyone can immediately without great study know those natural laws. And the statements of the fathers refer to such ignorance of natural law.

[3] There are other natural laws that are inferred from the first natural laws by few even of the experts, with great attention and study, and through many intermediate propositions. About these even experts sometimes have conflicting opinions, some thinking them to be just and others unjust; and ignorance of such a natural law excuses, especially in omitting to do something that should be done if one were not ignorant of the law, unless the ignorance is affected or crass and supine.[28] An emperor should therefore diligently apply himself to acquire knowledge of such natural laws, since the other natural laws – that is, in the first and second senses – will easily occur to him when it is necessary. And so that he may acquire perfect skill in such laws and in secular affairs, it is beneficial that he should have with him many wise advisers, on the example of the Romans, who (as was quoted above) appointed three hundred and twenty men, who used to deliberate every day, giving advice about the multitude. For as Solomon testifies, Proverbs 15[:22], "Plans are brought to nothing where there is no advice, but where there are many advisers they succeed"; and in Proverbs 11[:14] he says that "there is safety where there is much advice."

Student It seems to conflict with the teaching of the wise man for the emperor to be obliged to have many advisers. For in Ecclesiasticus 6[:6] we read: "Be in peace with many, but let one in a thousand be your adviser."

Master It is answered that advice is sought about various matters and for various reasons. Sometimes advice is sought concerning secret matters dangerous to reveal except to faithful and discreet friends. Sometimes, however, advice is sought about public matters, matters that can be revealed without danger to the unfaithful, to

---

[28] For the expressions "crass" and "supine" see *Digest*, 22.6.6; on "affected" ignorance see Thomas Aquinas, *Summa theologiae*, 1-2, q. 6, a. 8.

enemies, and to the foolish. Again, sometimes the advice of others is sought so as to have the agreement of the advisers, and when it is had the decision is made more authoritative and is accepted by others with more veneration and love, reverence, or fear. And sometimes advice is sought so that the one seeking advice may carry out the decision through the advisers. Sometimes the advice of others is sought so that the one seeking advice may acquire from their answer knowledge of law or fact that he does not know, and so that when he has it he may perceive what should be done. And sometimes the advice of others is sought so that the one seeking advice can probe and test the discretion or prudence or faithfulness or affection or will, either toward himself or toward others, of the advisers themselves.

When, therefore, advice is sought concerning secret matters dangerous to reveal, the advisers should be few – only those who are tested, faithful, friends and discreet. When, also, advice is sought so that the decision may be entrusted to the advisers for execution, few are needed, namely only [advisers who are] faithful, wise, and friends. And the text quoted above from Ecclesiasticus is to be understood of these two cases. But when advice is needed about public matters or things that can be revealed without danger, and advice is needed only so that the agreement of the advisers may be had and so that when it is had the decision may be made more authoritative, or so that the inquirer may acquire by the advisers' answer knowledge of law or fact of which he is ignorant, or so that he may test and probe their discretion or prudence or faithfulness or affection or will, then the advisers should be many; indeed, in such a case it will sometimes not be absurd to seek advice even from the unskilled or malevolent, since sometimes from their answer, even when they are unwilling and intend to deceive, a wise man will see what he should do: just as a wise man takes instruction not only from the good deeds of the wise but also from the bad deeds of the foolish, as Solomon testifies in Proverbs 24[:30]. He says: "I passed by the field of the slothful man, and by the vineyard of the foolish man: and behold they were all filled with nettles, and thorns had covered the face thereof, and the stone wall was broken down. When I had seen this I laid it up in my heart, and by the example I received instruction."

Chapter 16

Student Though we could, I think, make a large volume about the skill or prudence necessary to an emperor, yet let the above suffice for the present. I turn, therefore, to justice, which, as I believe, is necessary to an emperor. And I wish to know whether an emperor should always and in every case carry out the rigor of justice.

Master It is answered that an emperor should sometimes pass over justice completely, or defer it for a time; sometimes, however, it befits him – indeed, he is obliged of necessity – to temper the rigor of justice with mildness; but sometimes he is obliged, of necessity for salvation, to carry out the rigor of justice.

Student These things could be demonstrated, I think, by countless arguments and texts, but for the sake of brevity let us put them aside. For the present I wish to hear diverse opinions about one matter only, namely, whether all penalties for any crime whatever are at the emperor's choice when he exercises justice, so that it is permissible for him to inflict a pecuniary penalty, or another, for any crime whatever.

Master Concerning this diverse opinions are found. One is that all penalties are at the emperor's choice, so that it is permissible for him in any case whatever for any crime whatever to inflict any kind of penalties whatever. This seems to be supportable by the following argument. Where the penalty is not defined in the law, the penalty to be inflicted is entrusted to the choice of the inferior judge: and not unreasonably, because from the fact that there is not an explicit law according to which he ought to punish, it follows that he should punish according to his choice. But the emperor is above all positive laws. Therefore he is not obliged to punish according to any positive law, and, consequently, whenever he is obliged to punish anyone's crime, he can inflict any kind of penalties whatever according to his choice.

There is another opinion that in doing justice the emperor cannot always inflict for every crime any kind of penalties whatever according to his choice. For the emperor should not always be content with a pecuniary penalty but is bound to inflict another; similarly, also, it should not always be enough for him to inflict a penalty of beating, deportation, proscription, or exile, but he is bound to impose a penalty of death, mutilation, imprisonment, or perpetual detention. And often it is not permissible for him to remit such penalty by reason of friendship, by reason of consanguinity, by reason of nobility, or other circumstance. The reason for this is as follows. Just as where a definite penalty is not enacted in the law an inferior judge should proceed "preserving equity" (*Extra, De transactionibus*, last chapter), so, because the emperor is above positive laws and is not above natural equity, if in doing justice he does not wish, for a reason, to inflict the penalty enacted in the law, he is obliged of necessity to inflict a penalty "preserving equity," according to what he sees that the common good and the safety of subjects (and especially of the good) demand. But often a pecuniary penalty, or a penalty of deportation, proscription, or exile would not castigate a malefactor without some loss to the common good and danger to the obedient and good, as Ambrose testifies. In his *De officiis*, quoted in the *Decreta*, 23, q. 4, c. *Est iniusta*, he says, "If anyone, moved by the pleas of his children and affected by the tears of his wife, thinks that a robber should be pardoned who still evinces a desire for robbery, will he not hand over the innocent to destruction, setting free one who plans the destruction of many?" Hence also, Jerome, as we read in dist. 45, [c. 17], speaking of those who spare the bad, says: "When they spare one, they work the ruin of the whole Church. What goodness is that? What mercy is it, to spare one and lead all into danger?" From these [passages] we gather that if an emperor inflicts on a malefactor king or prince who is a relative or otherwise allied with him, or on someone else, who still evinces a desire to disturb the empire or the common good or the innocent, only a pecuniary penalty, or any other whatever by which he is not perfectly restrained from carrying out an evil will, he sins mortally and reprehensibly infringes equity, which he is obliged to follow. In such a case he is bound to inflict on such a malefactor (whether he is a king or prince who is a relative, or someone else) the penalty of physical death or perpetual imprisonment or some other penalty by which he is altogether restrained from evil deeds and from the power of doing evil.

Student It seems that it would be permissible for the emperor to remit a penalty even as serious as [is due] to one who had fallen into the crime of treason or committed any other outrage, because a judge in punishing should "turn toward the more humane side," *Extra, De transactionibus*, last chapter; and a sentence "that forbids mercy" must be avoided, dist. 50, *Ponderet*. It is therefore permissible for the emperor to show mercy to anyone whatever who has committed an outrage by remitting to him the penalty of death, or any other whatever.

Master It is answered that if the emperor knows that any criminal is perfectly reformed so that he gives up all will to do evil, and no one prosecutes his injury against him, the emperor can remit to him every penalty. But if he is not perfectly reformed, but it is feared with probability that he intends, when he has the power, to repeat his evil ways and to involve himself in his accustomed crimes or others, then it is not permissible for the emperor to remit to him every physical penalty, nor is it permissible to show him such mercy. By showing such mercy he would not turn toward the more humane side, nor would he be merciful, but he would have to be regarded as most cruel and most inhumane and most wicked, as blessed Augustine testifies. In *To Lotharius*, as we read in 23, q. 5, c. *Qui viciis*, he says: "One who, when vices are being fostered, spares and favors, so as not to grieve the will of sinners, is not merciful, any more than he who will not take a knife from a child so as not to hear him cry." Jerome also agrees with him. In *Upon Isaias*, which we read in the same *causa* and question, in c. [28] *Non est*, he says: "He is not cruel who slays the cruel." Such mercy is therefore an "unjust mercy," as Ambrose says;[29] indeed, it is a most wicked mercy, and worse than adultery, robbery, theft and very many other crimes regarded by everyone as enormities.

Student This opinion seems to me to have some plausibility. Relate, therefore, how the argument for the other opinion, which also does not lack all plausibility, is answered.

Master It is answered that where the law is not explicit inferior judges cannot and should not punish according to their own choice and at their own will, but in such cases the penalties are at their choice in such a way that equity is preserved; namely, so that the judge punishes with such a penalty as is more beneficial to the commonwealth and to the preservation of justice, by which the wrongdoer is corrected more effectively. For according to Augus-

---

[29] The source of the quotation from Ambrose has not been found.

tine, as we read in the *Decreta*, 23, q. 5, *Prodest*, "In both punishing and pardoning this alone is well done, that the life of men is corrected."

Chapter 17

Student If we dealt at length with the other virtues and characteristics with which it is appropriate for an emperor to be adorned we would make our work too prolix. Therefore, since, I judge, those two, namely skill or discretion or prudence, and justice, are most of all necessary to an emperor for ruling his subjects usefully – indeed, they seem practically sufficient, since those cannot be separated from the others when they are appropriate – let us pass very briefly over the others, so that we may come more quickly to more hidden things that have been examined less by others, especially since in the work *Concerning the Best Way of Learning*,[30] in the tract "On the Way of Learning Moral Philosophy" and the tract "On the Way of Learning Legal Matters," those who have them will have been able to find many things about the virtues necessary to rulers. First, therefore, let us see briefly about truth,[31] which it befits an emperor to maintain. Say, therefore, whether according to some opinion an emperor should be outstanding by such great truth that, just as it is not permissible for him to assert something false or to promise deceitfully or fraudulently anything he does not intend to perform, so it would not be permissible for him to revoke in any way something promised, or not fulfill it, or postpone it.

Master Some think [that], although the emperor should not fulfill things promised badly or things he promised licitly and afterwards considers are beginning to be harmful but should rescind them (just as, also, if he learns something better than things he had said before, he should not be at all ashamed to correct them suitably and should not wait to be corrected by others), yet he should not in any way revoke other promises or postpone them without manifest reason. He should also take care not to assert or promise anything quickly or lightly unless he is certain that it should be asserted or promised.

[30] This work has not been identified.
[31] That is, both telling the truth and being true to one's word.

Student Let us see about power, riches, and liberality together, whether they are appropriate to an emperor. For it seems that liberality conflicts with riches, because it pertains to a liberal man to pour out riches, and by this riches are exhausted.

Master Some think that without riches the imperial office cannot be well administered, for if "jurisdiction without coercion must be counted as nothing," *Extra, De officio iudicis delegati,* c. *Pastoralis,* and c. *Ex litteris,* much more is imperial authority nothing without coercion; and coercion cannot be exercised without power; therefore power is required in an emperor. And power seems most of all to be strengthened by riches, because power without friends, or at least without people who are obedient, does not seem able to last; and friends and people who obey are acquired by riches, as Solomon testifies. In Proverbs 19[:4] he says: "Riches make many friends, but from the poor man even those he had depart"; and in the same chapter he says: "Many honor the person of him that is mighty, and are friends of him that giveth gifts; the brothers of the poor man hate him, moreover his friends also have departed far from him."[32] And in Ecclesiastes 6[33] we read: "Wisdom is more useful with riches . . . for as wisdom is a defense, so money is a defense"; and in chapter 10 it is said that all things obey money. Riches are therefore appropriate to the imperial excellence for the sake of acquiring friends and people who obey. But friends and people who obey are not acquired and held by riches unless they are liberally poured out, for if riches are not poured out they do not make friends; but if they are unreasonably consumed by prodigality the friends are quickly lost. Therefore liberality seems appropriate to the imperial majesty for acquiring and holding friends and people who are obedient.[34]

Student Is courage necessary to an emperor?

Master The courage that is a virtue of the soul should be outstanding in an emperor, but physical fortitude, which is strength of body, is not so necessary in an emperor; for although it is very appropriate for an emperor to excel in physical fortitude and in skill in battle, it is, however, not simply necessary and should not

---

[32] Proverbs 19:6.
[33] Ecclesiastes 7:12.
[34] Liberality is intermediate between meanness and prodigality; see Aristotle, *Nicomachean Ethics,* IV.1.

be preferred to other excellences but should be put after wisdom, justice and other virtues, as the wise man testifies. In Wisdom 7[35] he says: "Wisdom is better than strength, and a wise man is better than a strong man." And in Ecclesiastes 9[:16] Solomon says: "And I said that wisdom is better than strength ... Better is wisdom than weapons of war." And in Proverbs 16[:32], "Better is the patient man than the strong man, and he who rules his soul than the destroyer of cities."

Book 3

Chapter 5

Student If the right to elect the highest pontiff can belong to the emperor, say, in accordance with that opinion, whence he has it. **Master** Your question can be understood in two ways: in one way so that the meaning is, Whence does the emperor have it that he is *capable of* this power or right?, in the other way so that the meaning is, Whence does he *have* this right, namely the right of electing the highest pontiff? If it is understood in the first way, – namely, Whence does the emperor have it that he is capable of this power or right? – it is answered that he has such a capacity from the very fact that he is Christian, Catholic, of sound mind, and a Roman. For if he were emperor and were not a Christian, he would not be capable of this right, because no one but a Christian can have the right to elect the highest pontiff; for things pertaining to the Christian religion should not be handled by outsiders (except that in a case of necessity even a non-Christian could baptize). If, also, he were emperor and a Christian but not a Catholic, but a heretic, as long as he was such he would not have the power or right to elect the highest pontiff, because no heretic, remaining a heretic, is capable of this right. If, also, he were emperor, a Christian, and a Catholic, but were not of sound mind – that is, did not have the use of reason but had gone mad – as long as he remained such he would not be capable of such right or power, at least so that it could issue in action. For although

[35] Wisdom 6:1.

if previously he had such power or right and afterwards went mad he would not by that very fact lose such power or right, nevertheless, if he were from the beginning out of his senses, such power or right should not be conferred on him, and it could not be conferred on him in such a way that he could, while his insanity lasts, perform the act of such power.

But if your question is understood in the second way – namely Whence does the emperor have (or can he have) such a power or right? – it is answered in two ways: in one way, that the emperor can have such a power or right from the highest pontiff, because the highest pontiff could grant the right to elect the pope to a cleric, or to clerics, to a layman, or to laymen, as it pleased him. This is proved in three ways, first as follows. He who is head of all Christians in spiritual matters has power to control and determine who is to elect the head of all, especially since Christ did not specifically and explicitly decide who should elect that head. But the pope is the head of all Christians in spiritual matters; therefore it pertains to him to decide who should elect the highest pontiff, and consequently the emperor can have the right to elect the highest pontiff from the pope alone.

Second, as follows. He who can appoint the highest pontiff can commit to whom he wishes the power to elect the highest pontiff, and his successor can grant to whom he wishes the right to elect a successor. But blessed Peter appointed the highest pontiff to succeed himself, namely blessed Clement; therefore his successor also could grant to whom he wished the power to elect the highest pontiff.

Third, as follows. Through the sacred canons, many of which were quoted above in chapter 3 of this third book, the pope granted the right to elect sometimes to kings and sometimes to others, and not illicitly; therefore no one can have the right to elect the highest pontiff except from the pope.

In the other way it is said that, by the very fact that he is Christian, Catholic, of sound mind, and a Roman, the emperor has the right and power to elect the highest pontiff, unless he himself tacitly or explicitly renounces that right, or unless the election of the highest pontiff or the power of granting the right to elect has been granted with the consent of the Romans to a determinate person or determinate persons; so that the Romans do not have from the pope the power or right to elect the highest pontiff. This is proved by the following argument. Christ ordered the Church in such a way that it would never fail in anything necessary and so that no man could deprive it by his negligence or malice of anything whatever that is necessary. But not least among the other things necessary to the Church is that there should be some who, when the highest pontiff dies, have the right to elect the highest pontiff to succeed. In this matter, therefore, Christ did not fail the Church, and he did not put it into anyone's power that he could by his negligence or malice deprive the whole of God's Church of this necessary thing. But if no one had the right to elect the highest pontiff except from the pope, then the pope could by his negligence or malice deprive the whole of God's Church of the power or right to elect the highest pontiff: for he could first, for some cause, reasonable or unreasonable, deprive those who now have the right to elect the highest pontiff of that right, and before giving the right to others he could be forestalled by death, or he could by negligence or malice defer the granting of that right to the end of his life; and thus the right to elect the highest pontiff would not remain with anyone. Of this necessity to the Church the Church could therefore (by being forestalled by the pope's death or by his negligence or malice) be left deprived, so that without a special miracle neither the universal Church nor the particular church[36] could have a pope. From this it is inferred that the right to elect the highest pontiff is not from the pope, and therefore the Romans have the right to elect, not from the pope, but by the very fact that they are Christians and Catholics. **Student** By that argument it is proved that the Romans do *not* have the right to elect the highest pontiff. For if they had it, then by negligence or malice the Romans could deprive the whole Church of the right to elect the highest pontiff, for they could renounce that right without granting the right to elect the highest pontiff to any others whatever; therefore the Church would then be left without a right to elect the highest pontiff.

Also, all the Romans who had the right to elect the highest pontiff could become heretics or convert to another sect, and when that happened they would lose the right to elect the pope; therefore

---

[36] That is, the church in the city of Rome.

the whole Church of God would be left without a right and power to elect the highest pontiff.

Further, if it is not from the pope that the Romans have the right to elect, I ask by what law do they have the right to elect the highest pontiff? Either by divine law or by human. Not by divine law, because we do not read in the divine Scriptures that God gave them such a right. And not by human law. For human law is either civil or canon law; civil laws are the laws of emperors and kings, canon laws are the laws of the highest pontiffs; therefore the Romans would have the right to elect either from emperors or kings or else from highest pontiffs. But they do not have the right to elect from the emperors; therefore they have such a right to elect from the highest pontiffs alone. And thus the right to elect is from the pope alone.

These are the reasons why it seems that that opinion and the argument advanced for it do not seem to have probability. But, nevertheless, relate how they are answered.

Master To the first of them it is answered that that opinion does not say that in *every* case *only* the Romans have the right to elect the highest pontiff. To explain this it is said that it must be known that the highest pontiff is not only the prelate and bishop of the Romans, but is also prelate and bishop of all Christians; and therefore, on occasion, the election of the highest pontiff could belong to any Catholics whatever, whose prelate and bishop he is. When, therefore, it is said that if the Romans had the right to elect the highest pontiff they could by negligence or malice deprive the whole Church of God of the right to elect the highest pontiff, it is answered that this argument would establish its conclusion if no one else but the Romans had in any case a right to elect the highest pontiff: as it is, however, although when the Romans are Christians and Catholics they have the right to elect the highest pontiff, yet if they renounced that right or became heretics, by that very fact other Catholics, whose bishop and prelate the pope also is, could elect the highest pontiff.

Student If other Catholics have the right to elect the highest pontiff because the highest pontiff is bishop and prelate of all Catholics, [1] why do they not always elect the highest pontiff together with the Romans, since those who have the right to elect should all elect the prelate? And [2] why do the Romans elect more than the others, if the others have the right to elect just as the Romans do?

Master The answer in accordance with that opinion to the second question that you ask opens the way to answering your first question. I will therefore first relate, in accordance with that opinion, how the second is answered. To this it is said that the highest pontiff is in a way the Romans' own bishop – that is, inasmuch as the Romans do not have another bishop and all others except them have bishops of their own; therefore the election of the highest pontiff reasonably belongs to the Romans alone, when they are Catholics. However, by the very fact that someone is bishop of the Romans he is bishop of all Catholics; therefore, although on occasion others have the right to elect, they do not have the right to elect together with the Romans, because, although they always have a right to elect the highest pontiff, they do not have the right to elect except for a case when the election does not belong to the Romans.

Student My question still does not seem to have been answered. For the question is *why* others besides the Romans do not have the right to elect except for a case when the election does not belong to the Romans, since the highest pontiff is the immediate prelate of all just as he is of the Romans.

Master To this it is answered that according to right reason the election of someone to be made ruler should always, if possible, be granted to a few who can easily meet, lest, if it were granted to many who could not easily meet, the election would be deferred because of the difficulty of meeting, to the notable detriment of the common good and of those whom the person to be made ruler has to rule. Because, therefore, the Romans are few in comparison with the other Catholics, and because (as has been said) the highest pontiff is likewise in some way the Romans' own bishop (because they do not have another bishop as other Catholics do), other Catholics, therefore, not unreasonably, do not have the right to elect the highest pontiff except when the election does not belong to the Romans – that is, because the Romans, either by renunciation of their right or by apostasy or heretical wickedness, lack the right to elect.

From this the answer is clear to your first question. For other Catholics do not always elect together with the Romans because, although they have the right to elect, they do not have the right to elect for every case, but only for the case when the right to elect does not pertain to the Romans. From these things it is inferred that – whether they were able to resign the right to elect the highest pontiff or were all to become heretics or apostates from the faith – the Romans could not deprive God's Church of the right to elect the highest pontiff, because for such a case other Catholics would have the right to elect.

Chapter 6

Student Say how answer is made to my premise[37] that the Romans have the right to elect the highest pontiff neither by divine law nor by human law.

Master To this it is answered that the Romans have the right to elect the highest pontiff by divine law, extending "divine law" to include all natural law.

Student To me that answer seems obscure. I therefore want it explained, in accordance with that opinion. And first explain, in accordance with it, why it is said, "extending divine law to include *all* natural law," and second why all natural law can be called divine law.

Master The first is said because of the three modes of natural law. For, in one way, that is called natural law which is in conformity with natural reason that in no case fails, such as "Do not commit adultery," "Do not lie," and the like.

In another way, that is called natural law which is to be observed by those who use natural equity alone without any custom and human legislation. This is called "natural" because its contrary is contrary to the state of nature as originally established, and if all men lived according to natural reason or divine law it[38] should not be observed or done. In this second way, and not in the first, all things are common by natural law, because in the state of nature as originally established all things would have been common, and if after the fall all men lived according to reason all things should have been common and nothing owned, for ownership was intro-

---

[37] See above, p. 284.
[38] The contrary.

duced because of wickedness, 12, q. 1, c. *Dilectissimis*. Isidore speaks in that way[39] in Book VI of the *Etymologies*, included in the *Decreta*, dist. 1, *Ius naturale*, when he says that according to natural law there is "common possession of all things and the one liberty of all." For common possession of all things and the one liberty of all do not exist by natural law in the first way, for then no one could licitly appropriate anything to himself and no one could be made a slave by any law of nations or civil law, because natural law in the first way is immutable, invariable, and indispensable, dist. 5, para. *Nunc autem*, and dist. 6, para. *His itaque respondetur*. But it is certain that some are made slaves licitly by the law of nations, as blessed Gregory testifies. In 12, q. 2, c. *Cum redemptor*, he says, "It is soundly done if, by the beneficence of the manumitter, men whom from the beginning nature brought forth free, and the law of nations placed under the yoke of slavery, are made free in the nature in which they were born." From these words we gather that by natural law all men are free, and yet by the law of nations some are made slaves. From this it is inferred that natural law, taking the word in one way, is not immutable; rather, it is permissible to enact the contrary, so that the contrary is done by law.

In a third way that is called natural law which is gathered by evident reasoning from the law of nations or another [law] or from some act, divine or human, unless the contrary is enacted with the consent of those concerned. This can be called natural law "on supposition": as, according to Isidore (as quoted above), "natural law is the return of a thing deposited or of money lent, the repelling of violence by force." For these are not natural laws in the first way, or in the second way either, because they would not have existed in the state of nature as originally established and would not exist among those who, living according to reason, were content with natural equity alone without any custom and human legislation, because among them nothing would be deposited or lent and no one would inflict force on another. They are therefore natural laws on supposition, because, supposing that things and money have been appropriated by the law of nations or by some human law, then it is gathered by evident reasoning that a thing deposited and money lent should be returned, unless for a reason the contrary

---

[39] That is, the second way.

is decided by him or those concerned. Similarly, supposing that some one in fact unjustly inflicts violence on another (which is not in accordance with natural law but against natural law), then it is gathered by evident reasoning that it is permissible to repel such violence by force.

Because of these three modes of natural law, they say that the Romans have by divine law the right to elect the highest pontiff, extending "divine law" to *every* natural law. For if it were extended only to natural law spoken of in the first way (as natural law is taken in dist. 5, para. 1, and dist. 6, para. *His itaque respondetur*, and dist. 8, para. *Dignitate vero*, and dist. 9, para. 1, and in many other places), the Romans would not have the right to elect the highest pontiff from divine law alone.

Student Because I have not elsewhere heard that distinction of natural law, I wish to make objections against it, to understand better from the solution of objections in accordance with that opinion whether it contains anything of the truth. That distinction seems, therefore, to conflict very obviously with Isidore's words in the chapter *Ius naturale* quoted earlier. First, because Isidore says, "Natural law is common to all nations, because it is everywhere held by an instinct of nature and not by any enactment." These words cannot suit the second member of the above distinction, because things whose contrary can be permissible according to the law of nations are not common to all nations and are not held everywhere by an instinct of nature, because they are not held where the contrary is observed according to the law of nations. Also, because Isidore says in the same place, "But this, or anything similar to this, is never regarded as unjust, but as natural and fair." This cannot be true of either the second or third members. For what is called natural law in the second way can be unjust, because the contrary can be in accordance with the law of nations; for what is contrary to the law of nations must be regarded as unjust. And what is called natural law in the third way can be unjust, because the contrary is in accordance with the law of nature in the second way. For it is in accordance with natural law in the second sense that restitution of money borrowed or of a thing lent should *not* be made, since it is in accordance with natural law in that sense that no money should be lent and nothing deposited; because according to the natural law, taking the term in that way, all things are common, and thus according to that law no money can be lent and nothing deposited. These are the arguments that move me against the foregoing distinction; but say how they are answered.

Master They are answered in two ways. In one way that some words in the chapter *Ius naturale* should be understood only of natural law spoken of in the first way, and thus do not seem to establish anything against the foregoing.

In the other way it is said that the words you quote in your objection are said of every natural law, but they should be understood soundly. When, therefore, Isidore says, "Natural law is common to all nations," etc., he means that natural law spoken of in the first way is common to all nations in such a way that all nations are indispensably obliged to it, and therefore "it is had by instinct of nature," that is, of natural reason, which is never mistaken. And natural law spoken of in the second way is common to all nations in such a way that all nations are obliged to it, *unless* for reasonable cause they decide on the contrary, and therefore it exists "by instinct of nature," that is, of natural reason, *until* the contrary is enacted by human ordinance; for reason dictates that all things are common until they are appropriated with the consent of men. But natural law in the third way is common to all nations *on supposition* – namely, if all nations enact or do something from which a [natural] law in that sense is gathered by evident reasoning; and therefore "it is had by an instinct of nature," i.e., of natural reason, *supposing* that from which it is thus inferred.

Similarly it is said of the words you quote second, "But this, or anything similar to this," etc., that they can be understood of the second member, because such a natural law is "never unjust, but is regarded as natural and fair," *unless* the contrary is, for some reasonable cause, established by some human law. Also, natural law spoken of in the third way is in some way "never unjust, but is" always "regarded as natural and fair," because, *supposing* that from which it is inferred by evident reasoning, it is "never unjust but is" always "regarded as natural and fair," *unless* the opposite is decided on by him or those concerned.

Student It seems that those things are said unsuitably, because according to them the same word occurring once in the foregoing words of Isidore is taken equivocally.

Master This is not regarded as unsuitable, because the gloss on dist. 63, c. *Nosse* notes this. It says, "Note, a word occurring here once is used equivocally, as in dist. 28, *Presbyterum*."

Student You have explained in accordance with the opinion stated above why it said that the Romans have the right to elect the highest pontiff by divine law, extending divine law to every natural law. Now say, in accordance with the same opinion, why it says that every natural law can be called divine law.

Master They say this, first, because every law that is from God, who is the creator of nature, can be called a divine law; but every natural law is from God who is the creator of nature; therefore etc. Also, because every law that is contained explicitly or implicitly in the divine Scriptures can be called a divine law, because "divine law is contained in the divine Scriptures," dist. 8, c. *Quo iure*; but every natural law is contained explicitly or implicitly in the divine Scriptures, because in the divine Scriptures there are certain general propositions from which, either alone or with other [premises], can be inferred every natural law, spoken of in the first way, in the second way, and in the third way, though it may not be found in them explicitly.

Student You have explained in accordance with the above-stated opinion the two things that seemed obscure to me. Now say, in accordance with the same opinion, how the Romans have from divine law the right to elect the highest pontiff.[40]

Master To this it is said that the Romans have the right to elect the highest pontiff from natural law spoken of in the third way. For *supposing* that someone is to be set over certain persons as prelate, ruler, or rector, it is inferred by evident reason that, unless the contrary is decided on by the person or persons concerned, those whom he is to be set over have the right to elect the one to be set over them, so that no one should be given to them against their will. It seems that this can be proved by numberless arguments and examples, but I will bring forward a few.

An example to this [effect] is that no one should be set over the whole body of mortals except by their election and consent.[41]

---

[40] This was the answer given to the question at the beginning of this chapter.
[41] "The whole body of all mortals" is the Roman Empire; it was universally accepted that the Roman emperor should be elected.

Further, what affects all should be dealt with by all; for someone to be set over all affects all, therefore it should be dealt with by all.

Again, to those whom it concerns to make themselves laws it belongs to elect a head, if they wish; but any people and city can make themselves their own law, which is called "civil" law, dist. I, *Ius civile*; therefore also a people and city can elect themselves a head. And thus it always belongs to those whom someone is to be set over to elect the one to be set over them, unless the contrary is decided on by the person or persons concerned. (This is said because they can, at least in many cases, resign their right and transfer their right to another or to others. In this way, although from natural law spoken of in the third way or in the second way the people had the right to make laws, yet they transferred that power to the emperor, and so it was in his power to transfer the right to elect the emperor to another or to others.[42] Similarly, if those whom someone is to be set over are in such matters subject to some superior, that superior can decide that they do not have the right to elect, although they had the right to elect by the law of nature spoken of in that way[43] – namely, unless the contrary had been decided on either by themselves or by the superior.)

And thus it seems to them that the proposition taken before must be regarded as evident. But the highest pontiff is in a way especially to be set over the Romans, because they do not have another bishop. Therefore, by natural law spoken of in that way – that is, by natural law on supposition, namely, on the supposition that they should have a bishop – they have the right to elect him, unless the contrary is enacted or decided on by the Romans themselves or by some other, superior to the Romans, who has power in this matter. For the Romans themselves can resign their right and also transfer the right to elect the highest pontiff to another; they could also transfer to another the right of appointing the electors of the highest pontiff. Also, someone superior to the Romans who had power in such matters could grant the right to elect to some persons other than the Romans; but that superior was Christ and not the pope, and therefore Christ and not the pope could deprive the Romans of the right to elect the highest

---

[42] That is, to the imperial electors.
[43] That is, in the third way.

pontiff. But Christ did not deprive the Romans of the right to elect their bishop; for when Christ set blessed Peter over all Christians, giving him power to select a see where he wished in such a way that in that place he would be in a way their own bishop, he did not deprive them of that right, which belongs to all whom some power, secular or ecclesiastical, is to be set over (unless the contrary is determined by those whom that power, secular or ecclesiastical, is to be set over, or by their superior); therefore, since blessed Peter selected the see of Rome, it follows that the Romans have the right to elect the successor of blessed Peter, who in spiritual matters is to be set over them especially. And thus the Romans have by divine law, extending divine law to every natural law, the right to elect the highest pontiff.

Student It seems that according to that opinion it would be better to say that the Romans have the right to elect their bishop by the law *of nations*, because it is by the law of nations that all of those whom someone is to be set over have the right to elect the person to be set over them unless they resign their right or their superior decides on the contrary.

Master Although many things that belong to the law of nations are natural laws, taking "natural law" in the third way, nevertheless it is more properly said, according to that opinion, that the Romans have the right to elect their bishop by divine law or by natural law spoken of in the third way, rather than by the law of nations; because it does not belong to the law of nations to have a Catholic bishop, but this pertains to the divine law. Also, although it belongs to the law of nations that someone to be set over others should be elected by those whom he is to be set over, it belongs equally to the divine law, because it can be inferred from [premises] found in the sacred Scriptures together with other [premises].[44] Thus the two suppositions from which it follows that the Romans have the right to elect their bishop belong to the divine law, though in different ways, but only one belongs to the law of nations. And for this reason it is more properly said that the Romans have the right to elect their bishop by divine law or by natural law spoken of in the third way, rather than by the law of nations.

However, since the holders of this theory do not care to contend about words, they say that it is enough for them that the Romans

---

[44] Compare the classification of Catholic truths in I *Dial.* 2.2.

have the right to elect their bishop from this, that they should have a bishop, and that those whom someone is to be set over should elect him[45] unless they resign their right or the contrary is decided on by their superior. But whether it should be said that, properly speaking, the Romans have the right to elect by divine law, or by natural law spoken of in the third way, or by the law of nations, or by divine law and the law of nations together, does not make much difference. It seems to some, however, that it is properly said that they have the right to elect by divine law and the law of nations together. And therefore when you ask whether they have the right to elect by divine or human law, they say: from neither divine nor human law alone, but from both together, extending human law to [include] the law of nations[46] and not only civil and canon law.

Chapter 7

Student Now that that opinion has been explained at some length, let us see how the arguments brought forward on the other side in chapter 5 above are answered in accordance with it.

Master To the first it is answered that in respect of those things in which sufficient and useful provision is made for Catholics by divine law and natural law, the pope does not have power to change anything to the prejudice of any Catholics and to the detriment or danger of the common good; and therefore the head in spiritual matters of all Christians does not have full power to decide and decree by whom the head should be elected, since by divine and natural law the right of election belongs to the Romans – especially since if he had full power this could have detrimental and dangerous effects on the common good, as was shown before.

Student Why do they say that in this matter the pope does not have full power? According to them in this matter he has *no* power, since the Romans have the right to elect from divine law.

Master They do not say that there is no case in which the pope has power in respect of this matter; rather, they think that on

---

[45] The text says: "those whom someone is to be set over, by them he should be elected."

[46] According to some of the civil law texts the law of nations is natural law, which implies that it is not human law.

occasion the pope has power, even by Christ's ordinance and by the power granted to him by Christ, to decide who should elect his successor. To explain this they say that it must be known that Christ made sufficient provision for the Church in all necessary matters, and therefore, in entrusting the Church to blessed Peter he gave blessed Peter and his successors fullness of power in spiritual matters in respect of all things necessary to his Church – saving the right of others, when they wish and are able to exercise their right as they ought: so that in spiritual matters the pope can, in all necessary matters, remedy the failure of others who do not wish or are not able to exercise their right. And therefore, because the Romans have by divine law the right to elect their bishop, the pope does not have power to make decisions about that election to the Romans' prejudice when the Romans would wish and would be able to exercise their right for the common good. Similarly, because on occasion other Catholics have the right to elect the highest pontiff, the pope therefore also would not have power to make decisions about that election when, on such an occasion, the other Catholics wished to exercise that right appropriately. But if the Romans and other Catholics were not willing or were not able to exercise that right, then the pope would have power to make decisions about the election of his successor.

Student Why do they say that the pope has such fullness of power in respect of necessary matters and do not say absolutely that he has fullness of power in all matters?

Master They say this because they think that Christ gave a law of such perfect liberty that (now that the ceremonial and legal [commandments] of the Old Law are revoked) the pope has no power over Christians except in respect of things commanded or forbidden by God and in respect of things to be done of necessity, not in respect of things not to be done of necessity. Thus he cannot command anyone to do something supererogatory except in a case when it must be done of necessity, and then it would have to be regarded not as supererogatory but as necessary; for example, he could impose it on someone because of a fault to fast on bread and water or to enter a monastery or the like, but in such a case that would not be supererogatory for him but necessary, because the fulfillment of a due punishment must be counted among necessary things.

Student What do they say to this, which you took as a premise: that Christ did not explicitly decide who should elect the head of Christians, therefore he left this to the pope?[47]

Master It is said that because Christ decided nothing specifically or explicitly about this, he therefore wished that in this respect all should keep the rights they have by the law of nations – namely, that which the nations reasonably follow; and in this respect he therefore entrusted to the pope no power prejudicial to the Romans.

Student Say how the second argument brought forward above in chapter 5 is answered.

Master It is answered that the deeds of the saints are not always to be taken as a precedent, and it is therefore often not possible to prove from examples what should be done normally, though they can often be used to show what could be done on occasion. The fact, therefore, that blessed Peter appointed his own successor cannot prove what the pope can do from Christ's specific ordinance; however, we can draw from it what a pope could do who was in every way such as blessed Peter was. Hence Gratian says, as we read in 8, q. 1, para. *His omnibus*: "And that action of blessed Peter," that is, that he handed on the pontifical office to blessed Clement, "can be taken as a precedent by those who replace themselves with persons such as the one blessed Peter sought as a successor."

Student If the pope has the same power as blessed Peter had, why can he not replace himself with a successor just as blessed Peter did?

Master This is answered in two ways. [1] In one way, the answer is given by the gloss, in the place referred to above, on the word *Beatus*, where it asks, "Could the pope still appoint a successor to himself?", and it answers, "No, because this would be to change the state of the Church, as in 25, q. 1, *Que ad perpetuam*, and because he makes a law for a time when he will not be judge."

Student Does this answer satisfy others?

Master No, because neither argument for the answer is sound, as it seems to them. Not the first, because the pope *can* change the state of the Church in respect of things over which he has power from Christ. For just as a king can command something that neither anyone before him, nor he himself, had ever commanded, dist. 8, *Que contra*, so also the pope can command something new and can revoke, from reasonable cause, many things customarily done. The second argument also does not satisfy them, because that argument would prove that no bishop could select his successor even with the pope's permission, the contrary of which we read in 7, q. 1, *Petisti.*

Student Relate the other answer.

Master In another way [2] it is said that blessed Peter appointed his own successor by Christ's special revelation or inspiration, or he did so by the will and consent of the Catholic Romans, who had the right to elect.

Student Since neither of those things is shown from the Scriptures, this answer is despised as easily as approved.

Master To this it is said that what is not found in the Scriptures either explicitly or implicitly *and also* is not proved by clear argument is despised as easily as approved; but it is proved by clear argument that one or other of those things happened, therefore both should not be despised.

Student Say how they answer the third argument brought forward in chapter 5.

Master To this it is answered that although the Romans had the right to elect the Roman bishop from natural law spoken of in the third way, they could in many ways have transferred that right and the power of appointing electors to another or to others, just as all the canons of a cathedral church have the right to elect the bishop and yet can grant it to another: for they can grant that power in various ways, to one, or to two, or to several, from among themselves; they can also grant the power to elect to someone outside their body, *Extra, De electione, Causam que.* The Romans, therefore, could have granted to the highest pontiff the power of appointing electors; they could also have granted the right of election to some few from among themselves. Also, as was said before, the highest pontiff on occasion has power to make decisions about the election of his successor. Also, although the pope himself can have no say in the election of a pope, nevertheless, insofar as he is a Roman, he can together with the other Romans discuss and decide whom the right to elect should be entrusted to. Also, inasmuch as he is a Catholic, the pope can with the Romans and other Catholics, in a general council which represents all Catholic Christians, discuss and decide whom the power to elect the highest pontiff is to be granted to. And thus in many ways the pope can have power to grant to another or others the right to elect the highest pontiff, even though the right to elect belonged to the Romans.

It must be conceded, therefore, that sometimes the pope has granted to certain kings, and sometimes to others, the right to elect the highest pontiff. But he has not done this because he alone always has power to grant such a right, but because the Romans transferred the right to elect either to him alone or to him and others together (namely some Romans who represented the Romans, and others).[48] And thus, as we read in dist. 63, c. *Adrianus*, Pope Adrian – not alone, but himself and a synod held in Rome, in which there were many Romans – transferred to King Charles the right and power to elect the pontiff and to make decisions about the Apostolic See; also, as we read in the same distinction, c. *In synodo*, Pope Leo – not alone, but with all the Roman clergy and people – granted to Otto I, King of the Teutons, power to make decisions about the pontiff of the highest Apostolic See; and thus the Romans consented to this grant, as they were able to do, as was said before.

And therefore, although the emperor has, together with other Romans, the right to elect from the fact that he is a Catholic and a Roman, nevertheless it was sometimes the pope and other Romans who gave him the right to elect alone, without the other Romans. He could also have it from the pope alone, if the Romans transferred their right to the pope, or, also, if in making decisions about the electors of the highest pontiff the Romans proved negligent, to the detriment of the Church. And it is likely enough that the Romans have transferred such right and power to the pope, and therefore from that time the pope alone has been able to grant the power to elect the highest pontiff either to the emperors, or to neighboring bishops, or to the cardinals, or to the Roman clergy, or to the canons of some church in Rome, or to others, as it has seemed to him would further the advantage of the Church.

[48] That is, to the pope in a general council or synod.

Student If the Romans have the right to elect the Roman bishop from divine law, how can they transfer the right to the pope, since it is not permissible for anyone to contravene divine law?

Master It is answered that for anyone to contravene what belongs to divine law in such a way that it is explicitly commanded or forbidden in divine law, or is inferred only from things contained explicitly in divine law, is not permissible. But to contravene what is from divine law because it is inferred from something contained implicitly in divine law and from natural law spoken of in the second way is permissible, for reasonable cause, just as it is permissible, for a reason, to contravene natural law spoken of in the second way; for although, as the holy fathers testify, by the law of nature all things are common, nevertheless it is permissible to appropriate temporal things. In this second way[49] the Romans have the right to elect the Roman bishop, and not in the first way; therefore it is permissible for them, for a reason, to contravene this law.

---

[49] That is, from divine law in the second sense, which is inferred from divine law in the first sense together with natural law in the second sense.

Eight Questions
on the Power of the Pope

Eight Questions
on the Power of the Pope

Question III. Whether by Christ's institution it pertains to the pope and the Roman Church to entrust to the emperor and other secular rulers temporal jurisdictions, which otherwise they may not exercise?

Eight Questions on the Power of the Pope: Question III

Chapter 1

The third question is whether by Christ's institution it pertains to the pope and the Roman Church to entrust to the emperor and other secular rulers temporal jurisdictions, which[1] otherwise they may not exercise.

About this question there are conflicting opinions. One is that by Christ's ordinance it does pertain to the Roman Church – i.e., the pope – to entrust temporal jurisdictions to the emperor and other rulers, and that without his authority and commission they should in no way exercise them. This opinion should be held, it seems, by those who assert that the pope has in both spiritual and temporal matters the fullness of power spoken of above (Question I, chapter 2), so that by Christ's ordinance he can do everything not against an indispensable natural law or against a divine law that must be observed of necessity for salvation in the time of grace.[2]

That the pope can (according to them) entrust temporal jurisdictions to the emperor and other secular rulers plainly seems provable if the pope has such fullness of power, since such fullness of power includes power to entrust temporal jurisdictions, because that power does not go against natural law or conflict with divine law.

---

[1] For *ipsi alias* substituting *ipsi aliter eas* (cf. III.2.20, p. 100).
[2] For a discussion of this theory of papal fullness of power see *Short Discourse*, pp. 18 ff.

That, also, he is bound to entrust such jurisdictions, since he cannot exercise them himself, is shown: because otherwise he would be negligent in doing God's work entrusted to him by God and would not imitate Christ, who said to the Father, in John 17[:4], "I have completed the work you gave me to do." For if by Christ's ordinance he can do everything and he is obliged never to give up power granted to him – indeed, imposed on him – by God (according to the opinion of blessed Cyprian), he must carry out everything and act so as to strive to fulfill through others what he cannot carry out by himself.

And that the emperor and other secular rulers should not (according to them) exercise such temporal jurisdictions unless they are entrusted to them by the pope seems provable. For anyone who assumes an office of administration, dignity, and honor, even a secular one, without the ruler to whom it belongs to make decisions about such offices is rightly censured for ambition. But ambition, even in respect of secular offices and jurisdictions, is reproved even by the civil laws. If, therefore, by Christ's institution it pertains to the pope to make decisions about such offices, no one exercises them licitly without the pope.

Further, as we read in *Extra, De regulis iuris, Non est*, Book VI, "He is not without fault who involves himself in a matter that does not pertain to him"; but if it pertains to the pope to entrust such jurisdictions to the emperor and others, they pertain to none of them without the pope; therefore if any of them involves himself in such a jurisdiction without the pope, he is not without fault, and consequently involves himself wrongly; therefore no one should exercise such a jurisdiction without the pope.

Again, according to the Apostle in Hebrews 5[:4], no one "takes honor to himself"; this should be understood not only of spiritual or ecclesiastical honor but also of secular honor. This seems provable also from the reason the Apostle touches on there. For no one can take secular honor to himself more than Christ can take spiritual or ecclesiastical honor, since no one is worthier of secular honor than Christ is of spiritual honor. But "Christ," as the Apostle testifies, "did not glorify himself so as to be made high priest, but He [did] who said to him, 'You are my Son, this day have I begotten you' ".[3] Therefore no one should take secular honor to

---

[3] Hebrews 5:5.

himself without the pope, if it pertains to the pope to entrust such honors to whomever he likes. For otherwise he will not enter through the door,[4] that is by lawful appointment; he will therefore be a thief and a robber, and he will not be an emperor or prince but a tyrant and intruder.

The same opinion should be held by those who say that, although the pope does not have the fullness of power spoken of in Question I, chapter 2, and here in this chapter, lest the Christian law be a law of greater slavery than was the Mosaic law, yet he has fullness of power as far as concerns everything necessary for governing the community of the faithful, and, although he does not have power in matters of supererogation, he does nevertheless have power in everything without which the totality of the faithful cannot be ruled. For the community of the faithful cannot be ruled without secular rulers with temporal jurisdictions. If, therefore, the pope has such fullness of power by Christ's institution, it belongs to him to entrust such temporal jurisdictions; therefore, if, without him, someone took such jurisdiction to himself, he would take it to himself wrongly, and would exercise it wrongly.

In favor of this opinion it can be argued as follows. A community of persons able to have communion with one another in which all or many are prone to discord, dissensions, and disputes is not best ordered unless it is subject to one supreme rector, judge, and head upon whom the jurisdiction of all others depends. This seems provable in many ways. For one people, if it is best ordered, should be subject to one governor and not many. Solomon seems to suggest this when in Proverbs 11[:14] he says, "Where there is no governor the people will be ruined." For in saying "Where there is no governor," not "Where there are no governors," he seems to suggest that over one people one supreme governor should rule and not many. But the whole human race is one people. (For the unity of a people does not require that they live in one city or town; for as we read in 2 Paralipomenon 18[:3], King Josaphat said to King Achab, "As your people, so also my people," and yet neither king's people lived in only one city or town.) For the whole human race to be governed best, therefore, it must be subject, in respect of all things, to one supreme governor, upon whom the jurisdiction of all others depends.

[4] John 10:1.

The Savior seems also to suggest this in John 10[:16], when he says, "There will be one fold and one shepherd." By this we are given to understand that one supreme shepherd should be over one flock and community, however large.

Jerome also seems to think the same, in his letter to the monk Rusticus, as we read in 7, q. 1. *In apibus*. There he seems to assert that in every community there should be one supreme rector and judge, because according to him "the emperor is one, the judge of one province is one, and single are the bishops of every church"; therefore by like reasoning there should be one ruler of the whole earth upon whom all the jurisdiction of others depends.

It is also proved by argument. For if there is not one supreme rector or judge over the whole earth upon whom the jurisdiction of all others depends, then there are (or should be) at the same time many with no superior. But this seems to conflict with the best way of ruling. For if there are many with no superior, they are over either the same people or different people. If they are over the same – as, according to many, in a kingdom or province a king or other secular judge, and a patriarch or archbishop or other ecclesiastical judge, are over the same people (over the laity, at least), though one rules in secular matters and the other in spiritual matters – it seems that such a community is not best ordered. For a community is not best ordered in which subjects cannot obey their superior in matters in which they are bound to obey; but if many with no superior are over the same people, then in many cases, even when it would be beneficial, subjects will not be able to obey their superior, because it will be possible for those judges with no superior to summon the same subjects to themselves in different places for the same time, and they will not be able to obey each of them; therefore they must be disobedient to one of them. Therefore that community is not best ordered.

But if many with no superior are over different people – as different kings reign over different kingdoms – such a community, including subjects of different rulers with no superior, is not best ordered. For since human nature is prone to dissension, discord among the different [rulers] with no superior will easily arise, which will not be able to be settled by a superior. And discord among magnates without a superior is very dangerous, according to Aristotle, *Politics*, Book v, chapter 9,[5] because, as he says there, "The dissensions of notables make the whole city take sides"; for when such people disagree, they break up and divide the whole community. Therefore such a community is not best ordered.

It remains, therefore, that no community is best ordered unless it is under one head upon whom the jurisdiction of all others depends. But the totality of mortals is a community of persons able to have communion with one another, in which many are prone to discord and disputes; therefore it is not best ordered unless it is under one head upon whom all the jurisdiction of all others depends. But that one head cannot and should not be anyone but the highest pontiff: first, because the jurisdiction of the highest pontiff, at least in matters relating to the Christian faith and religion, depends on God alone; also because the supreme judge of all cannot be the emperor, or, consequently, anyone inferior to him, because the emperor may once again be, as he was once, an infidel and a pagan; but jurisdiction in spiritual matters in no way depends upon an infidel or pagan. Upon the highest pontiff alone, therefore, the jurisdiction of all others depends. And if the jurisdiction of all others depends on the highest pontiff, neither the emperor nor any other ruler should exercise any temporal jurisdiction unless it is entrusted to him by the highest pontiff.

Chapter 2

Another opinion is that neither the pope nor the Roman Church has power by Christ's institution regularly to entrust temporal jurisdictions to the emperor and other secular rulers, and that they can exercise them without him. But there are various modes of asserting this.

One is that neither the pope nor the Roman Church has this from Christ, but it is by Christ's institution that the pope (as also the Roman church) has absolutely no coercive power unless it is entrusted to him by the people or by the emperor or by someone else inferior to the emperor, and that in temporal matters the pope,

[5] 1303 b31-2.

if he commits any crime, secular or spiritual, is subject to the emperor or the people, to be regularly restrained by due penalty; and that the emperor and other secular rulers have power to exercise temporal jurisdictions without their being entrusted to them by the pope.

Another mode of assertion is that by Christ's institution the pope has power so that spiritual causes, both criminal and other, belong to him, and in them he has coercive power; but he does not have power to intervene either regularly or occasionally in temporal matters, unless it is entrusted to him by the people or the emperor or by some other secular.

A third mode of assertion is that the pope does not by Christ's institution have power regularly, but only occasionally, to entrust temporal jurisdictions to the emperor and other rulers, and that on occasion they should not otherwise exercise them.

These modes of assertion therefore agree in this, that neither the pope nor the Roman Church has by Christ's institution power regularly to entrust temporal jurisdictions to the emperor and other secular rulers, and they can exercise them without his commission. For this it is possible to argue as follows. No one has power to entrust temporal jurisdiction to his lord. But the emperor is the lord of the highest pontiff, since the pope is the vassal of him – i.e. the emperor – to whom he owes tribute, "unless by the imperial kindness he has immunity," 23, q. 8, *Ecce quod*. Pope Urban also seems to have confessed this, as we read in 23, q. 8, *Tributum*. Speaking of giving tribute to Caesar for himself and the other clergy, he says, "What was appointed of old is to be paid from the external goods of the Church to the emperors, for the peace and quiet by which they should protect and defend us." From these words we gather that the pope should give the emperor tribute, which is "proof of subjection," *Extra, De censibus, Omnis anima*. Therefore the emperor is the lord of the highest pontiff; and thus the highest pontiffs have sometimes called the emperor their lord, 11, q. 1, *Sacerdotibus*; dist. 63, *Salonitanae* and c. *Nobis dominus*.

Further, property passes "with its burden," *Extra, De pignoribus, Ex litteris*; therefore the pope, receiving cities and estates that owe tribute and service to the emperor, is by reason of such things subject to the emperor.

Again, the Christian religion frees no one from slavery, as was argued above, Question II, chapter 8. Therefore if the pope was subject to the emperor before he was made pope, he remains subject to the emperor and a slave, unless the emperor voluntarily grants him freedom and immunity.

But someone will say that a slave appointed to the papacy is set free from slavery, and also from all subjection, in favor of the Christian religion, just as a slave made priest is set free from slavery in favor of the Church. To this it is said that nothing unjust should be enacted in favor of religion or of the Church, because impiety must not be done on the pretext of piety, 14, q. 5, *Forte*, 1, q. 1, *Non est putandum*. Since, therefore, it is unjust and wicked that anyone should, without fault, be deprived of his right, the Church cannot enact that the emperor or another should be deprived of the right that he had in the person of the pope before he was appointed to the papal office, "lest," as the Apostle says, in I Timothy 6[:1], "the Lord's name and teaching be blasphemed." Pope Gelasius seems to follow this teaching, as we read in dist. 54, c. *Generalis*; he affirms that slaves should never evade their lords' rights on a pretext of religion, "lest it seem that by something established in the name of Christianity either the rights of others are invaded or public discipline is subverted." It seems, therefore, that if a slave becomes priest or highest pontiff, he is not delivered from slavery by either divine or natural law. Neither can he be delivered from slavery by canon law, because the canon laws can by no means abolish secular laws and rights of seculars that are not at all opposed to divine and natural law. Therefore, if a slave made pope or priest is delivered to freedom, it must be that his freedom is gained by the human law of the emperors.

Chapter 3

Having briefly reported these opinions, we must see how answer is made in accordance with them to the arguments brought against them. According to the opinion reported last, there are various ways of answering the argument brought forward above in chapter I in favor of the first opinion.

In one way it is conceded that no community is best ordered unless it is subject to one supreme judge, and therefore it is conceded that, if all mortals should be governed by the best form of government, they should have one supreme judge, appointed by the choice of the totality of mortals or by the greater or sounder part. And this judge should not be the pope, but another who does not exercise the highest priesthood; and the pope and everyone else would be subject to him in all matters that belong to the office of supreme judge. So the pope, by Christ's institution, has no coercive jurisdiction or power, either regularly or occasionally, either in temporal or in spiritual matters – although he has from Christ the power to absolve from sin in the penitential forum, to administer the other Church sacraments, and to teach how we should live so as to acquire everlasting life.

This answer seems to be based on the divine Scriptures, for we read in them, it seems, that Christ prohibited all coercive power to his apostles when he said, Matthew 20[:25], "You know that the rulers of the peoples lord it over them, and the great men exercise power over them; it will not be so among you." From these words we gather that the apostles should have exercised no power over others; this should be understood especially of coercive power; therefore neither does the pope, Peter's successor, have by Christ's institution any coercive power. This also seems provable from the fact that Christ, of whom the pope is only the vicar, never exercised any coercive power but wished to be judged by a secular judge; therefore neither does his vicar have any coercive power, but he is subject in all things to a secular judge.

In another way it is answered that in spiritual matters the pope has full and even coercive power, and another judge has power only in temporal matters; and yet the community of mortals, despite this, can be best ordered; and therefore the statement "A community is not best ordered unless it is subject to one supreme judge" is denied.

And in another way, according to the second opinion reported above, it is said that no community of persons able to have discords among themselves would be best ordered if it *were* subject regularly and in *every* case to one supreme judge: for in such a community the supreme judge could do wrong with impunity, to the destruction of the whole community, and this conflicts with the best ordering of any community. Again, it does not conflict with the best ordering of a community if other persons besides the supreme judge have, even regularly, a coercive power not prejudicial to the power of the supreme judge. Further, it does not conflict with the best ordering of a community if someone is regularly exempt from the coercive jurisdiction of the supreme judge, provided he is subject occasionally – namely, when the common good would otherwise be endangered. From these [propositions] it is inferred that it does not conflict with the best ordering of a community for the supreme judge, and others inferior to him, to be subject occasionally to someone other than the supreme judge, who would have coercive power over them.[6]

Through this the above argument is answered as follows. No community of persons able to dissent is best ordered unless the whole of it is subject to one supreme judge *regularly or occasionally*, so that no one except the supreme judge is exempt from his power in such a way that in *no* case would it be permissible for the supreme judge to coerce him; but for someone to be exempt regularly from the power of the supreme judge but subject to him in case of necessity does not detract from the best ordering of any community, just as it does not detract from the best ordering of a community (general or particular) if the supreme member of that community is regularly exempt from the power of the whole community and is yet in case of necessity subject to that same community. And therefore the totality of mortals is not best ordered unless it is subject to one supreme judge in that way, although on occasion it may be beneficial to recede from that best arrangement at least for a time.

Chapter 4

However, because those statements do not seem clear at every point, but obscure, so that someone could doubt how they should be understood, to elucidate their meaning and thereby make it clearer whether they are true or false, we must say briefly, in accordance with that [second] opinion, which things are requisite to the best regime, prelacy, rectorship, or form of government,

---

[6] Thus the pope and other clergy might have some coercive jurisdiction, they might regularly be exempt from the secular ruler's jurisdiction, and on occasion the secular ruler might be subject to their jurisdiction.

which things conflict with it, and which should be regarded as compatible with it.

It is said, therefore, that it is required for the best regime, first, that it should exist for the sake of the common good of the subjects, not for the ruler's own good. For by this the best regime – both general, in respect of all mortals, and particular, in respect of certain persons – differs, not only from a regime that is illicit, vitiated, and unjust, but also from a despotic regime, i.e., lordly rule for the ruler's own good, and from all other regimes, even licit ones, not directed to the common good.

But the papal and episcopal regime, insofar as it exists by Christ's ordinance, is of this kind. Christ seems to have suggested this when he appointed blessed Peter as pope, saying to him, "Feed my sheep," as if to say, "I appoint you ruler over my sheep, not to take from them wool and milk, except for your necessities" (in accordance with the text of the Apostle, 1 Corinthians 9[:7], "Who feeds the flock, and does not eat of the milk of the flock?") "but to feed them." Christ also seems to have promised blessed Peter rulership of this kind when he said to him, as we read in Matthew 16[:18], "You are Peter, and upon this rock I will build my Church, and the gates of hell will not prevail against it. And I will give you the keys of the kingdom of heaven": as if to say, "I will promote you and put you over the rest only for the building up of my Church, not for dominating it" (as Peter himself suggests in his canonical epistle, 1 Peter 5[:3] when he says, "Not as dominating your charge") "so that you may lead it into the kingdom of heaven." And therefore by the words of Christ that follow, "Whatever you bind upon earth will be bound also in the heavens, and whatever you loose upon earth will be loosed also in the heavens," it is meant that power was promised to Peter over his subjects, not over others, for their building up, not for their destruction. And the Apostle says, in 2 Corinthians, last chapter [13:10], that such a power over his subjects was given to him by the Lord.

Accordingly blessed Peter received no power from Christ except for the sake of his subjects' good in attaining the kingdom of heaven, so that he would not have been able to impose anything on them by commandment except what was necessary to them for reaching the kingdom of heaven. And therefore Christ's authority was of no avail to him against the rights and freedoms of the faithful granted to them by God and nature, because he received power from Christ for building up, not for destroying the rights and freedoms granted to the faithful by God and nature: lest he should have seemed to be not merely their shepherd and slave but their lord, contrary to his own teaching by which he guided other bishops when he said, "Feed God's flock which is in your charge, caring for them not by constraint but willingly according to God, not for the sake of shameful gain but voluntarily, not as dominating your charge, but being a wholehearted example to the flock".[7] Accordingly, if blessed Peter had ordered anything, either generally or in particular, contrary to the rights and freedoms of the faithful, outside of a situation of necessity and of a usefulness that could be equated with necessity, such an order would have obliged no one; and if he had pronounced any sentence against those not acquiescing, it would have been null by the law itself, as having been passed "by someone not his judge," according to the rule in *Extra, De regulis iuris, Ea*, in Book VI: "Things done by a judge which do not belong to his office have no force." For if what a prelate demands of his subject is contrary to a freedom granted to him by the pope, that subject is free to refuse, *Extra, De excessibus praelatorum, Sane*, and 10, q. 3, *Quia cognovimus*; and "a sentence contrary to a privilege of the pope is null, as being passed by one 'not his judge,' " *Extra, De excessibus praelatorum, Cum ad quorundam*, in the gloss (and it seems to be taken explicitly from the text): *a fortiori* what Peter had demanded from his subject contrary to the freedom granted to him by God and nature that subject would have been free to refuse, and a sentence of Peter contrary to a privilege of God and nature would have been null, as being passed by one "not his judge," for in respect of the freedoms granted to the faithful by God and nature all were exempt from Peter's jurisdiction. Therefore, since the privileges and exemption that are granted by God and by nature should be more observed by everyone than those conferred by the pope or by blessed Peter, it seems to follow that every sentence of Peter contrary to such freedoms would have been null by the law itself, as having been passed by one "not his judge."

Such rulership, which looks only to the good of the subjects and not to the ruler's own good except insofar as it is included in

---

[7] 1 Peter 5:2–3.

the good of others, Christ did not at all prohibit to the apostles, although he imposed on them, either by commandment or as advice, that they should abstain from all rulership existing for the sake of the ruler's own honor and advantage. He said to them, as we read in Matthew 20[:25]: "You know that the rulers of the peoples lord it over them, and the great men exercise power over them; it will not be so among you. But whoever wishes to be the greater among you, let him be your servant, and whoever wishes to be first among you shall be your servant, just as the Son of Man did not come to be served but to serve." By these words Christ did not prohibit to the apostles every rulership, but rather showed that some rulership was to be sought by them, when he said: "Whoever wishes to be the greater among you," and "Whoever wishes to be first among you," for greatness and being first are known to pertain to rulership; the Apostle, who was not ignorant of Christ's teaching, suggested this manifestly in 1 Timothy 3[:1] when he said, "If anyone desires the office of a bishop, he desires a good work." But what sort of rulership Christ wished the apostles to seek he makes clear when he says, "Just as the Son of Man did not come to be ministered to" – by commands, threats, or terrors demanding secular honors, gifts, tributes, and services (especially not compulsory services), such as worldly rulers who do not embrace the best mode of ruling demand and extort from their subjects, too often even violently – "but to minister" – not only physically, even by humbly washing the feet of his disciples, but also spiritually: out of very great love, teaching those who believed in him for their advantage, not his own, advising them and most salutarily directing them by commands and prohibitions, which are known to pertain to rulership, as the Gospel writer Matthew testifies. In chapter 10[:5 ff] he says, "These twelve Jesus sent, commanding them, saying, 'Do not go on the road to the gentiles' . . . 'Do not possess gold,' " etc. This is also found explicitly in a great many other places of the gospel teaching.

Therefore, although he said that he had come "not to be ministered to, but to minister," Christ by no means removed from himself all prelacy or rulership, but only rulership for the sake of his own advantage, glory, or honor, as he himself often testified. Therefore, since he wished the apostles to be imitators of him in caring for the advantage of the faithful, he in no way prohibited them from all rulership, but instructed them by commandment or advice that in ruling they should seek to be useful to the faithful: not to dominate, loving their own advantage, glory, and honor – things such as worldly rulers, as we know, always or often seek. And the apostles exercised the purest form of such rulership, for the good of others. (But according to some, the successors of the apostles are by no means bound by the necessity of salvation to the purity of such rulership, without any admixture of any other kind of rulership that the ruler assumes for the sake of his own good, glory and honor, unless there were some who renounced all such rulership by vow or oath; though an assertion some make affirms that those who succeed the apostles in rulership are obliged to the purity of such rulership.)

Chapter 5

Secondly, according to the above opinion, it is required for the best regime (whether general, in respect of all mortals, or particular, in respect of some) that the ruler be one person, just as the regime is one. For this reason, according to philosophers, a royal regime, in which one person is preeminent, surpasses and excels both aristocratic and "constitutional" regimes, in both of which many preside.

It is possible to argue for this in many ways, but for the present let it suffice to bring forward only one argument, which is as follows. That regime must be regarded as best and as superior to the rest in which charity, friendship, peace, and concord among subjects is most of all cared for, fostered, increased, and preserved and in which sedition or discord, which is the corruption of every community, is especially avoided. For it is chiefly on account of these things that every regime beneficial to the common good is established, and the ruler should with the utmost effort plant and foster them in his subjects. And thus "the prince of peace," Christ, "upon [whose] shoulders is laid" the best "government,"[8] when he was about to withdraw physically from the apostles and the other faithful, especially imposed on them love and friendship,

[8] Isaias 9:6.

saying, "This is my commandment, that you love one another."[9] He also very often wished them peace, which is the effect of friendship and charity, and commanded it and taught them to desire it for others. For he said to them, as we read in John 14[:27], "I leave you peace; my peace I give to you"; in chapter 16[:33] he says, "May you have peace in me"; in Mark 9[:49] he says, "Have peace among you"; in John 20[:26] we read, "Jesus came and stood in the middle" of the disciples, "and said, 'Peace be unto you' "; and, as we read in Matthew 10[:12], he said to the apostles, "When you enter a house greet them, saying, 'Peace to this house.' "

And Christ, the author and rector of every community, declares that the corruption and destruction of any community comes from discord; and consequently concord is useful for the preservation of any community. As we read in Matthew 12[:25], he says, "Every kingdom divided against itself shall be made desolate, and no city or house divided against itself will stand." With these things Aristotle agrees, compelled by reason alone. In *Politics*, Book II, chapter 3,[10] he says, "We believe that friendship is the greatest of goods for cities, for thus they never make seditions." And in *Ethics*, Book VIII, chapter 1,[11] he says, "And it seems that friendship holds cities together, and legislators care more about it than justice: for concord seems to be something like friendship, and they seek this most of all." By these [passages] it is proved that government is most of all directed to preserving friendship, peace, and concord, and to removing discord, among those subject to the ruler.

And this comes about more if the ruler is one person than if there are many, as happens in an aristocracy. For if one alone is supreme ruler, no discord at all can come about in the first and head of all; for no one dissents from himself. But if there are several supreme rulers, whether they preside over different governments or one, whether aristocratically or "constitutionally," friendship and peace can be dissolved and discord and sedition arise among the principal rulers of the whole community, which is, as we know, more serious and more dangerous than any discord among subjects and the less powerful. For every discord among the less powerful

---

[9] John 15:12.
[10] 1262 b7–8.
[11] 1155 a22–3.

and subjects can be settled and healed by the ruler or rulers. But if discord has arisen among the supreme rulers, it easily spreads to everyone else, because, as Aristotle testifies in *Politics*, Book v, chapter 9,[12] "The dissensions of the notables make the whole city completely take sides; accordingly subjects must fear them and resolve the dissensions of chiefs and mighty men," namely by setting up one ruler over all, if they properly can. "In the leadership," i.e., among the rulers, "the fault comes about," to the danger and destruction of all, if they are in dissension. "But the leadership is said to be half of all";[13] and therefore in every community discord among the rulers must be regarded as most dangerous. Therefore it is requisite to the regime that is simply best that the person ruling be single, just as the regime is one. Several other things are requisite to the best regime, but for the present let it suffice to have dealt with these things briefly and in outline.

Chapter 6

Several things conflict with the best regime, a few of which must be touched on. The first of these is that it conflicts with it to have as subjects only slaves; indeed, it seems to some that it is not consistent with the purity of the best regime that any subject should be a slave without fault,[14] especially against his will. For the best regime is established chiefly for the good of subjects; but rule over slaves, which is also called despotism, exists chiefly for the good of the ruler; therefore such a regime must not be adjudged the best.

Further, a regime that is unjust and contrary to nature must not be esteemed as the best. But it is unjust and contrary to nature that someone should rule as slaves his betters or equals and similars in virtue and wisdom (or those of whom there can be a probable hope that they will become betters or equals and similars), as Aristotle seems plainly to assert in his *Politics*, Book iii.[15] Jerome also seems to testify to this when he says, as we read in the *Decreta*,

---

[12] 1303 b31–2.

[13] *Principium* is translated here and just above as "leadership" to fit the use Ockham makes of Aristotle's words. Aristotle probably meant "beginning."

[14] That is, without any fault of his own.

[15] 1287 a12–18.

dist. 25, para. *Nunc autem*, "Let someone be chosen," namely as ruler and prelate, "in comparison with whom the rest may be called a flock"; and in 1, q. 1, *Vilissimus*, we read, "He who is more outstanding in honor must be regarded as most contemptible unless he excels in knowledge and holiness." Thus the wise man in Ecclesiasticus 32[:1], instructing and guiding a ruler and prince, says, "Have they appointed you ruler? Do not be exalted; be among them as if you were one of them." Therefore it seems to conflict with the best regime that all the subjects of the one ruler should be slaves.

To prove this, Aristotle's argument in *Politics*, Book 1,[16] by which he tries to prove that rule over freemen is better than rule over slaves, also seems sufficient. For "the rule is better that is of better subjects," as rule over men is better than rule over beasts. But free men are better than slaves; therefore rule over slaves is not to be judged the best.

But against this someone will perhaps object that the most perfect obedience in subjects does not conflict with the best regime, for then the best regime could not be found in the most perfect religious order, which promises the most perfect obedience; but the most perfect obedience is the obedience of slaves, because anyone who promises and vows the most perfect obedience promises to obey in all things, and slaves are obliged to this; therefore rule of slaves does not conflict with the best regime. To this it is answered that the most perfect religious profession does not promise simply to obey in all things just as slaves are obliged to obey in all things, for then a prelate could compel such a religious to lead a secular life; but the most perfect religious profession promises to obey in all things that are not contrary to God and to its rule, especially in matters that pertain to God, to good morals, and to life under the rule.

Chapter 7

From that it follows, according to the above opinion, that it conflicts with the best regime that the ruler should have the fullness of power described above in Question 1, chapter 6, namely, so that

---

[16] 1254 a25–6.

he could by right, if he wished, command and impose on his subjects all things that do not go against or conflict with indispensable and immutable natural law or with divine law to which all Catholics are obliged. For all who are subject to someone with such fullness of power over them are his slaves in the strictest sense of the term, for no lord can by right have a power over his slaves greater than this power. But it conflicts with the best regime that all the subjects should be slaves; therefore it also conflicts with it that he should have such fullness of power.

Chapter 8

It remains to ask next what things should be regarded, according to the foregoing opinion, as compatible with the best regime, though they do not belong to its essence but can be present or absent.

To make this clear, it must above all be known that although many things pertain to the ruler of whom we are speaking – namely to give his rights to each person and preserve them, to enact necessary and just laws, to appoint subordinate judges and other officials, [to determine] which arts should be exercised, and by whom, in the community subject to him, and to command the acts of all the virtues, and many other things – nevertheless, he seems to have been appointed most principally to correct and punish wrongdoers. For if, in some community, no one had to be punished for any fault or crime, an adviser to good and a teacher would be enough, and a ruler would seem altogether unnecessary.

This is gathered from the sacred Scriptures. For the law and the ruler seem to have been established most principally for the same purpose. But the law is established, not for the good, but for correcting and punishing the bad, as the Apostle testifies. In 1 Timothy 1[:9] he says, "The law was not made for the just man, but for the unjust and for those who are not submissive"; and in Galatians 5[:18], "If you are led by the spirit," that is by reason, doing nothing against reason and good morals, "you are not under the law"; and in 2 Corinthians 3[:17] he says, "Where the spirit of the Lord is, there is freedom," namely so that the law of another ruler cannot bind (thus "have charity and do what you will"), and consequently you are not bound by any law if you have been fortified with charity, "which does not act wrongly"; and in dist.

4, c. *Factae* we read, "Laws are made so that human audacity may be restrained," etc.; and Augustine, as we read in 23, q. 5, *Ad fidem*, says, by laws "you are not compelled to do good, but forbidden to do evil." Therefore, similarly, a ruler should rule chiefly, not for the good, but for restraining the bad. The Apostle seems to assert this explicitly in Romans 13[:3], saying, "Rulers are not a terror to good works but to evil . . . And if you do what is evil, fear; for he does not carry a sword without reason. For he is God's minister, an avenger to execute wrath upon anyone who does evil." The wise man also seems to suggest this in Ecclesiasticus 7[:6], saying, "Do not seek to be made a judge, unless you have the strength to attack iniquities."

Chapter 9

In view of these things, it is said that it does not conflict with the best regime but is compatible with it, if the jurisdiction or power of some person or persons within the community does not at all depend upon the supreme ruler of that community or was not established by him, provided no one who does wrong in that community is thereby able to escape just and due punishment. For something that does not detract from the common good, though it somewhat reduces the honor or power of the ruler, does not seem to conflict with the best regime, since whoever exercises the best rule is obliged not to seek his own power or honor but the common good and the good of others, so as to imitate the Apostle when he says, in 1 Corinthians 10[:33], "Seeking what is advantageous not to myself but to many"; he also says, in Philippians 2[:4], "Each one considering not the things that are his own but those that belong to others." And no wonder, for "charity," which should flourish in the ruler toward his subjects, "does not seek the things that are its own," 1 Corinthians 13[:5]. The emperor[17] also suggests this about himself, saying, "We undertake willing labors to prepare peace for others," *Auth., Ut divinae iussiones subscriptionem habeant gloriosi quaestoris*, in the beginning, coll. 8; he also passes sleepless nights, "so that his subjects may remain in

---

[17] That is, Justinian.

total peace," *Auth.*, *Ut iudices sine quoque suffragio*, in the beginning, coll. 2.

But for jurisdiction, power, or office to exist in a community (especially from a superior) and not to depend upon the highest ruler of that community does not go against or conflict with the common good, provided no one who does wrong thereby escapes due punishment. For since such jurisdiction or power should benefit the common good, it makes no difference who establishes it, provided it is duly and rightly exercised and in no way neglected – which is all fulfilled if no wrongdoer in that community can escape the punishment of the supreme judge or of another. For it makes no difference to the common good who lawfully appoints the leader of the army or the leader of the soldiers, provided he wages wars wisely and vigorously for the safety of the commonwealth; and it makes no difference to the common good who lawfully appoints an inferior judge, provided he justly carries out what is just. And thus we see that this is followed in every community. For when someone undertakes supreme government over some community, he never appoints anew all who are to exercise any jurisdiction, power, or office in the community. He leaves those he finds appointed by his predecessor, or someone else, to carry out their duties, and he allows some to be appointed anew by others if that is the custom or the law; because, as has been said, whom someone has lawful power from does not detract from the common good, provided he diligently does the things that benefit the common good according to the power he has received. It therefore does not conflict with the best regime if some power or jurisdiction in a community does not at all depend upon the supreme ruler, provided the common good is in no way exposed thereby to danger (as will not happen if whoever exercises such power is unable thereby to avoid necessary correction if he does wrong).

Chapter 10

From the foregoing it is inferred that it does not conflict with the best regime for someone in the community to be regularly exempt from the coercive power of the supreme ruler provided he is subject to the supreme ruler occasionally, so that he cannot insolently do wrong. For such exemption does not detract from the common good, because if someone who is thus exempt does wrong, he cannot evade the punishment necessary to the common good. And from this it is further concluded that it does not conflict with the best regime for the correction or punishment of someone thus exempt from the power of the supreme ruler to be primarily the business of another, or others, not the supreme ruler, provided that if they fail (whether through malice, lack of power, or reprehensible ignorance), he can be punished at least occasionally by the supreme ruler. For this does not detract from the common good; for it makes no difference to the common good who lawfully punishes a criminal. Since, therefore, a ruler having more power than a teacher and adviser is established most principally to correct and lawfully punish wrongdoers "so that human audacity may be restrained and the innocent may be safe among the wicked," it is inferred that the things spoken of above do not conflict with the best regime, since through them wrongdoers are in no way able to have an impunity dangerous to the common good.

Chapter 11

Indeed, although the above opinion holds the foregoing views about the best regime, both general, in respect of the totality of mortals, and particular, in respect of some, nevertheless it says that such best regime should not always be established, either in the whole community of all mortals or in a particular community. For just as often some things are simply good and yet are bad for many because of their indisposition (for to drink wine and eat meat are good and yet are bad for many sick people), so the simply best regime is not best for all, indeed for some it is harmful, and it sometimes leads to the corruption and endangering of the common good. This can happen both from the wickedness of subjects and from the wickedness and inadequacy of the person to be appointed to such rule. For sometimes subjects who from ambition desire to rule without right, or who are stirred up by some other wickedness, would not at all tolerate the best regime and would rather turn to seditions and discords corrupting the commonwealth. And sometimes a person adequate in goodness and discretion could not be found, and then some other regime exercised by many together, for example aristocratic or "constitutional" government, should be established for the time; for that should be done for the time which for the time more advances the common good. And thus, by the will of God, who controls all things according to the suitability of times, the kingdom of the children of Israel, which at first was one, was afterwards divided into two kingdoms.

If, however, the best regime, whether of all mortals or of some, has been established, it must not afterwards be destroyed without the most urgent reason. Thus it could be interrupted for many reasons for which it could nevertheless not be destroyed. Accordingly, prescription could not destroy it, since all prescription against the best regime seems iniquitous. And therefore, if prescription does not run against many lesser things, much more should it not run against the best regime, though it should run in its favor: just as prescription does not run against freedom but for freedom, for whoever has stood in the status of freedom for ten years must be regarded as a free man, *Extra, De coniugio servorum, Licet.*

Chapter 12

The opinion previously stated holds that through the above the things said in chapter 3 become clearer, and the whole argument adduced in chapter 1 is destroyed. For when, first, it is taken [as a premise] that a community of persons able to have communion with one another in which all or many are prone to discord, dissensions, and conflicts is not best ordered unless it is subject to one supreme rector, judge, and head upon whom the jurisdiction of all others depends, it is answered that it is not necessary to the best ordered community that all jurisdiction should depend upon the supreme ruler, in accordance with what was said above in chapters 10 and 11.

And when this is proved by the text of Proverbs 11[:14], "Where there is no governor the people perish," it is answered that this proves that the whole human race is not simply best ordered, and the simply best regime is not established over it, unless it is subject to one supreme ruler by whom anyone else is, at least in *some* case, punished if he does wrong. But the unity of the people subject to the best regime does not require that the jurisdiction of all others should depend upon the first ruler; for someone can be exempt in this respect, though he should not be exempt in every case from punishment to be inflicted by the supreme ruler as first ruler of the whole community. Through the same [distinction] an answer is given to the text of John 10: "There will be one fold and one shepherd": for one supreme shepherd should be over one flock, and yet someone may be exempt from his rule in some case, namely when his exemption does not detract from the common good. And Jerome should be understood in the same way; for in every community one should be supreme rector and judge, and yet, without detracting from the best regime, someone can be exempt in some things.

And when it is proved by argument that there should be a supreme upon whom the jurisdiction of all others depends – because if in the whole world there is not one thus supreme, then there are or should be many without a superior, which seems to conflict with the best form of government, because they would rule either over the same or over different subjects, both of which seem unsuitable – it is answered that if the whole world were ruled by the best regime, although it would not be necessary for there to be one supreme upon whom in respect of institution and commission the jurisdiction of all others would depend, it would however be necessary for there to be one supreme ruler to whom every other should be subject as to a supreme ruler at least occasionally, by reason of some wrongdoing, though not by reason of every crime and in every case. And therefore there would not be many simply first with no superior; but there would be one simply first in respect of all, although different ones might be subject to him in different ways; for one of them could be exempt in many things without danger to the common good, and others could lack such exemption. Also, the one exempt could without prejudice to the common good have great power, even coercive, in no respect simply and regularly dependent upon the supreme ruler, because it would be enough if he were subject by reason of some wrongdoing to the supreme as to a ruler. And thus there would not be many simply supreme with no superior; therefore the argument brought forward to prove that it conflicts with the best regime in any community that there should be in that community several with no superior, whether they are over the same subjects or different ones, does not succeed against that mode of asserting the opinion.

But perhaps someone will object on the other side that the argument does succeed also against this mode of the opinion. For if one is supreme, and another with power over many, even coercive power, is exempt in the above way from the one who is supreme, then the subjects of the exempt [ruler] are either exempt from the jurisdiction of the supreme ruler or they are not exempt from his jurisdiction. If they are exempt from the jurisdiction of the supreme [ruler], therefore the supreme [ruler] by no means rules all, and, consequently, in respect of the whole community there is not the best regime. And if they are not exempt from the jurisdiction of the supreme ruler, then the above argument succeeds; for it will be able to happen that the supreme ruler and the exempt [ruler] call the same subjects to their courts at the same time; therefore they will obey either both, which is impossible, or neither, and then they will be disobedient to both, or they will obey one and not the other, and then they will inflict irreverence and injury on the one they do not obey.

To this it is answered that, without any imperfection of the best regime, it will be able to happen that the subjects of such an exempt [ruler] are exempt in many things (not in all) from the jurisdiction of the supreme ruler, *and* that they are not exempt;[18] and therefore, whether they are exempt or not, it is answered to the above argument that if the supreme ruler and the [ruler] thus exempt summon or cite the same subjects to their courts at the same time, then either they express the reason for the summons in such summons, or they do not express it. If they do not express it, they should go to the supreme ruler, because they are not obliged to obey the [ruler] thus exempt except "saving the rights of all others," just as the laity are not obliged to obey the pope except "saving the right of the secular ruler." In such a case his subjects therefore do not inflict injury upon the [ruler] thus exempt if they do not go to him, just as a bishop called to a synod does not cause injury to the one who calls him if he is impeded by a royal command, dist. 18, *Si episcopus*, where the gloss notes that "here deference is paid to the royal office, as in 12, q. 2, *De rebus*, dist. 63, *Salonitanae*. For the authority of a greater ruler excuses" –

---

[18] That is, either arrangement is consistent with the best regime.

as the gloss notes on dist. 63, c. *Salonitanae* – "as in 14, q. 5, *Dixit*." And if those who thus call the same subjects at the same time do express the reason for the summons, a general rule cannot be given for every case to decide whom they should go to, because often necessity excuses one called to a superior, and often the one called is not at all excused; accordingly often necessity excuses one called by a superior, yet when he is called by an inferior necessity does not excuse him, because no necessity appears by which he can be excused. Therefore, when those thus called can be excused, it should be left to the discretion of a prudent person [to decide] which he should appear before, because in such matters, because of the multiplicity of the cases that can happen, it is not possible to give a general rule that never fails. Nevertheless, it is said that they should appear before the supreme ruler unless reason dictates that because of some urgent necessity – for example, because of a weightier matter or something similar – they are excused for not appearing before him and not [for not appearing] before the other.

But perhaps someone will say to this: If a [ruler] thus exempt is only occasionally subject to the supreme ruler, by reason of some wrongdoing, it follows that he is not more subject to him [the supreme ruler] than the supreme ruler is to him, because occasionally, by reason of some wrongdoing, he can himself punish the supreme ruler, namely when all others have failed and the correction or punishment of the supreme ruler could not be passed over under dissimulation without danger to the whole commonwealth. To this it is answered that [the ruler] thus exempt would be subject to the supreme ruler rather than vice versa, because the first ruler would have power to punish [the ruler] thus exempt, not only from necessity, when all his subjects failed, but also by reason of the supreme rulership; but the [ruler] thus exempt would have power to correct the supreme ruler only from necessity, not by reason of his office, when all others, or the people, failed.

And when it is taken as the minor [premise] of that argument that the one supreme judge or ruler should not be anyone but the highest pontiff, it is answered that if the totality of mortals were best ordered and subject to the best regime, then, given the reasonable ordinance by which Christ determined that the highest pontiff and other clergy should in no way be involved in secular business except in case of necessity, the one supreme ruler or judge ought not be the highest pontiff but a secular ruler, lay and Christian. That he should be a layman, and not the highest pontiff or even a cleric, is proved by the fact that, as was proved above, Question I, chapter 4, outside the case of necessity or of utility comparable with necessity, the clergy should be strangers to secular business. That he should be a Christian is clear from the fact that otherwise he would try not to foster but to destroy the common spiritual good, which goes against and conflicts with the best regime over the totality of mortals.

But when it is said that the jurisdiction of the highest pontiff, especially in matters that pertain to the faith and the Christian religion, depends upon God alone, it is answered that, just as the possibility of understanding in various ways the statement that baptism and other sacraments depend upon God alone was in some way touched on above, Question II, chapter 3, so the statement that the jurisdiction of the highest pontiff depends upon God alone can be understood in different ways – for the present, in three ways. In one way, that the highest pontiff receives his jurisdiction from God without human ministry, so that he can in no case be appointed or deposed by man; and his jurisdiction does not depend upon God alone in that way, since no one except blessed Peter was appointed to the papacy without human choice. In another way it can be understood that such jurisdiction depends upon God alone in respect of appointment, with the concurrence of human ministry – namely, canonical election; and that opinion concedes that the jurisdiction the pope has by Christ's ordinance depends in that way upon God alone. Third, that it depends on God alone not only in that way, but also in respect of deposition, so that the pope cannot be deposed by anyone in any case except by God alone; and it does not depend upon God alone in this way, since the pope himself, and also another, can on occasion depose him. For he can depose himself both by heretical wickedness and by voluntary renunciation. And just as he can be accused by a man of any crime whatever, if it is notorious and causes scandal to the Church and he is incorrigible (as the gloss notes on dist. 40, c. *Si papa*), so in such a case he can be judged, or deposed and removed, by man; for every accusation must be made before a judge. And the pope should not be disturbed about this, lest he seem to seek to be preeminent and not to be useful; lest, against the teaching of Christ given to the apostles for themselves and for all the prelates of the Church, he should wish salt that has lost its savor not to be thrown out and trampled on by men; lest, against Christ's commandment, he should not wish the putrid member to be cut off for the health of his mystical body; lest he desire an erring brother corrected in charity not to be regarded as a heathen and a publican even though he has not heard the Church; lest he show that he does not want the rotten flesh cut off, the scabby sheep driven out of the fold, the ferment cleared out that corrupts the whole mass, but wishes himself to be spared and the whole Church led into ruin – all of which it is fitting to banish from the desires of the pope, who is bound to lay down his life for his subjects.

Therefore, according to that opinion, although the pope is rightly exempt from the power and jurisdiction of the supreme ruler in matters through which he has to provide for the welfare of all, so that he cannot be obstructed in them by anyone (and if the supreme ruler wishes to be useful and not to be preeminent, he is obliged to accept and praise this exemption), nevertheless, by reason of wrongdoing – not of any wrongdoing whatever (lest his authority seem contemptible, and lest for some small action, perhaps amended, he could be hindered from [furthering] the common utility), but of serious and very great wrongdoing, especially wrongdoing often repeated, that would abound in noteworthy danger, especially to the common good – it is beneficial that the pope should be able to be deposed and removed by human judgment, especially if he appears incorrigible and the Church is scandalized by him.

And it seems reasonable that such judgment concerning the pope should pertain first to some certain persons of the clergy; if they fail, whether through wickedness or through reprehensible negligence or through lack of power, this pertains to the supreme ruler, if he is a sincere and fervent follower of the faith and the Christian religion. And if he fails (whether through wickedness or through reprehensible negligence), the deposition of the pope (or at least his detention or prohibition from becoming insolent with impunity) pertains either to the whole congregation of the faithful or to any faithful persons whatever able to have enough temporal power over him, so that a suitable remedy can be found in the Church (as [it can] against the sin of any Christian, little or great), in accordance with the text of the Apostle in 1 Corinthians, 5[:13], "Throw out evil from yourselves" (and he also says, "Throw out the old ferment"[19]) – unless temporal power fails. In that case Jerome's advice must be observed, which we read in 11, q. 3, *Quando ergo*, namely that Christians, even those with understanding and prudence, should be silent, "lest they give holy things to dogs and throw pearls before swine, who will turn and trample on them; and let them imitate Jeremias when he said 'I sat alone, because I was full of bitterness.' "

And evidence that by reason of wrongdoing the pope in some case receives the court of the supreme ruler, who should be a layman, is taken from the divine Scriptures, in which we read that when Christ and the apostles were accused of crimes they were judged by secular judges, even unbelievers. And although they denied the crimes attributed to them, it is not found that they asserted or protested that they were not obliged in such a case to answer before such judges; indeed, they seem rather to have suggested that in such cases they were subject to them. For Christ said to Pilate, as we read in John 19[:11], "You would not have any power over me unless it were given to you from above." In these words Christ seems to have suggested that in that case Pilate had lawful and ordinate power over him given from above (that is, by God, according to the exposition of some teachers, or by a true emperor, according to the exposition of others). Therefore the power Pilate had over Christ in that case was not only permitted and usurped, but granted and given. The Apostle also seems to have asserted the same thing about himself when he was accused of a crime before unbelieving judges. As we read in Acts 24[:10], he said to the governor, "Knowing that you have been a judge over this nation for many years, I will with good courage answer for myself." He did not say, "I am not obliged to answer before you," but he said, "I will answer for myself"; therefore he seems by deed and word to have recognized that in that case he was his judge. And as we read in chapter 25[:10–11], he said to the governor Festus: "I stand at Caesar's judgment-seat, where I ought to be judged. I have done no injury to the Jews, as you well know.

---

[19] 1 Corinthians 5:7.

For if I have injured them, or done anything deserving death, I do not refuse to die. But if there is nothing in these things they accuse me of, no one can deliver me to them. I appeal to Caesar." In these words Paul recognized both Festus and Caesar as his judges. Since, therefore, it is wrong to say that Paul lied in word or deed, Caesar was, in truth, Paul's judge.

But perhaps someone will say that from this a manifest absurdity would follow, namely that the emperor, even an unbeliever, would be the pope's judge in a case of faith; for Paul's case, which was dealt with before the governor, was a case of faith, for he was accused by the Jews on account of the Christian faith. To this it is answered that a case of faith would be rightly dealt with before a faithful emperor if others failed, because, as we read in dist. 96, *Ubinam*, a question of faith "pertains not only to the clergy but also to the laity and to absolutely all Christians." And before an unbelieving emperor a case of faith could be treated, not insofar as it related solely to the truth divinely revealed, but insofar as it could touch upon morals and detract from the commonwealth and bring injury upon the common good or upon any person. The proconsul Gallio seems to have prudently suggested both of these things; as we read in Acts 18[:14–15], when Paul was accused by the Jews, he said to them: "If, indeed, it were some matter of injustice, or a terrible crime, O Jews, I would rightly bear with you. But if they are verbal questions about names of your law, see to it yourselves. I will not be judge of them." Thus, therefore, it is said that on occasion, by reason of wrongdoing, the pope would be subject to the emperor.

To all other canons and texts from which it is inferred that the pope must not be judged by anyone, it is answered that they should not be understood generally without any exception, but with their exceptions, as also countless other rules and also a great many texts of divine Scripture should be understood, even though they are uttered, not only indefinitely, but even in general words and with universal signs. And thus the gloss to 9, q. 3, c. *Nemo*, lists some exceptions, namely when the pope submits himself, as in 2, q. 7, *Nos, si*, and when he entrusts himself to his confessor; also in a case of heresy. And this last [exception] is included by the gloss to dist. 40, c. *Si papa*, which adds another (spoken of above) that comprehends countless others, namely, "if any crime of his, whatever it is, is notorious and he is incorrigible and the Church is scandalized" by him.

But between the exception concerning heresy and other crimes there is a great difference to be noticed. For because of heresy, however hidden, he is, by the law itself and without any human sentence, deprived of the papacy and every church prelacy, as being in truth not within the congregation of the faithful either in merit or in number, though according to the false opinion of those who do not know that he is a heretic he is thought to be the head of the Church; indeed, what is more, he incurs by the law itself the sentence of excommunication and all other penalties pronounced in unlimited terms by the sacred canons and the highest pontiffs against heretics, especially bishops. Thus the gloss says on 24, q. 1, c. 1, "This is a case in which a pope can bind a pope, in which the pope falls under the canon 'of sentence passed.' There is no objection from the rule that 'an equal cannot loose or bind an equal,' because if the pope is a heretic, inasmuch as he is a heretic he is less than any Catholic, because the law censures the deed even without sentence." But on account of other crimes a pope is not by the law itself deprived of the papacy but must be deprived by sentence.

Chapter 13

Now that we have seen how, according to the second opinion reported above in chapter 2, answer is made to the argument brought forward in chapter 1, we must see how answer is made according to the first opinion to the things argued in favor of the second opinion in chapter 2.

To the first, when it is said that the emperor is the lord of the highest pontiff, it is answered that it is not true. For the pope is not a vassal of the emperor nor his slave and does not owe him tribute by right, except perhaps to avoid scandal; but other clergy who have from the emperor estates, villas, and possessions beyond their needs are subject to the emperor, as Gratian says in the paragraph quoted before. And thus is understood Urban's decree in 23, q. 8, *Tributum*. And when it is said that some highest pontiffs have called emperors their lords, it is answered that they did so out of humility.

To the second, when it is taken [as a premise] that property passes with its burden, it is answered, according to those who say that the pope has that fullness of power discussed in Question I above, that this is true, when the property passes from the lordship or right of one to the new lordship or right of another; but in that way no temporal thing can pass into the lordship of the pope, since the pope is lord of all temporal things, which are possessed by anyone else by his permission. And therefore, according to that opinion, no emperor or king or other can, properly speaking, give a possession or any property whatever to the highest pontiff; but he can resign to the pope property he possessed by the pope's permission, just as, according to Innocent IV, Constantine "humbly resigned to the Church that inordinate power which he had before used illegitimately outside the Church." However, according to those who deny to the pope that fullness of power but attribute to him that by which he can do all things necessary for governing the community of the faithful, it is answered that property passes with its burden unless it is freed of its burden in favor of the faith or of the pope or of the Church or of some other spirituality, just as a slave priest is freed from slavery in favor of the clerical order, yet in such a way that he is fined by the loss of his *peculium*, dist. 54, *Ex antiquis*.

And when it is taken [as a premise] that the Christian religion frees no one from slavery, it is answered that this is not true. But when it is said that nothing unjust should be enacted in favor of religion or of the Church, it is conceded; but it is said that for someone to be deprived of his right without fault is not always unjust or wicked, when there is a reason and when such a right is completely in the power of a superior, as the rights of all are completely in the power of the pope. To Gelasius it is answered that Gelasius means that slaves should not evade their lords' rights on a pretext of religion without the authority of the highest pontiff, and thus this is enacted by canon law.

And when it is said that canon laws can by no means abolish secular laws and the rights of seculars, it is answered, according to the opinion that attributes to the pope the fullness of power spoken of above in Question I, chapter 2, that canon laws can abolish and overturn all secular laws and all the positive rights of seculars and give them to whom the pope pleases, and in such a way that of right the pope could at will take away even all kingdoms and all other rights whatever and all temporal things from those who possess them and keep them for himself or give them to anyone else whatever – in such a way that, though he would sin in doing this, nevertheless the deed would hold by right, and kings and all others would be bound to obey him in such things. But according to the other opinion, which says that the pope does not have such fullness of power but has the fullness of power by which he can do all things necessary for governing the community of the faithful, canon laws can for cause abolish secular laws and the rights of seculars, but not without reasonable and manifest cause.

Appendix: Text and translation

The translation of Ockham's political terms[1]

Ockham's Latin includes a great variety of political terms. Some express ideas of ruling: *rex, rector, regere, regimen, rectoria; princeps, principari, principans, principatus; dominus, dominari; gubernare, gubernator, gubernacula; praesidere, praesidens, praeses; imperare, imperator; praeesse; dux; caput; superior; praepositus; praelatus, praelatio*. Some express subjection: *subesse, subdere, subditus, subiectus*. Some express the idea of appointment to a position of rule or to some other office, or the establishment of an office or practice: *promovere, provehere, praeponere, praeficere, praeferre, constituere, instituere, assumere, sublevare, sublimare, facere, ordinare*. And there are others.

The members of the "*rex*" and "*princeps*" families of terms are often interchangeable. *Rex* always means "king." *Princeps* meant originally "the first man," but in the middle ages often "prince," or more generally a ruler; it was a common word from classical times. *Regere* originally meant "to make straight," "to guide," "to direct"; in classical and medieval Latin it means "to rule," not only as king but in any position of power. (*Regnare*, which has been translated as "to reign," meant "to rule as king.") *Principare* or, more commonly, *principari*, is the corresponding verb derived from *princeps*. It does not seem to have been much used before the middle ages: dictionaries do not record any occurrence in a classical author and only a few in Christian authors (including Lactantius and Augustine); in Dutripon's concordance to the Vulgate Bible it

---

[1] See Gewirth's "Introduction" to his translation of Marsilius of Padua, pp. lxvi–xci.

has only one entry (Mark 10:42, where it translates the Greek *archein*). It occurs in William of Moerbeke's translation of Aristotle's *Politics* and in Thomas Aquinas's commentary on the *Politics*; it is common in Ockham's political writings.[2]

Principatus was common from classical times; Ockham uses it in various contexts for the status of being a ruler ("rulership"), for the work that rulers do ("government," "rule"), and for the mode in which the ruling function is organized (the "form of government" or "regime"). *Regimen*, the corresponding word derived from *regere*, was apparently not much used by classical authors, but in Ockham's time it was common. It seems to have been interchangeable with *principatus* and is translated in the same ways (in one place, where it means a service due from ruler to subject, *regimen* is translated as "governance"). *Rector*, like *princeps*, means a ruler of any kind. It is usually translated as "ruler," but in some places (especially where other commoner words for "ruler" also occur) it is translated "rector," meaning not the rector of a parish but the head or ruler of any organization or state. *Rectoria* is synonymous with *principatus* and *regimen*.

Gubernare (like *regere*) originally meant "to direct," for example to steer a boat; Thomas Aquinas uses it usually with a nautical image in mind. In Ockham it means the same as *regere* and *principari*; it is translated as "to govern." *Gubernator* ("steersman") is translated as "governor." *Gubernacula* is translated as "government."

Praeesse means "to be over" – not just spatially but by ruling; it is translated as "to be over" or "to rule (over)." *Praesidere* is usually translated as "to preside (over)," and *praesidens* as "president." However, these terms should not be taken to suggest merely the functions of a chairperson or ceremonial head; in classical Latin *praesidere* often suggested military protection, for example by the governor of a province, and *praesidium* meant a garrison. *Praeses* is translated as "ruler" or "governor." *Dominari* is translated as "to be lord (over)" or "to rule (over)"; when it seems to be used with unfavorable connotations it is translated as "to lord it over" or "to dominate."

---

[2] *Principari, principatus,* and *princeps* are especially common in III *Dial.*, I, 2.3–9, in which Ockham explains Aristotle's classification of forms of government; *regere* and *rex* are commoner in theological contexts, such as *OND*.

Praelatus ("prelate") is the perfect passive participle of *praeferre*, "to prefer," hence "to promote" (to some office, in preference to other candidates); a prelate is one who has had preferment. The word could have been used for a holder of any office, cleric or lay (Du Cange defines *praelatus* as *magistratus, qui populis praeest*), but in fact it seems always or almost always to be used for someone with authority in the Church. It did not imply great authority or pomp; any superior was a prelate. *Praelatio* is translated as "rulership" or (if a synonym is also used) "prelacy."

Instituere and *constituere* seem to have been interchangeable in many contexts; sometimes they mean "appoint," sometimes "establish" (thus an office may be established and some individual appointed to it). *Constitutus* sometimes means "living in." *Ordinare* also means, in some contexts, to appoint to an office; in other contexts it means "to ordain" (i.e. to make an "ordinance" or law), in others "to grant."

In summary:

assumere	to appoint
caput	head
constituere	to appoint, establish
dominari	to be lord (over), to have lordship (over), to rule (over), to lord it over, to dominate
dominus	lord
gubernare	to govern, manage, direct
instituere	to appoint, establish
institutio	appointment, institution
ordinare	to ordain, order, appoint, decide (on), manage
ordinatio	ordinance, ordering, grant, decision, arrangement
praeesse	to be over, to rule (over)
praeferre	prefer, appoint
praeficere	to set over, to appoint
praelatio	rule, rulership, prelacy
praelatus	prelate
praeponere	to place over, to set over, to appoint
praeses	ruler, governor
praesidere	to preside (over)
princeps	ruler, leader, chief, prince
principans	ruler
principari	to rule
principatus	rule, rulership, government, regime

rector	ruler, rector
regere	to rule
regimen	rule, government, form of government, governance
rex	king
subdere	to subject
subditus	subject
subesse	to be under, to be subject to
subiectus	subject
sublevare	to raise up, to appoint
sublimare	to elevate, to appoint, to make

It will be apparent that many of these words, as we understand them, are interchangeable, at least in some contexts. English does not seem to have as copious a vocabulary of political terms as Latin did. We have not attempted, therefore, to establish any one-to-one correspondence between Latin terms and English. Neither do we use the same English word for every occurrence of the same Latin word, because in some contexts the usually appropriate word may be inappropriate. For example, "government" has faint connotations of legitimacy or normalcy that sometimes make the expression "tyrannical government" inappropriate, and for some reason it seems inappropriate to speak of the father "governing" the children; but in both of these contexts Ockham uses *principatus*, for which "government" is generally the most idiomatic translation.

Ockham practises *variatio*, i.e. the shift from one synonym to another to avoid close repetitions of the same word. A change of terms therefore does not necessarily indicate a change of meaning. In the translation some variation has been lost because sometimes the same English word translates different Latin words, but on the other hand the one Latin word is sometimes translated by different English words in different contexts.

Sometimes Ockham puts several synonymous words together in the same sentence or short passage.[3] This is not, we think, to suggest distinctions he wishes to make, but to convey a single idea that can be expressed in various ways, or perhaps to draw attention to analogies between things normally referred to in certain contexts by means of different special terms. Some examples:

---

[3] In some cases duplication may be due to copyists, who seem to have tried to fix mistakes sometimes by adding *et*, *vel*, or *seu* followed by the correct word. For example, at 818.44 the Frankfurt manuscript has *interficere et inficere*.

"Let us therefore make a little inquiry about it, beginning with its first part: namely, whether Christ made blessed Peter the [*caput*] head, [*principem*] leader, and [*praelatum*] prelate of the other apostles and of all the faithful" (III *Dial.*, I, 2.1).

"Just as laws should be established for the common advantage, ... so [*principes*] rulers, [*rectores*] rectors, and [*domini*] lords, both seculars and ecclesiastics, should be placed over others for the common advantage" (III *Dial.*, II, 1.5).

"A community of persons able to have communion with one another in which all or many are prone to discord, dissensions, and disputes is not best ordered unless it is subject to one supreme [*rectori*] rector, [*iudici*] judge, and [*capiti*] head upon whom the jurisdiction of all others depends" (*OQ*, III.1).

"We must say briefly ... which things are requisite to the best [*principatum*] regime, [*praelationem*] prelacy, [*rectoriam*] rectorship, or [*regimen*] form of government" (*OQ*, III.4).

"There are two primary kinds of constitutions, just as there are two primary kinds of [*principatuum*] governments or [*praelationum*] prelacies and of [*principantium*] rulers or [*praelatorum*] prelates or [*rectorum*] rectors" (III *Dial.*, I, 2.6).

"It is more beneficial for the community of the faithful to be ruled by the government that is more like natural [*regimeni*] government and [*principatui*] rule; ... But the [*regimen*] government or [*principatus*] rule of one person, namely when one alone [*regit*] governs many and [*praesidet*] rules over them, is more like natural rule than the [*regimen*] government or [*principatus*] rule of many." (III *Dial.*, I, 2.9).

If Ockham intended any distinctions of meaning among these alternative expressions we have not been able to see them. Readers who wish to make and test conjectures about shades of difference among these terms must therefore go back to the Latin text.

Amendments to the text of *Dialogus*[4]

Sigla

??:   conjectural emendation

[4] Latin text of the *Dialogus* (including corrected text of the portions translated in this volume) and additional translation of *The Work of Ninety Days* are available through the Internet at http://www.mq.edu.au/HPP/Ockham.

A: MS Auxerre, Lat. 252 (213)

B: MS Basle A VI 5

D: MS Dijon 340 (249)

F: MS Frankfurt, Staatsbibliotek, Lat. quart. 4

G: William of Ockham, *Dialogus*, in Melchior Goldast, *Monarchia S. Romani Imperii*

Gs: *Corpus iuris canonici*, Lyons, 1671

L: MS London, Lambeth 168

Ly: William of Ockham, *Dialogus*, in *Opera plurima* (Lyons, 1495)

M: MS Paris, Mazarine 3522 (478)

N: MS Naples, VII, c. 31

R: MS Paris, Nat. Lat. 15881

T: MS Toulouse 221

V: MS Vatican Lat. 4115

Vg: *Biblia Sacra iuxta Vulgatam Clementinam*

W: MS Vatican Lat., 4098

Z: refers to a printed edition of the text Ockham quotes (see Bibliography under Eusebius, Susemihl).[5]

m after symbol for MS: correction (interlinear or marginal) made in the MS by original writer or some other

References

"788.28 aliquibus" refers to G, page 788, line 28, at the word "aliquibus." (Line numbering is sometimes doubtful; we have counted so that the last line on the page is line 64.) If the same word occurs in a line more than once, the occurrence referred to is the first, or the first after an earlier word referred to in that line. "−" means delete the word(s) following; "+" means insert

---

[5] In adopting readings from modern editions we do not assume that Ockham himself used good texts. We have adopted a modern editor's version when it makes the quotation clearer without changing anything on which Ockham's argument depends.

the word(s) following; ">" means replace the word(s) before this sign with the word(s) following. Variants noted in any of these ways have been adopted as the basis of the translation.

Some variants not adopted that might in fact be correct readings are also noted. They are either preceded by a colon or enclosed in square brackets. Thus "788.28 aliquibus: quibusdam F" means that at page 788 line 28 G has "aliquibus" and F has "quibusdam," but "aliquibus" is retained. Square brackets within a variant quoted from another manuscript enclose another variant for the word or words just before the bracket. For example, "789.1 ... gubernet universitatem fidelium [infidelium L] LMF" means that L, M, and F agree, except that where M and F have "fidelium" L has "infidelium." Variants that make no difference to the grammar of the text or to the translation have not been noted; for example, "reprobare conantur" is not noted as a variant of "nituntur improbare." There are many variants in the manuscripts that are not adopted and not noted.

For Tract I, only three manuscripts are available namely L, M, and F; M seems generally the best; the early printed editions are closest to L. For Tract II the best of the manuscripts listed above seem to be V and N (which are very close); W and M also seem good, and A seems a good representative of the rest. We have consulted the other manuscripts listed but not read right through them. There are other manuscripts listed in Baudry, *Guillaume d'Occam*.

Professor Knysh, who kindly read through this appendix in an earlier version, suggested changes adopted at: 791.48, 791.56, 793.7, 794.42, 795.50, 798.56, 800.6, 803.63, 806.46, 806.53, 808.19, 809.36, 809.48, 809.49, 810.7, 810.56, 811.17, 811.60, 815.13, 815.20, 816.53, 819.6, 826.62, 856.32, 856.37, 865.36, 889.49, 889.61, 871.15, 871.22, 871.46, 872.60, 873.32, 874.19, 874.28, 874.46, 875.31, 875.35, 875.38, 875.59, 876.23, 876.24, 877.50, 878.15, 879.28, 880.49, 883.18, 885.10, 888.62, 213.16, 214.23, 215.32, 216.2, 217.1, 217.12, 217.16, 936.14.

Variants

III *Dial.*, I.2,

Chapter 1

788.28 aliquibus: quibusdam F 788.28–9 ipsam quo ad alias partes eius exquisite discutere: ipsamque ad singulas partes eius exquisite

discutere est M; ipsasque ad singulas eius partes requisite discutere
est F 788.29 pertractare + propono ?? [cf. 467.46, 634.44, 926.8]/
ipsa: MF add diffuse 788.33 nitaris > nitere MF 788.55 naturalia >
corporalia MF 788.56 quorum > quia MF 788.58 questionem >
conclusionem ?? 788.61 dixit > dicit MF 788.64 – visibili, qui
sensibiliter pascat imo etiam LMF 789.1 Christi + qui sensibiliter
pascat et gubernet universitatem fidelium [infidelium L] LMF 789.3
gubernatores – ubi LMF 789.7 communitas illa > communitati
illi ??/ potest + absque LMF 789.8 contrariari > variari MF
789.10 ordinare > ordinasse MF/ videtur + qui praecepit ut
legitur MF 789.12 iudicium > iudicum Vg [iudicium L; iudicem
MF]/ videris + verba MFVg 789.13 veniens > veniesque MFVg
(venies L. Cf. 789.23) 789.15 fideles > infideles ??/ spectant
+ absque LMF 789.19 quoniam infidelis > qui LMF 789.21
auctoritas... adducta... militet: auctoritates... adductae... mil-
itent L; auctoritates... adducta... militet ostendenda M;
auctoritates... adducta... militet ostendenda F 789.23 generis +
et LMFVg 789.28 debere > debuit ?? 789.33 alio > aliorum LMF
789.34 inducat: indicat M (LF = G) 789.36 videtur > tenetur
MF [videtur L] 789.38 quoniam infideles > quod LMF 789.39
inducerent > induceret universos MF 789.42 8 > 18 MFVg 789.44
quadragenarios > quinquagenarios Vg 789.46 nos > me MFVg
789.54 istarum + responsionum MF 789.59 qui + in MF/ quam >
quem MF 790.2 fideles + huiusmodi MF 790.3 posset: debet MF
790.4 qui: quia MF/ omnibus + talibus LMF 790.13 deliquerunt >
deliquerint LM [delinquerent F] 790.14 spectet > spectat MF/
ante + ascensionem domini F 790.19 de appellationibus + c. de
appellationibus Extra de praebendis MF/ ultima > ultimo LMF
790.20 caput + omnium MF 790.21 archiepiscopi, diaconi >
archipresbyteri, singuli archidiaconi Gs 790.28 manifestum > mani-
festius MF 790.29 – colligitur et MF

Chapter 2
790.46 – ista MF 790.51 et > in MF/ virtute et + in MF 790.52
aliquis: aliquibus MF 790.54 inaequalibus > inaequales LMFZ
790.55 – sunt MFZ/ inaequalem > inaequale Z 790.56 vel >
nihil Z 790.58 eorum: MF add non/ quae > qui MF 791.2
agilitate > aequitate Vg 791.3 cum: est MF 791.4 temporali +
que F [quis M]/ copiosis + non habetur MF/ possit: potest MF
791.7 nullo – modo LMF/ praeest > praeesset MF 791.11 nunc >

inter MF 791.23 existimant + omnes MF 791.35 communia >
utilia MF (cf. 804.20) 791.37 plena talium certaque > plenorum
talium certa MF 791.38 quia... ait > quia ut... testatur MF/
ducat – et LMFLy 791.42 unumquodque igitur oportet > unum
quidem igitur comparatus Z [unum quidem igitur [F omits] oportet
MF]/ fore > forte LMFZ/ deteriora > deterior LMFZ 791.43
comparata > comportata Z/ haec > hoc et LMFZ 791.44 una >
multa MFZ 791.46 naribus > auribus ?? [cf. 791.45] 791.47 et >
quam multi multis oculis et multis auribus [naribus MF]. Similiter
inconveniens est MF 791.48 vident + quam unus MF 791.52 –
verbis MF 791.53 et > etiam MF 791.55 imminerit > imminent
LM 791.56 ut + a MF/ regantur > regatur MF 791.58 malicia >
maliciis ?? [cf. 792.2] 791.61 imperiis > impiis LMFLy/ 29 + ait
MF 791.62 hic > hinc LMFLy 791.64 tamen > autem MFVg
792.7 virtutis > vir LMFZ 792.8 magis studiosus > singulum Z
[LM have a space; F omits]/ sed + ut Z/ comportare censum >
comportate coenae Z/ qui > quae ex Z 792.9 elargiti > elargitae
LMFZ/ unamquamque > unumquemque Z/ fini > fieri Z 792.10
– et MFZ/ prorsus > et multos sensus Z 792.11 – sic MFZ
792.14 utrum + unus Z 792.15 – sit MFZ/ respondetur >
respondet LMFLy/ sed: vel Z 792.20 omniumque > omnium Z
792.21 regnum + eligibilior utique erit [est MF] civitatibus aristocratia quam regnum MFZ

Chapter 3
792.31 – etiam MF 792.32 utitur + grecis MF 792.33 ignota >
ignotae LMF 792.36 alii qui > aliqui MF/ exponunt > exponendo
LMF 792.50 dominator > dominari MF/ non eadem > in MF
792.51 –sed MF 792.54 legalis scientia > legales scientiae LMF
792.55 locutio – illae LMF/ quibus > qua ?? [quae MF] 792.64
non + principaliter LMF 793.7 legem + iustam MF 793.16 sed
+ quando principatur MF 793.22 exponitur sic. In > exponitur,
sic in (McGrade) 793.29 pertinent > essent MF 793.30 secundum
quod > sed LMF [secundum quam Ly] 793.32 serva: sua LM
793.34 quando + domus eius MF 793.36 quod + sicut LMF

Chapter 4
793.53 attigi > attingit MF 793.59 leges > legem ??

Chapter 5

794.4 – est MF 794.14 naturaliter > manualiter LMF 794.16 principatum > principatu LMF

Chapter 6

794.26 propriae > primae LMFLy 794.27 et principantium sive praelatorum: L omits 794.29 et > vel ?? 794.31 transgressio > transgressus MF 794.41 nec + etiam MF 794.46 bonum + principatus autem tyrannicus non est propter bonum commune MF 794.54 praedicto + potest uti subiectis [subditis F] et bonis eorum qualitercunque sibi placet propter bonum commune, sed MF 794.54–5 subiectis et bonis eorum qualitercunque > eis ut MF 794.61 nisi > non nisi ?? 795.8 monarchiae > monarchae ?? 795.11–13 commune et in quantum unus solus principatur, habet aliquid de principatu regali. In quantum vero bonum proprium etiam intendit habet aliquid de principatu tyrannico et despotico > proprium et non commune [F adds est et] habet aliquid de tyrannide [tyrannico F] vel despotico principatu. Inquantum autem in multis intendit bonum commune habet aliquid de principatu temperato et recto, et ideo, cum unus solus principetur, habet aliquid de principatu regali MF [commune habet aliquid de principatu tyrannico et despotico et inquantum unus solus principetur habet aliquid de principatu regale L] 795.14 regalis – et LMF 795.17 modo > non LMFLy/ voluntatem + suam MF 795.21 – scilicet primus LMF 795.31–2 imperandi + ipsum LMF 795.32 habentes: M has a gap, LF omit 795.36 si enim secundum legem > sive enim [vero F] aliquis sit primo rex secundum voluntatem suam sive secundum legem, si MF [sive enim secundum legem, si L] 795.42–3 aliquis dominetur regaliter et aliquis despotice inconveniens non videtur > aliquis aliquibus dominetur regaliter et aliquibus despotice inconveniens non videtur ?? [aliquibus dominetur regaliter et aliquid despotice inconveniens non videtur L; de aliquibus dominetur regaliter et aliquid despotice inconveniens non videtur M; de aliquibus dominetur regaliter et aliquid de despotico inconveniens esse videtur F]

Chapter 7

795.50 3 > 4 LMFLy/ 1 > 5 MF 795.54 quae – ad LMFLy 795.57 principentur > principarentur ?? [principantur MF]/ dicen-

tur esset > dicendi essent LMFLy 795.58 sit > fit F 795.59
servando > habendo MF/ ad + aliquam LMF 795.61 semper +
reprehensibile LMFLy

Chapter 8
796.7 quod: LMF omit; politia enim Fm

Chapter 9
796.28 − iam LMF 796.31 antequam + ad MF 796.34 itaque > ita
quod LMFLy 796.35 una > aliqua MF 796.37 nullus + imperator ??
[M has dots after nullus] 796.44 possunt > possint M 796.45 etiam:
MF add vobis quedam 796.46 quae dicentur > dicantur LMF 796.53
quare > quia MF 796.55 quia magis > magis autem MF [quia magis
autem L] 796.57 paterfamilias > patremfamilias ??/ principatur >
principari LMFLy 796.58 regalis − et LMFLyZ 796.59 quidem + est
LMFLyZ 797.4 quare > quia MF/ regalis + non LMF 797.10 quoniam + autem MFZ 797.11 praeest: praeesse Z 797.12 principatur:
principatus Z/ colligit > colligitur LMFLy 797.19 scimus > senius Z/
minore > iuniore Z 797.21 masculum ad foeminam > masculinum ad
femininum Z 797.22 principatum: principata LMF 797.25 negare >
evacuare MF 797.34 − naturaliter seu MF 797.42 − quia in utroque
principatu est unus principans MF 797.48 communitatem > communitati F

Chapter 10
797.60 omnem > esse Z 797.61 eiusdem > ethicorum ?? 797.62
animi quid > aliquid MF 797.64 domus + divisa per discordiam
et odium contra se non stabitur etc MF

At end of chapter 10 L has: hic multa deficiunt scilicet residuum
huius decimi undecimum et duodecimum capitula. M and F have:
Hic caret in parte suppleatur igitur etc. The MSS omit chapters
11 and 12.

Chapter 11
798.11 nullus: nonnullus Ly

Chapter 12
798.24 alius + non Ly 798.33 utilissimus > vilissimus Ly

Chapter 13
798.47 et > neque LMF 798.49 ipsum + ibidem MF 798.53 −
ut MFZ 798.54 et > ut Z/ melius + semper MFZ 798.56 quando:

qui M, si F 798.60 ante haec > autem hoc MFZ 798.61 neque
+ est Z 798.62 intrari > necessarium Z [necessarii MF] 798.63
aliquando subiiciuntur > qui aliquando principentur aliquando sub-
iciantur ?? [qui [L omits] aliquando principantur aliquando subician-
tur [subiciuntur L] LMF] 798.64 – omnibus MFZ 799.2 et alii
+ semper MF

Chapter 14
799.36 omni > toto MF 799.40 quo > quale MF 700.42 instruc-
tor > institutor MF 799.44 iudex et > iudex vel LMFLy 799.46
sanctior + et sapientior MF 799.49 – tamen LMF

Chapter 15
799.58–9 quae ... videntur > quae supra c.ii recitantur, quae
contra secundum modum ponendi qui supra c.xi recitatur, et pro
quo nunc ultimo allegasti, militare videntur ?? [quae contra
secundum modum ponendi supra c.xi recitantur et pro quo ultimo
allegasti militare videntur L; contra quae secundum modum ponendi
supra c.11 [ii F] recitatur et pro quo nunc allegasti militare videtur
[F omits militare videtur] MF] 799.60 dicitur + enim MF 799.61
si ... aliquis > si nullus in populo Christiano invenitur MF 799.62
inveniatur > invenitur MF 799.63 beneficium > officium MF
800.6 apparet > appareret MF 800.9 possint > possit LMF 800.23
Aristoteles + igitur M [ergo F] 800.25 solum aequalibus > solum
inaequalibus LMFLy 800.27 similibus + et aequalibus MF 800.31
iustitia > iniustitia MFLy/ iusta > iuste MF 800.43 proprium +
corpus MF 800.47 bonum est > locum habet MF 800.51 virtus >
dignitas MF

Chapter 16
800.57 allegari > militare MF 800.61 veritate > virtute LMFLy
800.62 – quasi MF 800.64 virtutem + et sapientiam MF 801.4
forte > fortiter MF 801.6 rationem > auctoritatem LMF 801.9
mali + semper MF 801.10 est + semper MF 801.11 vilissimus
+ respondetur quod prelatus vilissimus MF 801.19 diaconi >
diacones LMF 801.20 – conceditur LMF 801.21 sanctam + Ad
alias auctoritates per modum consimilem respondetur LMF 801.24
turbationes + dissensiones MF

Chapter 17
801.43 non dicitur quod > dicitur quod hoc [LLy omit] non
LMFLy 801.45 contigit > contingit LMF 801.51 2 > III LMFLy/

et > c. MF 801.52 sic > sit MFZ/ et alios > vel aliorum Z/
differenter > differentem Z/ ea > eam MFZ 801.57 puto > puta
LMF 801.62 – hominum LMF 802.7 nam + cum LMF/ fit >
sit LMF 802.9 – si ?? 802.11 quia > tamen MF/ illi + quare
MF 802.13 sicut > sic ?? 802.17 principetur + sibi MF/ similibus
+ nec est iustum naturale quod ille principetur sibi similibus MF
802.19 procederet > procedet LMF 802.20 sicut + saepe MF
802.24 similibus + nec est iustum illum debere principari sibi
similibus MF 802.25 termino discreto contento > termini discreti
contenti M [termini discreti F; termino discreti contenti L] 802.26
disiuncta > disiunctiva LMFLy 802.29 si sit > quae est ?? 802.34
quod > quia LMF 802.36 ut habent alium > et [MF omit et]
quandoque alium LMF 802.37 ignorantur > ignoranter LMF
802.38 equivalens > equipollens MF/ converso + vel MF 802.39
loquuntur > sequuntur LMFLy 802.43 sic > si LMFLy 802.48
quartum > xiii LMFLy 802.50 principatum > principatu LMF
802.55 modo > malo LMFLy 802.57 regulariter > regaliter (1476
edition)/ 803.15 praeferri > praeesse MF 803.16 minus perfectus:
unus vel alius MF 803.23 sortem > sortes MF 803.28 virtute:
LMF add nec

Chapter 18
803.41 dicunt: debent LMF 803.50 valeret > valerent LMF 803.53
unde in laude > unde et in laudem LMFLy 803.56 omnibus +
aliis MF 803.62 optimis + viris MF 803.63 ab uno + bono MF/
– qui aliter non est bonus ?? 803.64 ad > in LMF/ – quod MF
804.1 super > per LMFLy

Chapter 19
804.18 tertiam > primam LMF 804.19 melius vel certius > certius
et melius MF 804.20 nociva sunt + penitus LMFLy 804.25
quamvis + in casu MF 804.30 – sufficienter MF 804.30–1 consilio
+ sufficienter bono MF 804.36 bonus aut optimus > optimus aut
bonus MF 804.40 quisquam > quisque LMFLy 804.44–5 – et
participans MF [si esset participans L] 804.55 – modis LMF
805.5 consilio + praestando MF 805.8 dixit > dicit LMFLy 805.13
et > a LMFLy 805.17 quam + voluntas MF 805.25 – et quia
MF 805.26 perversus + et LMF 805.31 modo + hoc MF 805.33–
4 immineat > immineret MF 805.47 quando > quandoque MF

805.49 fermenti > fermentum MFVg 805.51 multitudine + quan-
tumcunque parva MF 805.52 unius > unus MF 805.52-3 –
sequitur quod similiter LMF 805.54 – Patet consequentia LMF
805.61 non sufficit: sufficit M; sufficit non F 805.64 consulant et
faciant > consulent et facient MF [consulent et faciant L] 806.5
incurrerent > incurrent LMF 806.8 et eligibilior: MF omit 806.9
quando > et [etiamsi ??] regitur ab uno optimo vel bono, sed
intendit concludere quod interdum melior est et eligilior aristocratia
quam regnum. Quia MF 806.11 tunc > ideo MF 806.12 unus +
regaliter ?? [regulariter MF]/ ille + unus MF/ potest > posset
LM [possit F] 806.18 aristocratiam: MF add tantum/ in regnum
+ et LMFLy

Chapter 20

806.28 – scilicet MF 806.40 Discip. + Pro ista opinione aliquas
[alias M] allegationes adducas. Magist. LMF 806.41 consanguinitate, reprehensibilem > consanguinitate et affinitate, Non debet
reprehensibile Gs [consanguinitate et affi. non debet F] 806.46
etiam supra > ecclesia super MF 806.53 non: ideo MF 806.54
cuicunque + alii MF 806.56 est > esset LMF 807.1 ex hoc +
quod LMF 807.3 impedit > expedit LMF 807.4 quod > quo
LMFLy 807.5-6 – tamen LMF 807.7 ethicis + et in politicis
MF 807.18 qui + diu LMFLy 807.18-19 aliquorum: MF omit
807.29 damnandi > dominandi LMFLy 807.30 – sicut MF 807.43
–habet . . . et MF 807.46 21 > 31 Gs [21 LMF] 807.47 regale >
regulare LMFLy 807.47-8 utitur > nititur LFGs 807.48 60 dist . . .
dist. 60 > 40 dist . . . dist. 40 LMF [60 Gs – an error]/ 4. dist.
2 iurisiurandi > 4, q. 3, para. iurisiurandi ?? [4, q. 3, si testes,
para. item iurisiurandi Gs (item is an error); 4 di. 2 iurisiurandi
L; 4, q. 2, para. iurisiurandi MF] 807.50 10 > 16 LMFGs/
nulli > nonnulli LMFGs/ est enim hoc > et est hic MGs 807.51
3. + para. 2 MGs 807.54 – est LMFLy 807.56 allegato >
praeallegato MF 807.57 nisi in > in fine nisi Gs 807.59 parti +
Christianorum MF 807.62 potest > posset LMF 807.63 fideles:
fideles et MF 807.64 pars + tunc MF/ divinae > Christi LMF/
ordinationi > ordinatione LM 808.2 potest > posset LMF 808.11
– si MF 808.19 regula + illa MF 808.22-3 caveatur + expresse
MF 808.23-4 – et de lege dei naturali ?? 808.25 ordinationi: LMF
omit 808.29 44 > 24 LMF

Chapter 21

808.41 nitaris > nitere MF [niteris L] 808.43 – suum MFVg 808.44 Christi + Ergo omnes Christiani non habent potestatem tollendi ordinationem Christi MF 808.46 unde + et LMFLy 808.47 incipit > incepit MF 808.53 habeat + unum MF/ Quod sub Christo > sub Christo quod MF 808.57 cum et > tamen ut Z 808.62 est singularis > est cuius a singulis Z 809.1 vel potest esse > nec esse potest vera M 809.2 licitus et > et licitus M 809.5 nobis > vobis MFGs/ beati + tamen MFGs 809.5–6 approbemus > conprobemus MGs 809.7 dici possit > potest dici MF/ quam ea quae sit > ea sit quam MFGs 809.8 constituta > constitutam MFGs/ etiam sit nota > etiamsi nota et LMFGs (M omits et) 809.10 successionem > successiones MF 809.12 successiones + episcoporum MF 809.14–5 constituere > statuere MF 809.23 capite + traditum MF 809.27 – et sunt verba Hieronymi LMF 809.30 pontificem > pontificium MF 809.33 habere > facere ?? 809.36 quemlibet > quomodolibet MF

Chapter 22

809.48 per ea quae conata sunt > per eam quae condita fuit MF/ – probare ??/ 21 > 20 MF 809.49 et + ideo MF 809.54 recipi > excipi ?? 809.55 praecipit > praecepit LMF 809.56 qui > si quis Vg 809.57 percutiat > percutiet FVg/ ubi > ut ?? 809.59 illa + Christi MF 809.64 – quia LMF 810.1 praeceptum > praecepta MF 810.2 expressum fuit > expressa fuerunt LMF 810.3 omni + conditione MF 810.4 inveniri potest > invenitur MF 810.7 ubi dicit > dicens MF/ dominus + Jesus MF 810.11 liceret > licet MF 810.20 Christus + expresse MF 810.25 dixit + ergo MFVg 810.28 quod + scilicet MF 810.33 persecutiones > persecutionem LMF/ praesertim + promissa M [praetermissa F] 810.33–4 imitanda > dimittenda F 810.36 – totam MF

Chapter 23

810.55 praeceptum + divinum MF 810.56 scilicet + casu MF/ – vel MF 810.58 divinum + et Christi MF 810.59–60 Christo . . . baptizare > Christo propter necessitatem et utilitatem liceret venire contra preceptum divinum. Praetera, si propter necessitatem et utilitatem liceret venire contra preceptum divinum, omnia sacramenta Christi mutare propter necessitatem et utilitatem liceret.

Quia nullus obligatur ad sacramenta quaeque nisi propter preceptum divinum, ergo propter necessitatem et utilitatem liceret non baptizare ?? [Christo mutare propter necessitatem et utilitatem liceret venire contra preceptum divinum quia nullus obligatur ad sacramenta quaeque nisi propter preceptum divinum, ergo propter necessitatem et utilitatem liceret non baptizare M; Christo mutare propter necessitatem et utilitatem liceret. Praetera, si propter necessitatem et utilitatem liceret venire contra preceptum divinum quia nullus obligatur ad sacramenta quaeque nisi propter precepta divina, ergo propter necessitatem et utilitatem liceret non baptizare F; L=G] 810.61 possit > posset MF 810.62 possit > posset MF 810.63 possit... possit > posset... posset MF 811.2 circa > contra LMF 811.5 licet > licebit MF

Chapter 24
811.17 scilicet + de MF/ circa > contra LMF 811.28–9 divini + naturalis MF 811.31 scit + verum MF 811.33 – et ideo MF 811.38 possit > posset MF 811.42–3 aliorum – et LMF 811.45 servare > servari MF/ 43 > 23 LMF 811.53 nullam > nullum LMF 811.60 contra: MF add dominum [deum Knysh] vel 811.61 contrarium + tenere MF 812.1 modo + papa MF 812.5 sed + sensus ??/ – articulos MF/ qui > que M 812.7 interpretati > interpretata LM 812.10 aut > et M 812.14 adduxisti > adduxi MF 812.26 tamen: cum tamen MF 812.29 argumento > sensu MF 812.32 intelligi > excipi MF 812.34–5 aliquid... aliquid > aliquod... aliquod LMF 812.44 et + aliud MF 812.46 Christi + nisi MF

Chapter 25
813.9 haberentur > sederent MF 813.16 – est Gs 813.18 licet > nec MF 813.20 6 > 7 LMFLy 813.22 ori > ore LMF 813.23 et > ita Gs/ episcopus > episcopo Gs 813.28 plures > duo MFGs/ supra + eodem LMFGs/ – dicens MFGs 813.37 legitur > loquitur MF 813.41 factus > facto MFGs 813.43 Novatianus > Novatus MFZ 813.45 appellabant > appellarunt Z 813.46 presbyterorumque > presbyteriorum quoque Z 813.47 signatur > significatur Z 813.47–8 certamen initur > statuitur MFZ 813.48–9 humanam > inhumanam Z 813.49 etiam > esse Z/ ita > infra MF 813.50 etiam > autem MFZ 813.52 intra + se Z 813.52–3

decideri > deciderit LMFLyZ 813.53 Cornelius > Celerinus Z/
circa + omnia Z 813.55 adhuc > ad hoc Z 813.56 consecrato >
execrato Z/ festinatione > satisfactione Z/ reversi sunt >
reverterunt Z 813.57 scilicet > sed Z/ laicis + viris MFZ 813.59
erat > sit Z [erit LMF]/ capere > cupere Z 813.61 simplicibus >
simplicissimis Z 814.1 aliquantulum > aliquantum Z/ incurreret >
incurrerit Z 814.2 confusus > perfusus Z/ aliqua > reliqua LMFZ
814.3 potuit > potuerit Z 814.9 civitas > civitatis LMFLy 814.10
ecclesiam + catholicam MF 814.17 monstrantur > monstratur
LMF 814.28 quomodo > quam Z 814.31 sed + etiam MF 814.38
− vera MF

Chapter 26
814.52 esset > essent LMFLy 814.53 essent > esset LMFLy
814.55–6 fundata + et LMFLy 814.57 utilitati > utilitate LMF
814.58 Romanum > Romanorum LMF 815.13 de > a M 815.16
faciliter > convenienter MF 815.20 causaliter > casualiter MF
815.25 ratione > Romanae MF (cf. 809.21–3)/ auferetur > auferr-
ent M [auferret F] 815.34–5 administrationi augustini > administra-
tionem augustino Gs 815.36 causa + iusta LMFLy 815.39–40 ab
uno quam a pluribus > a pluribus quam ab uno MF 815.41
principatur > principatus LMFLy 815.42 quia > quam LMFLy
815.44 principetus > principetur LMFLy 815.45 quia: qui LMF/
nondum > non autem (the quotation is found there) 815.47 −
aliquo LMF

Chapter 27
815.59 − non ?? 815.61 simul + plures LMF 816.8 quamvis >
quantumque MF 816.28 idem + ad aliam MF/ − quia LMF
816.28–9 interdum + quando MF 816.30 − ideo LMF 816.31
affectus > effectus LMFLy 816.33 − cum MF 816.33–4 maiori . . .
minor > minor [pars add. L] maiori ratione LMF

Chapter 28
816.53 24 > 20 M 816.55 habendi > ponendi LMFLy 816.57–
8 quibuscunque + et quotcumque LMFLy 816.61 alio > apostolico
MF 817.3 tunc > tamen LMF 817.12 prima > i.e. MFGs/ in >
i.e. LMLy 817.27 aliud > aliquid MFGs

Chapter 29

817.48 aliqua + alia MF

Chapter 30

818.9 tactas: tractas L/ superius: MF add contra regnum est unius capitis omnium Christianorum [a reader's comment?] 818.29 huiusmodi + omnia MF 818.33 potest imminere > immineret MF 818.37 Anselmus > Anterus papa MFGs 818.54 credendum > verendum MF 818.61 nec ... nec > sive nec ... sive MF 818.63 sit > erit MF/ uno > uni LMFLy 819.6 in verbis > ex verbis MF 819.10 totus > totius LMF

III **Dial.,** I.3

Chapter 8

824.44 videtur + posse LMF 824.46 minus: magis MF 824.50 nostrorum > meorum LMF 824.54 1 > 10 LMF 824.58 necessaria > necessario LMF 825.2 hoc > haec LMFVg 825.3 3 > 4 MF 825.4 Elchiam sacerdotem magnum > Eldam prophetam uxorem Sellum MF 825.6 dicantur > dicatur LMF 825.23 oportet > oporteret MF 825.26–7 quoniam > terminanda quia sapientes in concilio generali MF 825.28 – de ipsa MF 825.31 ergo > sed LMF 825.32 et – quam 825.33 – cum LMF 825.41 revelantur > revelentur MF 825.45 dirigantur > diriguntur MF 825.48 7 > 1 MF 825.50 principio potest > principio poterit MF 825.49 – ex quo patet quod MF

Chapter 9

826.3–4 tum ... mundo > tum quia dicit non sunt defuturi in mundo et non dicit non sunt defuturi in concilio generali MFm 826.6 est > sit MF 826.12 posset > possit MF 826.14 revelationes + fuisse LMFLy/ apostolis + et MF/ – posse MF 826.18 viderunt > viderant MF 826.22 si > sibi LMFLy 826.23 omnibus > hominibus LMF 826.24 – et LMF 826.25 spiritu > enim spiritui MFVg 826.26 spiritui > spiritu LMFVg 826.30 revelata > revelatae MF 826.32 aliquod > aliquid LMF 826.33 monuit > movit F 826.34 monet > movet F 826.35 et canonice > canonice et Catholice MF 826.43–4 fuerunt > fuerint MF 826.50 non tamen > sed non LMF 826.50–1 etiam cui constat: cui non constat MF;

cui constat L 826.58 concilium + generale MF 826.59 sed + est
MF 826.62 apostolorum + et MF 827.2 generale + imperfecte
tamen et aliquo modo concedi potest quod concilium generale MF/
− tamen LMF

Chapter 10

827.18 possunt > possint MF 827.21 quemadmodum + per LMF/
−et LMF 827.24 ascenderunt > ascenderint MF 827.26 necessarium > necessarius MF 827.27 quia + aut MF 827.30 quod +
taliter MF 827.32 proponitur + diffiniendum M 827.36 scrutantes
+ scripturas LMF/ − enim M/ ne > quia M 827.37 catholicus
+ ne M 827.39 23 > 22 MGs 827.40 fecit . . . speravit: MF omit,
LGs=G 827.41 + Deficit residuum istius decimi capituli [M adds
etc] MF

Chapter 11

827.49 si + eius LMF 827.51 − respondetur quod ?? [quod MF]/
per > si per LMF 827.55 generali + sive aliis qui essent extra
concilium generale MF/ − concedo antecedens LMF/ tum > nam
LMF 827.58 potuerunt > poterunt LMF/ digne > digni M/
extiterit > extiterint MF 827.58–9 − celebratum LMF 827.61
habere > sumere MF 828.3 fuerint > fuerunt MF 828.3–4 poter-
int > poterunt MF 828.8–9 convenerant > convenerunt MF 828.9
quia + non M/ celebratur > celebrabatur ?? 828.17 − nego
antecedens LMF/ item si quaesierint > quotiesque quaesierint ??
[item quia quae sunt MF] 828.18 errare possunt > errant M
[errare F; erraret L]/ − nihilominus . . . patet LMF 828.19 data
+ a LMF 828.21 − solum LMF 828.25 secundo + quia MF
828.28 − igitur LMF 828.29 huiusmodi + verum intellectum MF

III **Dial.**, I.4

Chapter 8

855.30 tamen > cum ?? 855.31 vos + et post MF 855.32 euntes
+ ergo MFVg 855.36 generale deroget speciali > generali deroget
speciale LM [generale deroget speciale F] 855.39 dederit + ceteris
MF 855.42 quibus > qualibet M/ verbis + quibus ?? 855.43
potestatem − in MF 855.50 generali > huic quod conceditur in

generali MF/ conceditur: MF omit 855.54 si + in MF 855.60
apostolo + qui/ − ubi LMF

Chapter 9

856.20 ipsum > Petrum MF 856.22 − quod MF 856.27 dixit >
dicit MF 856.32 7 > et (Knysh) 856.37 Petrus + conversioni MF
856.39 cetera sed > ceterasque LMF 856.47 tradidit > credidit
LMF 856.51 ratione > responsione MF 856.54 dixit > dicit MF
856.59–60 acceperit . . . scripserit > scripserit . . . acceperit ??

Chapter 10

857.13 pascendo > pascendos MF 857.14 beneficii + vel MF
857.19 commisisset minime > minime commisisset MF 857.27
posset > possit MF 857.28 88 > 34 F 857.31 oves + ad gregem
reducere perditas MF 857.34 sequitur > sequuntur LMFVg 857.38
− et evidenter MF 857.44 − pastore qui MF/ aedificando + eas
MF 857.44–5 − Christi oves pavisset MF

Chapter 11

857.56 sententia + supra MF 857.62 − etiam MF 858.6
prolatum . . . intelligi > per verbum indiffinite prolatum MF

Chapter 22

864.48 eius > eis M 864.48–9 − scilicet maior LMF 864.58 ipsis
+ apostolis MF 865.4 apostolorum + et LMF 865.5 virtutum >
virtutis Z/ urbem + Romam Z/ animadversum > adversum LM
865.6 deducit + ducem MF 865.7 et ambrosius > beatus ambrosius
MF 865.9 allegatis > allegatas LMF 865.13 tenuerint > docuerint
M 865.16 temporibus > tempore LMF 865.19 tribuenda >
ascribenda M (ascribenda distribuenda F) 865.24 et > nec LMF
865.25–6 doctorum + graecorum MF 865.33 − fidei MF 865.33–
4 populo + potest autem veritas fidei salvari in paucis de populo
MF 865.36 populo: MF add qui totum populum Christianum

III **Dial.**, II

Prologue

889.46 quem > quae NFB [quem V] 889.48 maiorum > aliorum
VNMA 889.49 intendimus > nitemur VNM/ altricari > altercari

VNM/ tres > quinque VNMA 889.52 iure − seu VNMA 889.53
investigat > investiget VNM/ perscrutatur > perscrutetur VNMA
889.54 potestatis + Quartus indaget [indagat LB] an quicunque
fuerit imperator Romanorum iura Romani imperii contra quem-
cunque impugnatorem invasorem vel quomodolibet impeditorem
[defensorem LFBD] etiam contra papam, cardinales et clerum, si
iura Romani imperii impugnaverint invaserint vel impedierint, non
obstante quacunque sententia ordinatione constitutione vel processu
papae et cardinalium vel quorumcunque aliorum, armis et [arma
A] potentia, si non potest aliter, de necessitate salutis teneatur
defendere, et [etiam V] si turbata fuerint, restaurare. Quintus tractet
[tractat LB; tractatus est M] de rebellibus proditoribus destruc-
toribus divisoribus usurpatoribus Romani imperii vel alicuius partis
ipsius VNMA(etc.) 889.58 quatuor > quinque VNMA 889.59 con-
sultius + totaliter VNM 889.60 cum > quia tamen VNM 889.61
alio > aliis VN/ erat > erit VNMA 889.62 faciendum > facienda
VNMA 889.63 futurae > futura VNM 889.64 latentes > latere
VNMA **(Page numbers here are not in sequence)** 871.1 anima-
buntur + que VNMA/ fuerunt > fuerint VNMA 871.2 impro-
bando > reprobando VNM 871.4 quaerendas > quaerenda VNMA
871.5 stolidas > solidas et VNM/ fanticastas > fantasticas VNM/
recitabimus > recitabis VNM/ conabor > coneris VNM 871.8
veritati > veritatis VNMF/ quia + et VNMA/ excitantur > exercit-
antur NW/ ingenia + et VNMA 871.9–10 splendescat: splendescet
MAB(VN=G) 871.10 et arguendo > ac querendo VNM 871.13
ut > quae sicut VNM 871.14 totum > tecum VNM 871.15 ut >
non Vm [ut debito V; ut dubito N]/ iustitiae + detrimentum VN/
essem > esset VNA 871.16 explicare > explicarem NMA/ ut >
sicut VNM/ vis + quam VNMA 871.17 − quid VNMA/ approban-
dum > approbandam VNMA 871.18 et > ut VNMA 871.19
invidia > invidiae VNMA 871.20 acerbius + et VNMA/ non:
VNW omit/ famulante > stimulante N [stimulantis V] 871.21
quaerit > quiverit VNMA 871.22 cum igitur > tu igitur cum
VNM

ɪɪɪ **Dial.,** ɪɪ.ɪ

Chapter 1
871.32 Romani: quoniam AFTDW (VNM=G) 871.34 usurpav-
erunt > usurpaverint VNM 871.35 − et VNM 871.35-6 − an

expediat... orbis VNMARW (LBDTF=G) 871.36 aut > an
VNMA 871.38 – hanc VNMA 871.39 censetur > censeretur NW
871.42 posse: NW omit/ universo + mundo VNMA 871.43 iustius
+ severius VNM 871.44 maxime > principaliter VNM/ – in VNM
871.46 dicens > docens VN 871.47 ubi sic inquit > dicens VNMA
871.50 damnantis > dominantis MVNALy 871.51 principis >
patris VNMLy/ habeant > habent VNMA 871.52 – quieti MAGs/
ita > ratio VNM 871.53 unde + et N/ principes: MA add et
871.54 tuto > tute VNMA 871.55 – de haereticis VNM/ scilicet >
ideoque VNGs 871.57 salubrius, efficacius, iustius, ac severius >
iustius, severius et efficacius ac salubrius VNMA 871.59 et securi-
oris: secularis VNM (FD=G)/ ut + in VNMA 871.60 – ut
VNMA 871.62 promptiores > proniores VNM/ sustinendum >
suscitandum VNM 871.63 periculosiores + et difficiliores ad sedan-
dum VNM 871.64 comites > communitates VmN/ qui > qui et
que VND/ subditos – qui VNA 872.1 – sunt VNA 872.2 habet >
habeat VNM 872.3–4 – ministrantur VNMA 872.4 et > ita VN
[ita et D] 872.6–7 studiis > in hiis VNAGs 872.7 communem >
communis VNMGs/ idem + ut habetur VN [habetur MFD] 872.11
6 + dicens VNM/ contemptibiles > contemptibiliores Vg 872.12
contemptibiles > contemptibiliores Vg/ – ex VNM/ qui + sunt
VN 872.13 – vocantur VNM/ negotia > iudicia VN 872.14 patres
+ et VNMA 872.15 etiam > enim VN 872.16 accipiat > arripiat
VNMA [arripuit FGs] 872.17 hominum + homo VNAGs/ distinctis: dignitatibus distinctis Gs 872.18 successu > cursu
VNMAGs/ temporalium + tantummodo VNMGs 872.20 cor-
poralibus > secularibus VNBGs 872.21 fere + sub omnibus VNM/
4 > 10 VNMA 872.22 praedicta > praedictus VNM/ – ponit
MVNA 872.23 – cum MVNA 872.24 – Domini VNMA (Gs=
G)/ conveniunt > conveniant VN/ et aliis quasi > aliisque VNMA
872.26 denique + et VNM 872.27 – legitur et VNM 872.29 –
obedire VNM 872.30 laicos + et principes [principales V] seculares
subesse VNM/ igitur + et VNMA/ universo orbi > universitati
[universi M] mortalium VNM/ – uni imperatori VNM 872.31 –
subesse VNM/ temporalia: NW omit 872.33 tenendum > haben-
dum VNM/ in... in > de... de VN/ parvis + sicut idem iuris
est in toto et in parte, in magnis et parvis VN/ appellationibus +
c. de appellationibus VNM 872.34 quod > ut VNMA 872.36–37
communicationem > communionem VN 872.37 posset > possit
VNA/ invenire > cuilibet subvenire VNMA [subvenire LF] 872.38

summo principi: supremo principi VN; summo pontifici M 872.40
2 > 11 VNM/ – in VNM/ omnibus + talem VN/ est + unus
VNMA 872.41 – aut VNMA 872.44 – ut VNMA/ communicationem > communionem VNMA 872.45 – etiam VNMA 872.46
eadem > ipsa ADTFW [eadem... ait: et VNM] 872.47 dicens >
dicendo VNMA 872.48 plus > plures VNMA/ debent > debet
NW 872.49 communicationem > communionem VNMA/ possunt
+ unum corpus VNMAFm 872.50 efficiunt unum > efficiant bene
VNM 872.51 corpus et + etiam VNMA 872.53 poterit > poterunt
VNM 872.54 adinvicem > ab invicem VNM/ communionem +
adinvicem VNMA 872.56 valeant > debeant VNMA 872.57 duode-
cim. + ait VNM 872.58 sed + etiam VNM 872.60 debent + hinc
VNMF/ 10 > 18 VN 872.61 – mundi VNMA 872.62 debet >
debent VNMA/ hinc + etiam VN 872.64 – ex VNMA 873.1
Johan > Job VNMALy 873.2 ipse > populi VNVg/ fecit > facit
VNM 873.3 regnum > regimen VNMA 873.4–5 fidelium > mortalium VN (cf. 873.6 below) 873.5 per quod > ac VNMA/ conserv-
antur > conservatur VNMA 873.6 fidelium > mortalium VNM
873.7 fuerint: habuerint VN/ – unum MVN 873.8 speciale >
partiale VN 873.9 Lucae 11 > Matt.12 VNMA 873.11 obedire:
subesse VN 873.15 aut > ac VNM/ suum + negavit VNMA
873.16 facilius > de facili VNM 873.21 tamen quae et > causam
que et c. VNMA/ periculosum + autem VN/ unde + et VN
873.22 iudicium iudicum MV/ 873.27 summum > supremum
VNM 873.28 per > par VN 873.32–3 pax... non poterit > nec
pax... poterit VN 873.35 – cum VNM 873.37 accusatione >
accusationibus VNMAGs 873.39 reges + et principes VNMA/
fuerint + uni VNMA 873.42 universitatem mortalium > universos
mortales VNM 873.43 mortales + talis VNM 873.46 loquitur >
legitur VMA/ ad hoc + divinae VMA 873.52 promittit > permittit
VNMA 873.53 unus + princeps VNA 873.55 similiter > simpliciter
VNMA 873.56 universitatem > universitati VNMA 873.57 est >
erit VNM 873.58 totius + mundi VNM 873.58–9 secundum >
ad VNMA 873.59 debacchare > debacchari VN 873.63 posset
maiorem habere > maiorem haberet VNM/ potestatem >
potentiam VNM/ quam + habet VN 873.64 – unum VNMA
874.1 impedire > impedit quin VNM/ orbi > mundo VNMA
874.2 expediat > expedit VNM/ orbi > mundo VNMA 874.3–4
est iniquum... esset contra ius > est iniquum. Sed non est

iniquum unum omnibus aliis dominari, quia si esset iniquum esset
contra ius VNBDW 874.4 non + est VNMA 874.6 esset > est
VN/ nec + est VNM 874.9 quare: quando AB

Chapter 2

874.18 recitasti > tetigisti VNM 874.19 idcirco > ideo VN 874.20 non
expedit: F adds unum principem mortalem in temporalibus toti mundo
praeesse, et quod non expedit 874.22 scire > audire VNM/ − primo
VNMA 874.24 perniciosum − est VNW/ malitiosum > malum
VNMA 874.25 non est a Deo vetitum sed ordinatum > est a Deo. Deus
enim VN [a Deo. Deus M] 874.26 − dominus VNM 874.28 parvis − et
VNM 874.30 illis > illi VNM/ utuntur > utitur VNM 874.31 solum >
populum VNMALy 874.32 dominicis > divinis NMLF [dominiis corrected to dominicis V; dniis A] 874.33 ad Samulem > Samueli VNMA
874.34 regam > regnem VNMA 874.39 igitur + nec VNMA 874.40
− non VNMA 874.43 sequatur > sit ius VNMA/ ius gentium + ius
gentium ?? 874.46 cum > tum VN/ − iura gentium seu VNMA 874.47
imperator + potenter NMAF [potenti V; non potenter L] 874.50
quae > qui VNMFW/ dicuntur > debent VNMA 874.52 uni domino
+ sunt VNMA 874.53 − adinvicem VNMA 874.55 unum > idem VN/
communionem + seu societatem pacificam VNM 874.56 etiam sustinendo > suscipiendo VNMA 874.56-7 sunt fideles + et quidam infideles VNMLy 874.57 prohibente + qui VNA 874.58 − cum VNA
874.58-9 nec . . . pacificam > nec debent cum eis communionem seu
societatem pacificam habere VNMA 874.59 domino > ipso rege regum
et domino dominantium VNMW 874.60 gladium + veni enim separare
hominem adversus patrem suum. VNM 874.62 eorum > earum VNM
874.62-3 misceantur uxoribus eorum > misereantur earum NW
874.64 13 + inquiens VNM 875.1 iudicio + suscipiendo VNM 875.2
litigant > litigabant VNMA 875.3 fratrem + et fratrem VNMA 875.4
− verbis VNM 875.5 infidelibus + et VN 875.5-6 − communionem et
VNMA 875.8 debite debite > debitam . . debitam VN/ nullus + unus
VNM 875.9 cum + etiam VN/ regni + respectu totius mundi VNMA
875.10 tuum + digne VNMVg 875.11 potest > poterit VNMA

Chapter 3

875.20 − circa hanc VNW 875.23 et > etiam VNM 875.25
manifeste > magnifice VM 875.26 Dominus > Deus ut habetur
VNM 875.28 sunt + tibi VNVg 875.30 − verbis VNM/ − pru-

dentia et VNAF 875.31 magis > maior VN/ requiritur > reperitur
VN 875.33 – mihi VN 875.34 autem + in VN/ alia > divina
VN 875.35 praecedunt > praecellunt V 875.37 improbationem >
responsionem VNMA/ quia + ut VN/ – quod VNMA 875.38
divina et + in M 875.40 describat > describet VNMVg 875.41
volumine + et VNMA 875.42 autem > etiam VNM 875.43 medit-
are > meditaberis VNM

Chapter 4

875.54 principem + neque NMFA [nec V] 875.58 vel > et VNMA
875.59 motiva > aliquod motivum N/ – idem VNFA/ regnum >
regimen VNMA 875.60 expediens > utilius VNMA 875.61 omnium
+ melius VN 875.64 – 2 dist de quibus VNMFTDA (L=G) (A
copyist's guess? *Recte* 20 d. de quibus)/ huic > hinc NMFA 876.1
14 > 24 VN/ assentit > asserit VNMA/ etiam + in laudem
Romanorum VNMA 876.2 – post . . . Romanorum VNMA/ dicit >
dicitur VNMALy 876.2–4 – quicunque . . . quia MSS 876.5 –
semper VNMA 876.6–10 – et committunt . . . dominabatur MSS

Chapter 5

876.21 interdum + autem VNMW/ expedit > expediat VMW
876.23 partibus > regionibus VN/ assertionem > opinionem VN
876.24 istam assertionem > ista opinio VN 876.26 etiam ipsi >
ipsi etiam VNM 876.28 – tanquam VNMA/ communis +
aliquando VNM 876.29 – aliquando VNM/ – videtur VNM
876.30 procurari > procuraretur VNM 876.31 residentes > presid-
entes VN/ saepe minus > equanimius VN [eque minus LA] 876.32
quia > qui VNMA 876.33 praefulgenti > praefulgeret VNM 876.38
illo: primo ABF/ – Israeliticum VN [Israeliticum aliquando MFDA]
876.40 enim: autem MLA; autem changed to enim F/ et +
etiam VN 876.41 regnaverunt > regnavit VNA [regnaverit M]/ –
principem VN 876.43 enim: VFA omit (N=G)

Chapter 6

876.57 quibusdam > quibus NWMFA/ multis > nonnullis VNM
876.60 repugnet + eidem VNMA 876.61 videntur + esse VNM/
istam: BTFW add Magister 876.62 artarentur > arcerentur NW
876.63 cunctis + mundi VNMA/ securius > severius VNM
876.63–4 pertractemus: BTFW add Discipulus 876.64 Magister.

respondetur + ad ipsam VN [ad eam M] (**There is another p. 877 below**) 877.1 accidit > accidat VNM/ cunctis + mortalibus VNM 877.3 – igitur VNMA/ dicunt: debent ABF 877.4 alios: ARF omit/ – est NVW 877.5 vivere + inter malos VNMA/ – et NVW 877.7 monarchiam > monarcham NW 877.10–24 Discipulus. Ut expressius ... mihi recita. Magister: MSS omit 877.24 casus: VNMA omit 877.25–33 viros ... satis sint: MSS omit and add et malis inique faveret 877.33 In his duobus igitur casibus: in istis casibus MSS; LAF add videlicet/ – principe VN/ – scilicet VNM 877.35 mundi + sive propter maliciam multitudinis nolentium obedire uni VN 877.36 assumendi: AB add sive 877.37–8 apud istos > opinionem istam VNM 877.38 cognosco > conicio Vm (corrected from convicio) [convicio NM] 877.40 – modos seu VNM 877.42 volentis > valentis VNT 877.43 principis > principantis VNM 877.44 sic > si VNM/ princeps + totius mundi, non esset aliquis VNM 877.47 – bene VNM 877.48 apparet > appareret VN [apparerent A]/ posset > possent VN 877.49 imperium – et VNM 877.50 imperatoriam: ABF add etiam/ – dignitatem seu VNM 877.51 mundi + sive VNMA/ vel > sive VNMA/ magister + de hoc VNM 877.52 destrui + vel cassari VNMA 877.53 responderent > respondeant VNM

Chapter 7

(**There is another p. 878 below**) 878.5 turbari – et VNM 878.8 potentior > maximae potentiae VNA/ tenendum > tuendum VNMALy 878.9 quod + quia VNM 878.12 secundam + autem VNM 878.13 homines proni: proniores ABF 878.15 accidere > acciderent N [acciderint V] 878.21 modi alii > modis aliis VNMA/ cessarent + si VNMA 878.22 praesidentem > praeessent VNMA/ etiam > enim VN/ – quod VNA/ inter > interdum VNMA + etiam VN [et M]/ aliquid > aliquem VNMA 878.23 eis + esse VN/ propositum > praepositum NMAF/ provocarent > provocare ut VNMA/ ut > suo VNM 878.24 bella > prelia VM 878.25 sunt > sint VN 878.26 praesidentes essent > praesiderent VNMA 878.27 vivant > vivent VNMA

Chapter 8

878.35 mortalium > viventium VNM/ unum + principem VN 878.37 ita + semper VNMA 878.41 non + ex ordinatione VNMA

878.44 deberent > debent VN/ uno > uni VNM 878.46 quia:
quando NM; quando V, deleted; quandoque A 878.48 resolvitur >
dissolvitur VNMGs 878.52 – ita VNM 878.54 poterit > posset
VN [possit M] 878.55 bene > et ideo VN [ideo AM] 878.56 –
ad VNMA/ sed non > non tamen VNM/ – et sic VNMA 878.57
vacare et + ideo VN 878.58 debito + uni VNMA 878.60 tempus
+ et VNMA/ solum + ad VNMA/ etiam + ad VNMA/ magnum
+ tempus VNM/ sic > sicut VNM/ rationabili > aliquando
VNMA/ dilata + est VNM 878.61 aliquando > interdum VNMA/
unde + et VN 878.62 licita > licite VNMA/ potest > posset VN/
ad > per VNMA 878.63 ducentum > ducentos VNM/ potest >
posset VNM **(There is another p. 877 above)** 877.1 summum >
ad VNM 877.4–5 potuerunt > poterunt VNM 877.5 ad + totius
VNM/ sublimaretur > sublimetur VN 877.7 posset > possit N
877.8 posset > possit VN 877.9 promoveatur > provehatur VNM

Chapter 9
877.17 cuilibet + uni VNM 877.18 cum > et VM/ toto: VN add
mundo 877.20 consimile > simile VNMA 877.22 c. + Terrulas
et c. VNA/ deinde > unde et VN [unde M] 877.23 quod nocet >
quid VNGs [quod M] 877.24 rubricis > rescriptis V/ proposi-
tione > proponente VN 877.25 ius > iuris VNM 877.26 nunc
autem non est > numquam autem vel non V/ 877.27 particulari >
partiali VN/ superius > prius VNM 877.30 particulari > partiali
VNMA 877.31 – semper VNMA 877.33 sic > ita VNMA 877.35
propriam > commodum proprium VN

Chapter 10
877.43 posset > possit VNM 877.44 ratione > responsione VNMA
877.46 – esse VNM/ videtur + et VNMA 877.47 rationalis >
rationabilis VNM 877.48 omnes alias > rationes illas VNM 877.49
– omnes VN/ – qui VNMA/ possunt > possint VN 877.50
omnia > omnes VNM 877.51 sed per hoc nequaquam concludi
videtur quod > per hoc excludi videtur quod nequaquam VNM
[sed per [propter F] hoc nequaquam excludi videtur quo ABLFT]/
volentes > valentes VN 877.52 – seculari VNM 877.53 quare >
quia VNMA 877.53–4 propter iram > perperam VN 877.54 ideo
+ quia VNM/ propinquitatis > propter iniquitatem VNM 877.56
regimine + pro VNM 877.58 et > etiam VN 877.60 tolletur >

tolleretur MA 877.61 ad > per VNMA/ elicitur > eliditur VNM
877.62 sis > sit VNMALy/ unius: unum NWM 877.64 habeant >
habuerint VNM (There is another p. 878 above) 878.1 supremum
non habentes > supremi VNA [summi M]/ regularem > regulariter
VNM 878.4 delinquerent > delinqueant V [deliquerint NM] 878.6
respondetur + per hoc VNMA/ quod + hoc VN 878.8 regnat >
regnaret NVW 878.9 qualis esset > quod quilibet VNMA/ − si
VNMA 878.10–11 universitas + mortalium VNM 878.11 est >
erit VN/ inter + omnes VN 878.13 connexio + de facto VN
878.18 quod quandoque > quia tamen VNMA 878.20 et ad tempus
cesset > cesset ad tempus VNMA/ sublevetur > sublimetur VNM
878.22 hoc + esset VNMA/ influentiam hominum > insuf-
ficientiam humanam [hominum A] VNMA 878.23 vel > sed VNMA
878.25 possit > posset VN/ ad > pro NVW 878.26 est > esset
VNMA 878.26–7 esset + quia VN 878.27 aut contra + ius VNM
878.28 est > potest esse VN [est potest esse M] 878.30 modificatione + specificatione VNMA 878.31 deum alienum > deos alienos
VNM/ moechaberis + non falsum testimonium dices, non mentieris
VN 878.32 − vel VNM/ declaratione > determinatione VNMA/
alieno + etiam VN 878.34 absolutum − et VNM/ aliqua +
conditione VN 878.35 et huiusmodi > seu determinatione VNM/
oportet > potest esse VNMA 878.37 aliquis + licite VNMA 878.40
ita etiam > et ideo VN [et it MA]/ esset > est VNM 878.41 −
rationi et VNM

Chapter II

878.48 − praesidere vel VNMA 878.49 solvuntur > dissolvuntur
VNM 878.50 − probari seu VNM 878.51 rationem > illarum
rationum VN 878.52 et disponit etc. > processit VNM 878.52–3
fecit > facit VNMA 878.56 − conservandum et VNM 878.60
petitio + populi VNMA 878.61 ideo petebant > ideo petierunt
VNM 878.62 habetur > legitur VNM 878.63 et sequitur > et
post eodem capitulo sic legitur VNM 878.64 rex + enim VNMAVg
879.3 die quae > die qua VNMAVg 879.4 facient > faciunt
VNMAVg 879.7 impii > iniqui VNM/ depellendi > repellendi
VNMA 879.11 − iudicem seu VNM 879.12 in > de VNMA/
suorum > eius VNMA 879.14 verbis > quod displicebat eis VN/
dixerunt + ecce VNMA 879.16 dictis > allegatis VN 879.17 −
dari VNM 879.18 plus > prius VN 879.19 quando non + expedit

VNM/ latet > lateat VNMA 879.20 – vera NVW 879.23 impru-
denter > impudenter VN 879.24 deum > os domini VNMA 879.27
remansissent > permansissent VNMA/ quia > qui VNM 879.28
innocentiae et + statum VN 879.31 est > erit NW/ – naturae
VNA 879.33 ad quartam > quarta ratio VNMA 879.35 – haec
VNM/ repelli > refelli VNMA 879.36 ipsum > quandoque VNM
879.37 – et licitum VNM 879.38 modificatione vel conditione >
conditione modificatione VNM 879.39 – specificatum seu determi-
natum VNM 879.40 distinctione > determinatione VNM 879.41–
2 modificatione etiam > conditione, modificatione, specificatione
seu determinatione VNM 879.43 causato > cum tanto VNMA
879.44 9 quod > 9 para. 1 VNM [9 c. i A]/ ita quod > itaque
VNMA/ dominari > dominetur ??/ iurgia > coniugia VNM 879.47
invariabile > immutabile et immobile VNMA 879.48 – licet VNM
879.49 fideles quidam – sunt VNM 879.53 debeant > deberent
VNMA 879.54 imperatoris vel curatoris > creatoris VNMB 879.55
iudicium infidelis > iudicem infidelem VNMA 879.56 – si VNMA/
licitum – esset VNMR/ fidelibus: infidelibus VN (MA=G)/ infidelium > fidelium VNMA 879.58 fidelium > fidelem VNM/
sustinendo > suscipiendo VNMA 879.59 videtur > esset VN
879.60 quia + licet VNMA/ debent > debeant VN 879.62 duc-
entes: ducendo VNM 879.63 obedientes: obedientiam V; obedierunt
NM; obedierint A 879.64 nec > et VNM 880.1 fideles > fidelibus
VNMA 880.3 tum > tertio VNMA 880.4 alii alii autem > infideles
aliquando enim [autem MA] omnes VNMA 880.5 gerendum >
gerendam VNM 880.6 gerendum > gerendam VNM 880.7 quam >
quantum M (VNA=G) 880.9 dispendio > defectu VN/ regnum
+ etiam VN 880.11 posset + digne VNMA + et MA

Chapter 12
880.20 an > quod scilicet VNMB [scilicet quod A]/ mundo: MA
add per 880.21 scilicet: VNA omit/ ecclesiasticum: AB omit/ alia
adducas > responde VN (MABL omit) 880.22 temporalibus sive
+ in VNMA 880.25 peritior + etiam VNMA 880.27 deberet >
debeat VNM 880.29 sacerdotes + ex VNMA 880.32 ad hoc >
adhuc VNMA 880.33 impediri + et quod principale motivum
concludat VNMA/ quoniam > nam VNMA 880.35 praecellere +
quia maxime ad sapientem pertinet praesidere VNMALy 880.36
super > filiis VNVg 880.38 talis + in VNMA/ arte > arce Gs

880.41 verbis sequitur > colligitur VNM 880.44 respondetur +
tibi VNMA 880.46 recipiant > susciperent VN/ debent > debebant
VN [debeat M; debeant A] 880.49 vel mo. + secularibus se negotiis
immisceant V 880.51 scientia > notitia VNMA/ prohibentur >
prohibeantur VNM 880.52 insistant > insistatur VNMA 880.53
literarum > scripturarum VNMA 880.55 quaedam > te quidem
VN/ praenotatis > praefocatus VNGs 880.59 – in VN 880.60 ext.
1 c. in ordine > 11 q. 1 c. Te quidem in ordinatione VNM 880.62
fias ne + in VNMA/ – cautione VNMA

Chapter *13*
883.5 plura > plurima VNA 883.8 similter > simul VNMA 883.9
videtur > videretur VN 883.10 solum > sani VN 883.11 deberet:
debent M 883.13 sapientis > sapientum VNMA 883.16 – tantum
VNMA 883.17 – nimis et VN 883.18 corruptio + iustitiae VN
[gap M]/ – quasi VNM 883.20 altero > alio VNM 883.22 pacis et
+ corruptione VN [turbatione M] 883.25 puniendus > corrigendus
VNMA 883.26 multa + sunt VNMA 883.27–8 – scilicet VN
883.29 quaerendi + et pandendi VNMA 883.31 consulendi >
regendi VNMA 883.33 quaerendi > quaerentes VNMA 883.34
fecerunt > fecerint VN 883.35 ut > et VNM/ 322 > 320 VNM
883.36 summum > suum VNMA 883.37 providens > prudens
VNMA

Chapter *14*
883.46 fides + peritia VN 883.47 –peritia VN 883.48 propono +
quero igitur VNM 883.50 – etiam VN/ in > de VNMA 883.51
posset > possit VNM 883.52 – multae VNMA

Chapter *15*
883.62 – mundi si fuerit VNA 884.3 potest > debet VNM 884.4
– perfectius VNA/ ista habere scilicet > habere VNA 884.5
aliqualem > aliquarum VN 884.6 legem vel > legere et VN [legere
vel MA] 884.9 tenetur notitiam > debet peritiam VNMA 884.13
quod + imperator VNDA 884.19 secundum > iuxta VNMA/
tenentur + et V 884.21 legum + civilium VNMA 884.23 tunc >
etiam VNMA 884.25 – desistere vel VNM 884.26 debeat >
deceret eum VNMA 884.27 esset + in VNMD 884.27–8 imperatori
aut regi > imperatore et rege VNMA 884.28 ut > quod VNMA

884.29 a + cura VNMA/ commissis > commissa VNMA/ subditos > subiectos VNM/ et regni > vel [et M]) regimen VNMD/
regnum alteri > regni alii VNMA 884.30 insistat > insistatur
VNMA 884.31 impendit et de ipso: impendent et de eis VN 884.34
inscriptis > in scripturis VNA 884.38 naturali + et discretione ac
industria naturali VNMB/ excellit > excedit VNM 884.40 intelligit
quod in > in taliter VNA/ promovendo + omni VN [cum MA]/
literatura, facundia, eloquentia, experientia et memoria > literature,
facundie, eloquentie, experientie et memorie VNA 884.41 quilibet
excellens > quantumlibet excellenti VNMA/ cum > licet VNMA
884.42 etiam > presertim VNMA 884.43 debeat > debent M
[deberet VNA]/ ad mundi > regni VNM 884.47 secularium +
negotiorum VNMA 884.48 contigit > contingit VNM 884.53 excus-
aret: excusat V 884.54 30 > 38 VN/ q. 1 > q. 4 VNM/ qui >
para. NMB [c. V]/ – omnis NVW 884.56 aut + etiam VNM
884.57 duplici > triplici VN (MA=G)/ PSex > a VNM 884.57–8
immobilibus > in moralibus VNM 884.58 sequuntur et sumuntur >
sequuntur vel sumuntur MA [sumuntur vel respondent VN]/ iura
+ naturalia VNMA 884.59 de ipsis + non cogitare et VNMA/
cogitare > cogitasse VN 884.60 cognoscit > occurrunt VN 884.62
quia > quare VNMA 884.63 enim + quis VNM/ nitetur >
temptatur VMDT [temptetur NA] 884.64 et > etiam VNW 885.1
concludit > occurret VN [ostendit MAD]/ occiderit > occidit
VNM 885.3 – deliberatione seu VNMA 885.6 iuris + naturalis
VNMA/ intelligitur > intelliguntur MA/ maior > maiorum VNA
885.9 quibusdam – ea esse VNM 885.10 ignoraret > ignoraretur
ius VN 885.11 crassa et affectata > affectata, vel crassa et supina
VNMA 885.12 iura + naturalia VNM 885.13 ostendentur > occur-
rent VN/ nec > ut autem VNM/ peritiam – et VNMA 885.14
– notitiam VNMA/ acquiri > acquirat VNM/ – etiam VN/
plures > quamplures VN 885.15 32 > 320 VNMA/ – et VN
885.17 secundo > 11 VN 885.18 doctrina > doctrinae NW/
imperatorem + debere VN 885.19 legitur > habetur VNM 885.21
secreto quod > secretis que VNMA 885.22 interdum + autem
VNM/ vel > et NVW 885.23 – tot VNMA 885.24 efficiatur >
efficitur VNM 885.24–5 etiam > et VNMB 885.25 ordinatione >
veneratione VNM/ amoris > amore VNMA 885.29 multotiens >
aliquotiens VNMA 885.30 eorum consilia et eorum > ipsorum
consiliariorum VN 885.31 contra > erga VNA/ quod > quae

VNMA 885.33 autem > etiam VN/ demandetur > mandetur
VNMA 885.34 – tantum VNA 885.36 revelari + et VNMA 885.39
habeat experientiam ut > experiatur et VNMA 885.40 numero >
imo VNA 885.41 – etiam VNMA/ est > erit VN/ absurdum +
etiam VNMA/ impiorum > imperitorum VNMA 885.42 nocere
volentibus > nolentibus VNAD [volentibus M] 885.46
operuerunt > operuerant VNAVg

Chapter 16

885.55 semper + et VNM 885.59 possunt > possent VNMA
885.60 sed + eas VNMA/ omittamus > dimittamus VNM 885.64
pro > in VNMA/ – et VNMA (Page numbers here are not in
sequence) 888.1 videtur: videntur NW/ ratione + posse VM 888.2
committitur: commitetur NW 888.3 puniri > punire VNMA 888.4–
5 – crimen alicuius VNM 888.5 consequens + quandocumque
VN [quandoque MA]/ – et VNMA 888.8 debet + imperator
VNA/ debet > tenetur VNA 888.9 – scilicet VNM 888.11 amicitiae
nec + ratione VNMA 888.11–12 voluntatis > nobilitatis VN 888.12
aut > nec VNMA 888.13 translationibus > transactionibus VNM
888.15 scilicet > si VNA 888.16–17 subditorum viderit postulare,
et maxime bonorum: subditorum bonorum praecipue viderit postulare VN; subditorum saepe [B omits] viderit postulare et praecipue
bonorum MB; A=G 888.18 obedientium + et VN/ – et VNMALy
888.20 – et VNGs/ filiis: suis MA/ etiam > et VNA 888.20–1
coniunctis > coniugis VNA [coniuges M] 888.21 ac > cui VNA
[et cui M]/ effectus > affectus VNMAGs 888.25 inferendo >
infligendo VNMA/ alicui > aliter VNM 888.26 alieno appareret >
alii cui aspiret VN [alii cui appareret MAB; alicui appareret T]
888.27 pecunialem > pecuniariam VN [M omits]/ persecutione >
prosecutione VN 888.28 reprimeretur > reprimatur VNMA 888.29
igitur > tenetur VN [tenetur igitur A]/ malefactor > malefactori
VNA 888.30 alienus > alius VNMA 888.31 mala faciendi >
malefaciendi VNM/ – debet VNMA 888.34 commissum > commisisset VNM 888.35 sententia: sententiam VNMA (as in Gs –
but the syntax is different) 888.36 pondere > ponderet VNMA
888.37 – hic VN 888.41 itineribus > criminibus VNM 888.42
liceat > licet VNMA 888.43 minimam > misericordiam VNMALy
888.44 sed + esset VNM/ impius > impiissimus VM/ teste +
beato VN 888.44–5 Lucanum > Lotharium VNGs 888.45 parcet >

parcit VNMA 888.46 accipere > rapere NMAGs [recipere V] 888.47 Esa > Isayam VNM/ legitur: imponitur VNW; ponitur M 888.49 et rapinis >. rapina VNM 888.50 videtur + mihi VNMA/ aliqualiter > aliqualem VNM/ apparentiam + ideo VNMA 888.52 secundum + suum VNMA 888.53 debent > poene sunt VN [poene debent M; bene debent A]/ arbitrari > arbitrarie VN 888.55 dicitur > habetur VNMA 888.55–6 licite > bene VNMA 888.56 – bene VNMA

Chapter 17
888.62 tractemus > tractaremus VN 888.63 ideo > ideoque cum ut VNM [ideoque cum ABDT]/ quod VNM/ scilicet peritia et discretio > scilicit peritia seu [et M] discretio sive prudentia et iustitia VNM [ARBDTF omit; L=G] 888.64 tamen > cum VNBD 889.1 brevissime + de aliis VNM/ transeamus: tractabimus M 889.2–3 dicendi > addiscendi tractatu de modo addiscendi moralem philosophiam et tractatu de modo addiscendi VNM 889.3 potuerunt > potuerint VNM 889.4 veracitate > veritate V/ quandocunque > quam VNMA 889.5 an per aliquam sententiam > secundum aliquam sententiam an VNM/ imperator + tanta VNMA/ veracitate > veritate V 889.8 – solvere VN/ perpenderit + incipere VN 889.9 teneatur > debeat VNMA 889.10 illorum > illis ??/ invenerit + ipsis VNMA/ – eis VNM/ impendere > imponere VNM 889.17 quia > si enim VNM 889.22 7 > eodem VN 889.25 dicit > dicitur NW/ optimae > opportune VNMA 889.27 nec > si enim divitiae non effundantur non VNM/ addunt amicos: adducuntur amici M/ et nisi > si autem VNM [et iam AW; at ubi B]/ prodigalitatem + irrationabiliter VNMA 889.29 – sic VNM 889.32 praecellere: pollere VN/ nec > sed V 889.33 praeponendae > postponendae NVW 889.35 19 > 16 VN 889.35–6 patiens sapiens > patiens VNVg [sapiens MA]

III **Dial.**, II.3

Chapter 5
930.62 primo dic quid sit > dic VNMA 930.63 dupliciter... intelligi > questio tua potest dupliciter intelligi VN [questio modo tota potest dupliciter intelligi M; AB=G] 930.64 ut sit capax > ut sit sensus unde habet imperator ut sit capax huiusmodi VNMA/

scilicet + ius VNM 931.1 intelligitur > intelligatur VNA/ modo + scilicet VNMA 931.4–5 pontificem + per VNMA 931.5 tractare > tractari VN/ decet > debent VNMALy 931.6 possit > posset etiam VNAD [posset et M] 931.8 haberet: habet NW 931.8–9 enim > etiam VNDA 931.12 – ex VNMA 931.13 conferre > conferri VNMA 931.14 possit > posset VNMA 931.14–5 intelligitur > intelligatur VNMA 931.18 – quia VNM 931.19 constituere > statuere VNM/ caput + omnium VN 931.20 Christus + non VNM 931.21 Christianorum + in spiritualibus VN/ debeat > debet VNMA 931.22 – papam vel VNMA 931.23–5 qui potest . . . eligendi successorem > qui potest summum pontificem ordinare potest committere cui vult potestatem eligendi summum pontificem et eius successor potest concedere cui voluerit [vult M] ius eligendi successorem VNMA 931.26 successorem > successurum VNM/ potest > potuit VN/ vult > voluerit VNM 931.27 sunt + superius VNM 931.28 aut > aliquando VNA 931.29 imperator: VNW omit 931.30 ius + et potestatem VN/ nisi + ipse VNM 931.31 vel potestas et > vel potestas concedendi VN [concedendi vel potestas et M; concedendi vel possibilitas et ATD] 931.32 – alicui VN 931.33 potestatem + sive VNMA 931.34 – non VNM 931.35 – vel defecerit VNMA/ vel > et VN 931.36 possit > posset VNMA/ ecclesiae + hoc VNMA 931.38 possit > posset VNMA 931.39 necessario + totam VNMA/ si: quia VNW (aliter si V) 931.40 nisi: VN omit (Vm inserted in margin, and deleted) 931.41 ecclesiam + dei VNMA 931.42 non > modo VNM 931.45 necesse est > necessario VND/ – ne VNM 931.46 malitiam + eius VN/ speciali + nequaquam VN [nunquam MAF] 931.57 – summum pontificem VNMA/ papa + quero VNMA 931.61 – huiusmodi VMA 932.2 habeant > habent VNMA 932.3 aliorum > est prelatus et episcopus omnium Christianorum VNMA 932.4 potest > posset VNMA 932.7 ratio: responsio M 932.8 eo quod > quando VNMA 932.8–9 habent > habeant VN 932.10 et – etiam VNM 932.11 eo > propter hoc VNMA 932.14 ius + eligendi VNMA/ id > responsio ad secundum VNM [per responsionem ad secundum AB] 932.15 secundum > primum VNMAB 932.16 illam + primo VNMA 932.17 alium – in VN 932.20 Christianorum > Catholicorum VNMA/ – et VN 932.20–1 habent > habeant VN 932.21 tamen + habent ius eligendi VNMA 932.23 Discip. . . . . Romanos > Discip. adhuc questioni mee non videtur satisfactum. Hoc enim

queritur, quare alii a Romanis non habent ius eligendi nisi pro
casu quando electio non spectaret ad Romanos VN (TL=G) 932.24
aeque bene > ita VNM 932.26 concederetur: consideratur Ly
(VNMA =G) 932.28 quibus est rex > quos habet regere MA
[quos habet VN] 932.30 rationabiliter > non irrationabiliter VNM
[non rationabiliter A] 932.32 quando > quia scilicet VNM/ iuris
+ sui VNM 932.33 id > primum VNMA/ ideo + alii VN 932.36
si possunt > sive possent VNM 932.37 possunt > possent VNM/
ecclesiam + dei VNM/ quin > quia VNMA/ in > pro VNMA
932.38 – summum pontificem NVW

Chapter 6
(This chapter has been translated from the text established from
V and M by H.S. Offler, published in "The Three Modes of
Natural Law in Ockham: A Revision of the Text," *Franciscan
Studies*, 37 (1977), 207–18. The page and line references following
are to that edition.) 212.1 excepi > accepi NMAW 212.11 distingui-
tur > dicitur VNMA 212.18 homines + omnes NMA 213.16
poterit > potest N [poterit V] 214.23 modo + quod enim non fiat
restitutio commodatae pecuniae nec depositae rei est de iure naturae
secundo modo N/ illo – secundo NV 214.31 dicto: NMA add et
quaedam de aliis, et ideo verba quae accipis obiciendo [quae obicis
A] de iure naturali primo modo dicto tantummodo debent intelligi
215.3 intelligitur > intelligit VNMW 215.8 rationali > rationabili
VNMA 215.32 dixit > dicit N [dixit V] 216.19 [contrarium] >
contrarium VNM 216.20 unde > ut VN 217.1 tertio + modo VN
217.6–7 secundo > illo VN 217.12 tertio > illo VN 217.16 vel >
et VNM

Chapter 7
References following are to Goldast.) 935.14 inductas > adductas
VNMA 935.16 aliquam > aliquod V [MAD omit, N illegible to
us] 935.18 in > a VNMA/ debet > debeat VNM 935.19 haber-
ent > haberet VM 935.23 habet > habeat VN 935.24 etiam quod
papa > quod papa etiam VNMA 935.26 – illos VNDA 935.27 –
suae VNDA/ necessariis + et VN 935.28 – suam VN 935.29
debite > debito modo VN 935.30 spiritualibus possit supplere >
possit supplere in spiritualibus VNMA/ illorum > aliorum VNM
935.33 in: pro VNMA 935.34 ideo + etiam VNAD [et M]/ habet >

haberet VNMA 935.35 – optime et VN 935.36 non habet >
haberet VNM 935.37 – in VNM 935.40 ceremonialibus + et
legalibus VNM 935.41 et ... sunt facienda > et quo ad illa quae
de necessitate sunt facienda non ad illa quae non sunt de necessitate
facienda [D omits] ADTF [et [Vm inserts non] quo ad illa quae
non [M omits] sunt de necessitate facienda VNM] 935.43 debet >
deberet VNA [debent M] 935.44 praecipere > imponere VNM
935.46 promissionis > punitionis VNMA/ ad + hoc VNM/
accepi > accepisti ?? (cf. 931.20) 935.47 relinquitur > reliquit VN
[relinquit M; A=G] 935.48 quod + quia VN/ et > vel VNM
935.49 cuilibet > quibuslibet VN/ si > quae VNMA 935.51
adductam > inductam VNMA 935.52 communia > conseqentiam
VNA 935.53 illis > exemplis VN/ huiusmodi > communi VN
935.54 posset > possit MA 935.55 probare > probari VNMA/
posset > potest VND 935.56 hoc autem > hinc VNM/ – dist. VN
935.58 quid ... successorem > qui tales sibi substituunt qualem
successorem beatus Petrus VNMA 935.59 habet: haberet MD
935.60–1 ad hoc ... modo > ad hoc dupliciter respondetur uno
modo respondet glossa VNDA 935.62 statum: statutum VM/ –
patet VNMA 935.64 ista in nullo placent > ista responsio placet
VNMA [AB add dicitur quod devolverentur]/ dicitur ... scilicet >
non VNA [non scilicet M] 936.1 ratio: responsio V [pars Vm;
responsio replaced by ratio A]/ statutum > statum NMA 936.4
consueuerunt > consueuerant VNMA 936.5 probatur > probaretur
VN [probarem M] 936.7 respondetur > dicitur VN/ – si VNMA
936.8 Christi + vel VNM 936.9 non ... ea > per scripturas non
ostenditur eadem VN 936.10 quam probari nititur > qua probatur
VNMA/ Mag. + Ad hoc respondetur quod [per V] illud quod in
scripturis nec explicite nec implicite reperitur, nec etiam patenti
ratione convincitur, eadem facilitate contemnitur qua probatur sed
VN/ – dicitur VNMA/ istorum fuisse > praedictorum fuerit VNM
[istorum fuerit AD] 936.11 – et VNMA/ quomodo > qualiter
VNMA 936.13 habuerunt > habuerint NV 936.14 et + etiam VN
936.16 id > illud VNM 936.17 eligendi + alicui [MA omit] extra
idem collegium VNMA 936.24 pontificem + concedenda et ita
multis modis potest papa habere potestatem concedendi alii vel
aliis ius eligendi summum pontificem VN 936.26 vel > et VN
936.27 quod > quia VNMA 936.28 simul + aliquos Romanos
scilicet VN [scilicet alios Romanos M]/ et aliis > et alios VNMA/

illud ius eligendi: VNW omit 936.29 etiam > et VN 936.30 fuere > fuerunt VND/ – Francorum VNMA 936.31 – summum VNM/ habetur > legitur VNM/ 7 > e VN 936.32 toto > cuncto VNMA 936.32-3 Theutonicorum + potestatem VN 936.33 concessione concesserunt > concessioni consenserunt VNDA 936.34 eo > hoc VNMA 936.35 habuit > habuerit VNM/ – potestatem et VNM/ habuit > habuerit VNM 936.36 quia > quod VNMA 936.38 electione > electoribus VNMA 936.40 ius > potestatem VNMA 936.41 Romanae > Romae VN 936.42 convenire > expedire VNM 936.47 – etiam VNDA/ – rationabili VNDA 936.49 modo + secundo VNBT 936.49-50 – secundo modo VNA

Bibliography

Aristotle, *Politics*: *see* Susemihl

Baudry, Léon, *Guillaume d'Occam. Sa vie, ses oeuvres, ses idées sociales et politiques* (Paris, 1949)

Bévenot, Maurice, ed., Cyprian *De Lapsis* and *De Ecclesiae Catholicae Unitate* (Oxford, 1971)

Biblia Sacra iuxta Vulgatam Clementinam, ed. A. Colunga and L. Turrado (Madrid, 1965)

Corpus iuris canonici, ed. A. Friedberg (Leipzig, 1879) (for gloss: Lyons, 1671)

Corpus iuris civilis, ed. T. Mommsen, P. Krueger, and R. Schoell (Berlin, 1954) (for gloss: Lyons, 1627)

Cyprian: *see* Bévenot

Digest: The Digest of Justinian, Latin text ed. T. Mommsen with the help of P. Krueger, English translation ed. Alan Watson (Philadelphia, 1985)

Duns Scotus, Johannes, *Opera omnia* (Rome, 1950 ff.)

Dutripon, F. P., *Vulgatae editionis Bibliorum Sacrorum Concordantiae* (Paris, 1980)

Eusebius, *Werke*, vol II, *Die Kirchengeschichte*, ed. E. Schwartz; the Latin translation of Rufinus prepared by Theodor Mommsen (Leipzig, 1903) (Die Griechischen Schriftsteller der Ersten Drei Jahrhunderte, 9.1)

Friedberg: *see Corpus iuris canonici*

Marsilius of Padua, *Defensor pacis*, tr. A. Gewirth (Toronto, 1980)

Miethke, Jürgen, *Ockhams Weg zur Sozialphilosophie* (Berlin, 1969)

The Oxford English Dictionary, second edn., ed. J.A. Simpson and E.S.C. Weiner (Oxford, 1989)

Reuter, Timothy and Silagi, Gabriel, *Wortkonkordanz zum decretum Gratiani* (Munich, 1990)

Susemihl, F., *Aristotelis Politicorum libri octo cum vetusta translatione Guilelmi de Moerbeka* (Leipzig, 1872)

Bibliography

William of Ockham, *Dialogus*, in Melchior Goldast, *Monarchia S. Romani Imperii* (Graz, 1960)

Dialogus, in *Opera plurima* (Lyons, 1495)

Epistola ad Fratres Minores, in *Opera politica*, vol. I

Expositio in librum Perihermeneias Aristotelis, ed. Angelus Gambatese and Stephanus Brown (in William of Ockham, *Opera philosophica*, vol. II)

Ockham's Theory of Propositions: Part II of the Summa logicae, tr. Alfred J. Freddoso and Henry Schuurman (Notre Dame, 1980)

Octo quaestiones, in *Opera politica*, vol. I

Opera theologica et philosophica, *Opera philosophica* (St. Bonaventure, NY, 1967 ff.)

Opera politica, ed. R. F. Bennett, H. S. Offler, and J. G. Sykes (Manchester, 1940–)

Opus nonaginta dierum, in *Opera politica*, vols. I (*altera editio*) and II

A Short Discourse on Tyrannical Government, ed. A. S. McGrade, translated by John Kilcullen (Cambridge, 1992)

Summa logicae, ed. Philotheus Boehner, Gedeon Gál, and Stephanus Brown (in William of Ockham, *Opera philosophica*, vol. I)

General index

absolute and ordinate power of God, 12

absolute commandments: see natural law

abuti 5, 9, 10

acts, of eating, 22, 23; of using, 5, 6, 26; successive, 10

Ad conditorem 3, 4, 19, 21, 49

Adam, 39, 40, 41, 42, 63 *see also* state of innocence

Adam's alleged ownership in Paradise, 10, 67

advantage, 95, 96, 101, 102 *see also* necessity and utility

advice, xxiv, xxv, xxvii, 167, 168, 169, 269; need for, 124, 166, 167, 268, 274; sought for various reasons, 168, 274, 275

affirmative and negative precepts, 256

ambiguity, 33, 48, 49

ambition, 304, 322

anticipation, 41, 43, 44

apostles, their renunciation of ownership, 10; their alleged ownership of estates, 9, 10; subject to Peter except in preaching, baptizing and binding and loosing from sin, 220, 223; subject to correction by Peter for wrongdoing, 221, 223; their preaching journey, 11; when appointed to apostolate, 12

apostles' creed, 74, 114

apostolic foundation of the Church, 179, 195

apostolic rulership in the Church, 179

appeal, 9

appropriation *see* power to appropriate

argument from the opposite sense, 189

aristocracy, 132, 142, 143, 162, 171

aristocracy and kingship, differ more through difference of the rulers' power than through their number, 196; which is better, 171, 172, 198

Avignon, 3, 8

banausi, 137

believers and unbelievers, whether they can have community and peaceful society, 247, 265; can be under the same temporal government, 265

belonging, various senses of, 52, 53, 54

best ordering of a community *see* best regime

best regime, xxxii, xxxiii; must exist for the common good of subjects, 312; cannot have only slaves as subjects, 317, 318; must provide for the punishment of any wrongdoer, 320, 321, 322, 323; must be a monarchy, 315, 316; not compatible with subjection of the community in every case to one supreme judge, 310; the ruler cannot have fullness of power (in the sense that he can do anything not opposed to divine or natural law), 318, 319; does not require that all jurisdiction derive from supreme ruler, 320, 321, 323; compatible with

373

Index of persons

Abel, 62, 63, 67, 69
Abraham, 67, 69, 129, 188, 189, 216
Achab, 305
Adams, M., xxxviii, xxxix
Adrian, Pope, 297
Alexander III, Pope, 176
Alexander IV, Pope, 7
Ambrose, Saint, 53, 87, 104, 150,
    157, 228, 277, 278
Anacletus, Pope, 178, 227
Anselm, Saint, 100
Aristotle, 37n, 54n, 127, 128, 129,
    130, 132, 133, 138, 140, 141, 142,
    143, 144, 145, 146, 147, 150, 151,
    153, 155, 158, 159, 160n, 162,
    166, 167, 169, 171, 207, 280n,
    307, 316, 317, 318, 371
Augustine, Saint, 25, 27, 30, 35, 45,
    48, 49, 50, 52, 58, 62, 67, 68, 71,
    72, 74, 83, 84, 98, 110, 111, 113,
    173, 179, 181, 182, 191, 197, 216,
    227, 228, 238, 243, 278, 320
Augustinus Triumphus, xii

Basil, Saint, 53
Baudry, L., 371
Bede, Saint, 86, 177, 183
Bennett, R., 372
Bernard, Saint, 93, 98, 100, 102, 105
Bévenot, M., 371
Black, A., xxxix
Blythe, J., xxxix
Boehner, P., 372
Brown, S., 372

Burns, J., xxxix

Caesar, 330
Cain, 62, 63, 67, 69
Charles, King, 297
Chrysostom, Saint John, 84, 100, 102
Clement, Saint, 45, 46, 97, 227, 282
Constantine, 105, 332
Cornelius, 190, 192
Cyprian, Saint, 129, 178, 190, 194,
    228, 240, 304

Damascene, John, 39, 44
Daniel, 208
David, 251
Dionysius, 38, 60
Duns Scotus, Johannes, 7n, 371
Dutripon, F., 371

Elias, 13
Eusebius, 222, 227, 228

Festus, 81, 329
Francis of Assisi, Saint, xxxix
Freddoso, A., xxxix, 372
Freppert, L., xxxix
Friedberg, A., 371
Fulgentius, Saint, 87

Gál, G., xxxix, 372
Gallio, 330
Gambatese, A., 372
Gelasius, Pope, 309, 332
Gewirth, A., 371, 334n

380

Index of references to the Bible

Books are listed alphabetically, 1 Corinthians after Canticles.

Index of references to canon law

Decreti prima pars

Numbers in brackets give the chapter and the column in volume 1 of
Corpus iuris canonici, *ed. A. Friedberg (Leipzig, 1879), or (for references*
to the gloss) in volume 1 of the edition of 1671.

dist. 1 [col. 1], 24
dist. 1, *Ius civile* [c. 8, col. 2], 69,
   202, 291; gloss [col. 5], 202
dist. 1, *Ius generale* [c. 2, col. 1], 50
dist. 1, *Ius genetium* [c. 9, col. 3], 246,
   264
dist. 1, *Ius naturale* [c. 7, col. 2], 55,
   57, 287, 288, 289; gloss [col. 4–5],
   42, 261
dist. 3, *Omnis* [c. 4, col. 5], 154; gloss
   [col. 9], 154n
dist. 4, *Erit autem* [c. 2, col. 5], 250
dist. 4, *Factae sunt leges* [c. 1, col. 5]
   238, 320
dist. 4, *In istis* [c. 3, col. 5], 50
dist. 5, para. *Nunc autem* [*Nunc ad*]
   [col. 7], 265, 287, 288; gloss [col.
   13], 264n
dist. 6, para. *His itaque* [col. 11], 50,
   265, 287, 288
dist. 8, *Que contra* [c. 2, col. 13], 50,
   296
dist. 8, *Quo iure* [c. 1, col. 12], 62,
   68, 290; gloss [col. 22], 66
dist. 8, para. *Dignitate vero* [col. 13],
   288

dist. 9, para. *Cum ergo* [col. 18], 264,
   288
dist. 10, *Certum* [c. 3, col. 20], 240
dist. 10, *Imperium* [c. 5, col. 20], 240
dist. 10, *Quoniam idem* [c. 8, col. 21],
   240
dist. 10, *Suscipitis* [c. 6, col. 20], 151,
   180, 240
dist. 11, *Consuetudinis* [c. 4, col. 23],
   22
dist. 11, *Palam* [c. 9, col. 25], 227
dist. 17 [col. 50], 211
dist. 18, *Si episcopus*, gloss [col. 78],
   325
dist. 20, *De quibus* [c. 3, col. 66],
   131, 168, 249n
dist. 20, para. 1 [col. 65], 187
dist. 21, *In novo* [c. 2, col. 69], 178
dist. 21, *Quamvis* [c. 3, col. 70], 256
dist. 21, para. 1 [col. 67], 177
dist. 22, *Omnes* [c. 1, col. 73], 93,
   180n, 202, 256
dist. 22, *Sacrosancta* [c. 2, col. 73],
   256
dist. 25, *Qualis* [c. 4, col. 94], 189;
   gloss [col. 126], 189

Decreti secunda pars

Numbers in brackets give the chapter and the column in volume 1 of Corpus iuris canonici, *ed. A. Friedberg (Leipzig, 1879), or (for references to the gloss) in volume 1 of the edition of 1671.*

23, q. 8, para. *Ecce quod* [col. 959], 308

24, q. 1, *Achatius*, gloss [col. 1382], 331

24, q. 1, *Loquitur* [c. 18, col. 971], 178

24, q. 1, *Pudenda* [c. 33, col. 978], 179

25, q. 1, *Quae ad perpetuam*, gloss [col. 1438], 180

25, q. 1, *Sunt quidam*, gloss [col. 1439], 185, 187

Decretales Gregorii IX

Numbers in brackets give the book, title and chapter, and the column in volume II of Corpus iuris canonici, ed. A. Friedberg (Leipzig, 1879), or (for references to the gloss) in volume II of the edition of 1671.

Prologue, para. *deoque lex proditur* [col. 1], 238; gloss [col. 5], 258

De accusationibus, Qualiter et quando [V.1.17, col. 738], 243

De aetate et qualitate praeficiendorum, Quaeris [I.14.6, col. 127], 176

De appellationibus, Cum cessante [II.28.60, col. 437], 175; *De appellationibus* [II.28.11, col. 413], 127, 240

De censibus, Omnis anima [III.39.2, col. 622], 308

De coniugio servorum, Licet [IV.9.3, col. 692], 323 *De consanguinitate, Non debet reprehensibile* [IV.14.8, col. 703], 172

De constitutionibus, Cum accessissent [I.2.8, col. 9], 202; *Translato* [I.2.3, col. 8], 258; gloss [col. 16], 258n

De consuetudine, Cum consuetudinis [I.4.9, col. 41], 22; *Cum dilectus*, gloss [col. 94], 186; *Cum olim* [I.4.6, col. 38], 202; *Cum tanto* [I.4.11, col. 41], 246, 264; gloss [col. 95], 265n; *Quanto* [I.4.4, col. 37], 177

De donationibus, Fraternitatem [III.24.2, col. 533], 180

De ecclesiis aedificandis, Ad audientiam, gloss [col. 1400], 203

De electione, Causam que [I.6.8, col. 52], 296; *Licet* [I.6.6, col. 51], 175; *Significasti* [I.6.4, col. 49], 183; *Venerabilem* [I.6.34, col. 79], 94

De excessibus praelatorum, Sane [V.31.5, col. 836], 313; *Cum ad quorundam*, gloss [1784], 313

De feriis, Conquestus est nobis [II.9.5, col. 272], 176

De his quae fiunt a maiori parte capituli, Quum in cunctis ecclesiis [III.11.1, col. 506], 175; gloss [col. 1100], 175, 176

De iudiciis, Novit [II.1.13, col. 242], 93

De iureiurando, Etsi Christus [II.24.26, col. 369], 183; *Querelam* [II.24.10, col. 362], 177

De observatione ieiuniorum, Consilium nostrum [II.46.2, col. 650], 177

De officio iudicis delegati, Causam quae [I.29.17, col. 163], 242; *Ex litteris* [I.29.29, col. 173], 280; *Insinuante* [I.29.25, col. 170], 242; *Pastoralis* [I.29.28, col. 172], 280; *Prudentiam tuam*, gloss [col. 344], 249n

De pignoribus, Ex litteris [III.21.5, col. 527], 308

De postulatione praelatorum, Bonae memoriae, gloss [col. 104], 24

De praebendis et dignitatibus, Maioribus [III.5.8, col. 466], 127, 240; gloss [col. 1028], 127n

De privilegiis, Quia circa [V.33.22, col. 865], 224

De regularibus, Licet [III.31.18, col. 575], 221

De regulis iuris, Omnis [V.41.1, col. 927], 256; *Quod non est* [V.41.4, col. 927], 177

De renunciatione, Nisi cum pridem, para. *Propter malitiam* [I.9.10, col. 108], 154; gloss [col. 234–5], 15n, 154n

Liber sextus decretalium

*Numbers in brackets give the book, title and chapter, and the column in
volume* II *of* Corpus iuris canonici, *ed. A. Friedberg (Leipzig, 1879).*

Index of references to civil law

Numbers in brackets refer to the page numbers in the appropriate volume of Corpus iuris civilis, *ed. T. Mommsen, P. Krueger and R. Schoell (Berlin, 1954), or, for the gloss, to the edition of 1627.*

Cambridge Texts in the History of Political Thought

Titles published in the series thus far

Aristotle *The Politics and The Constitution of Athens*
(edited by Stephen Everson)
  o 521 48400 6 paperback
Arnold *Culture and Anarchy and other writings*
(edited by Stefan Collini)
  o 521 37796 x paperback
Astell *Political Writings* (edited by Patricia Springborg)
  o 521 42845 9 paperback
Augustine *The City of God against the Pagans* (edited by R.W. Dyson)
  o 521 46843 4 paperback
Austin *The Province of Jurisprudence Determined*
(edited by Wilfrid E. Rumble)
  o 521 44756 9 paperback
Bacon *The History of the Reign of King Henry VII*
(edited by Brian Vickers)
  o 521 58663 1 paperback
Bakunin *Statism and Anarchy* (edited by Marshall Shatz)
  o 521 36973 8 paperback
Baxter *Holy Commonwealth* (edited by William Lamont)
  o 521 40580 7 paperback
Bayle *Political Writings* (edited by Sally L. Jenkinson)
  o 521 47677 1 paperback
Beccaria *On Crimes and Punishments and other writings*
(edited by Richard Bellamy)
  o 521 47982 7 paperback
Bentham *Fragment on Government* (introduction by Ross Harrison)
  o 521 35929 5 paperback
Bernstein *The Preconditions of Socialism* (edited by Henry Tudor)
  o 521 39808 8 paperback
Bodin *On Sovereignty* (edited by Julian H. Franklin)
  o 521 34992 3 paperback
Bolingbroke *Political Writings* (edited by David Armitage)
  o 521 58697 6 paperback
Bossuet *Politics Drawn from the Very Words of Holy Scripture*
(edited by Patrick Riley)
  o 521 36807 3 paperback
The British Idealists (edited by David Boucher)
  o 521 45951 6 paperback
Burke *Pre-Revolutionary Writings* (edited by Ian Harris)
  o 521 36800 6 paperback
Christine De Pizan *The Book of the Body Politic*
(edited by Kate Langdon Forhan)
  o 521 42259 o paperback

Guicciardini *Dialogue on the Government of Florence*
(edited by Alison Brown)
  0 521 45623 1 paperback
Harrington *The Commonwealth of Oceana* and *A System of Politics*
(edited by J. G. A. Pocock)
  0 521 42329 5 paperback
Hegel *Elements of the Philosophy of Right*
(edited by Allen W. Wood and H. B. Nisbet)
  0 521 34888 9 paperback
Hegel *Political Writings* (edited by Laurence Dickey and H. B. Nisbet)
  0 521 45979 3 paperback
Hobbes *On the Citizen*
(edited by Michael Silverthorne and Richard Tuck)
  0 521 43780 6 paperback
Hobbes *Leviathan* (edited by Richard Tuck)
  0 521 56797 1 paperback
Hobhouse *Liberalism and Other Writings*
(edited by James Meadowcroft)
  0 521 43726 1 paperback
Hooker *Of the Laws of Ecclesiastical Polity*
(edited by A. S. McGrade)
  0 521 37908 3 paperback
Hume *Political Essays* (edited by Knud Haakonssen)
  0 521 46639 3 paperback
King James VI and I *Political Writings*
(edited by Johann P. Sommerville)
  0 521 44729 1 paperback
Jefferson *Political Writings*
(edited by Joyce Appleby and Terence Ball)
  0 521 64841 6 paperback
John of Salisbury *Policraticus* (edited by Cary Nederman)
  0 521 36701 8 paperback
Kant *Political Writings* (edited by H. S. Reiss and H. B. Nisbet)
  0 521 39837 1 paperback
Knox *On Rebellion* (edited by Roger A. Mason)
  0 521 39988 2 paperback
Kropotkin *The Conquest of Bread and other writings*
(edited by Marshall Shatz)
  0 521 45990 7 paperback
Lawson *Politica sacra et civilis* (edited by Conal Condren)
  0 521 39248 9 paperback
Leibniz *Political Writings* (edited by Patrick Riley)
  0 521 35899 x paperback
The Levellers (edited by Andrew Sharp)
  0 521 62511 4 paperback
Locke *Political Essays* (edited by Mark Goldie)
  0 521 47861 8 paperback

Locke *Two Treatises of Government* (edited by Peter Laslett)
0 521 35730 6 paperback
Loyseau *A Treatise of Orders and Plain Dignities*
(edited by Howell A. Lloyd)
0 521 45624 X paperback
Luther and Calvin on Secular Authority (edited by Harro Höpfl)
0 521 34986 9 paperback
Machiavelli *The Prince* (edited by Quentin Skinner and Russell Price)
0 521 34993 1 paperback
de Maistre *Considerations on France*
(edited by Isaiah Berlin and Richard Lebrun)
0 521 46628 8 paperback
Malthus *An Essay on the Principle of Population*
(edited by Donald Winch)
0 521 42972 2 paperback
Marsiglio of Padua *Defensor minor* and *De translatione Imperii*
(edited by Cary Nederman)
0 521 40846 6 paperback
Marx *Early Political Writings* (edited by Joseph O'Malley)
0 521 34994 X paperback
Marx *Later Political Writings* (edited by Terrell Carver)
0 521 36739 5 paperback
James Mill *Political Writings* (edited by Terence Ball)
0 521 38748 5 paperback
J. S. Mill *On Liberty,* with *The Subjection of Women* and *Chapters
on Socialism* (edited by Stefan Collini)
0 521 37917 2 paperback
Milton *Political Writings* (edited by Martin Dzelzainis)
0 521 34866 8 paperback
Montesquieu *The Spirit of the Laws* (edited by Anne M. Cohler,
Basia Carolyn Miller and Harold Samuel Stone)
0 521 36974 6 paperback
More *Utopia*
(edited by George M. Logan and Robert M. Adams)
0 521 40318 9 paperback
Morris *News from Nowhere* (edited by Krishan Kumar)
0 521 42233 7 paperback
Nicholas of Cusa *The Catholic Concordance*
(edited by Paul E. Sigmund)
0 521 56773 4 paperback
Nietzsche *On the Genealogy of Morality*
(edited by Keith Ansell-Pearson)
0 521 40610 2 paperback
Paine *Political Writings* (edited by Bruce Kuklick)
0 521 66799 2 paperback

Plato *The Republic* (edited by G. R. F. Ferrari and Tom Griffith)
    0 521 48443 X paperback
Plato *Statesman* (edited by Julia Annas and Robin Waterfield)
    0 521 44778 X paperback
Price *Political Writings* (edited by D. O. Thomas)
    0 521 40969 1 paperback
Priestley *Political Writings* (edited by Peter Miller)
    0 521 42561 1 paperback
Proudhon *What is Property?*
(edited by Donald R. Kelley and Bonnie G. Smith)
    0 521 40556 4 paperback
Pufendorf *On the Duty of Man and Citizen according to Natural Law*
(edited by James Tully)
    0 521 35980 5 paperback
The Radical Reformation (edited by Michael G. Baylor)
    0 521 37948 2 paperback
Rousseau *The Discourses and other early political writings*
(edited by Victor Gourevitch)
    0 521 42445 3 paperback
Rousseau *The Social Contract and other later political writings*
(edited by Victor Gourevitch)
    0 521 42446 1 paperback
Seneca *Moral and Political Essays*
(edited by John Cooper and John Procope)
    0 521 34818 8 paperback
Sidney *Court Maxims* (edited by Hans W. Blom, Eco Haitsma Mulier
and Ronald Janse)
    0 521 46736 5 paperback
Sorel *Reflections on Violence* (edited by Jeremy Jennings)
    0 521 55910 3 paperback
Spencer *The Man versus the State* and *The Proper Sphere of
Government* (edited by John Offer)
    0 521 43740 7 paperback
Stirner *The Ego and Its Own* (edited by David Leopold)
    0 521 45647 9 paperback
Thoreau *Political Writings* (edited by Nancy Rosenblum)
    0 521 47675 5 paperback
Utopias of the British Enlightenment (edited by Gregory Claeys)
    0 521 45590 1 paperback
Vitoria *Political Writings*
(edited by Anthony Pagden and Jeremy Lawrance)
    0 521 36714 X paperback
Voltaire *Political Writings* (edited by David Williams)
    0 521 43727 X paperback
Weber *Political Writings* (edited by Peter Lassman and Ronald Speirs)
    0 521 39719 7 paperback

William of Ockham *A Short Discourse on Tyrannical Government*
(edited by A. S. McGrade and John Kilcullen)
　0 521 35803 5 paperback
William of Ockham *A Letter to the Friars Minor and other writings*
(edited by A. S. McGrade and John Kilcullen)
　0 521 35804 3 paperback
Wollstonecraft *A Vindication of the Rights of Men* and *A Vindication of
the Rights of Woman* (edited by Sylvana Tomaselli)
　0 521 43633 8 paperback